THE MAMMOTH BOOK OF
Native Americans

THE MAMMOTH BOOK OF
Native Americans

JON E. LEWIS

CAR̲ . . . . S

New York

Carroll & Graf Publishers
An imprint of Avalon Publishing Group, Inc.
245 W. 17th Street
New York
NY 10011
www.carrollandgraf.com

First Carroll & Graf edition 2004

First published in the UK by Robinson,
an imprint of Constable & Robinson Ltd 2004

ISBN 0-7867-1290-2

Printed and bound in the EU

For Freda, Tristram and Penny

Contents

Chronology

c. 30,000BC
First humans enter North America, via Bering land bridge

c. 8000BC
Ice Age ends; mastodon, giant horse, sabre-toothed tiger, miniature horse and other fauna become extinct

5000BC
Eskimo-Aleut and Na-Dene people migrate to North America from Asia

1500BC
Indians of the north-eastern woodlands adopt practice of burying their dead

1000BC
Maize becomes food staple of Mexican Indians; agriculture established in Mogollon highlands of American Southwest; the beginning of Adena culture

200–500AD
Hopewell civilization flourishes in Midwest and East

750AD
Mississippian Culture in ascendancy

850–1150

Zenith of City of Cahokia, on site of present day St Louis

800–1100

Maize becomes major crop in Eastern woodlands

900

Rise of Anasazi civilization in Southwest

c. 1000

Pueblo communities of Acoma and Hopi established

1075

Anasazi road-building begins at Chaco Canyon

c.1130

Anasazi evacuate Chaco Canyon

c.1450

Confederacy of the Iroquois born

1492

Columbus lands in Bahamas; population of North America as high as 18 million

1500

Algonquian-speaking nations push sedentary Iroquian people from the north-east

1513

Ponce de Leon lands in Florida

1521

Second Ponce de Leon expedition forced to evacuate Florida by Calusa tribes

1528

Panfilo de Narvaez lands at Tampa Bay, Florida, but retreats after Indian attacks

1539–43

Hernado de Soto lands in Florida and rampages westwards through the Timucua, Creek, Mobile, Apalachee and other nations; de Soto buried next to the Mississippi in 1542

1540–42

Francisco Vasquez de Coronado leads Spanish expedition from Mexico, penetrating as far north as Kansas.

1598

Juan de Onate founds Spanish settlements in northern New Mexico

1599

Vincente Zaldivar attacks Acoma ('Sky City') pueblo, killing 800

1600s

Navajo adopt sheep farming and the reintroduced horse (c.1659)

1607

English colonists establish permanent settlement at Jamestown, Virginia

1609–13

War between Powhatan and Jamestown settlers; peace sealed by marriage of Princess Pocahontas to John Rolfe

1609

Samuel de Champlain kills three Iroquois chiefs with a single bullet on shore of Lake Champlain

1612

Jesuits begin arriving in New France (Canada)

1617

Pocahontas dies on trip to England

1620

English Pilgrims land at Plymouth

1622

Opechancanough of the Powhatan attacks Virginian settlements (until 1632)

1637

Pequot War against English to maintain hunting grounds, Connecticut

1644

Second Opechancanough War sees demise of the Powhatan Confederacy

1650–1777

Iroquois Confederacy at height of influence

1663

Bible translated into Massachusetts ('Mamusse Wunneetupanatamwe Up-Biblum God Naneeswe Nukkone Testament Kah Wonk Wusku Testament') by John Eliot

1675–6

King Philip's War; after early successes, Wampanoags and Narragansetts slaughtered and enslaved

1680

Revolt of the Pueblos

c.1700

Comanche established on Southern Plains and horsed

1712

Tuscarora War in North Carolina

1731

French capture Great Sun of the Natchez and sell him into slavery

1737

'The Walking Purchase' defrauds the Delaware of twelve hundred square miles of land.

1738

Smallpox strikes the Missouri region causing 90 per cent mortality amongst the Arikara

1742

Joseph Brant (Thayendanegea) of the Mohawk born

1750

Plains Cree horsed

1754-63

French and Indian War ends in victory for Britain

1763

Pontiac's Rebellion, Great Lakes

1769

Spanish establish missions in California; over the next 60 years Native population of California between Dan Diego and San Francisco declines from seventy-two thousand to eighteen thousand through disease and forced labour

1770

Cheyenne horsed on Northern Plains

1775

Revolution begins

1777

Shawnee raids against white settlements in 'Kentucke' reach peak

1779

Retaliatory campaign by Generals Clinton and Sullivan raze 40 pro-British Iroquois towns in Mohawk Valley

1783

America granted independence from Britain

1786

Tlingit on NW coast first encounter whites

1791

Miami Chief Little Turtle inflicts 900 casualties on US force led by General St Clair; worst US defeat in any war against the Indians

1794

Ohio-region Indians lose Battle of Fallen Timbers

1795

Under terms of the Treaty of Greenville Indians forfeit slice of southern Indiana and most of Ohio

1799

Handsome Lake of the Seneca receives vision in which Jesus tells him 'Now tell your people that they will become lost when they follow the ways of the White man'

1800

Indian population estimated at 600,000 by Bureau of Indian Affairs

1803

Louisiana Purchase from France places 828,000 square miles of the trans-Mississippi and its tribes under US dominion

1804–6

'Voyage of Discovery' by Lewis and Clark to Pacific Ocean

1809–11

Tecumseh of the Shawnee campaigns for Native American unity; his brother and ally Tenkswatawa defeated at Tippecanoe, Indiana, by Governor Harrison

1812–15

War of 1812 between Britain and USA

1813

Tecumseh killed in battle of the Thames fighting alongside British

1814

'Redstick' Muskogee warriors defeated by combined US and Cherokee force at Horshoe bend

1816–18

First Seminole War

1819

Florida acquired from Spain.

1821

Sequoyah invents Cherokee syballary

1822

Red Cloud born

1830

Indian Removal Act requires displacement of Eastern Indians to Indian Territory (present-day Oklahoma)

1831
Sitting Bull born

1832
Black Hawk's War between US and Fox and Sauk

1835
Minority of Cherokee leaders sign Treaty of Echota

1837
Smallpox epidemic devastates tribes of the West, including the Mandan, of whom only 39 survive

1838–9
30,000 Cherokee driven from Georgia to Indian Territory along 'Trail of Tears'; the Chickasaw, Creek, Choctaw and other tribes are also relocated

1842
Seminole, last of the free tribes of the Southeast, end their guerrilla war and agree to removal from Florida, although some scattered bands remain to fight a Third Seminole War; Oregon Trail established from Independence, Missouri, to Pacific Northwest with branch to California

1848
James W. Marshall discovers gold at Sutter's Mill, California

1849
Gold Rush to California begins

1851
Indian Appropriation Act leads to reservation system becoming widespread

1860
Paiute War in Nevada

1861

Civil War (until 1865)

1862

Battle of Apache Pass between California Volunteers and Apache under Cochise and Mangas Coloradas; Homestead Act gives US citizens over 21 the right to 160 acres of public domain; Little Crow leads uprising of Santee Sioux in Minnesota, which is eventually defeated at Wood Lake

1863–4

Manuelito leads Navajo War

1864

Following their surrender, the Navajos make the 'Long Walk' to Bosque Redondo; Comanche fight Kit Carson in battle of Adobe Walls in Texas Panhandle; Colorado Volunteers massacre peaceful camp of Cheyennes and Arapahos at Sand Creek

1866

The Five Civilized Tribes forced to cede western section of Indian Territory in reprisal for some members' support of the Confederacy during Civil War; Fort Laramie Council between US government and Northern Plains tribes; Red Cloud's Sioux ambush US army near Fort Phil Kearny on Bozeman Trail in 'Fetterman Massacre'

1867

Medicine Lodge Treaty assigns reservations to Cheyennes, Arapahos, Kiowas, Kiowa-Apaches and Commanches

1868

US abandons forts on Bozeman Trail in tacit admittance of defeat in 'Red Cloud's War'; Roman Nose of Cheyenne dies in skirmish with volunteer scouts at Beecher Island ('The

Fight in Which Roman Nose Died'); George A. Custer and 7th Cavalry massacre Black Kettle's Cheyenne near Washita River, Indian Territory, in Southern Plains War

1869
Trans-continental railroad completed; Ely Parker of the Seneca appointed Indian Commissioner; first Ghost Dance movement involves tribes of Great Basin and West Coast

1870s
First recorded use of peyote amongst Indians of the US (the Lipan Apache)

1871
Congress passes law-depriving tribes of their status as separate nations

1872–4
Modoc War in lava beds of Northern California sees 165 Indians led by Captain Jack stand off vastly superior US force until artillery usage forces Modoc capitulation

1874
Cochise of the Apache dies; Comanche and allies under leadership of Quanah Parker attack buffalo hunters at Adobe Walls but are repelled by superior Sharps rifle in Red River War

1875
Quanah Parker of the Quahadi Comanche agrees to enter reservation

1876
Black Hills War begins after gold miners invade Sioux lands; Custer and 7th Cavalry defeated at Little Big Horn

1877

After a relentless campaign by US army Crazy Horse of the Sioux ceases hostilities but is killed in custody two months later; Chief Joseph's band of Nez Percé surrender after fighting for nearly 1000 miles in bid to flee to Canada

1878-9

Flight of the Northern Cheyennes from Indian Territory

1879

Carlise School founded in Penyslvania to assimilate Indians into white society

1881

Sitting Bull, Sioux victor of Little Big Horn, surrenders to US forces after leaving exile in Canada

1882

Indian Rights Association formed

1885

Sitting Bull joins Buffalo Bill's Wild West Show

1886

General Nelson A. Miles accepts the surrender of Apache warriors led by Geronimo

1887

Dawes Act divides reservations into individual holdings and opens millions of acres to white settlement

1889

First land rush into Oklahoma, formerly Indian Territory

1890

Sioux Ghost Dancers massacred by units of the 7th Cavalry at Wounded Knee, South Dakota; Indians at nearby Pine Ridge reservation flee in panic, December; Census records the Indian population as 248,253 and announces end of the frontier

January 1891
Sioux refugees surrender to Nelson Miles and return to Pine Ridge

1893
Buffalo almost extinct, only 1000 remain on Plains

1900
Indian population down to 237,000

1909
Geronimo dies

1910
Indian population of US creeps up to 277,000

1913
'The Navajo War'

1915
'The Ute War'

1916
Ishi, the last surviving member of the Yahi band of California, dies

1918
Native American Church founded

1922
John Collier founds the American Indian Defence Association

1924
Indian Citizenship Act passed

1934

Indian Reorganization Act passed, part of Roosevelt's 'New Deal' for Native Americans

1935

Last of the 'Bronco Apaches' gives up the old free life in the Sierra Madre

1941–5

25,000 Native Americans see active service with US forces during World War II

1944

National Congress of American Indians founded in Denver

1946

US Congress begins to implement 'termination' and 'relocation' policies

1968

American Indian Movement founded; Kiowa N. Scott Momaday publishes *House Made of Dawn*, which wins Pulitzer Prize for Literature in following year

1969–71

Indian militants occupy Alcatraz Island

1970

US president Richard Nixon formally repudiates termination

1972

'Trail of Broken Treaties' protest ends in occupation of the Bureau of Indian Affairs, Washington DC

1973

Activists from American Indian Movement and local Oglala Sioux stage armed protest at Wounded Knee ('Wounded Knee II')

1974
Indian Financing Act passed by US Congress

1975
Indian Self-Determination and Education Assistance Act passed; the sacred Blue Lake returned to Taos Pueblo

1978
American Indian Religious Freedom Act passed

1979
Seminole open 1700-seat bingo parlour

1981
President Reagan cuts funds for Indian social programmes by 40 per cent

1990
Native American Graves Protection and Repatriation Act passed

2000
Census records four million Americans who classify themselves as 'Native Americans'

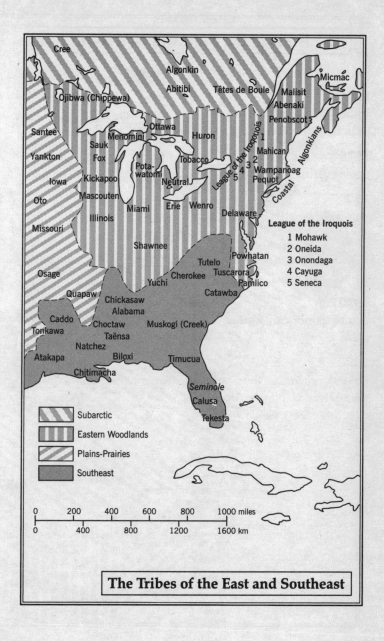

Cree

Algonkin

Abitibi   Têtes de Boule

Micmac

Ojibwa (Chippewa)   Malisit
                                               Abenaki
                                     Penobscot

Santee   1
           Menomini   Huron   Mahican
Yankton Sauk   2
         Fox   Ottawa   Wampanoag
                  Tobacco   4 3
Iowa   Kickapoo Pota-   Neutral 5   Pequot
                   watomi
Oto   League of the Iroquois
         Mascouten   Miami   Erie Wenro
Missouri   Illinois   Delaware

                                               League of the Iroquois
         Shawnee
Osage   Powhatan   1 Mohawk
                        Tutelo   2 Oneida
         Quapaw Cherokee Tuscarora   3 Onondaga
                   Yuchi   Pamlico   4 Cayuga
         Chickasaw   Catawba   5 Seneca
Caddo   Alabama
Tonkawa Choctaw   Muskogi (Creek)
         Taënsa
Natchez   Biloxi
Atakapa   Timucua
Chitimacha

              Seminole
              Calusa
              Tekesta

▨ Subarctic

▤ Eastern Woodlands

▧ Plains-Prairies

▦ Southeast

0   200   400   600   800   1000 miles
0   400   800   1200   1600 km

The Tribes of the East and Southeast

The Tribes of the Northwest and North

- Eskimo
- Subarctic
- Northwest Coast
- Plateau
- Plains-Prairies

Western Eskimo

Koyukon

Ingalik

Aleut

Tataina

Tatana

Ahtena

Eyak

Tlingit

Tagish

Haida

Tsimshian

Tahltan

Bella

Coola

Kwakiutl

Nootka

Salish

Kutchin

Han

Hare

Copper Eskimo

Tutchone

Mountain

Yellowknife

Ca

Kaska

Dogrib

Slave

Sekani

Carrier

Beaver

Chipewya

Shuswap

Sarsi

Okanagan

Plains Cree

Kutenai

Blackfoot

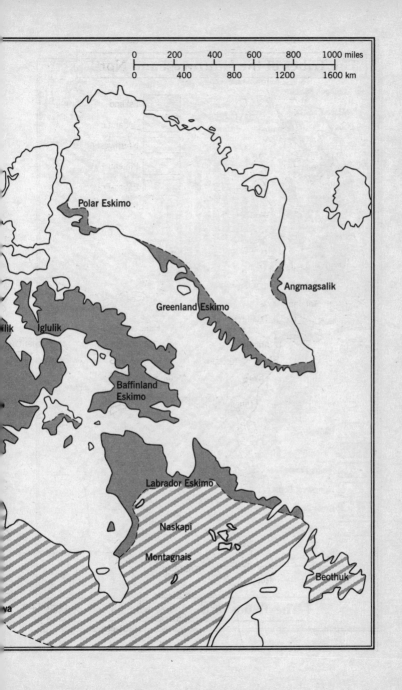

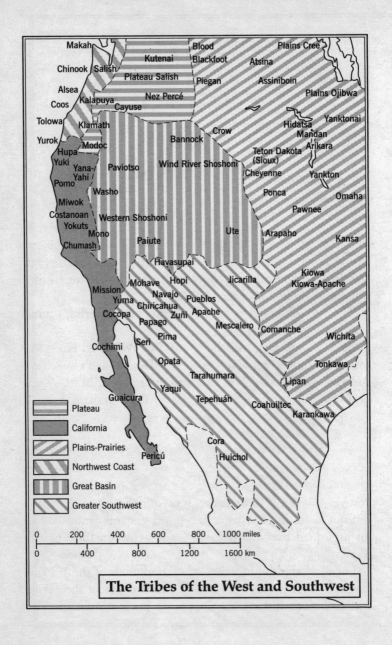

The Tribes of the West and Southwest

Introduction

The bright winter's day of 29 December 1890. A detachment of the 7th Cavalry – Custer's regiment – stand guard over huddled, refugee Sioux. Yellow Bird, a Sioux shaman, throws a handful of dirt in the air.

The itchy-fingered cavalry open fire, killing perhaps three hundred Sioux.

Such, in synopsis, was the "battle" of Wounded Knee. As everyone knows, not least because of Dee Brown's epic *Bury My Heart at Wounded Knee*, at that remote creek in Montana occurred the last engagement in the "Indian Wars". Alongside the Sioux in the mud was killed a dream: the dream of Indian freedom.

That much is true, but Wounded Knee has come to overshadow as much as it lights, and all its symbolisms have become lop-sided. Against prevailing assumption, the story of Native Americans did not end at Wounded Knee, just as it did not begin in 1854 when the Sioux became embroiled in an argument over a white emigrant's cow on the Oregon Trail.

For too long, the history of the aboriginals of the US has become synonymous with the extended death of the Plains Indians. What of the stone cities of the ancient Anasazi? The political democracy of the 15th century Iroquois? And the struggle of the eastern tribes against the Anglo-Americans? The bloodiest conflict between Indians and Whites was not out on the Great Plains, but in the woods of New England when King Philip (Metacom) warred against the Puritans in 1675.

Moreover, America's natives have endured some of their hardest struggles *after* 1890 – against their population freefall to 250,000 in 1900, against government-sponsored "termination" in the 1950s, against subsistence existence on the reservations in the 1980s (when unemployment regularly topped 80% at Pine Ridge). In 1890, the Indians of the United States might have dropped their Remingtons and their warclubs, but they still sought control of their destiny. When, in the 1970s, Indian activists took up the "peacepath" to legally challenge treaty iniquities, their goal was the same as, say, Red Cloud's a hundred years before. Only the means differed.

There's something else about Wounded Knee. Just as it was one episode among a million in the thirty thousand-year-history of the Indians of the US, it was also an absolutely typical encounter between Whites and Natives. When Yellow Bird threw his dust in the air, he was making a Ghost Dance motion. The 7th Cavalry believed it to be a signal for the Sioux to attack them. Ever since the Europeans landed in the "New World" in 1492, their relations with the Indians have been based on misunderstanding, fear and prejudice.

Despite the best effort of some Whites, the prevailing Euro-American opinion concerning America's aboriginals over the last half-millennium is that they were ne'er-do-well "savages" who inconveniently squatted on desirous land, from which they should be removed. Sometimes this was done by force;

usually the White's microbes did the job anyway. Something like a viral holocaust descended on post-Columbian America. As much as 90% of the old population was wiped from the face of the "New World" by disease and its faithful attendant, famine.

To the more romantically minded – or just plain further removed – America's first inhabitants were sometimes conjured as "noble savages", free spirits in human form. Whether "savage savage" or "noble savage" the Indian was reduced to stereotype. Unfortunately, time has done little to diminish such impluses by Whites. You only have to consider the New Age veneration of Native culture as being the epitome of "greenness" to see that. Although well-intentioned, the New Agers have simply made another stereotype. Native cultures varied considerably, and many were distinctly politically incorrect (cannibalism and a profligate overstocking of horses which literally ate and drank *bos bison americanus* out of existence in some places, for example).

And so to this history of the Indians of the United States. In its writing, I have tried to avoid the pitfalls adumbrated above. I have tried to remember that the first Americans had a way of life as well as a way of death, that their story is long and continuing, and that it is only the White convenience that catergorises them as "Indians". To themselves, they were and are 500 different nations, composed of millions of individuals. Where possible I have let these individuals speak for themselves.

When the old and defeated Fox and Sauk chief Black Hawk met President Andrew Jackson, he declared "I am a man, and you are another". This has been my guiding sentiment on the long trail of pages which follow.

Jon E. Lewis

PART I

A World Made of Dawn

Native America, from Creation until AD 1492

Pleasant it looked
this newly created world.
Along the entire length and breadth
of the earth, our grandmother,
extended the green reflection
of her covering
and the escaping odors were pleasant to inhale

Winnebago song

Prologue

The first settlers of the land that would become known as America walked there. It was a time when the waters were locked in ice, and the seas had fallen so low that a land bridge spanned the narrow Bering. Strait. "Bridge" is perhaps a misnomer, Berengia was a sizable mass; it was a dry perambulation to the New World for the Siberia nomads, who constituted a mere handful of families. From them would descend, according to recent DNA analysis, 95 per cent of Native Americans.

Perhaps the pioneers set foot in America 30,000 years ago; perhaps 12,000 years ago. The only real scientific certainty is that the pioneers were anatomically modern humans – *homo sapiens sapiens* – not stoop-browed Neanderthals or the like; humans did not evolve in America, they arrived there. From the Yukon, as the Pleistocene ice receded, there was exposed a corridor to Montana, down which the pioneers moved, and from thence south and out, until one fine day they reached the bottom of Argentina. Always they were lured forward not by god or gold, but game, in the vast shapes of the mastodon, the mammoth, the giant buffalo and their like, which the pioneers hunted with their distinctive fluted spear-heads, the spears themselves powerfully propelled from a wooden spearthrower, or *atlatl*. Eventually, through over-hunting or global warming (because of a new tilt to the Earth's axis) circa 10,000 years ago, the giant herbivores were forced into extinction, causing these so-called Clovis people (after the New Mexico archeological site) to give up their way of life, to diversify into the hunting of smaller game and even into farming.

Such is the gist of the White account of the settling of America by Indians, with the codicil that there were two later waves of emigration, as adduced from DNA and linguistic evidence, those of the Eskimo-Aleut and the Na-Dene.

American Indians account for their Creation differently. Among the people of Acoma Pueblo, it is told that the sisters Iatiku and Nautsiti emerged from a hole in the ground, *sipapu*, and when Nautsiti left the region after being tempted by the evil Snake, Iatiku bore many children, each of which became an Acoma clan. The Iroquois relate how Skywoman, *Ata-en-sic*, was pushed from her domain to live on an island made by Muskrat and Turtle, where she gave birth to her daughter – the beginning of the world. For some tribes on the Northwest coast, humanity emerged from a giant clam and was welcomed by Raven's song of greeting. The Blackfeet say that Old Man made a woman and child of clay, "told them to rise and walk; and they did so".

The seeming diversity of Amerindian Creation myths notwithstanding, they have much universality about them. In almost all of them, the Maker – the Great Spirit, Wakan Tanka, however named – spiritually binds the people to all the remainder of his works. Put another way, Indians and Nature are one, indivisible, made so by God. When the Earth is cut, the Indian weeps. This spiritual, near mystical, union with the land is the heart of Indian religion, aesthetics, morality; improper conduct throws the connection out of kilter, bringing harm to the tribe; reverence, beautiful art, correct deeds harmonize the tribe and their land.

The sacred interconnectedness of the Indian to his environment was beyond the ken of the whites when they came in AD 1492; five hundred years of tragedy was the result. They "sicken and die" said Geronimo of the Apache, when they were moved off their land. Exactly the same could be said of all the other Indian nations in post-Columbian America.

Also common to Amerindian Creation myths is the belief that each nation was created on its own land, which was the centre of the world, and special to them. Geronimo put it thus: "For each tribe of men Usen [God] created He also made a home. In the land for any particular tribe He placed whatever would be best for the welfare of that tribe . . . the Apaches and their homes [were] each created for the other by Usen himself."

If White Man's anthropology does not confirm Geronimo's proposition, it does acknowledge the beautiful adaptation of the post-Clovis Indians to the regions to which they trekked, the wild rice-gathering of the Great Lakes Indians, the salmon-hunting of the totem-pole-building Tlingit, the harvesting of Mesquite pods by the Cahuilla. As the tribes built relationships with their land so they themselves changed, and became diverse in stature and different in language. From the single aboriginal voice of the first settlers, there came a myriad tongues, the Algonquian, the Siouan, the Iroquoian, the Athapascan, the Piman, the Shoshonean, Shahaptian, the Caddoan, the Salishan and others. Distinct by way of life, by physicality, by language, the post-Clovis aboriginals became a kaleidoscope of 500 nations. Although the Whites liked to talk of "the Indian" when they gate-crashed America in 1492, the original inhabitants had long been Native Peoples who, outside the commonality of their spiritual binding to the Earth (and a domestication of animals which started at the dog and ended at the turkey with nothing else in between), could be as different to each other as the French European was to the English European.

Corn Mother Comes

"When a child was born his Corn Mother was placed beside him, where it was kept for twenty days, and during this period he was kept in darkness . . . Early on the morning of the twentieth day, the mother, holding the child in her arms and the Corn Mother in her right hand, and accompanied by her own mother – the child's grandmother – left the house and walked to the east. They stopped, facing east, and prayed silently, casting pinches of cornmeal to the rising sun. When the sun cleared the horizon the mother stepped, forward, held up the child to the sun, and said, 'Father Sun, this is your child.'" – *Hopi ceremony*

The passing of the giant beasts of the Clovis era made for a new beginning for America's first inhabitants. They turned to many ways of survival, but most notable of all was the ceaseless manipulation by some Indians of wild plants. Although the popular image of the Native American is a befeathered hunter, it is a startling and salutary fact that 60 per cent of the contemporary world's food comes from plants domesticated by Amerinidian, above all, the potato, the tomato and the maize (corn) plant.

Corn, the very staff of life for pre-Columbus Indians, derived from a wild grass of the highlands of Mexico called *teosinte*, it took approximately 7,000 years for the fingertip-sized *teosinte* ears to be turned, by genetic selection – through the ruse of picking always the best heads, and crossing corn with hardy grass – into large, body-sustaining cobs. For almost the entire period, Native Peoples would have integrated *teosinte* – growing into a hunting and gathering economy, but by about 1,000 BC corn-cropping was sufficiently advanced to become the prime food of Mexico. And from Mexico corn-agriculture quickly diffused into the American Southwest, to found no less than three major farming civilizations, the Mogollon, the Hohokam and the Anasazi.

The Mogollon lived and farmed in the upland meadows and forests of the New Mexico–Arizona border, where their new settled way of life allowed them to become expert makers of the famous Mimbres pottery, the earliest pieces of which date from AD 750. Despite the baseness of their yucca fibre-brushes, Mogollon potters achieved extraordinary, delicate geometric and naturalistic designs (classically black on white, later polychrome), often compared to the art of Ancent Greece. Mimbres pottery was commonly placed in the graves of the dead, a "kill" hole punched through the bottom of the pot to release the spirits of its painted figures.

The Mogollon initially lived in semi-subterranean pits, covered by brush and mud plaster, arranged in villages; over time, however, the pit-houses evolved into above-ground dwellings built with stone, with the pit itself acquiring a new role as a *kiva*, a ceremonial meeting place for male kin.

Mogollon culture faded from the Southwest around AD 1250, by which date it had profoundly influenced both the Hohokam and Anasazi.

The Hohokam inhabited the burning Sonora desert, west of the Mogollon Mountains, although archaeologists dispute whether they were migrants from Mexico ("Hohokam" means "Those who have gone") or evolved from local desert Indians. Whatever, the Hohokam, who flourished between AD 200 to AD 1450 were full-on farmers, who mastered irrigation to make the desert bloom. Trapping the waters of the Gila, the Salt and their subsidiaries, the Hohokam watered their corn, bean, cotton and squash fields through hundreds of miles of canals up to twenty-five feet wide. As the Hohokam flourished, a distinct pattern of settlement arose, in which a town was surrounded by satellite villages, suggesting a political unit ruled by single potentate on the Mexican model. There were other Mexican connections; the Hohokam traded with northern Mexico, especially the Gulf of California tribes (from whom the Hohokam obtained shells, which were fashioned into personal adornments and religious items), and built ball courts like those of the Maya and other Mesoamericans. The game played on these courts was similar to basketball. Hohokam archaeological sites have given up balls made of rubber – a material foreign to Arizona.

As much of a mystery lies in the fate of the Hohokam, as in their origins. Most scholars believe that total crop failure around AD 1450 through drought or through increased soil salinity, caused the Hohokam to disband. In all probability, the modern Pima and Papago (O'Odham) Indians are their descendants.

Meanwhile, to North of Hohokam territory, on the high Colorado Plateau where the Four Corners of Arizona, New Mexico, Utah and Colorado meet, arose the greatest civilization of the Southwest, that of the Hisatsinom. Or, as the Navajo named them, the Anasazi, "The Ancient Ones".

THE ANCIENT ONES

Originally desert nomads, the earliest Anasazi, the "Basket Makers", began living in pit-houses of a distinctive round shape around AD 500. Some 200 years later, the Anasazi underwent a phenomenal cultural flowering They took up pottery, developed irrigation, farmed maize, farmed cotton, made cotton cloth, and they began to build above ground with stone and adobe. They had become the people of the Pueblos.

The essential Pueblo dwelling was a rectangular room, constructed out of stone laid in mud mortar; its joy was that it could be adjoined or even topped by another such. In other words, the basic unit could make an apartment block. Which is exactly what happened, most impressively at Pueblo Bonito in Chaco Canyon, New Mexico, where a D-shaped complex rose five storeys high and housed maybe 1,500 people. Until 1882 it was the biggest apartment block in America.

Chaco Canyon was the epicentre of Anasazi civilization; aside from Pueblo Bonito, the ten-mile length of the valley contained eight other towns ("Great Houses") and the overall population was some 5,000 people. Radiating from the canyon to the rest of the Anasazi world were extensive, straight-arrow roadways, 400 miles of them, down which trading goods flowed and pilgrims tramped. Some of the religious rituals were played out in the pueblos' plazas, others took place in cylindrical *kivas* similar to those of the Mogollon. The *kiva*, which was descended into by the smokehole in the roof, was a room for ceremony and also an earthly representation of the Anasazi's original dark underwater home. In the floor of every *kiva* was dug a hole, symbolizing *sipapu*, the entrance to the world. Some kivas, such as the Great Kiva at Chetro Keti, were fifty feet in diameter, able to accommodate 500 people, the roof supported by enormous timbers dragged by hand from the mountains forty miles away.

The Chacoan civilization was bright and brief. Within 200 years it had gone, and the canyon was abandoned to shadows. Exactly why the Anasazi quit – in quite orderly manner – the canyon is unknown. A blistering 50-year drought from about AD 1130 is a likely cause. There was also turmoil in the turquoise trade which generated much of Chaco's wealth, when the major customers, the Toltecs in Mexico, fell to the "barbarian" Chichimecs.

This was not quite the end of the Anasazi. At Mesa Verde, in southern Colorado, the Anasazi were still to fashion their remarkable cliff-dwellings; one of these alone, the Cliff Palace, contained 220 rooms and 23 *kivas*. To farm their fields on the mesa top, the Mesa Verde Anasazi had to climb sheer rock faces. In all likelihood, the Anasazi's adoption of cliff-dwelling was prompted by the aggression of nomadic tribes.

By AD 1300 the cliff-dwellings too had been abandoned. Again the "why" is a mystery. One reason advanced is that Anasazi settlements had simply become too large for the democratic-minded Anasazi to cope with. Accordingly, they walked away from their cliff-civilization, to Hopi, Acoma, and to the east, where the big river flowed.

According to Native myth, the Anasazi centres were abandoned because Snake, who oversaw rain and fertility, left the people. So most of them followed his trail, until they reached a river, where they once more built stone towns, albeit on a less grand scale than before.

In 1540, when Coronado stumbled on the Rio Grande

Valley, he found no less than one hundred stone towns
("pueblos") inhabited by the descendants of the Anasazi.

They live there still.

The Mound Builders

Across in the Southeast, meanwhile, another great corn-fed civilization had arisen, that of the Temple Mound Builders, so named for the religious edifices which topped their great earth tumps. Also called the Mississippian culture in nod to its stronghold in the bottomlands of the Mississippi and Ohio, it arose around AD 750, lasted into the historic period, and would penetrate as far westwards as Oklahoma, and north-wards to Wisconsin.

The Temple Mound Builders did not spring pure-formed out of the air, but were the culmination of other local cultures, dating back to at least 1000 BC and the Adena of Ohio, who constructed earthen mounds as burial sites for their deceased. Many traits of Adena culture were carried on by a successive mound-building culture, the Hopewell, which radiated out from Ohio to Indian villages in the midwest and east. More sophisticated agriculturalists than the Adena, the Hopewell (to whom the Corn Mothers came in about AD 100), were also major-league artisans, securing obsidian from Yellowstone, tortoiseshell from the Gulf of Mexico, silver from Ontario, bear teeth from Wyoming, all fashioned for adornment, religious ritual or as grave goods. One of the Hopewell people's most distinctive artefacts was a tubular stone pipe with animal effigies; in the pipe they smoked tobacco, not for pleasure but for ceremony. It was due to the Hopewell that pipe-smoking became universal amongst the Indians of North America.

Their mounds were more impressive than those of Adena, looming as high as forty feet into the sky, their massive size suggesting that a priestly class of overseers existed to mobilize and organize the massive labour force required for their construction. More impressive even than the Hopewell's mounds were their elaborate earthen banks, built to define and protect their sacred sites. Of these, the Great Serpent Mound, near Chillicothe in Ohio, is the exemplar, a dramatic snake effigy which twists and coils along a ridge for a quarter of a mile, before its jaws seize a gigantic egg.

By AD 500 the Hopewell culture was in terminal decay. In its stead arose the Mississippian, the benefactors of a new strain of corn, which was so dramatically productive it became almost the sole sown crop. As in the Southwest, the shift to major cropping of corn encouraged more complex political and social structures; nowhere was this more clearly seen than in the Mississippian capital of Cahokia.

CAHOKIA

Over the river from modern-day St Louis, Cahokia gathered within its pallisaded walls over 10,000 people, ruled over by a small nobility, themselves under the tutelage of an absolute monarch, the Great Sun chief. Whereas the Adena-Hopewell cultures had built earthen mounds for funerary use, the Mississipians built theirs as the base for houses and temples; the Great Sun at Cahokia lived on the flattened top of the Monk's Mound, which covered 16 acres, was 100 feet high and contained 22 million cubic feet of earth, all of it raised by hand. There were another 100 smaller mounts in Cahokia.

Cahokia was the capital of the Temple Mound people from around AD 850 to 1150, during which period they aggressively expanded their civilization. Like the Hopewell the Mississippians sat at the centre of a spider's web of trade routes – along which goods were carried by foot or by traders in dugouts – which reached up to the gold streams of Canada and down to the conch waters of the Gulf of Mexico. Lavish ceremonial centres appeared at Etowah (Georgia), Spiro (Oklahoma), and Moundville (Alabama) and other points in the Southeast, for it was the rituals and motifs of the Death Cult that bound the various Mississippian chiefdoms together. The Cult was well named; one of its principal practices was the torture-sacrifice of enemy warriors, whose severed heads would later be displayed on poles around the temple. Purification came from an emetic, the cassina-based "Black Drink", taken "until the blood comes".

But just as empires rise, so they surely fall. By the time the conquistadors tramped to the Mississippi, Cahokia had long been left to the weeds. So had Moundville and Etowah. Yet across the south, the Whites encountered numerous still-extant nations of Temple Mound Builders, including the Taensa, the Cherokees, Timucuas, Coosas, Muskokees, Mobiles, Quapaws, and Chickasaws. Of them all, it was the dog-eating Natchez nation, some 5,000 strong, who practised the old Mississippian culture in its strongest form, complete with caste system ruled over by the Great Sun. Even into the eighteenth century, French accounts tell of the Great Sun carried around on his litter, resplendent in swan-feather headdress, and so absolute a ruler that if he demanded "the life of any one of them [his subjects] he comes himself to present his head". The Natchez were a fascination to the

French, who wrote more about them than any other Indian nation of the lower Mississippi. A great deal of the ink was devoted to the extreme promiscuity of Natchez girls, although the preening tattooed Natchez warriors and the cross-dressed homosexuals had their share. Eventually, in 1731, the Natchez fell out of favour with the French, who sold the Great Sun into slavery in Santo Domingo; most of the rest of the Natchez went into exile among the Cherokee, Chickasaws and Creeks. After 2,000 years, the temple mound tradition of the Southeast was at its end.

While Mississippian society was always strictly hierarchical (the mass of the Natchez, incidentally, were termed "Stinkards"), in the woodlands of the East, a very different, even democratic, civilization flowered.

The League of Five Nations

Dekanawideh [Deganawida], *the determined man, "setting his teeth together," as his name would indicate, vowing to master himself and save his people from destruction, wandered from the crowd, and reached the side of a smooth clear-running stream, transparent and full of fishes. He sat down, reclining on the sloping bank, gazing intently into the waters . . . He was deep in thought and did not notice, perched on the top-most point in the pinery, the Great White Eagle . . . Under the bird's keen eyed scouting protection Dekanawideh's "great idea" evolved itself into specific form. Drafting a plan as he sat on the grass, trusting merely to his memory did not prove satisfactory.*

Taking an eagle feather, placing it upon the ground, "That," he said, "shall represent the great idea . . ."

Such is the story handed down for the ages, not from father to son, but from mother to children.

— JOHN OJIJATEKHA BRANT-SERO
Mohawk historian, 1901

The Iroquois were ancient inhabitants of the Woodlands of what is now New York State. Surrounded by Alonquian-speakers, the Iroquois nations – the Senecas, Mohawks, Oneidas, Onondagas and Cayugas – were skilled husbanders of the region's game and flora, and increasingly successful farmers of corn (seventeen varities of it, no less), squash, sunflower and beans. By about AD 1300 the Seneca tribe alone was harvesting more than a million bushels of corn per annum.

The tending of the Iroquois' gardens and fields was done by the women. Indeed, women controlled Iroquois, or Hodenosaunee, society. Kin relations and property were inherited through the mother, and each clan (a *de facto* extended family) was presided over by "mother of the household", the oldest woman. The clans lived in longhouses, covered in elm bark, which were oftentimes 150 feet or more in length; on ground-level beds slept the clans, while upper-storey platforms were used for the storage of food, goods and clothes. When a man married, he left his own clan to live in the longhouse of his wife. To prevent domestic strife, it was taboo for him to speak with his mother-in-law. If he was killed in war, his wife was entitled to an enemy captive as compensation; she could marry him or torture him as she chose. (The Iroquois were great torturers; sometimes they punished captives for days by ever more imaginative methods.) Even the chiefs were chosen by a council of "Mothers".

Women were also part of the tribe's priesthood, the Keepers of the Faith. As befitted a people who tended more and more to farming, the pre-Columbian Iroquois held regular communal observances in which the Three Sisters – Corn, Beans and Squash – were feted and thanked. Meanwhile, the malign spirits which always lurked near were driven out by the healing False-Face Society, who impersonated the spirits with hideous wooden masks, or by the Husk Faces, whose masks were of braided maize-husk. Evil could also be combatted by the accumulation of *orenda*, the spiritual force which was present in all things. To further help the individual and the tribe in time of illness, shamans or "medicine men" were utilized, whose curing powers came through dreams.

In dealing death to their neighbours, the Iroquois were unremittingly ferocious. So blood-red, indeed, were their stone-headed tomahawks that the Iroquois nations threatened to annihilate each other in a cycle of revenge feuds. They were saved from their own private oblivion by a Huron holy man named Deganawida, who had a vision in which he saw the Five Nations united under a Tree of Great Peace. Together with a Mohawk noble-convert, Hiawatha (as immortalized in Longfellow's "Song of Hiawatha"), he spread the word of peace and government to the five tribes, who eventually held a great council, at which Deganawida the Peace maker planted a white pine tree:

1. I am Dekanawidah and with the Five Nations' Confederate Lords I plant the Tree of Great Peace. I plant it in your territory, Adodarhoh, and the Onondaga Nation, in the territory of you who are Firekeepers.

I name the tree the Tree of the Great Long Leaves. Under the shade of this Tree of the Great Peace we spread the soft white feathery down of the globe thistle as seats for you, Adodarhoh, and your cousin Lords.

We place you upon those seats spread soft with the feather down of the globe thistle, there beneath the shade of the spreading branches of the Tree of Peace. There shall you sit and watch the Council Fire of the Confederacy of the Five Nations, and all the affairs of the Five Nations shall be transacted at this place before you, Adodarhoh, and your cousin Lords, by the Confederate Lords of the Five Nations.

2. Roots have spread out from the Tree of the Great Peace, one to the north, one to the east, one to the south and one to the west. The name of these roots is The Great White Roots and their nature is Peace and Strength.

If any man or any nation outside the Five Nations shall obey the laws of the Great Peace and make known their disposition to the Lords of the Confederacy, they may trace the Roots to the Tree and if their minds are clean and they are obedient and promise to obey the wishes of the Confederate Council, they shall be welcomed to take shelter beneath the Tree of the Long Leaves.

We place at the top of the Tree of the Long Leaves an Eagle who is able to see afar. If he sees in the distance any evil approaching or any danger threatening he will at once warn the people of the Confederacy.

The Great Law

So was the Confederacy of the Iroquois born. The date was around 1450. The territory governed by the Confederacy was envisioned as a giant longhouse that stretched from Lake Erie to Lake Champlain, with the Mohawks the Keepers of the Eastern Door, the Senecas the Keepers of the Western Door. The Onondagas, positioned at the centre, were the "fire keepers" for all the Hodenosaunee, the "people of the longhouse". To the Onondagas also fell the keeping of the wampum belts that recorded tribal treaties and history. (White wampum came from the whelk shell; the more valuable purple wampum came from the shell of the quahog clam.)

The Confederacy brought more to the Iroquois than peace; it brought democracy and government. Although certain posts were hereditary, clan mothers selected fifty male *rotiyanehr* to represent the clans at the Grand Council, where the Mohawks and Senecas sat to the east of the council fire, the Oneidas and Cayugas to the west. Decisions were be consensus, or the casting vote of the Onondagas:

9. All the business of the Five Nations Confederate Council shall be conducted by the two combined bodies of Confederate Lords. First the question shall be passed upon by the Mohawk and Seneca Lords, then it shall be discussed and passed by the Oneida and Cayuga Lords. Their decisions shall then be referred to the Onondaga Lords (Fire Keepers) for final judgement.

The same process shall obtain when a question is brought before the council by an individual or a War Chief.

10. In all cases the procedure must be as follows: when the Mohawk and Seneca Lords have unanimously agreed upon a question, they shall report their decision to the Cayuga and Oneida Lords who shall deliberate upon the question and report a unanimous decision to the Mohawk Lords. The Mohawk Lords will then report the standing of the case to the Firekeepers who shall render a decision as they see fit in case of a disagreement by the two bodies, or confirm the decisions of the two bodies if they are identical. The Fire Keepers shall then report their decision to the Mohawk Lords who shall announce it to the open council.

The *rotiyanehr* were chosen as being the wisest, fairest, most altrusistic of the clan's men. According to the Great Law, "With endless patience, they shall carry out their duty. Their firmness shall be tempered with a tenderness for their people.

Neither anger nor fury shall find lodging in their minds, and all their words and actions shall be marked by calm deliberation".

Any *rotiyanehr* who fell below such high standard were removed, sometimes ruthlessly so:

This string of wampum vests the people with the right to correct their erring Lords. In case a part or all the Lords pursue a course not vouched for by the people and heed not the third warning of their women relatives, then the matter shall be taken to the General Council of the women of the Five Nations. If the Lords notified and warned three times fail to heed, then the case falls into the hands of the men of the Five Nations. The War Chiefs shall then, by right of such power and authority, enter the open council to warn the Lord or Lords to return from the wrong course. If the Lords heed the warning they shall say, "we will reply tomorrow." If then an answer is returned in favor of justice and in accord with this Great Law, then the Lords shall individually pledge themselves again by again furnishing the necessary shells for the pledge. Then shall the War Chief or Chiefs exhort the Lords urging them to be just and true.

Should it happen that the Lords refuse to heed the third warning, then two courses are open: either the men may decide in their council to depose the Lord or Lords or to club them to death with war clubs. Should they in their council decide to take the first course the War Chief shall address the Lord or Lords, saying: "Since you the Lords of the Five Nations have refused to return to the procedure of the Constitution, we now declare your seats vacant, we take off your horns, the token of your Lordship, and others shall be chosen and installed in your seats, therefore vacate your seats."

Should the men in their council adopt the second course, the War Chief shall order his men to enter the council, to take positions beside the Lords, sitting between them wherever possible. When this is accomplished the War Chief holding in his outstretched hand a bunch of black wampum strings shall say to the erring Lords: "So now, Lords of the Five United Nations, harken to these last words from your men. You have not heeded the warnings of the women relatives, you have not heeded the warnings of the General Council of women and you have not heeded the warnings of the men of the nations, all urging you to return to the right course of action. Since you are determined to resist and to withhold justice from your people there is only one course for us to adopt." At this point the War Chief shall let drop the bunch of black wampum and the men shall spring to their feet and club the erring Lords to death. Any erring Lord may submit before the War Chief lets fall the black wampum. Then his execution is withheld.

The Great Law

Iroquois democracy, it should be noted, enjoyed universal suffrage. Every Iroquois, regardless of position or gender, had a vote. By the Iroquois Constitution or *Great Law*:

93. Whenever a specially important matter or a great emergency is presented before the Confederate Council and the nature of the matter affects the entire body of the Five Nations, threatening their utter ruin, then the Lords of the Confederacy must submit the matter to the

decision of their people and the decision of the people shall affect the decision of the Confederate Council. This decision shall be a confirmation of the voice of the people.

94. The men of every clan of the Five Nations shall have a Council Fire ever burning in readiness for a council of the clan. When it seems necessary for a council to be held to discuss the welfare of the clans, then the men may gather about the fire. This council shall have the same rights as the council of the women.

95. The women of every clan of the Five Nations shall have a Council Fire ever burning in readiness for a council of the clan. When in their opinion it seems necessary for the interest of the people they shall hold a council and their decisions and recommendations shall be introduced before the Council of the Lords by the War Chief for its consideration.

96. All the Clan council fires of a nation or of the Five Nations may unite into one general council fire, or delegates from all the council fires may be appointed to unite in a general council for discussing the interests of the people. The people shall have the right to make appointments and to delegate their power to others of their number. When their council shall have come to a conclusion on any matter, their decision shall be reported to the Council of the Nation or to the Confederate Council (as the case may require) by the War Chief or the War Chiefs.

97. Before the real people united their nations, each

nation had its council fires. Before the Great Peace their councils were held. The five Council Fires shall continue to burn as before and they are not quenched. The Lords of each nation in future shall settle their nation's affairs at this council fire governed always by the laws and rules of the council of the Confederacy and by the Great Peace.

The Iroquois Constitution had an influence beyond the Indian world. It was held in high esteem by White colonists, and its echo can be detected in the US Congress' seeking of consensus between the Senate and the House on the passage of bills.

That said, the Confederacy had a selfish military purpose, as well as a high political principle. It allowed the united Iroquois to place thousands of warriors in the field, who from 1649 onwards ruthlessly subjugated the Hurons, Eries, Illinois, Tobacco, and others. Hundreds of prisoners were tortured and killed; equally, hundreds of others were adopted.

Yet it was not just Indians who would come to dread the sound of the Iroquois war-cry. Over the next 150 years, the White intruders to the east would find the People of the Longhouse their most democratic but also their most intractable enemy.

The Buffalo Plains

The Great Plains stretch lonely and unforgiving for 2,000 miles from Texas to Alberta, walled in the west by the Rockies and beginning in the east where the Woodlands of the Iroquois dwindle out. Covered by grass, oftentimes scorched by the sun in the big sky, the Plains seemed to offer little to the post-Clovis Indian.

Save one irresistible lure. Twenty five million *bos bison Americanus*. A scale-model of the Pleistocene-era buffalo, the shaggy bison provided protein, robes, fuel (chips), awls (bones) and scores of other goods. A dozen cured buffalo hides made a tipi home. Buffalo leather could also make war shields, kettles and even coracle-like boats. The brains in the skull, cracked open with a buffalo hoof, helped tan the hide. Horns were used for drinking cups. Large bones were weapons. The Blackfeet tribe extracted no fewer than eighty-eight commodities from the buffalo, excluding food.

The trick was to kill the 900 kg beast. Early Plains Indians – who were pedestrians – commonly hunted the buffalo by stampeding the herd into a funnel-shaped drive which led over a cliff-edge. The Blackfeet called such a killing site a *pis'kun*, or deep blood kettle. Some kettles, such as the *Estipah-Sikikini-Kots* ('Where-he-got-his-head-smashed-in') kettle in southern Alberta were used for millennia by the Plains tribes, and would have been places of enormous ceremonial importance; there medicine men (shamans) would have invoked the spirits for help in the slaughter, and enticed the buffalo to their doom by *iniskims*, buffalo-attracting stones. Since Indians believed that the buffalo, like every animal, was an other-than-human person, the beast had to give its consent to die, which was obtained by prayer and reverence.

That said, thousands of buffalo would have been killed at each *pis'kun* annually, with much wastage. The fur-trader Alexander Henry observed that in a kill on the Vermilion River "the bulls were mostly entire, none but the good cows having been cut up"; Alexander was writing in AD 1809, but there is little reason to suppose that archaic Indians were more economical than their ancestors.

For the Indians who exclusively hunted buffalo, life was truly nomadic, with their tipis and scant possessions hauled around by dogs. There seem to have been few such tribes; most Indians in aboriginal days were part-time buffalo-hunters, travelling out of the woods and mountains for a twice-yearly hunt. In February they took buffalo for robes; in the autumn, when the buffalo were fat off summer grass, for meat.

From the early centuries AD, maize civilization started to spread to the Plains. Prominent among the maize-growers were the Caddoans, who pushed into eastern Texas, where they built their beehive "grass-houses" and erected palisades and moats around their villages. Yet even for these Hopewell farmers, the buffalo was a temptation too much, and they would leave regularly their static packed villages for the hunt. Alongside all the other uses of the buffalo already mentioned, the Caddo found another: they used the beast's scapulae for hoes.

The Great Plains, as far as the archaeologist's trowel can

tell, were always in people motion. Tribes came and went, moved on, migrated and emigrated. A snapshot in time, say 1540, provides the following disposition of tribes. In the north and west were the distinctly unagricultural Blackfeet and Shoshoni, plus wandering bands of Comanche and Apache; around Lake Winnipeg were the Ojibwa and Cree; to the south of Winnipeg, in descending order, were the Sioux (then Minnesota rice and maize eaters), the Pawnee, Omaha, Iowa, Missouri, Kansa, Osage, Witchita and Caddo; living along the Missouri in earth-lodges were the semi-agricultural Arikara, the ancient Mandan, and the Hidatsa; this is not to forget the Tonkawa and Karanka of south Texas, who ate buffalo and occasionally each other. Perhaps 150,000 Indians in total lived on the Buffalo Plains.

In 1540 the conquistador Coronado blundered on to the Plains, whose vast expanse then drummed with a sound long forgotten in North America: that of horses' feet. The first horse on earth had evolved on the self-same soil 40 million years before, but had become extinct in its homeland towards the end of the Pleistocene era. The Spaniard's reintroduction of the horse changed life on the Plains unforgettably and exhilaratingly.

When in 1603 the Spanish began to settle in earnest along the Rio Grande, they forbade the Indians the use of the horse. Neither the Indians nor the horse were tractable to Spanish wishes. Horses escaped, Indians raided. By about 1640 the southern Apache were mounted, and not long afterwards the Kiowa were trading horses to the Witchita, and so the horse revolution proceeded north. The Comanche were horsed by about 1700, the tribes of the central Great Plains by the 1720s.

With the horse, the buffalo was no longer a big chore, just a big target. Moreover, *equus* made it easy to follow the buffalo on its migration, and easy to carry off the haul at the kill; whereas a dog could carry seventy-five pounds of meat the horse could carry hundreds of pounds. Tribes surged onto the Plains to become horse-riding exultant nomadic hunters of the buffalo. At least nine tribes – including the Teton Sioux, the Crow and Arapaho – abandoned digging-sticks entirely. "We lost the corn," say the Cheyenne, who fled farming in North Dakota in circa 1770 to become fully-fledged equestrians by the time the explorers Lewis and Clark encountered them in the Black Hills in 1804. Of course, the new arrivals did not enter a population vacuum; as the Shoshoni complained to Lewis and Clark, that tribe had been "driven into the mountains by the Pawkees [Piegan] or the roving Indians of the Sascatchawain" who were equipped with guns garnered from the Whites in the East.

Buffalo, horse and gun. It was these three items that birthed the historic Plains Indian culture. Typical of this culture – which borrowed heavily from the Shoshoni – was complete exploitation of the buffalo, emphasis on warfare as a way of achieving social status, scalping, sun dances, and whole-time use of the tipi.

The tipi of the pedestrian Plains Shoshoni was a mere eight feet in diameter, its small size regulated by the fact that a dog had to transport it; the true tipi, as pulled by a Big Dog (as some tribes called the horse) was larger, at fifteen feet, and consisted of a large semi-circular cover over a conical frame of three or four poles, depending on tribal preference. A picture of life inside a Plains tipi in the 1830s has been left us by the artist and traveller George Catlin. He writes here of a Sioux "wigwam":

Inside of these tents, the fire is placed in the centre, the smoke escaping out at the top; and at night the inmates all sleep on buffalo-skins spread upon the ground, with their feet to the fire; a most safe, and not uncomfortable mode. When you enter one of these wigwams you have to stoop rather awkwardly; but when you are in, you rise up and find a lofty space of some twenty feet above your head. The family are all seated, and no one rises to salute you, whatever your office or your importance may be. All lower their eyes to your feet, instead of staring you in the face, and you are asked to sit down.

A robe or a mat of rushes is spread for you, and as they have no chairs you are at once embarrassed. It is an awkward thing for a white man to sit down upon the ground until he gets used to it, and when he is down, he don't know what to do with his legs.

The Indians, accustomed to this from childhood, sit down upon, and rise from, the ground with the same ease and grace that we sit down in, and rise from, a chair. Both men and women lower themselves to the ground, and rise, without a hitch or a jerk, and without touching their hand to the ground. This is very curious, but it is exceedingly graceful and neat. The men generally sit cross-legged; and to sit down they cross their feet, closely locked together, and extending their arms and head forward, slowly and regularly lower their bodies quite to the sitting posture on the ground: when they rise they place their feet in the same position, and their arms and head also, and rise to a perfectly straight position, apparently without an effort.

The women always sit with both feet and lower legs turned under and to the right or the left, and, like the men, lower and raise themselves without touching the ground.

When you are seated, to feel at ease your legs must be

crossed, and your heels drawn quite close under you, and then you can take the pipe when it is handed to you, and get a fair and deliberate glance at things around you.

The furniture in these wigwams is not much, but it is very curious in effect, and picturesque, when we look at it. The first startling thing you will meet on entering will be half-a-dozen saucy dogs, barking, and bristling, and showing their teeth, and oftentimes as many screaming children, frightened at your savage and strange appearance.

These hushed, you can take a look at other things, and you see shields, and quivers, and lances, and saddles, and medicine bags, and pouches, and spears, and cradles, and buffalo masques (which each man keeps for dancing the buffalo dance), and a great variety of other picturesque things hanging around, suspended from the poles of the tent, to which they are fastened by thongs; the whole presenting, with the picturesque group around the fire, one of the most curious scenes imaginable.

In front of these wigwams the women are seen busily at work, dressing robes and drying meat. The skin-dressing of the Indians, both of the buffalo and deer-skins, is generally very beautiful and soft. Their mode of doing this is curious: they stretch the skin, either on a frame or on the ground, and after it has remained some three or four days with the brains of the buffalo or elk spread over the fleshy side, they grain it with a sort of adze or chisel, made of a piece of buffalo bone.

After the process of "graining", and the skin is apparently beautifully finished, they pass it through another process, that of "smoking". For this, a hole of some two or three feet in depth is dug in the ground, and a smothered fire kindled in the hole with rotten wood, producing a strong and peculiar sort of smoke; and over this a little tent, made of two or three buffalo-skins, and so closed as to prevent the smoke from escaping, in which the grained skins hang for three or four days. After this process, the dresses made of these skins may be worn repeatedly in the rain, and will always dry perfectly soft – a quality which, I believe, does not yet belong to dressed skins in civilized countries.

"Drying meat" is done by cutting it into thin slices and exposing it in the sun, hung upon poles, where it dries, and is successfully cured, without salt and without smoke.

Life Among the Indians

The Sioux liked to decorate the outside of their tents with pictographs, believing these had supernatural powers to ward off misfortune and sickness. Sometimes use of pictographs was restricted to men of rank; only high-status Blackfeet, for instance, were allowed to paint the cross of the Morning Star at the top of their tipis.

Status among Plains Indian men came almost exclusively from war honours. Accordingly, warfare was a way of life for the Plains Indian male. On occasion the resultant wars between the tribes could be deadly – the west never was Arcadia: at Crow Creek in South Daokota in 1325, 500 Arikara were massacred by other Indians – but usually they were ritualized, perculiarly bloodless affairs. There were certain differences between the tribes as to what was the most daring exploit in war, but generally to "count coup" – that is, to harmlessly touch an enemy with a hand or weapon – was the top glory-winner, with rescuing a downed comrade second, and stealing enemy horses third. Soldier societies jealously administered the war honours, which were recorded on tipis and warbonnets (a fashion item thought to have originated with the Teton Sioux). Men not inclined to the rufty-tufty warriordom had no other career prospects apart from shamanism or transvestism. *Berdache* not only dressed as women but performed women's work.

Scalping had religious purpose. Scalps empowered the taker, but were also a means by which mourning could be ritually transferred from the tribe to its enemy. Scalp dances were not enjoined in joy but in relief that normal life could begin again. As befitted a religious rite, scalping imposed exacting obligations on the taker, who might be required to live on a diet of thickened milk, fish and no sex for months. The Sioux, incidentally, liked to scalp more than the top of the head; if they had time in battle they would de-skin the entire face as well.

Most raids for scalps and for honours occurred in the summer, which was also the time for assembly and ceremony. The greatest of the Plains ceremonies was the Sun Dance, another Sioux institution which became widespread the Plains across. Overseen by the men's and women's societies, the Sun Dance required participants to go without food and water for days (usually four) whilst staring fixedly at the top of a central pole which toted some representation of the sun. Some partakers also tortured themselves as Catlin recorded in 1843:

An inch or more of the flesh on each shoulder, or each breast was taken up between the thumb and finger by the man who held the knife in his right hand; and the knife, which had been ground sharp on both edges, and then hacked and notched with the blade of another, to make it produce as much pain as possible, was forced through the flesh below the fingers, and being withdrawn, was followed with a splint or skewer, from the other, who held a bunch of such in his left hand, and was ready to force them through the wound. There were then two cords lowered down from the top of the lodge, which were fastened to these splints or skewers, and they instantly began to haul him up; he was thus raised until his body was suspended from the ground where he rested, until the knife and a splint were passed through the flesh or integuments in a similar manner on each arm below the shoulder, below the elbow, on the thighs, and below the knees.

In some instances they remained in a reclining position on the ground until this painful operation was finished, which was performed, in all instances, exactly on the same parts of the body and limbs; and which, in its progress, occupied some five or six minutes.

Each one was then instantly raised with the cords, until the weight of his body was suspended by them, and then, while the blood was streaming down their limbs, the bystanders hung upon the splints each man's appropriate shield, bow and quiver, and in many instances, the skull of a buffalo with the horns on it was attached to each lower arm and each lower leg, for the purpose, probably, of preventing by their great weight, the struggling, which might otherwise have taken place to their disadvantage whilst they were hung up.

Illustrations of the Manners, Customs and Condition of the
North American Indians, 1848

To fortunate Sun Dancers a vision would be given. Sitting Bull of the Hunkpapa Sioux received one in 1876 in which he envisioned dead US soldiers "falling into our camp".

And they did so, on the Rosebud and on the Little Big Horn. By that time the Indians of North America had been fighting the Whites for more than 350 years, ever since a certain Ponce de Leon landed in Florida.

PART II

Encounter

Native America, 1513–1840

But if you do not [submit] . . . we shall powerfully enter into your country, and shall make war against you . . . We shall take you, and your wives, and your children, and shall make slaves of them.

The Spanish Requerimiento

Where today are the Pequot? Where are the Narragansett, the Mohican, the Pocanet, and other powerful tribes of our people? They have vanished before the avarice and oppression of the white man, as snow before the summer sun . . . Will we let ourselves be destroyed in our turn, without making an effort worthy of our race? Shall we, without a struggle, give up our homes, our lands, bequeathed to us by the Great Spirit? The graves of our dead and everything that is dear and sacred to us? . . . I know you will say with me, Never! Never! . . .

Sleep not longer, O Choctaws and Chickasaws, in false security and delusive hopes . . . Will not the bones of our dead be plowed up, and their graves turned into plowed fields?

Tecumseh, Shawnee chief, July 1811

Prologue

It was on 12 October 1492 that the isolation of the Indians was ended forever, when a lost Christopher Columbus bumped into the Bahamas. Believing himself to be in the East Indies, he termed the natives of the archipelago, "Indios".

The inappropriateness of the name, the sheer accidental nature of the encounter never augured well.

These "Indios" Columbus found to be primitive yet charming: "So tractable, so peacable, are these people", Columbus wrote to his sponsors, the King and Queen of Spain, "that I swear to your Majesties there is not in the world a better nation. They love their neighbours as themselves, and their discourse is ever sweet and gentle, and accompanied with a smile; and though it is true they they are naked, yet their manners are decorous and praiseworthy."

Despite, or perhaps because, of the "tractable, so peacable" nature of the Arawaks, Columbus promptly proceeded to claim their land in the name of Spain, force their conversion to Christianity and then enslave them. On his first voyage, Columbus took ten Arawaks home as slaves. All but two died.

The Arawaks had also given Columbus a fatal gift: gold. Within a year, Columbus was back in the Caribbean, putting the Indians to work (as slaves) digging and panning for gold. So hard was the labour, so brutal were their overseers that the Indians of Hispaniola (Haiti, the Spaniard's first base) revolted. Five hundred years of war between Native and Invader had begun.

The Spaniards put down the insurrection with spectacular savagery, massacring entire villages, hanging individuals on the 340 gallows they erected, burning others, and shipping thousands off to Spain. Wrote one Spaniard sympathetic to the Indians, the famous missionary Bartolome de Las Casas: "It was a general rule among the Spaniards to be cruel; not just cruel, but extraordinarily cruel so that harsh and bitter treatment would prevent Indians from daring to think of themselves as human beings or having a minute to think at all. So they would cut an Indian's hands and leave them dangling by a shred of skin and they would send him on, saying, 'Go now, spread the news to your chiefs.'" They would test their swords and their manly strength on captured Indians and place bets on the slicing off of heads or the cutting of bodies in half with one blow. They burned or hanged captured chiefs.

Those whom the Spaniards spared disease (probably swine influenza) did not. "So many Indians died that they could not be counted", wrote a Spanish observer, "all through the land the Indians lay dead everywhere. The stench was very great and pestiferous." The first Americans had no resistance to European dieases. Many plagues – influenza smallpox, measles and others – would overwhelm them in the years to come.

How many native people lived on Hispaniola when Columbus arrived is unknown. Possibly there were eight million of them. By 1520, there were 20,000. By 1535 there were none.

The same fate consumed all the inhabitants of the surrounding islands in the Caribbean. And it awaited the Indians on the mainland of the Americas, in Peru, in Mexico, and then in what would become the United States.

Blood on the Flowers

Florida is one of the bountiful places on Earth, possessed as it is by the sun and the waters. So abundant is the life in its seas that Indians of the region were able to build, against all laws of anthropology, static, complex societies based on fishery not agriculture. Pre-eminent among the tribes were the Calusa, with their vast shell-island capital at Calos (near Fort Myers), where the chief's hall was able to sit 2,000 "without being very crowded".

The Calusa were great sailors, trading over the Keys and as far as Cuba. They would have heard early about the strange cruelties of the bearded strangers.

In 1513 the conquistador Juan Ponce de Leon landed in Florida (named by him after the April "Feast of Flowers", Pascua Florida, when he discovered it). Failing to find gold, he fell back on raids for the conquistador's second favourite commodity, slaves. Here too, de Leon was luckless; when he landed in San Carlos Bay, the alerted Calusa warriors attacked in eighty canoes, and after two days of pitched battle forced the conquistadors off. Thus was the first blood spilt between European and Native American in the United States.

Eight years later, in 1521, de Leon returned to Calusa

country, this time as the would-be leader of a Spanish settlement. Behind a barrage of Spanish fire-power, a fort was built but the settlers succumbed steadily to the Calusa's poisoned arrows. When de Leon himself was injured in the thigh, they fled to Havana, where de Leon died of his wound.

For fifty years the Spanish left the Calusa alone, choosing instead to invade the lands of the tattoed Timucuan on Florida's Gulf coast and build a fort at St Augustine (the first permanent white settlement in the USA). Then in 1566 Pedro Menendez de Aviles sailed into the Calusa's main harbour, indicating a desire to parlay.

Both sides hankered after diplomacy. Spanish guns had made the Calusa's enemies, the Timucuan, powerful enough to threaten Calusa tributary towns; alliance with Spain would enable the Calusa to retain their dominance. For his part Menendez wanted the gold and the captives the Calusa took from the frequent Spanish wrecks along their coasts. To bind the alliance, the Calusa chief Carlos II, proposed that his sister should be married to Menendez. The Spaniard baulked at the miscegenous idea, and was only tempted into matrimony when Carlos offered his people's conversion to Christianity. Menendez, accompanied by his new Calusa wife, now baptized Dona Antonia, beat an undignified hasty retreat to Havana.

Outside of Greek mythology, Dona Antonia became one of the few women to cause a war. She was alternatively abandoned and then held hostage by Menendez, who further angered the Calusa by politicking with their enemies, the Tocobagas. "Menedez has two hearts," Dona Antonia complained. "One for himself and one for Tocobaga, but none at all for me or my brother."

Determining to rid Calusa of the Spaniards, Carlos II ejected a Jesuit missionary and attempted the seizure of a

Spanish galleon. Menendez reacted with all the terror of the conquistador challenged. After tricking Carlos to a meeting, he beheaded him and installed a puppet chief at musket-point. Civil war among the Calusa ensued, before the mass receded into the jungle, burning their capital behind them in an Indian turn at scorched earth. Bereft of Calusa provisions and manpower, the enraged Spaniards held the country, but meaninglessly so: starving, they had little option but to quit, salving their pride by condemning the Calusa's lands as unfit for agriculture.

With the Spanish gone, the Calusa trickled back to their capital, and went on much as before. Years later, they traded with more peaceable Spaniards, but never converted to Christianity. Eventually the European's diseases triumphed where Menendez's arms had not. By the eighteenth century, the once mighty Calusa were reduced to small bands and were driven by English-backed Indians from north Florida into the Keys. A few hundred surivived to be incorporated into what are now the Miccosukee and Seminole nations.

The Calusa were not the only vanished tribe of Florida. The Timucua, after being gathered into Spanish missions for conversion, rebelled unsuccessfully in 1656, their population further depleted by pestilence and the pure lucklessness of being caught in imperial wars of the white invaders. By 1736 the Timucua had vanished. So too had the Apalachee, from near Tallahassee, who were subjugated and carried into exile by the English and their Creek mercenaries in 1704. Today, the Apalachee exist only in a word. Appalachian.

DE SOTO'S RAMPAGE

Juan Ponce de Leon's failure to find the yellow metal did not deter other conquistadors for questing for gold in the land of flowers.

Hernando de Soto landed at Espiritu Santo, Florida, in the summer of 1539, along with 550 soldiers and gangs of workmen. They included smiths, to make slave collars. De Soto brought horses, attack dogs, and pigs too, the latter doubling as larder and scourge of Indians in ambush. Turning north, de Soto began hacking his way through the packed Timucuan nation, with its statehouses and vast crop fields, grabbing all and sundry to act as manacled bearers. Uncomprehending chiefs were read the *Requerimiento,* the legal device the Spanish used to sanction their conquests in the name of God and Iberia, before submitting by the grace of the conquistador's fire-power. Many resisted. The Timuacan chief of Acuera informed de Soto that "I and all my people have vowed to die a hundred deaths to maintain the freedom of our land." Unfortunately for the Timuacans they lost the pitched battle they took to the Spaniards. When their chief was captured, he gamely managed to land de Soto such a blow with his fist that he knocked two of the conquistador's teeth out. At this, de Soto's men fell on the Timucuan captives, slashing them with their swords, bit by bit, until they died.

After wintering near Tallahasee, the Spaniards continued with their trail of death and destruction, entering into what are now Georgia and South Carolina in spring 1540. At Cofitachequi on the Savannah River, the Spaniards encountered the Creeks, who were "more civilized than any [Indians] . . . seen in all the territories of Florida, wearing clothes and shoes". A young Creek chieftainess, adorned in feathers and furthers, came to greet de Soto with canoes laden with gifts. So captured was de Soto with the loveliness of the chiefteness that he called her "the Lady of Cofitachequi". According to de Soto's secretary, "She was a young girl of fine bearing; and she took off a string of pearls which she wore on her neck, and put it on the Governor as a necklace to show her favour."

Certainly, the chieftainess hoped that such diplomacy, such largesse would cause de Soto to spare her nation. It did not. He ordered his men to plunder the graves at the temple mound, and dig out the chests of pearls they had learned were buried there. De Soto then kidnapped the chieftainess to act as his guide through the Appalachian Mountains. The Lady later escaped, taking with her a large box of plundered pearls.

After a stumbling and starving detour through Cherokee country, where the "Tsalagi" gave them dogs to eat, the Spaniards turned southwest to Creek country again, entering Mississippian civilization of Coosa in July 1540.

Accompanied by a thousand men in feathered headdresses, dressed in a robe of marten skins, the paramount chief of the Coosa greeted de Soto, and escorted him to the Coosa capital. With a wiliness beyond his youthful years, the Coosa chief proved de Soto's equal in diplomatic manoeuvering, and managed to persuade him out of his country.

De Soto and his column of soldiers and slaves then tramped onto towards Choctaw territory, where he seized the Mobile chief, Tascalusa. There were the usual Spanish demands for gold and bearers. These the Tascalusa agreed to gather at the town of Mabila.

And so a trap was set for de Soto. Behind the fortifications of Mabila was an army of warriors. Over the stockade walls they poured, forcing the Spaniards to retreat, until de Soto steadied them. The battle which followed was the greatest de

Soto's men fought with the Indians. Eventually, the Spaniards drove forwards into the town, breaking down its wooden walls with their battle axes, crowding the Mobile into their houses. To the blast of trumpets and the beating of drums, de Soto ordered the buildings afired. Amid the terrible swirling smoke and flames, the Mobile, a Spaniard recalled, "fought with a desire to die".

After nine hours, as the sun set, the sound of battle died away. In the silence and smoke, even the hardbitten Spanish soldiers stood shocked. Around them, between the burned out buildings, the streets were deep with thousands of Mobile dead, perhaps as many as ten thousand of them. The Spaniards suffered only two fatalities.

De Soto's men spent the winter in Chickasaw country. So aggrieved were the Chikasaw by de Soto's depradations that they slaughtered nearly all his horses and eleven of his men. Recovering, de Soto marched off once more, reaching the Mississippi in May. As de Soto's men built barges on the shore for the crossing, they were visited by chiefs of the Azuixo (the Arkansas):

The Indians came presently down the river; they leaped on shore, and declared to the Governor, that they were subjects of a great lord, whose name was Aquixo, who was lord of many townes, and governed many people on the other side of the river, and came to tell him on his behalfe, that the next day he with all his men would come to see what it would please him to command him.

The next day with speed, the cacique came with two hundred canoes full of Indians with their bowes and arrowes, painted, and with great plumes of white feathers, and many other colours, with shields in their hands, wherewith they defended the rowers on both sides, and the men of warre stood from the head to the sterne, with their bowes and arrows in their hands. The canoe wherein the cacique was, had a tilt over the sterne, and hee sate under the tilt; and so were other canoes of the principall Indians. And from under the tilt where the chiefe man sat, hee governed and commanded the other people. All joyned together, and came within a stones cast of the shore. From thence the cacique said to the Governour, which walked along the rivers side with others that waited on him, that he was come thither to visit, to honour, and to obey him. because he knew he was the greatest and mightiest lord on the earth: therefore he would see what he would command him to doe. The Governour yielded him thankes, and requested him to come on shore, that they might the better communicate together. And without any answere to that point, hee sent him three canoes, wherein was great store of fish, and loaves made of the substance of prunes, like unto brickes. After he had received all, he thanked him, and prayed him againe to come on shore, and because the caciques purpose was, to see if with dissimulation he might doe some hurt, when they saw that the Governour and his men were in readinesse, they began to goe from the shore; and with a great crie, the crossebowmen which were ready, shot at them, and slue five or sixe of them. They retired with great order; none did leave his oare, though the next to him were slaine; and shielding themselves, they went farther off. Afterward they came many times and landed: and when any of us came toward them, they fled unto their canoes, which were verie pleasant to behold for they were very great and well made, and had their tilts, plumes, paveses and flagges and with the multitude of people that were in them they seemed to be a faire armie of gallies.

Across the Big River, it was plunder and kidnap as usual for de Soto. In Arkansas, the people abandoned their towns as he neared, but his raiding parties stole the unwary and the unprepared. Only gold still eluded him. After months careering around Arkansas, the disillusioned de Soto began the return journey. On reaching the Mississippi again, at Guachoya, he "took to his pallet". Even in illness, he demanded the rights of the conqueror, sending a message to the town on the opposite bank that he was the "Child of the Sun" and should be obeyed. The chief of the haughty Natchez tribe, inheritors of the old earth-mound culture, was distinctly underawed, and told de Soto to go and dry up the river if he truly was the Child of the Sun. Too enervated to punish such trans-Mississippi insolence, de Soto had an innocent village nearby razed to the ground. Commented one Spaniard: "The cries of the women and children were such as to deafen those who pursued them . . . About one hundred men were slain; many were allowed to get away badly wounded that they might strike terror into those who were absent."

De Soto committed no more depredation, for he died shortly afterwards. His men journeyed around Louisiana and east Texas, then elected to escape down the Mississippi. On the river they were attacked by flotillas of painted Natchez canoes, their awnings fluttering in the river breeze, and even when they passed from Natchez territory they were not safe. Other tribes attacked and harassed the Spaniards, killing ten of them, until they were finally driven out into the Gulf on 18 July 1542.

The de Soto expedition was over. Its impression on the

tribes of the southeast was deadly and indelible. Disorientated by the failure of their religions and their chiefs to protect them, hopelessness spread through the people. But not as quickly as the microbes the Spaniards left behind.

When another Spaniard, Tristan de Luna, visited the southeast less then twenty years after de Soto, he found it a ghost land. Temple mounds were unkempt, maize fields were unworked, the roads empty. The Coosa capital, which once boasted 500 houses, was near deserted. Some Old World disease, even perhaps the one which killed de Soto himself, had annihilated the Indians of the Southeast.

Blood on the Stone

While de Soto put the Southeast to sword and flame, another conquistador had plunged into the interior of North America. This was Francisco Vasquez de Coronado, who rode up out of Mexico in 1540 in the search for the legendary Seven Cities of Cibola, where the streets were reputedly paved with gold.

Coronado's expedition had a colourful genesis. Twelve years earlier, the freebooting Panfilo de Narvaez had scoured Florida for *oro*, before his expedition floundered in disease and Indian attacks (he had, ill-advisedly, thrown the ancient mother of the Timuacan chief to his dogs). Fleeing for the sanctuary of the Mexican settlements, the makeshift craft of Narvaez's men were blown ashore on the Texas coasts, near the mouth of the Sabine. There they were killed or enslaved by the local Indians. After the passage of six years, four Spaniards, led by Cabeza de Vaca and including the black servant Estevan, escaped and spent two years wandering the southwest. It was during this journeying that they heard of the fabulous Indian cities to the north, where the people lived in immense towns with multistoried buildings. De Vaca and his companions had some reputation as medicine men, and were feted by the local tribes and eventually escorted to the Sonora

Valley trail to Mexico. The odysseans reached Mexico City in July 1536, where their tale of gilded cities to the north caused gold fever. Soon was dispatched a reconnaissance under Fray Marcos de Niza and Estevan, neither of them of sober judgement. To Fray Marcos's eager ears, Estevan reported that he had reached the fabled City of Cibola; in truth, he had reached the stone "pueblo" of Hawikuh (where the Zuni chief later killed him). The credulous Fray Marcos then sped back to Mexico to report that he had found a land which was the "largest and best of all those discovered", and where the "house doors were studded with jewels".

Thus it was that in February 1540 the thirty-year-old governor of New Galicia, Francisco Vasquez de Coronado, departed Compostela for the Seven Cities of Cibola. Accompanying him were 300 soldiers, a party of priests and a small host of the contradictions which would bedevil the encounter between the Whites and the Indians. Unlike many conquistadors, Coronado did not set out with genocide in his heart; both his personality and his orders from Spain urged humanity. Meanwhile, marching alongside Coronado's men were one thousand Indians who sought to profit over others of their race by serving the Spanish cause.

With Fray Marcos as their guide, Coronado's conquistadors meandered north, until they reached Hawikuh. The Zuni were not welcoming. Astonished by their first sight of horses (which the Zuni thought must be man-eaters, because of their gargantuan faces and teeth), the Zuni herded their women and children onto a nearby mesa, while the priests rushed out and put a sacred line of cornmeal on ground, shouting to the Spanish to halt with their monsters. Paying no heed, the Spaniards hastened on. A Zuni war horn sounded, and arrows and stones pelted down on the Spaniards, who replied with their battle cry of "Santiago" and charged at the Zuni lines.

Within the hour, the Zunis had been routed by Spanish guns and horses. Hawikuh was taken.

To Coronado's bitter disappointment, "Cibola" was not a city of gold, merely, in the words of the expedition's chronicler, "a little crowded village, looking as if it had been crumpled all up together". The Zuni pueblo may have been only made of mud, yet it was the centre for an extensive agriculture, and the foodstores were overflowing, to the relief of the hungry Spanish invader. "There we found something we prized much more than gold or silver; namely plentiful maize and beans, turkeys larger than those in New Spain [Mexico], and salt better and whiter than I have ever seen in my whole life," reported the chronicler.

Coronado's expedition remained at Hawikuh for four months, during which time he received delegations and gifts from numerous towns, who hoped to satisfy the white gods of which their prophecies had sometimes spoken. The conquistadors, meanwhile, still yearned for gold, and sent out desperate expeditions. One party, led by Garcia de Cardenas, came upon the Grand Canyon, but frustrated could proceed no further. Soldiers under Pedro de Tovar explored the mesa-top towns of the Hopi. Another detachment, under Hernando de Alvarado, tramped east and entered the Pueblos along the Rio Grande, which the invaders named Tiguex after its Tigua (Tiwa) Pueblo inhabitants. As always, there was no yellow metal. There were, however, watered meadows and well-stocked towns, and the conquistadors, having exhausted the larder of the Zuni, moved to winter in Tiguex territory.

Ordering the Indians out of the Alcanfor Pueblo, Coronado requisitioned the buildings for his troops. The Indians had offered hospitality, in return they were ejected from their homes. More high-handedness was to come. As cold weather licked at the Pueblo, Coronado ordered the local Tiwa towns to provide clothing for his men – even stripping cloaks off the Indians' backs.

Relations had reached breaking point. They snapped when a Spaniard raped an Indian woman, and her husband's complaint was ignored.

Understanding, at last, that the White strangers were mortals not deities, the Indians rushed to fortify the outlying Tiguex pueblos and attacked a fundamental of Spanish power: the horse herd. The Tiguex uprising spread quickly. Coronado, in reply, ordered his soldiers "not to take them [the Indians] alive, but to make an example of them so that the other natives would fear the Spaniards". At the town where the woman had been raped, Coronado's men pounded their way in, setting the buildings alight. Suffocating on the smoke, the Indians staggered out to be captured by Coronado's lieutenant, Garcia Lopez de Cardenas. Acccording to the Spanish chronicler: "[Cardenas] . . . ordered two hundred stakes to be prepared at once to burn them alive. Nobody told him about the peace that had been granted them . . . not thinking that it was any of their business. Then when the enemies saw the Spaniards were binding them and beginning to roast them, about a hundred men who were in the tent began to struggle and defend themselves with what there was there and with the stakes they could seize. Our men who were on foot attacked the tent on all sides . . . and then the horsemen chased those who escaped. As the country was level, not a man of them remained alive. . ."

It was now the end of December. Some Tiguex fled to the Sangre de Cristo mountains, others barricaded themselves into two pueblos, where they were besieged. One Pueblo, Moho, held out for fifty days, until its water was gone. A night exodus was intercepted by the Spanish, who slew all they could, save for some women and children taken as slaves. To ensure the Indians marked his might, Coronado had the other Tiguex pueblos burned down. So passed the Tiguex from the face of the Earth.

The following spring, Coronado set out for the fabled land of "Quivira", where the chief "took his afternoon nap under a great tree on which were hung a number of little gold bells, which put him to sleep as they swung in the air". Two Indians, a Witchita named Sopete and Pawnee nicknamed "Turk", were his guides. For days the mighty procession of conquistadors followed the Pawnee Pied Piper, over the Texas Panhandle and past the disbelieving Apache, until at Tule Canyon Coronado realized that he had been fooled. The Turk had sought to lose the Spaniards in the vastness of the Plains.

Coronado had the Turk clapped in irons. By compass he directed the expedition to Quivira himself. To Coronado's fury, there no gold, no jewels, no furs – nothing worth a conquistador's while, only some bee-hive grass-covered lodges belonging to the Witchita. Raging with anger, Coronado's men garrotted the Turk. Letting Sopete go to his people, the demoralized conquistadors turned south for another impoverished winter in the Tiguex Pueblos.

By early next spring, the conquistadors were on the trail back to Mexico. Behind them, the land lay wounded and the tribes shattered and fearful. But if the Indians hoped the Spaniards had gone for ever, they were to be disappointed.

Sky City

For four decades, the Pueblos were allowed to tend their wounds. Goldless, they had no interest for the Spanish. Until, that is, the Spanish court decided that they were godless and should be saved. Accordingly, the Crown authorized Don Juan de Onate, the husband of one of the Cortes' grand-daughters, to occupy the land of the Pueblos for King and God. "Your main purpose," the instructions to Onate read, "shall be the service of God Our Lord, the spreading of his holy Catholic faith and the reduction and pacification of the natives of the said provinces." Another whirlwind was about to storm through the land of the Pueblos.

Onate eventually set out in January 1598, a vast train of troops, colonists, friars, cattle and carts behind him. Encountering the Pueblos, he was received with hospitality and gifts; their spiritual world healed, the Pueblo people forgave past Spanish excess.

Present excesses were a different matter. In a manner reminiscent of Coronado, Onate ordered the Indians to evacuate a town, which he renamed San Juan and took as his garrison and capital. His black-robed friars forcibly converted the (probably uncomprehending) Indians, to the chagrin of their religious leaders. Even after receiving a generous donation of turkeys and corn from the Acoma pueblo, the Spaniards demanded more. A gift was a gift: a demand was an insult.

In December 1528, the Acoma refused to provide water, wood and food for a second assessment ordered by Onate's lieutenant, Juan de Zaldivar. Eventually Zaldivar persuaded the Acoma to sell him corn, and entered the pueblo to collect it. Some incident – possibly a sexual assault on an Acoma woman, possibly the Spanish theft of a turkey – caused Acoma warriors to kill Zaldivar and fourteen Spanish soldiers

On hearing of this "outrage", Onate ordered a punitive expedition to be sent against the Acoma. Chosen as leader was Zaldivar's brother, Vicente. By a decree of 10 January 1599, Zaldivar was ordered: ". . . inasmuch as we have declared war on them without quarter, you will punish all those of fighting age as you deem best, as a warning to everyone in this kingdom. All of those you execute you will expose to public view at places you think most suitable . . . If you should want to show lenience after they have been arrested, you should seek all possible means to make the Indians believe that you are doing so at the request of the friar with your forces. In this manner they will recognize the friars as their benefactors and protectors and come to love and esteem them, and to fear us."

Twelve days later, the Spaniards arrived to inflict their retribution on Acoma, which towered four hundred feet above them on the mesa top. For more than five hundred years, Aku (Sky City) had floated in the desert air like an hallucination. One of the most ancient Pueblos, it was also unconquered. One Spaniard described it so:

The village was very strong, because it was up on a rock out of reach, having steep sides in every direction . . .

There was only one entrance by a stairway built by hand
... There was a broad stairway for about 200 steps, then a
stretch of about 100 narrower steps, and at the top they
had to go up about three times as high as a man by means
of holes in the rock, in which they put the points of their
feet, holding on at the same time by their hands. There
was a wall of large and small stones at the top, whch they
could roll down without showing themselves, so that no
army could possibly be strong enough to capture the
village. On the top they had room to sow and store a large
amount of corn, and cisterns to collect snow and water.

Sky City was invulnerable to all people. Except for those
from another land equipped with gunpowder, cannon, and
armour.

Launching a diversionary attack on the narrow steps up to
the city, Zaldivar dispatched a small team to scale the rear
mesa, dragging behind them a cannon. Whence at the top,
the cannon was directed at the city, shot after shot pounding
the stone and mud buildings. Meanwhile, the main Spanish
force took advantage of the Acomas' confusion and stormed
up the steps into the city. For three days, there was building-
by-building fighting, with desperate Acoma warriors trying to
contain the cannon by throwing their bodies at its mouth.
Later a soldier with Zaldivar recalled the battle at Sky City:

In the attack of the preceding Thursday more than 300
men were killed, and from Saturday to Sunday, more
than 200 more. We began to set fire to the pueblo and
to destroy it, forcing them to retire to the strongest parts.
The estufas [kivas] of the pueblo had been fortified until
the first one was about as strong as the peñol [mesa]
itself . . . In good order [with two artillery-pieces], we

forced the Indians to fight and they attacked with great fury. Twice we drew back, with them upon us, but they always fared badly. The result was that more than 800 persons died, and the prisoners taken numbered 500 women and children, and 80 men. The latter were tried and punished. With this the land was pacified thanks to God our Lord.

The punishment meted to the Acoma for their "treason" was draconian. All males over twenty-five had one foot amputated, the mutilation done in public *pour encourager les autres,* and also sentenced to twenty years of personal servitude. All Acoma between twelve and twenty-five were condemned to twenty years' slavery. All girls under twelve were given to the friars, all boys to Zaldivar.

Next to incur the wrath of Onate were the Tompiros, whose reluctance to donate him food and blankets caused Onate to fire their pueblo. Then he sent Zaldivar to battle against them, who dutifully razed three of their pueblos to the ground, and slaughtered a thousand Indians in a six-day running fight, the sand thick with bodies, blood and swarming flies.

Onate succeeded in cowing the pueblos, but not in defeating them. Thousands of Indians took to the mountains, and the food supply of the Spaniards dwindled, since the Spaniards would not sully their own hands with toil. When Onate returned in September 1601 from his personal wild-goose chase to Quivira, he found his colony hungry and mutinous. Among the complainants were the Franciscan friars, because their missionary work had been undone by the brutality of the settler-soldiers. The Indians asked the friars, "if . . . Christians cause so much harm and violence, why should [we] become Christians?"

At length, Onate was forced out as governor, and convicted for his cruelty towards the Indians. A new governor moved the capital to Sante Fe, where he built thick walls (fortuitously, as it would turn out), and succoured the friars in their feverish conversion work. Not dissimilar to the Indians in their deep spirituality and love of ritual, the Franciscans cleverly and successfully grafted their Catholicism onto the Native ceremonial cycle. Less astute was the friars' fanatical bent towards merciless physical chastisements, even unto death, for any display of "idolatry" – masks, fetishes, wooden dolls – and "licentiousness"; the people of the Pueblos, to Franciscan consternation, were polygamous and non-monagamous. Moreover, the Franciscans sought to fashion Pueblo male and female roles to life in the European image. Men were denied hunting and war, and put to work as sheepherders and builders; the women laughed at such emasculation. If the Indian men protested to the friars, the black-robes only humiliated them more, oftentimes twisting their testicles in public.

In 1680 the people of the Pueblos revolted. Led by Pope, an Indian who had been lashed for "sorcery", 8,000 Indians turned on their overlords, stealing their horses, destroying their settlements, until only Sante Fe was a refuge. Eventually, behind a barrage of gunfire, 200 Spaniards broke out and escaped down to Mexico, their route passing through countryside littered with dead friars and smoking churches.

Although the Spanish reconquered New Mexico in 1692, they did so in a different manner than hitherto; in the words of the expedition's leader, Don Diego de Vargas, the conquest passed off without "wasting a single ounce of powder, unsheathing a sword, or . . . costing the Royal Treasury a single maravedi". De Vargas' softly softly approach was caused by neat, distilled political need; the

Spaniards were threatened in North America by Apache, French and English expansion, and a stable northern frontier was an imperial necessity. So, instead of fighting the Pueblos, Spain employed their services as auxiliaries; instead of extirpating their religion they left it alone. The Pueblos played the game, too, using Spanish power as protection against marauding Apache and Navajo, operating the externals of Christian ritual alongside their own observances, and becoming deft herders of Spanish-introduced sheep.* Nearly 200 years passed in such uneasy but such eminently practical co-existence, until Spanish power was broken in the land of New Mexico by the Anglos. The consequence of co-existence was longer lived: the Pueblos retained their identity and their religious practices more successfully than almost any other group of Native Americans. To this day, kachinas, dances, and kiva rites harmonize the Pueblo Indian with the world.

*Only the remote Hopi were not brought back into the Spanish fold.

Blood on the Wood

Why will you take by force what you may obtain by love? Why will you destroy us who supply you with food? What can you get by war? . . . We are unarmed, and willing to give you what you ask, if you come in a friendly manner . . .

I am not so simple as not to know it is better to eat good meat, sleep comfortably, live quietly with my women and children, laugh and be merry with the English, and being their friend, trade for their copper and hatchets, than to run away from them . . .

Take away your guns and swords, the cause of all our jealousy, or you may die in the same manner.

Powhatan, 1609

Although the Spanish were the first Whites to settle in what would become the United States, the country's conquest ultimately lay with others. Spain was too riven with intellectal difficulties, too possessed by skimming of the land's metallic wealth to develop a coherent colonization policy. France, too, tended to look upon the New World as place to plunder – be it gold, furs or Newfoundland cod – and to trade. As a result, the whole of the Eastern seaboard from Canada down to

Florida – a temperate terrain ideally suited to large-scale agricultural settlement – was unclaimed.

It was the fortune and fate of Britain that when she came to build her empire, this land was free. Or at least free from Whites, for it was of course lived upon and loved by the tribes of the northeast, principally the Algonquian peoples. The first British expeditions failed, but in 1606 the London Company was granted the right by James I "to deduce a colony of sundry of our people" in America, north of the 34th parallel. Three ships made their way across the ocean in 1607. "The six and twentieth day of April about foure a clocke in the morning," wrote Master George Percy, "wee descried the Land of Virginia . . . faire meddowes and goodly tall trees, with such Fresh-waters runninge through the woods as I was almost ravished at the first Sight thereof."

After landing, the settlers built a village, James Fort, named in honour of the monarch. And within a mere two weeks were attacked in force by the Powhatan Confederacy, an alliance of thirty one Algonquian tribes led by Wahunsonacock – known to the English as Powhatan, after his nation. The Powhatan already had experience of the Whites, from passing slave-traders and priests and they knew from the Secotan to the south, where the English colony under Ralph Lane had been planted and "lost", what European weaponry and germs could do.

The English settlers drove off the Powhatan assault with their cannons and muskets. Where the Powhatan failed, famine succeeded. So poor were the 150 colonists at farming – most of them were gentry and soldiers – that nearly half of them were dead by September. And more would have gone to their graves, save for some local Powhatan taking pity on them. "It pleased God (in our extremity)," wrote Captain John Smith, the colony's leader, "to move the Indians to bring us Corne, ere it was halfe ripe, to refresh us, when we rather expected . . . they would destroy us."

Destruction of James Fort was no longer the wily Powhatan's desire. Appreciating that the colony, if brought into membership of the Powhatan Confederation, could be a fine source of guns and metal, he instead flattered and provisioned it.

Unfortunately, Powhatan was only feeding the hand that would bite him. When a fire destroyed the James Fort foodstore, John Smith demanded that the Pamunkey, one of the principal tribes of the Powhatan Confederacy, sell him corn. Their chief, Opechancanough refused – at which Smith seized him by the hair and pushed a pistol into his face, while his men took the corn anyway.

More insolence and intimidation by the colonists ensued, and the inevitable war between the proud Powhatan and the Whites broke out in the fall of 1609. For months the Powhatan besieged James Fort (later Jamestown), until reinforcements arrived in summer 1610, and the English, fired up on revenge and religious fervour, took the war to the "ungodly" Powhatan. Despite their grievous losses, the Powhatan stuck it out until 1613, when Powhatan's beloved daughter, Pocohontas, was kidnapped. Now Powhatan sued for peace, which was sealed by Pocohontas' marriage to the settler John Rolfe, "for the good of the plantation". It was conveniently ignored that Pocohontas – a nickname meaning "frisky"; her real name was Matowaka – was already married to a brave, Kocoum. Whatever, Rolfe learned from the Powhatan the cultivation of tobacco, and through him the colony had its source of fortune. In 1616 Rolfe took his bride to London, where "Lady Rebecca" as she had been baptized, dazzled everyone from Ben Jonson to James' queen. A year later, on the passage back to Jamestown, Pocohontas died of smallpox. She was 21.

The grief-stricken Powhatan abdicated leadership of the Confederacy and died within the year, leaving his half-brother Opechancanough as paramount chief. Unlike the conciliatory Powhatan, Opechancanough was an implacable enemy of the "coat-wearing people", and whipped up hatred against them with the help of the charismatic, feather-robed Pamunkey war-chief, Nemattanew. It was easily done, for the colonists' appetite for land was insatiable. And they took the best of it; early in the life of James Fort the "cutt-throats" (another popular Algonquian name for the English) had felled through herculean effort forty acres of land, but thereafter they found it easier to seize the Indian's fields, and let their livestock run over the Indian's unfenced gardens.

In the spring of 1622 the Powhatans struck in sudden fury. Recalled one contemporary, Anthony Chester:

Several days before this bloodthirsty people put their plan into execution, they led some of our people through very dangerous woods into a place from which they could not extricate themselves without the aid of a guide, others of us who were among them to learn their language were in a friendly way persuaded to return to our colony, while new comers were treated in an exceedingly friendly manner.

On Friday before the day appointed by them for the attack they visited, entirely unarmed, some of our people in their dwellings, offering to exchange skins, fish and other things, while our people entirely ignorant of their plans received them in a friendly manner.

When the day appointed for the massacre had arrived, a number of the savages visited many of our people in their dwellings, and while partaking with them of their meal the savages, at a given signal, drew their weapons and fell upon us murdering and killing everybody they could reach sparing neither women nor children, as well inside as outside the dwellings. In this attack 347 of the English of both sexes and all ages were killed. Simply killing our people did not satisfy their inhuman nature, they dragged the dead bodies all over the country, tearing them limb from limb, and carrying the pieces in triumph around.

Jamestown itself might have been wiped off the face of the country, save for a converted Indian, Chanco, warning an English friend.

The surviving English then sent out three punitive expeditions a year, captained by men under oath to make no peace whatsoever. Along the York and lower James rivers, the Indians were for all intents and purposes exterminated. Opechanough's capital was burned down, and 800 Indians slain in a single day. To ensure that the Indians starved, the English smashed their fishing weirs and canoes, and in a single day destroyed enough corn to feed people for a year.

Conjuring the Indians as mere brutes, the colonists exercised no restraint in their warring; they even set on the Indians "blood-Hounds to draw after them . . . Mastives to seaze them, which take this naked, tanned, deformed Savage, for no other then wild beasts.' Anything went. Two hundred Chiskiacks were invited to parlay, then given a poisoned toast to "eternal friendship". Moreover, the "Powhatan Uprising" gave the colonists full licence to take all the Indians' land. Wrote the colonist Edward Waterhouse: "We . . . may now by right of warre, and law of Nations, invade the Country, and destroy them who sought to destroy us: whereby wee shall enjoy their cultivated places . . . Now their cleared grounds in all their villages (which are situate in the fruitfullest places of the land) shall be inhabited by us". After ten years, the war ended in mutual exhaustion.

Peace or war, the Powhatan stood only to lose. The tide of White settlement lapped further and further into their tidewater lands, until the Powhatan were pushed into two corners. Not only were the Powhatan losing their lands, they were losing their people, courtesy of the Whites' diseases. In terminal crisis, the Powhatan Confederation made one last push against the colonists. Carrying the nonagenarian Opechancanough into battle on a litter, the Powhatan attacked the settlements in 1644, killing 500 English in a single day. But the English were now too many to kill. Opechancanough was eventually captured, and thrown into a cell in Jamestown for public display. After two weeks, an English guard shot him in the back and killed him.

With Opechancanough died the Powahatan Confederacy. The English broke up the league, assigned its tribes to small reservations, on which the Indians died of starvation and its ever-present friend, disease. Within a hundred years of the English arrival in Virgina, Powhatan survivors numbered as few as 600.

There were other tribes in Virginia, of course. They fared no better than the Powhatan.

Pilgrims and Pequots

It was Captain John Smith who dreamed up the name "New England" during his exploration of the East coast 1614. So taken was Smith with "this most excellent place" that "could I have but meanes to transport a Colonie, I would rather live there than anywhere"

The colony Smith dreamed of was eventually founded in 1620, when the Pilgrim Fathers landed at Plymouth. William Bradford, the first governor of New England, related their arrival in his *History of Plymouth Plantation*:

> Being thus arrived at Cap-Cod . . . they espied five or six persons with a dogg coming towards them, who were savages; but they fled from them and rane up into ye woods and ye English followed them . . . but ye Indeans seeing them selves thus followed, they againe forsooke the woods, and rane away . . . afterwards [the English] . . . directed their course to come to the other shore . . . and by the way found . . . a good quantitie of clear ground wher the Indeans had formerly set corne, and some of their graves. And proceeding furder they saw . . . heaps of sand newly padled with their hands, which they, digging up, found in them diverce faire Indean

baskets filled with corne . . . they returned to the ship . . . and tooke with them parte of the corne . . . and showed their breethren; of which . . . they were marvelusly glad, and their harts incouraged . . . the 6 of Desemr: they sente out their shallop againe . . . and as they drue near the shore they saw some 10 or 12 Indeans very busie aboute some thing . . . Being landed, it grew late, and they made them selves a barricade . . . But presently, all on the sudain, they heard a great and strange crie . . . and one of their company being abroad came running in and cried, "Men, Indeans, Indeans"; and with all, their arowes came flying amongst them . . . Afterwards, they gave God sollamne thanks and praise for their deliverance, and gathered up a bundle of their arrows . . . and called that place their first encounter . . .

Like the Indians of Virginia, the Indians of New England knew enough of the "Hairy-Mouths" ways even before they settled in their lands. Slavers and their microbes had already visited New England. The "graves" Bradford referred to were those of Indians killed by epidemics of "plague" even before the Puritans set a foot ashore. Indeed, there were so many Indian skeletons unburied that one early colonist thought he had arrived in "a new found Golgotha". Indian settlements – including Plymouth, or Patuxet, to the Indians – were ghost towns, the population having fled out of fear and despair.

Having beaten off their first Indian attack, the Pilgrims began to build houses and work the Indians' fields. Even so, nearly half of the Pilgrims died over the long winter. Their depression was only relieved by the providential visit of an Indian on 16 December, who "came bouldly amongst them and spoke to them in broken English".

This was Samoset, a Maine Indian who had been captured

by (and escaped from) slave-trading English. A few days later Samoset brought along Tisquantum, another ex-captive, and almost the sole surviving Patuxet. Despite their kidnappings, the men bore no ill will to the English. On the contrary, Tisquantum (whose name the monoglot English shortened to Squanto) was the Pilgrims' salvation. In the words of Bradford, who was no Indian-lover: "Squanto continued with [the English], and was their interpreter, and was a spetiall instrument sent of God for there good beyond there expectation. He directed them how to set their corne, wher to take fish, and to procure other commodities and never left them til he dyed."

Crucially, Squanto instructed the colonists in the using of fish as fertilizer. Moreover, he introduced them to the grand sachem of the Wampanoags, Massasoit, "a very lustie man, in his best yeares, an able body, grave of countenance & spare in speeche . . . His face was painted with a deep red like mulberry and he was oiled both head and face." (Massasoit was actually a title of address; the grand sachem's name was "Yellow Feather", Wasamegin.) With Squanto and Samoset interpreting, the Pilgrims and the Wampanoags made a pact of mutual assistance and peace, from which both sides stood to win. There were a bare 100 settlers amid thousands of Indians; the Wampanoags coveted English firepower to halt the expansion of their neighbours, the Narragansetts. That fall, the Pilgrims held a thanksgiving for their survival and invited Massasoit to the party. After three days of festivities, Wampanoags and Pilgrims agreed to hold such a celebration every year.

Such harmony could not last. The Wampanoag–Pilgrim pact was but destined to be the first on a trail of broken promises.

Yet before the English fought the Wampanoags, they

found other enemies in New England. In 1630 came the "Great Migration" of Puritans to Massachusetts, which pushed the English frontier into Connecticut Valley, into the country of the Pequot ("destroyers"), a division of the Mohegan. Once all-powerful, the Pequot had been devastated by smallpox and Dutch-politicking with their tributary tribes: the Pequot needed to re-establish their reputation and dominance. After murdering two drunken English traders in 1636, the Pequot under their sachem, Sassacus, launched a desultory attack on Fort Saybrook. Honour satisfied, the Pequot asked the English if they had "fought enough?" They had not. In June 1637 an English army of 240 colonists, with a thousand Indian allies, made a stealthy night attack on a stockaded Pequot town near Mystic River. John Mason, the English captain, later wrote an account of the night:

We then Marching on in a silent Manner, the Indians that remained fell all into the Rear, who formerly kept the Van; (being possessed with great Fear) we continued our March till about one Hour in the Night: and coming to a little Swamp between two Hills, there we pitched our little Camp; much wearied with hard Travel, keeping great Silence, supposing we were very near the Fort; as our Indians informed us; which proved otherwise: The Rocks were our Pillows; yet Rest was pleasant: The Night proved Comfortable, being clear and Moon Light: We appointed our Guards and placed our Sentinels at some distance; who heard the Enemy Singing at the Fort, who continued that Strain until Midnight, with great Insulting and Rejoycing, as we were afterwards informed: They seeing our Pinnaces sail by them some Days before, concluded we were afraid of them and durst not come near them; the Burthen of their Song tending to that purpose.

In the Morning, we awaking and seeing it very light, supposing it had been day, and so we might have lost our Opportunity, having purposed to make our Assault before Day; rowsed the Men with all expedition, and briefly commended ourselves and Design to God, thinking immediately to go to the Assault; the Indians shewing us a Path, told us that it led directly to the Fort. We held on our March about two Miles, wondering that we came not to the Fort, and fearing we might be deluded: But seeing Corn newly planted at the Foot of a great Hill, Supposing the Fort was not far off; a Champion Country being round about us; then making a stand, gave the Word for some of the Indians to come up: At length Onkos and one Wequash appeared; We demanded of them, Where was the Fort? They answered On the Top of that Hill: Then we demanded, Where were the Rest of the Indians? They answered, Behind, exceedingly afraid: We wished them to tell the rest of their Fellows, That they should by no means Fly, but stand at what distance they pleased, and see whether English Men would now Fight or not. Then Capt. Underhill came up, who Marched in the Rear; and commending ourselves to God, divided our Men: There being two Entrances into the Fort, intending to enter both at once: Captain Mason leading up to that on the North East Side; who approaching within one Rod, heard a Dog bark and an Indian crying Owanux! Owanux! which is Englishmen! Englishmen! We called up our Forces with all expedition, gave Fire upon them through the Pallizado; the Indians being in a dead indeed their last Sleep: Then we wheeling off fell upon the main Entrance, which was blocked up with Bushes about Breast high, over which the Captain passed, intending to make good the Entrance, ecouraging the rest to follow. Lieutenant Seeley endeavoured to enter; but being somewhat cumbred, stepped back and pulled out the Bushes and so entred, and with him about sixteen Men: We had formerly concluded to destroy them by the Sword and save the Plunder.

Whereupon Captain Mason seeing no Indians, entred a Wigwam; where he was beset with many Indians, waiting all opportunities to lay Hands on him, but could not prevail. At length William Heydon espying the Breach in the Wigwam, supposing some English might be there, entred; but in his Entrance fell over a dead Indian; but speedily recovering himself, the Indians some fled, others crept under their Beds: The Captain going out of the Wigwam saw many Indians in the Lane or Street; he making towards them, they fled, were pursued to the End of the Lane, where they were met by Edward Pattison, Thomas Barber, with some others; where seven of them were Slain, as they said. The Captain facing about, Marched a slow Pace up the Lane he came down, perceiving himself very much out of Breath; and coming to the other End near the Place where he first entred, saw two Soldiers standing close to the Pallizado with their Swords pointed to the Ground: The Captain told them that We should never kill them after that manner: The Captain also said, We must Burn them; and immediately stepping into the Wigwam where he had been before, brought out a Firebrand, and putting it into the Matts with which they were covered, set the Wigwams on Fire. Lieutenant Thomas Bull and Nicholas Omsted beholding, came up; and when it was thoroughly kindled, the Indians ran as Men most dreadfully Amazed.

And indeed such a dreadful Terror did the Almighty let fall upon their Spirits, that they would fly from us and run into the very Flames, where many of them perished. And when the Fort was thoroughly Fired, Command was given, that all should fall off and surround the Fort; which was readily attended by all; one Arthur Smith being so wounded that he could not move out of the Place, who was happily espied by Lieutenant Bull, and by him rescued.

The Fire was kindled on the North East Side to windward; which did swiftly over-run the Fort, to the extream Amazement of the Enemy, and great Rejoycing of our selves. Some of them climbing to the Top of the Pallizado; others of them running into the very Flames; many of them gathering to windward, lay pelting at us with their Arrows; and we repayed them with our small Shot: Others of the Stoutest issued forth, as we did guess, to the Number of Forty, Who perished by the Sword.

What I have formerly said, is according to my own Knowledge, there being sufficient living Testimony to every Particular.

But in reference to Captain Underhill and his Par-Lies acting in this Assault, I can only intimate as we were informed by some of themselves immediately after the Fight, Thus They Marching up to the Entrance on the South West Side, there made some Pause; a valiant, resolute Gentleman, one Mr Hedge, stepping towards the Gate, saying, If we may not Enter, wherefore came we here; and immediately endeavoured to Enter; but was opposed by a sturdy Indian which did impede his Entrance; but the Indian being slain by himself and

Sergeant Davis, Mr Hedge Entred the Fort with some others; but the Fort being on Fire, the Smoak and Flames were so violent that they were constrained to desert the Fort.

Thus were they now at their Wits End, who not many Hours before exalted themselves in their great Pride, threatning and resolving the utter Ruin and Destruction of all the English, Exulting and Rejoycing with Songs and Dances: But God was above them, who laughed his Enemies and the Enemies of his People to Scorn, making them as a fiery Oven: Thus were the Stout Hearted spoiled, having slept their last Sleep, and none of their Men could find their Hands: Thus did the Lord judge among the Heathen, filling the Place with dead Bodies!

And here we may see the just Judgment of God, in sending even the very Night before this Assault, One hundred and fifty Men from their other Fort, to join with them of that Place, who were designed as some of themselves reported to go forth against the English, at that very Instant when this heavy Stroak came upon them where they perished with their Fellows. So that the Mischief they intended to us, came upon their own Pate: They were taken in their own snare, and we through Mercy escaped: And thus in little more than one Hour's space was their impregnable Fort with themselves utterly Destroyed, to the Number of six or seven Hundred, as some of themselves confessed. There were only seven taken captive, and about seven escaped.

Of the English, there were two Slain outright, and about twenty Wounded: Some Fainted by reason of the sharpness of the Weather, it being a cool Morning, and the want of such Comforts and Necessaries as were needful in such a Case; especially our Chyrurgeon was much wanting, whom we left with our Barks in Narragansett Bay, who had Order there to remain until the Night before our intended Assault.

And thereupon grew many Difficulties: Our Provision and Munition near spent; we in the enemies Country, who did far exceed us in Number, being much enraged: all our Indians, except Onkos, deserting us; our Pinnaces at a great distance from us, and when they would come we were uncertain.

But as we were consulting what Course to take, it pleased God to discover our Vessels to us before a fair Gale of Wind, sailing into Pequot Harbour, to our great Rejoycing.

There was only one other engagement in the "Pequot war", when a party of Pequots were trapped in a swamp. On taking their surrender, the English enslaved them.

The Pequot nation was nigh on exterminated. The "destroyers" were no match for English guns or military ruthlessness. "Indeed," said Captain Mason of Mystic River, "it did hardly deserve the name of *Fighting*." Bewildered by the English blood-lust, their Indian allies at Mystic River actually sought to stop the slaughter of the Pequots, crying, "mach it, mach it: that is, It is naught [evil], because it too furious, and slays too man men".

Much of the future between the Indian and the White Man was cast at Mystic River. So complete was the English victory that the Puritans, adherents of Calvin's doctrine of predestination, ascribed God's will to their domination of the Indian and his land. God's sanction was only confirmed by the plagues He sent against the Red Man, but from which he largely spared the White. After Mystic River, the English endeavour over the Indian had God on its side.

It would, though, be wrong to believe that all colonists were Indian-haters. Many individual settlers were neighbours and friends of Indians (and vice versa), and it was from such social intercourse that Algonquian words and habits entered American culture: clambake, moccasin, squaw, and baked beans among them. One of the fiercest proponents of Indian land rights was the "eccentric" Roger Williams, founder of Providence Plantation (Rhode Island), who eventually obliged the colonies to pay for their purchases of the Earth. Then there was Thomas Morton, the non-Separatist who angered the Puritans by erecting a Maypole, and who so obviously preferred the company of the Massachusets to his own race. "The more Savages the better quarter, the more Christians the worse quarter" he wrote. Bradford had the "Lord of Misrule" deported in 1628, but his reflections produced one of the most valuable accounts of Native American life in the New England of the seventeenth century, *The Manners and Customs of the Indians,* 1637. Here Morton recalls the Indian's homes, apparel, reverence for age and reputation, and their agriculture:

Of Their Houses and Habitations: The Natives of New England are accustomed to build themselves houses much like the wild Irish; they gather poles in the woods and put the great end of them in the ground, placing them in form of a circle or circumference, and, bending the tops of them in form of an arch, they bind them together with the bark of walnut trees, which is wondrous tough, so that they make the same round on the top for the smoke of their fire to ascend and pass through; these they cover with mats, some made of reeds and some of long flags, or sedge, finely sewed together with needles made of the splinter bones of a crane's leg, with threads made of their Indian hemp, which there grows naturally, leaving several places for doors, which are covered with mats, which may be rolled up and let down again at their pleasure, making use of the several doors, according as the wind sits. The fire is always made in the middle of the house, with windfall commonly, yet sometimes they fell a tree that grows near the house, and, by drawing in the end thereof, maintain the fire on both sides, burning the tree by degrees shorter and shorter, until it be all consumed, for it burns night and day.

Their lodging is made in three places of the house about the fire; they lie upon blankets, commonly about a foot or 18 inches above the ground, raised upon rails that are borne upon forks; they lay mats under them, and coats of deer skins, otters, beavers, racoons, and of bears' hides, all which they have dressed and converted into good leather, with the hair on, for their coverings, and in this manner they lie as warm as they desire. In the night they take their rest; in the day time either the kettle is on with fish or flesh, by no allowance, or else the fire is employed in the roasting of fishes which they delight in. The air does beget good stomachs, and they feed continually and are no niggards of their victuals, and they are willing that any one shall eat with them. Nay, if any one that shall come into their houses and there fall asleep, when they see him disposed to lie down, they will spread a mat for him of their own accord, and lay a roll of skins for a bolster, and let him lie. If he sleep until their meat be dished up, they will set a wooden bowl of meat by him that sleeps, and wake him, saying, "Cattup keene Meckin." That is, 'If you be hungry, there is meat for you, whereof if you will eat you may." Such is their humanity.

Likewise, when they are minded to remove, they carry away the mats with them; other materials the place adjoining will yield. They use not to winter and summer in one place, for that would be a reason to make fuel scarce: but, after the manner of the gentry of civilized natives, remove for their pleasures; sometimes to their hunting places, where they remain keeping good hospitality for that season; and sometimes to their fishing places, where they abide for that season likewise; and at the spring, when fish comes in plentifully, they have meetings from several places, where they exercise themselves in gaming and playing of juggling tricks and all manner of revelries which they are delighted in; so that it is admirable to behold what pastime they use of several kinds, every one striving to surpass each other. After this manner they spend their time.

Of the Indians' Apparel: The Indians in these parts do make their apparel of the skins of several sorts of beasts, and commonly of those that do frequent those parts where they do live; yet some of them, for variety, will have the skins of such beasts that frequent the parts of their neighbors, which they purchase of them by commerce and trade. Their skins they convert into very good leather, making the same plume and soft. Some of these skins they dress with the hair on, and some with the hair off; the hairy side in winter time they wear next their bodies, and in warm weather they wear the hair outwards. They make likewise some coats of the feathers of turkeys, which they weave together with twine of their own making, very prettily. These garments they wear like mantels knit over their shoulders, and put under their arms. They have likewise another sort of mantel, made of moose skins, which beast is a great large deer, so big as a horse. These skins they commonly dress bare, and make them wondrous white, and stripe them with furs round about the borders, in form like lace set on by a tailor, and some they stripe with fur in works of fantasies of the workmen wherein they strive to excel one another. And mantels made of bears' skins is a usual wearing among the natives that live where the bears do haunt.

They make shoes of moose skins, which is the principal leather used to that purpose; and for want of such leather (which is the strongest) they make shoes of deer skins, as they dress bare, they make stockings that comes within their shoes, like a stirrup stocking, and is fastened above at their belt, which is about their middle. Every male, after he attains unto age which they call Puberty, wears a belt about his middle, and a broad piece of leather that goes between his legs and is tucked up both before and behind under that belt; those garments they always put on, when they go a hunting, to keep their skins from the brush of the shrubs, and when they have their apparel on they look like Irish in their trousers, the stockings join so to their breeches. A good well grown deer skin is of great account with them, and it must have the tail on, or else they account it defaced; the tail being three times as long as the tails of our English deer, yea four times so long, this when they travel is wrapped round their body and, with a girdle of their making, bound round about their middles, to which girdle is fastened a bag, in which his instruments be with which he can strike fire upon any occasion. Thus with their bow in their left hand, and their quiver of arrows at their back, hanging on their left shoulder with the lower end of it in their right hand, they will run away on a dog trot until they come to their journey's end; and, in this kind of ornament, they do seem to me to be handsomer than when they are in English apparel, their gesture being answerable to their own habit and not unto ours.

Their women have shoes and stockings to wear likewise when they please, such as the men have, but the mantle they use to cover their nakedness with is much longer than that which the men use, for, as the men have one deer skin, the women have two sewed together at the full length, and it is so large that it trails after them like a great lady's train; and in time I think they may have their pages to bear them up; and where the men use but one bear skin for a mantle, the women have two sewed together, and if any of their women would at any time shift one, they take that which they intend to make use of, and cast it over them round, before they shift away the other, for modesty, which is to be noted in people uncivilized; therein they seem to have as much modesty as civilized people, and deserve to be applauded for it.

Of Their Reverence, and Respect to Age: It is a thing to be admired, and indeed made a precedent, that a nation yet uncivilized should more respect age than some nations civilized, since there are so many precepts both of divine and humane writers extant to instruct more civil nations: in that particular, wherein they excel, the younger are always obedient unto the elder people, and at their commands in every respect without grumbling; in all counsels (as therein they are circumspect to do their actions by advise and counsel, and not rashly or inconsiderately), the younger men's opinion shall be heard, but the old men's opinion and counsel embraced and followed. Besides, as the elder feed and provide for the younger in infancy, so do the younger, after being grown to years of manhood, provide for those that be aged; and in distribution of acts the elder men are first served by their dispensator; and their counsels (especially if they be *powahs*), are esteemed as oracles amongst the younger natives. The consideration of these things, methinks, should reduce some of our irregular young people of civilized nations, when this story shall come to their knowledge, to better manners, and make them ashamed of their former errors of this kind, and to become hereafter more dutiful; which is, as a friend (by observation having found) have herein recorded for that purpose.

Of the Maintaining of Their Reputation: Reputation is such a thing that it keeps many men in awe, even amongst civilized nations, and is very much stood upon: it is (as one has very well noted) the awe of great men and of kings. And, since I have observed it to be maintained amongst savage people, I cannot choose but give an instance thereof in this treatise, to confirm the common received opinion thereof.

The Sachem or Sagamore of Sagus made choice, when he came to man's estate, of a lady of noble descent, daughter to Papasiquineo, the Sachem of Sagamore of the territories near Merrimack river, a man of the best note and estimation in all those parts, and (as my countryman Mr Wood declares in his prospect) a great Necromancer; this lady the young Sachem with the consent and good liking of her father marries, and takes for his wife. Great entertainment he and his received in those parts at her father's hands, where they were feasted in the best manner that might be expected, according to the customs of their nation, with reveling and such other solemnities as is usual amongst them. The solemnity being ended, Papasiquineo causes a selected number of his men to wait upon his daughter home into those parts that did properly belong to her Lord and husband; where the attendants had entertainment by the Sachem of Sagus and his countrymen: the solemnity being ended, the attendants were gratified.

Not long after the new married lady had a great desire to see her father and her native country, from whence she came; her Lord willing to please her, and not deny her request, amongst them thought to be reasonable, commanded a selected number of his own men to conduct his lady to her father, where, with great respect, they brought her, and, having feasted there a while, returned to their own country again, leaving the lady to continue there at her own pleasure, amongst her friends and old acquaintance, where she passed away the time for a while, and in the end desired to return to her Lord again. Her father, the old Papasiquineo, having notice of her intent, sent some of his men on embassy to the young Sachem, his son-in-law, to let him understand that his daughter was not willing to absent herself from his company any longer, and therefore, as the messengers had in charge, desired the young Lord to send a convoy for her, but he, standing, upon terms of honor, and the maintaining of his reputation, returned to his father-in-law this answer, that, when she departed from him, he caused his men to wait upon her to her father's territories, as it did become him; but, now she had an intent to return, it did become her father to send her back with a convoy of his own people, and that it stood not with his reputation to make himself or his men too servile, to fetch her again. The old Sachem, Papasiquineo, having this message returned, was enraged to think that his young son-in-law did not esteem him at a higher rate than to capitulate with him about the matter, and returned him this sharp reply; that his daughters blood and birth deserved more respect than to be so slighted, and, therefore, if he would have her company, he were best to send or come for her.

The young Sachem, not willing to undervalue himself and being a man of a stout spirit, did not stick to say that he should either send her by his own convey, or keep her; for he was determined not to stoop so low. So much these two Sachems stood upon terms of reputation with each other, the one would not send her, and the other would not send for her, lest it should be any diminishing of honour on his part that should seem to comply, that the lady (when I came out of the country) remained still with her father; which is a thing worth the noting, that savage people should seek to maintain their reputation so much as they do.

Of Their Custom in Burning the Country and the Reason Thereof: The savages are accustomed to set fire of the country in all places where they come, and to burn it twice a year, viz.: at the spring, and the fall of the leaves. The reason that moves them to do so, is because it would otherwise be so overgrown with underweeds that it would be all a coppice wood, and the people would not be able in any wise to pass through the country out of a beaten path. The means that they do it with, is with certain mineral stones, that they carry about them in bags made for that purpose of the skins of little beasts, which they convert into good leather, carrying in the same a piece of touch wood, very excellent for that purpose, of their own making. These mineral stones they have from the Piquenteenes (which is to the southward of all the plantations in New England), by trade and traffic with those people.

The burning of the grass destroys the underwoods, and so scorches the elder trees that it shrinks them and hinders their growth very much; so that he that will look to find large trees and good timber, must not depend upon the help of a wooden prospect to find them on the upland ground; but must seek for them (as I and others have done), in the lower grounds, where the grounds are wet, when the country is fired, by reason of the snow water that remains there for a time, until the sun by continuance of that has exhaled the vapors of the earth, and dried up those places where the fire (by reason of the moisture) can have no power to do them any harm; and if he would endeavor to find out any goodly cedars, he must not seek for them on the higher grounds, but make his inquest for them in the valleys, for the savages, by this custom of theirs, have spoiled all the rest; for this custom has been continued from the beginning.

And lest their firing of the country in this manner should be an occasion of damnifying us, and endangering our habitations, we ourselves have used carefully about the same time to observe the winds, and fire the grounds about our own habitations; to prevent the damage that might happen by any neglect thereof if the fire should come near those houses in our absence. For, when the fire is once kindled, it dilates and spreads itself as well against, as with the wind; burning continually night and day, until a shower of rain falls to quench it.

And this custom of firing the country is the means to make it passable; and by that means the trees grow here and there as in our parks; and make the country very beautiful and commodious.

Of Their Inclination to Drunkenness: Although drunkenness be justly termed a vice which the savages are ignorant of yet the benefit is very great that comes to the planters by the sale of strong liquor to the savages, who are much taken with the delight of it; for they will pawn their wits, to purchase the acquaintance of it. Yet in all the commerce that I had with them, I never proffered them any such thing; nay, I would hardly let any of them have a dram, unless he were a sachem, or a *winnaytue*, that is a rich man, or a man of estimation next in degree to a sachem or sagamore. I always told them it was amongst us the sachems drink. But they say if I come to the northern parts of the country I shall have no trade, if I will not supply them with lusty liquors; it is the life of the trade, in all those parts; for it so happened that thus a savage desperately killed himself; when he was drunk, a gun being charged and the cock up, he sets the mouth to his breast, and, pulling back the trigger with his foot, shot himself dead.

That the Savages Live a Contented Life: A gentleman and a traveller, that had been in the parts of New England for a time, when he returned again, in his discourse of the country, wondered (as he said) that the natives of the land lived so poorly in so rich a country, like to our beggars in England. Surely, that gentleman had not time or leisure while he was there truly to inform himself of the state of that country, and the happy life the savages would lead were they once brought to Christianity. I must confess they want the use and benefit of navigation (which is the very finest of a flourishing commonwealth), yet are they supplied with all manner of needful things for the maintenance of life and livelihood. Food and raiment are the chief of all that we make the use of; and of these they find no want, but have, and may have them, in most plentiful manner.

Just as there were Whites like Williams and Morton who befriended Indians, there were Indians who befriended Whites. Massoit of the Wampanoags had been one such. But in 1662 Massoit died, and after a brief interval the succession passed to his son Metacom, known to the English as King Philip. His inheritance was a pitifully shrunken nation, hemmed in on all sides. "But little remains of my ancestor's domain," said Philip. "I am resolved not to see the day when I have no country." Of equal resolve were the new-style authoritarian leaders of New England, men more rapacious and disrespectful than their forbears to the Indian. It was such men, the proprietors of the Plymouth Colony, who in 1671 decided on the utter subjugation of the Wampanoag, whose tribute status should henceforth be marked by a £100 a year gift.

From that moment onwards, war was certain.

King Philip's War

Various are the reports and conjectures of the causes of the present Indian warre. Some impute it to an imprudent zeal in the magistrates of Boston to christianize those heathen before they were civilized and enjoining them the strict observation of their laws, which, to a people so rude and licentious, hath proved even intolerable, and that the more, for that while the magistrates, for their profit, put the laws severely in execution against the Indians, the people, on the other side, for lucre and gain, entice and provoke the Indians to the breach thereof, especially to drunkenness, to which those people are so generally addicted that they will strip themselves to their skin to have their fill of rum and brandy . . .

Some believe there have been vagrant and jesuitical priests, who have made it their business, for some years past, to go from Sachem to Sachem, to exasperate the Indians against the English and to bring them into a confederacy, and that they were promised supplies from France and other parts to extirpate the English nation out of the continent of America. Others impute the cause to some injuries offered to the Sachem Philip; for he being possessed of a tract of land called Mount Hope

. . . some English had a mind to dispossess him thereof, who never wanting on pretence or other to attain their end, complained of injuries done by Philip and his Indians to their stock and cattle, whereupon Philip was often summoned before the magistrate, sometimes imprisoned, and never released but upon parting with a considerable part of his land.

But the government of the Massachusetts . . . do declare these are the great evils for which God hath given the heathen commission to rise against them . . . For men wearing long hair and perewigs made of womens hair; for women . . . cutting, curling and laying out the hair . . . For profaneness in the people not frequenting their meetings . . .

With many such reasons . . . the English have contributed much to their misfortunes, for they first taught the Indians the use of arms, and admitted them to be present at all their musters and trainings, and shewed them how to handle, mend and fix their muskets, and have been furnished with all sorts of arms by permission of the government . . .

> *Edward Randolph, emissary of James II, on the*
> *"causes of the present Indian warre", 1675*

When King Philip's War came, it came with the suddenness of a lightning storm bursting upon the land. On June 21, 1675, there were orchestrated Indian attacks on Taunton, Dartmouth, Middleborough and Rehoboth, which were all burnt to the ground. Quickly the war spread through New England, as town after town was set upon and set afire. Mary Rowlandson, wife of the minister of Lancaster, was taken captive when the town was attacked:

On the 10th of February, 1675, came the Indians with great numbers upon Lancaster. Their first coming was about sunrising.

Hearing the noise of some guns, we looked out; several houses were burning, and the smoke ascending to heaven. There were five persons taken in one house; the father and the mother and a suckling child they knocked on the head; the other two they took and carried away alive. There were two others, who, being out of their garrison upon some occasion, were set upon; one was knocked on the head, the other escaped. Another there was who, running along, was shot and wounded, and fell down; he begged of them his life, promising them money (as they told me), but they would not hearken to him, but knocked him in the head, and stripped him naked, and split open his bowels. Another seeing many of the Indians about his barn ventured and went out, but was quickly shot down. There were three others belonging to the same garrison who were killed; the Indians, getting up upon the roof of the barn, had advantage to shoot down upon them over their fortification. Thus these murderous wretches went on burning and destroying before them.

At length they came and beset our own house, and quickly it was the dolefulest day that ever mine eyes saw. The house stood upon the edge of a hill; some of the Indians got behind the hill, others into the barn, and others behind anything that could shelter them; from all which places they shot against the house, so that the bullets seemed to fly like hail, and quickly they wounded one man among us, then another, and then a third. About two hours (according to my observation in that amazing time) they had been about the house before they prevailed to fire it; they fired it once, and one ventured out and quenched it, but they quickly fired it again, and that took. Now is the dreadful hour come that I have often heard of, but now mine eyes see it. Some in our house were fighting for their lives, others wallowing in their blood, the house on fire over our heads, and the bloody heathen ready to knock us on the head if we stirred out. Now might we hear mothers and children crying out for themselves and one another, "Lord, what shall we do?" Then I took my children (and one of my sisters hers) to go forth and leave the house, but, as soon as we came to the door and appeared, the Indians shot so thick that the bullets rattled against the house as if one had taken a handful of stones and threw them, so that we were forced to give back. We had six stout dogs belonging to our garrison, but none of them would stir, though another time if any Indian had come to the door, they were ready to fly upon him and tear him down. The Lord hereby would make us the more to acknowledge His hand, and to see that our help is always in Him. But out we must go, the fire increasing, and coming along behind us roaring, and the Indians gaping before us with their guns, spears, and hatchets to devour us.

No sooner were we out of the house but my brother-in-law (being before wounded in defending the house, in or near the throat) fell down dead, whereat the Indians scornfully shouted and hallooed, and were presently upon him, stripping off his clothes. The bullets flying thick, one went through my side, and the same (as would seem) through the bowels and hand of my dear child in my arms. One of my elder sister's children (named William) had then his leg broke, which the Indians perceiving they knocked him on the head. Thus were we butchered by those merciless heathen, standing amazed, with the blood running down to our heels. My eldest sister being yet in the house, and seeing those woeful sights, the infidels hauling mothers one way and children another, and some wallowing in their blood; and her elder son telling her that her son William was dead, and myself was wounded, she said, "And, Lord, let me die with them"; which was no sooner said, but she was struck with a bullet, and fell down dead over the threshold. I hope she is reaping the fruit of her good labors, being faithful to the service of God in her place.

I had often before this said, that if the Indians should come, I should choose rather to be killed by them than taken alive, but when it came to the trial, my mind changed; their glittering weapons so daunted my spirit, that I chose rather to go along with those (as I may say) ravenous bears, than that moment to end my days.*

King Philip had prepared his war well. After his forced vassalage by the English in 1671 he had built a military alliance of tribes which united three-quarters of the region's Indians, including the Nipmucks, Pocassets, Sokokis, Hassanamesitts, Pocuintucks, Sacos, Kennebecs, Pigwackets, Arosauntacooks, Wawenocs, as well as his own Wampanoags. For a while the Narragansetts, the Wampanoags' old adversaries, held off in neutrality; until that is, the English launched an unprovoked attack upon them, killing upwards of six hundred Narragansett. Most of them were burned alive – "terribly Barbikew'd", recorded the Boston Puritan Cotton Mather – in a single incident.

So began the most devastating war, relative to the size of population, in America's history. To the surprise of the

*Rowlandson was released after eleven weeks of captivity.

colonists, the Indians were relatively well-armed with muskets (they did their own gunsmithing, on secret forest forges) and fought with a courage with earned grudging admiration.

For months, the Puritans were on the back step, the Indians attacking fifty-two of their ninety towns, but by summer 1676 Indian victories were only a distant Puritan nightmare. Metacom was ceaselesly harried by colonial militia, aided by "praying Indians", Mohawks and Mohegans, attacking his camps and supplies. Invariably, the militia ran amok. Wrote one eyewitness of an attack on an Indian camp by the Connecticut River:

Our souldiers got thither after an hard March just about break of day, took most of the Indians fast asleep, and put their guns even into their wigwams, and poured in their shot among them, whereupon the Indians that durst and were able did get out of their wigwams and did fight a little (in which fight one Englishman only was slain) others of the Indians did enter the River to swim over from the English, but many of them were shot dead in the waters, others wounded were therein drowned, many got into Canoes to paddle away, but the paddlers being shot, the Canoes over-set with all therein, and the stream of the River being very violent and swift in the place near the great Falls, most that fell over board were born by the strong current of that River, and carryed upon the Falls of Water from those exceeding high and steep Rocks, and from thence tumbling down were broken in pieces; the English did afterwards find of their bodies, some in the River and some cast a-shore, above two hundred.

To encourage this seventeenth-century "ethnic cleansing",

Connecticut offered "scalp bounties". For each enemy Indian's scalp the reward was "A coat, that is two yards of trucking [trade] cloth, worth five shillings per yard; and for every one brought in alive, two coats; for King Philip's head, twenty coats, and if taken alive forty coats".

By summer 1676 Metacom's war for liberation had become a fight for survival; the Indian allied army was haemorrhaging, starving, and Canonchet, the canny warleader of the Narragansett, had been caught and executed. "I like it well," he told the firing squad. "I shall die before my heart is soft or I have said anything unworthy of myself."

The fatal blow to Metacom fell on an August day of that summer, when a Massachusetts force attacked his camp, killing 173 Indians. Metacom himself escaped, but his wife and nine-year-old son did not and were captured. "My heart breaks," he told a friend. "Now I am ready to die."

Metacom's death duly came at dawn on 12 August 1676, when his sleeping camp was attacked by English militia. He was shot through the heart by an Indian auxiliary, his head severed and later put on a pole on the Plymouth blockhouse. By one of the grim ironies of which American history is fond, Metacom was killed in the old Wampanoag capital of Montaup – the self-same place where his father, Massasoit, all those years before had given life to the Pilgrims.

The Indians' defeat was total. It could not have been otherwise. Some contemporaries attributed Puritan victory to God, some to the scouting and warrior prowess of their Indian auxiliaries, the Mohawks, the Mohegans, and the "praying Indians". The truth was more prosaic: wars are invariably won by might. The Puritans were victorious because there were 50,000 of them – against 10,000 Indians, who even as King Philip's War was being fought were ravaged by disease. More than 40 per cent of New England's

Indian population was killed, fled or was removed in King Philip's War; 5 per cent of New England's White population died (a higher proportion than that suffered by the USA in World War II).

The footnotes to King Philip's War were tragedy in continuum.

After a fierce debate amongst the clergy, King Philip's wife and son were spared death, but sold into slavery in the West Indies instead. Into bondage with them went hundreds of other captives, mainly women and children.

Such enslavement of Native Americans was, by the mid-seventeenth century, a mainstay of the commerce of the English settlements, especially in the Carolinas. There the colonists proved past masters at encouraging the tribes to raid each other and sell the captives to the traders. Tribe after tribe – the Coosa, the Sampa, the Westo, Congaree, Santee and dozens more – disappeared in the resultant maelstrom. Within a century, there were no Indians left worth the catching, and the trade in Indians declined sharply from 1730. The legacy lasted longer. The economy of the south was built on the slavery of the Indians, and when the supply of Indians dwindled, it was easy enough to use slaves of another hue.

Clash of Empire

These Indians by their situation are a Frontier to some of [the English colonies], and from thence, if Friends, are Capable of Defending their Settlements; If Enemies, of making Cruel Ravages upon them; If Neuters, they may deny the French a Passage through their Country, and give us timely Notice of their Designs. These are but some of the Motives for cultivating a good Understanding with them . . .

Governor George Thomas of Pennsylvania, 1744

To the north of New England, through the endless woods, lay the domain of the most powerful Indian confederation in North America east of the Great River. The Iroquois. Since the formation of the League of the Iroquois in about 1450 its component Five Nations – the Mohawk, Cayuga, Onondaga, Oneida and Seneca – had assumed mastery of the northeast from Maine to Lake Michigan, from the Cumberland River to the Ottawa River. Such hegemonic bent was not entirely of the Iroquois' own instigation; profiteers in the fur trade with the Whites, the Iroquois – with donated Dutch and English guns – fought the "Beaver Wars" against their neighbours so as to better strip their streams of *Castor canadensis*.

Accomplished in war and commerce, the Iroquois were also strategically located between the competing colonies of New England and New France. The Iroquois, it could be said, were the power-brokers of the northern continent.

In general, the colonists of New France showed a gentler touch than the English in their dealings with the Indians. Whereas the English lusted for land, the French only wanted its bounty, notably its furs. And the French liked the Indians, often adopted their ways, and married into their tribes. One contemporary English traveller, Thomas Forsyth, Englishman, was moved to record:

. . . The French being settled in Villages in all parts of the Country and most of these settlers of villages were composed of people who were married to Indian women and followed a life similar to that of the Indians themselves such as hunting, fishing & by which means the Frenchman's children were related to both parties and nothing could stir among the Indian nations, but those Indian women who were married to the French hunters would hear who would relate it to their husbands, and from them to the commandant and so on, by which means the Government had always time to prepare and frustrate many a deep design that was laid for their total ruin. The French being thus settled in villages, those who cultivated the earth, worked their land in a common field, upon a very small scale by which means there never was any misunderstanding between the Whites & Indians about lands. In the fall of the year the Frenchman and his family and the Indian and his family would paddle their canoes off together and chuse out a proper place to hunt the ensuing winter. They would hunt together, eat & drink together, as

much so as if they were one & the same family, if the
Frenchman was in want of any thing that the Indian had
he would assist him and the Frenchman would do the
same in return . . .

At this day let a Frenchman come from Paris and
meet an Indian, the Indian will shake hands with him, as
cordially as if they had been acquainted for many years,
will inquire about France as if he had relations there,
indeeh there is no people who takes the pains the French
do to conciliate the friendship of the Indians. For
instance we see many young French Canadians, the first
year they winter among the Indians. They will eat,
drink, sleep and be high fellow well met with the Indians,
will learn in the course of a few months the Indian
language by which means the Indians become attached
to the Frenchman and the Frenchman to the Indians
and the French always had & always will have more
influence over the Indians than any other nation of
White people.

Thomas considered the "French System" altogether
superior to the English method of musket and racial
separatism.

While the English had hewed a slow frontier with axe and
musket, the French had fraternized and roamed, and by 1680
claimed the St Lawrence Basin, the Great Lakes, all lands to
their north, and most of the interior of the continent, courtesy
of La Salle's voyage down the Ohio and Mississippi Rivers.

Yet at the commencement of their dealings with the
Indians, the French had made one fatal mistake. It would
haunt their endeavours in America till the end. That mistake
came in 1609 when Samuel de Champlain, "the Father of
Canada", and two French companions accompanied a party

of Hurons and Algonquians up the Richelieu River, and to the lake that now bears Champlain's name. The Hurons, although an Iroquoian people, were mortal enemies of the Iroquois league. On July 29 a party of Iroquois (Mohawks, specifically) appeared. Champlain later recounted the ensuing battle:

When it was evening, we embarked in our canoes to continue our course; and, as we advanced very quietly and without making any noise, we met on the 29th of the month the Iroquois, about ten o'clock at evening, at the extremity of a cape which extends into the lake on the western bank. They had come to fight. We both began to utter loud cries, all getting their arms in readiness. We withdrew out on the water, and the Iroquois went on shore, where they drew up all their canoes close to each other and began to fell trees with poor axes, which they acquire in war sometimes, using also others of stone. Thus they barricaded themselves very well.

Our forces also passed the entire night, their canoes being draw'n up close to each other and fastened to poles, so that they might not get separated and that they might be all in readiness to fight, if occasion required. We were out upon the water, within arrow range of their barricades. When they were armed and in array, they dispatched two canoes by themselves to the enemy to enquire if they wished to fight, to which the latter replied that they wanted nothing else; but they said that, at present, there was not much light and that it would be necessary to wait for daylight, so as to be able to recognize each other; and that, as soon as the sun rose, they would offer us battle. This was agreed to by our side. Meanwhile, the entire night was spent in dancing and singing, on both sides, with endless insults and other talk; as, how little courage we had, how feeble a resistance we should make against their arms, and that, when day came, we should realize it to our ruin. Ours also were not slow in retorting, telling them they would see such execution of arms as never before, together with an abundance of such talk as is not unusual in the siege of a town. After this singing, dancing, and bandying words on both sides to the fill, when day came, my companions and myself continued under cover, for fear that the enemy would see us. We arranged our arms in the best manner possible, being, however, separated, each in one of the canoes of the savage Montagnais. After arming ourselves with light armour we each took an arquebus and went on shore. I saw the enemy go out of their barricade, nearly 200 in number, stout and rugged in appearance. They came at a slow pace toward us, with a dignity and assurance which greatly amused me, having three chiefs at their head. Our men also advanced in the same order, telling me that those who had three large plumes were the chiefs, and that they had only these three, and that they could be distinguished by these plumes, which were much larger than those of their companions, and what I should do what I could to kill them. I promised to do all in my power . . .

Our men began to call me with loud cries; and, in order to give me a passageway, they opened in two parts, and put me at their head, where I marched some 20 paces in advance of the rest until I was within about 30 paces of the enemy, who at once noticed me, and, halting, gazed at me, as I did also at them. When I saw them making a move to fire at us, I rested my musket against my cheek, and aimed directly at one of the three chiefs. With the same shot, two fell to the ground; and one of their men was so wounded that he died some time after. I had loaded my musket with four balls. When our side saw this shot so favourable for them, they began to raise such loud cries that one could not have heard it thunder. Meanwhile, the arrows flew on both sides. The Iroquois were greatly astonished that two men had been so quickly killed, although they were equipped with armour woven from cotton thread and with wood which was proof against their arrows. This caused great alarm among them. As I was loading again, one of my companions fired a shot from the woods, which astonished them anew to such a degree that, seeing their chiefs dead, they lost courage and took to flight, abandoning their camp and fort, and fleeing into the woods, whither I pursued them, killing still more of them. Our savages also killed several of them, and took ten or twelve prisoners. The remainder escaped with the wounded. Fifteen or sixteen were wounded on our side with arrow shots; but they were soon healed.

After gaining the victory, our men amused themselves by taking a great quantity of Indian corn and some meal from their enemies, also their armour, which they had left behind that they might run better After feasting sumptuously, dancing and singing, we returned three hours after with the prisoners. The spot where this attack took place is I.ake Champlain.

Champlain won the battle, but lost a continent in return. Thereafter, the Iroquois invariably viewed the French as the enemy. Just as invariably, the English conceived of the Iroquois as an asset in their quickening struggle for the control of North America, and concluded a formal alliance –

the "Chain of Covenant" – with them in 1677. For their part, the Iroquois proved astute at diplomacy and the maintenance of their independence.

After decades of indecisive wilderness clashes – King William's War, Queen Anne's War and King George's War – the French and British headed towards a final tussle for control of the continent. The immediate cause of hostilities was the French attempt to tighten their grip on the interior by building palisaded posts in the upper Ohio Valley – a vast area claimed by Britain and Virginia, and already infiltrated by their traders.

It was one such trader, an Irishman called George Croghan, who sparked off what the colonists called the French and Indian War. Croghan ordered a post to be built at the Miami Indian village of Pickawillany – in the very heart of French territory. For a while this prospered, but then in spring 1753 a new French Governor, Marquis Duquesne, ordered an attack on Croghan's post by French traders and Ottawa Indian allies. The post was destroyed and its defenders slain. A visiting Miama chief was unlucky enough to be killed, boiled and eaten. To prevent any future intrusions by Croghan and his trading ilk, Duquesne built a chain of four forts from Lake Erie to the Forks of the Ohio, sealing off the Ohio Valley from the trespassing Pennsylvanians. The last fort, on the Ohio Forks (the site of present-day Pittsburgh), Duquesne named after himself.

The French had thrown down the gauntlet. The British barely hesitated to pick it up. To lose the Ohio Valley would be to lose everything – the entire hinterland.

The French and Indian War began almost as the final log was being hauled into place at Fort Duquesne. Virginia's Scots Governor, Robert Dinwiddie, had already sent the 21-year-old George Washington with a warning to the French to vacate it. When they refused, Washington returned in April 1754 with a small force of militia men. En route to Duquesne they were met by a powerful Seneca chief, Tanacharison, who was leader of the Iroquois in Ohio, together with the Iroquois' dependent bands of Delaware.* The Iroquois had sought neutrality in the Whites' war, but French insults of the Half King – one French officer had informed him that "I despise all the stupid things you have said", and thrown a gift of wampum at him – encouraged friendliness towards Washington. Accordingly, the Half King's warriors joined Washington's militia in attacking a French scouting party, killing the commanding officer and nine of his men, after which the Half King departed for home.

Realizing that he had noisily lost his advantage of surprise, Washington reconsidered the wisdom of attacking the French fort and withdrawing to the treeless valley of Great Meadows, where he built an impromptu post, Fort Necessity. Sheltered behind a dirt bank, Washington waited for the French to come to him. They did, on 3 July 1754. They were also accompanied by hundreds of Indians, for the French had secured considerable support from Indian tribes with whom they traded. The outnumbered British fought for a day in the pouring rain, before being allowed an honourable surrender.

The next few years of the war were equally inglorious for the British, largely because of their ineptitude in courting the Indians. In 1755 the British commander, Major General

*The Delaware, Lenape, been shamefully removed from Pennsylvania in the 1737 affair of "The Walking Purchase"; citing a treaty supposedly signed by William Penn and Delaware chiefs in 1686, Pennsylvania colonists forced the Delaware to cede all lands around the forks of the Delaware River "as far as a man can go in a day and a half". The treaty was certainly fraudulent, and to emphasize their dishonesty the colonists found athletes to run – not walk, as the Delaware had supposed – for a day and half. One athlete managed sixty-four miles. That is, he won for the colonists 1,200 square miles of Delaware lands.

Edward Braddock, marched his troops towards Fort Duquesne as though on parade. He had just eight Indians with him, courtesy of his rudeness to the Indians. "He looked upon us as dogs," complained the Oneida chief Scarouady, "and would never hear anything that was said to him." Surprised by the French, along with their hundreds of Miami, Ottawa, Potawatomi, Ojibwa, Menominee, Huron, Shawnee, pro-French Seneca, and Delaware allies at Monongahela River, Braddock's redcoats were bloodily bested. Braddock himself was mortally wounded. His aide, George Washington, had a lucky escape with "four bullets through my coat and two horses shot under me".

Afterwards, the Indian allies of the French, especially the Delaware, began to raid British settlements, in some cases pushing back the frontier by 100 miles. "It is incredible," wrote one French officer, "what a quantity of scalps they bring us."

Despite defeat upon defeat, the British managed to turn the war around. Crucially, they secured the aid of the Iroquois.

William Johnson was an English fur trader who had settled in the Mohawk Valley. Through two marriages into the Mohawk tribe – one of his wives, incidentally, was Molly Brant, sibling of the soon to be famous Joseph – Johnson had become so influential in Iroquois affairs that the English commissioned him "Colonel of the Six Nations" [the original Five Nations having been joined by the Tuscarora]. In 1755 Colonel Johnson attended the Six Nations council, flung a war belt on the floor and asked for braves for unofficial fighting against the French. Among the volunteers was the sachem Hendrick (Theyanoguin), already in his seventies, who brought 400 warriors to Johnson's campaign against the French in the Champlain Valley, which culminated in the battle of Lake George. Looking over his assembled Mohawks, Hendrick is reputed to have said: "If they are to fight, they are too few; if they are to die, they are too many." Hendrick and many of the Mohawk did die, but the battle was won. Four years later, the Iroquois fought side by side with the British in the capture of Fort Niagra from the French. This was 1759. By now the French had definitively lost the war.

The finish of France in North America would also plunge the Iroquois into crisis. No longer did they provide a balance of power. There was only one power left. Britain.

Pontiac's Dream

"The only true method of treating the savages is to keep them in proper subjection and punish, without exception, the transgressors."

Sir Jeffrey Amherst, commander in chief of British forces

"Drive from your lands those dogs in red clothing [British soldiers]; they are only an injury to you. When you want anything, apply to me . . . Become good and you shall want for nothing."

The Master of Life to Neolin, the Delaware prophet

The Iroquois were not the only Indians disorientated by the departure of France from the New World. So too were the tribes who had fought for her in the French and Indian War. To pacify these tribes, British officers and Indian agents continued the French habit of gifting the Indians small quantities of powder and lead for hunting, and of food in hard times. This was not to the political taste of Sir Jeffrey Amherst, the British commander in North America, who considered the Indians "more nearly allied to the Brute than to the Human Creation". And stopped the gifts, declaring imperiously, "I do not see why the Crown should be put to that expense."

The Ohio country Indians had other grievances for, with the end of the war, white settlers were crowding into their territory.

In such disturbed times, the Delaware prophet, Neolin the Enlightened, found a ready audience. Like other visionaries, from Nemattanew to Wovoka, Neolin urged the Indians to turn their backs on ways and goods of the Whites, for the supernatural Master of Life had told him:

> The land on which you are, I have made for you, not for others: wherefore do you suffer the whites to dwell upon your lands? Can you not do without them? Before those whom you call your brothers [i.e., Europeans] had arrived, did not your bow and arrow maintain you? You needed neither gun, powder, nor any other object. The flesh of animals was your food, their skins your raiment. But when I saw you inclined to evil, I removed the animals into the depths of the forests . . .
>
> Drive from your lands those dogs in red clothing; they are only an injury to you. When you want anything, apply to me . . . Become good and you shall want for nothing.

One of those on whom Neolin's words fell like whips was the forty-year-old war chief of the Ottawa, Pontiac, who galvanized tribes on the western border into a grand alliance. Miamis, Hurons, Chippewas, Potawtomis, Menominees, Delawares, Foxes, Kickapoos, Weas, Sauk, Shawnees, Mascoutens, Mingos all joined with Pontiac's Ottawas in a plan for a simultaneous uprising against every British fort in the lake and Ohio country.

Such strategy and organization was almost unique in the annals of Indian–White warfare. As in the single blow of an axe, the forts of Michilimackinac, Green Bay, St Joseph, Sault Ste Marie, Miami, Ouiatenon, Le Bouef, Presque Isle, Venango, Fort Detroit, and Fort Pitt were all hit and attacked.

Some of the forts fell to full-frontal attacks, others were captured by strategem. At Michilimackinac, Chippewas and Sauks invited the garrison to watch a game of "ball play" (the fore-runner of lacrosse), during which the ball, as if by accident, landed inside the fort. Whilst retrieving it, the Indians turned on the garrison.

Alexander Henry, was a trader present at the fort and later captured by the Indians:

Mr Tracy had not gone more than twenty paces from the door, when I heard an Indian war-cry and a noise of general confusion.

Going instantly to my window, I saw a crowd of Indians within the fort, furiously cutting down and scalping every Englishman they found. In particular, I witnessed the fate of Lieutenant Jemette. I had, in the room in which I was, a fowling-piece, loaded with swan-shot. This I immediately seized, and held it for a few moments, waiting to hear the drum beat to arms. In this dreadful interval I saw several of my countrymen fall, and more than one struggling between the knees of an Indian, who, holding him in this manner, scalped him while yet living.

At length, disappointed in the hope of seeing resist-ance made to the enemy, and sensible, of course, that no effort of my own unassisted arm could avail against four hundred Indians, I thought only of seeking shelter.

Amid the slaughter which was raging, I observed many of the Canadian inhabitants of the fort calmly looking on, neither opposing the Indians nor suffering injury. From this circumstance I conceived a hope of finding security in their houses.

A Paris woman of M. Langlade's household beckoned me to follow her. She brought me to a door, which she opened, desiring me to enter, and telling me that it led to a garret, where I must go and conceal myself. I joyfully obeyed her directions; and she, having followed me up to the garret door, locked it after me, and with great presence of mind took away the key.

This shelter obtained, if shelter I could hope to find it, I was naturally anxious to know what might still be passing without. Through an aperture which afforded me a view of the area of the fort, I beheld, in shapes the foulest and most terrible, the ferocious triumphs of barbarian conquerors. The dead were scalped and mangled; the dying were writhing and shrieking under the unsatiated knife and tomahawk, amidst the shouts of rage and victory. I was shaken not only with horror at the sight, but with terror for myself. The sufferings which I witnessed, I seemed to be on the point of experiencing. No long time elapsed before, everyone being destroyed who could be found, there was a general cry of "All is finished!" And, at the same instant I heard some of the Indians enter the house in which I was.

Only Forts Detroit, Niagara and and Pitt (built on the ruins of Fort Duquesne) resisted the Indian onslaught; the British at Detroit, where Pontiac was in personal command of the attack, sustained a siege of nearly a year before relief, one of the longest sieges in American history.

"Pontiac's War", as the British termed it, was fought with rare ferocity. Some two thousand Whites were killed, many of them illegal settlers, as the Indians put the frontier from New York to Virginia to the torch. Panicky and possessed by hatred, white settlers killed all Indians to hand, even friendly ones. At Conestoga, Pennsylvania, at Christmas 1763, hooligans led by a Presbyterian Church minister massacred twenty Christian Susquehannocks, the last of their tribe. An eyewitness, John Penn, described their murder:

Those cruel men . . . by violence broke open the [workhouse] door, and entered with the utmost fury . . . When the poor wretches saw they had no protection . . . nor could possibly escape, and being without the least weapon for defence . . . they divided into their little families, the children clinging to the parents; they fell on their knees, protested their innocence, declared their love to the English, and that, in their whole lives, they had never done them injury; and in this posture they all received the hatchet! Men, women, and little children were every one inhumanely murdered! – in cold blood! . . . The bodies of the murdered were then brought out and exposed in the street, till a hole could be made in the earth, to receive and cover them.

To suppress Pontiac's rebellion, Amherst determined to "use every strategem in our power". Alongside orthodox military expeditions to retake the frontier, he also infamously pioneered germ warfare. Writing to Colonel Henry Bouquet, a British officer in Pennsylvania, Amherst inquired, "Could it not be contrived to send the smallpox among the disaffected tribes of Indians?" Some months later, smallpox was duly enlisted on the British side, when the commander of besieged

Fort Pitt invited the Delawares to a parlay, and gave them infected blankets from the hospital as a present. The resultant scourge severely undermined the Indian attack at Fort Pitt, whilst elsewhere in the war the Indian alliance was breaking up, as tribes lost heart, or simply tired of fighting and longed to go home. Some of the insurgents made peace in September 1764, acknowledging King George as their Father in the Treaty of Detroit. By the Treaty of Oswego, two years later, Pontiac and the other hostiles surrendered. His rebellion over, Pontiac journeyed to the land of the Illinois, where he was murdered by the tomahawk of a Peoria Indian in April 1769. The killer had been bribed with a barrel of liquor by an English trader to commit the deed.

Pontiac's War was not without result for the Indians. To give the insurgents no further cause for discontent, the wearied British Crown issued a proclamation on 7 October 1763 limiting White settlement to the east of the Appalachian crest. The land to the west was to be reserved as hunting ground for the Indians.

The proclamation astounded America. With the removal of France, thousands of colonists expected to swarm into the fertile "new Paradise" of trans-Appalachia. Many were volunteers who had served in the colonial militia with the lure of land as payment for service rendered. It now seemed that the interior would be barred to them forever. But when the shock died down, the colonists realized that the proclamation was unenforceable. They simply ignored it and marched over the mountains. They marched into Ohio, Tennessee, Pittsburgh, and along Daniel Boone's Wilderness Road into "Kentucke", where they invaded the extensive hunting domain shared by the Iroquois, Shawnee, Delaware and Cherokee. Cornstalk, the Shawnee war chief, made a desperate appeal to the Whites to leave the intertribal hunting ground alone: "We have never sold you our lands which you now possess", said Cornstalk, "and which you are now settling without ever asking our leave, or obtaining our consent. We live by hunting and do not subsist in any other way – that was our hunting ground and you have taken it from us. This is what sits heavy [on our] hearts and on the hearts of all nations."

The British response was to back the settlers and bring down "Lord Dunmore's War" on the heads of Indians in the disputed country. In the fall of 1774 Lord Dunmore marched three thousand Virginia militia into "the Dark and Bloody Ground", and gave battle to the Shawnees, along with their Mingo, Wyandot, Delaware allies at Point Pleasant on 9 October 1774. Defeated, the Shawnees were forced north of the Ohio, and in the following month signed a treaty relinquishing their hunting grounds in Kentucky.

Among those fighting with Cornstalk at Point Pleasant was the Mingo chief, Tachnechdorus (also known as John Logan), whose family of thirteen had been wiped out by white settlers at Yellow Creek. Until that time, Logan had been a good friend of the English, as he made clear in a message to Lord Dunmore which became known as "Logan's Lament":

I appeal to any white man to say, if ever he entered Logan's cabin hungry, and he gave him not meat; if ever he came cold and naked, and he clothed him not.

During the course of the last long and bloody war, Logan remained idle in his cabin, an advocate for peace. Such was my love for the whites, that my countrymen pointed as they passed, and said, "Logan is the friend of white men." I had even thought to have lived with you but for the injuries of one man. Colonel Cresap, the last spring, in cold blood and unprovoked, murdered all the relations of Logan, not even sparing my women and children. There runs not a drop of my blood in the veins of any living creature. This called on me for revenge. I have sought it; I have killed many; I have glutted my vengeance. For my country, I rejoice at the beams of peace. But do not harbor a thought that this is the joy of fear. Logan never felt fear. He will not turn on his heel to save his life. Who is there to mourn for Logan – Not one!

Despite the good service Lord Dunmore rendered the settlers at Point Pleasant, the colonists and the Crown were already and irrevocably on the trail to the War of Independence. It was a war in which the Indians would once again be enmeshed by machinating White powers. It was a war in which the Iroquois, among many other tribes, would feel the final blow to their power and their lands.

The White Man's War

"War is war. Death is death. A fight is a hard business."
Cornplanter, Seneca war chief, 1777

In the War of Independence, the Americans and the British both sought to woo the Indian to their side. Most Indian nations, meanwhile, sought neutrality. They knew from bloody experience that the wars of the Whites only brought ruin to the first Americans.

Few nations, however, were able to resist the lures and the pressures of the Revolutionary War as it unfolded. Not least the League of the Iroqouis.

Occupying strategic land close to the colonies, the Iroquois were a particular object of lobbying. Samuel Kirkland, a new England missionary, worked assiduously for the American cause and found a sympathetic hearing among the Tuscaroras and Oneidas. But the British had a stalwart friend in the Mohawk chief Theyendanegea, known to them as Joseph Brant, the protégé and brother-in-law of Sir William Johnson. Brant travelled the Six Nations arguing the British cause. Such division was unprecedented in the history of the League, and the crisis deepened when a smallpox epidemic struck Onondaga, the seat of the Iroquois' government, killing three sachems. The survivors put out the eternal fire at the centre of the Longhouse.

Sensing that the support of the Iroquois might be the means to victory, both the Americans and the British redoubled their efforts and overtures. Early in the summer of 1777 the Iroquois gathered at the invitation of the British at Oswego. Only the Oneidas and Tuscaroras refused to attend. Some chiefs, like the Seneca Cornplanter, urged neutrality. "War is war", cautioned Cornplanter. "Death is death. A fight is a hard business . . . I move therefore to wait a little while to hear more consultation between the two parties. [Britain and America]"

At this the angry – but astute – Joseph Brant called Cornplanter a coward. Honour, if not sense, required upholding. Everyone, Cornplanter included, rushed to joining the British war effort and prove their bravery. An early opportunity came on 6 August 1777, when an English force and four hundred Iroquois warriors led by Brant successfully attacked colonials and Oneidas at Oriskany Creek in the Mohawk Valley. Brant, a guerrilla leader of rare ability (and a scholar of note; he would later translate the Book of Common Prayer and St Mark's Gospel into Iroquois), then laid waste to the settlement of Cherry Valley. The Revolutionary cause was only saved when, in 1779, Washington felt he could spare enough troops to send to the northern frontier. He desired the "total destruction and devastation of [Iroquois] settlements". The means to this brutal end was General John Sullivan, whose retaliatory campaign in Iroquois country removed forty Iroquois towns from the face of the earth and burned 160,000 bushels of corn, plus apple, peach and pear orchards. Sullivan's men thought themselves in a kind of garden of Eden, so abundant, cultivated and civilized was the land of the League. They left it, according to one early account, "a scene of drear and sickening desolation." Survivors "were hunted like beasts", or starved during the long winter. Troops, for their amusement, skinned the bodies of dead Indians "from the hips downward, to make boot tops or leggings". Brant terrorized the colonial lands between the Mohawk and Ohio rivers until the end of the conflict.

Meanwhile, the Iroquois' sometime dependants, the Shawnee and Delaware took advantage of the White man's war to defend their lands, beginning raids in the summer of 1776 which forced the Kentucky stations to hastily erect ten-foot high stockades of pointed logs set vertically. No sooner was this "forting up" achieved than in the spring of 1777, the infamous "year of the three sevens", Chief Blackfish and 300 Shawnee invested Boonesborough so completely that the inhabitants were unable to plant crops. To secure the middle frontier, the Americans dispatched George Rogers Clark at the head of Virginia and Kentucky riflemen, but their burning of the principal Shawnee towns on the Ohio merely caused a vortex of retaliatory attacks on the Kentucky settlements. Bands of Indians roved the ever darker and bloodier ground, picking off travellers and careless settlers. Not until Clark's climactic victories of 1782 did the Americans subdue the Shawnee.

It was on the middle frontier that the infant United States made its first treaty with an Indian tribe. Under an agreement signed at Fort Pitt on 17 September 1778, the Delawares – who had been pushed into Ohio by the westwards tide of colonial settlement – acceded to the passage and provision of US troops, in return for a representative in Congress. Alas, the peace with the Delawares was short-lived. When frontiersmen massacred ninety Christian Delawares as they sung hymns in their church at Gnadenhutten, the Delawares went on the warpath, roasting captured Americans over beds of hot coals.

Neither did the Indians of the Southeast escape the ravening mouth of war. There, fighting began in the southern backcountry when Cherokees – against the wishes of their ally, the regional British superintendent of Indian affairs, Colonel John Stuart – swooped on Eaton's Station in North Carolina on 20 July 1776. After a treasonous but humanitarian warning to the hamlet by Stuart, the Indians were rebuffed, and so moved on to Fort Watauga. Milkmaids in the fields outside just made the safety of the Stockade, Kate Sherill being pulled over the wall by John Sevier, who shot her closest pursuer almost in the same motion. Again the Indians were rebuffed. Incensed by their double humiliation, Chief Dragging Canoe's warriors, along with Creeks, Choctaws, Tories and renegade trader Alexander Cameron, struck isolated farms and settlements all along the Watauga and Nolichucky rivers. The settlers struck back with equal savagery. South Carolina offered a bounty of £75 for Indian scalps. And in the fall some 5,000 militiamen from Virginia and the Carolinas swept down like an avenging storm on the Overhill, Middle and Lower Town Cherokee. By the treaty of DeWitt's Corner and Long Island, the Cherokee were forced to surrender 5 million acres of tribal land, including most of the Tennessee basin. Settlers poured in, and in 1780 Nashville was founded.

Nowhere did the Indians profit in the White man's war.* And the Indians did not profit in the peace which ended it.

By the Treaty of Paris of 1783, Britain granted America its independence, plus sovereignty over a domain which stretched from the Great Lakes in the north to the 31st

*The Indians had not even been able to stop White settlement in Kentucky, which had a White population of 70,000 by 1780.

parallel in the south, and west to the Mississippi. Conspicuously, there was not a word in the treaty about protection of the Indians who had fought for the Crown. What then befell the Iroquois was typical. Abandoned by the British and denied their New York lands by the American victors, Brant and many other Iroquois pro-British moved to Canada (where their descendants still live); those Iroquois who remained in New York did so on reduced lands – reservations, indeed – which were endlessly beset by speculators and government agents coveting them as payment to the veterans of Washington's army. To the victor went the spoils of war, in particular the Indian's lands.

Eventually, a rising chorus of Indian complaint over coercive land acquisitions in the "Northwest Territory" (as the region above the Ohio had become known) caused Congress in Philadelphia to experience a change of heart. By the Northwest Ordinance of 1787, it was asserted that the land of the Indian nations could not be taken without their agreement. Declared the Ordinance: "The utmost good faith shall always be observed toward the Indians; their lands and property shall never be taken from them without their consent; and in their property, rights, and liberty they shall never be invaded or disturbed unless in just and lawful wars authorized by Congress; but laws founded in justice and humanity shall, from time to time, be made, for preventing wrongs being done to them and for preserving peace and friendship with them."

Fine sentiments. Rarely would they work in practice, for one simple reason: the Indians rarely wanted to sell their land. To sate the Whites' land-lust, it would have to be prised from them by guile, bribery or the end of a gun. Proof – if proof were needed – was just around a bend of the Ohio River.

Under the terms of the Northwest Ordinance – one of the

most important laws in the history of White westwards expansion – the government began the surveying of land around Ohio, as a prelude to its sale to settlers. Conveniently ignored by the government was the singular fact that this land had been fraudulently obtained in the aftermath of the Revolution, and the Indians still claimed it as their own. To signal its commitment to the virtue of might over right, the government in 1789 built Fort Washington on the north bank of the Ohio (the site of modern Cincinnati). The Indians of the region – the Chippewas, Shawnees, Miamis and other tribes of the Lakes and Ohio – were already embroiled in rnnning fights against squatters and marauding Kentucky frontiersmen; the building of Fort Washington caused the discontented Indians to go on the warpath. Under Blue Jacket of the Shawnees and Little Turtle of the Miamis, Ohio Indians struck repeatedly at the frontier, slaying whole settlements, even attacking supply boats on the Ohio. Urging them on was Britain, anxious to surreptitiously stymie American expansionism and still clinging – in violation of the Paris treaty – to her northwest forts.

The United States had its first Indian war. To crush the insurgent tribes the new president, George Washington, sent out two military expeditions. Both fared badly. The first, in 1790, under the drunkard General Josiah Harmar, was mauled comprehensively in ambushes by the Miami and Shawnee warriors of Little Turtle and Blue Jacket. The next year, General Arthur St Clair, the gout-ridden governor of the Northwest Territory led 2,300 troops (and 200 prostitutes, listed as "cooks") out of Fort Washington on a march so slow – 5 miles a day – that some militia enlistments terminated before they had caught sight of a hostile Indian. Others simply deserted. Within a month, St Clair's army had shrunk to 1,400 men. At length, St Clair's expedition reached a tributary of the Wabash. Inept and inexperienced at Indian-fighting, St Clair let his men sleep in the wooded creek almost without guard. Throughout the night of 3 November 1791, warriors from the Miami, Shawnee, Delaware and other western tribes infiltrated the expedition's sleeping camp. At dawn, the war-whooping warriors rushed the Americans from three sides, and in three hours of battle, much of it fought hand to hand, killed 850 American troops, civilian teamsters and "cooks". The remainder fled in panic, St Clair on an ass, reaching Fort Washington in four days; the journey out had taken five weeks.

It was the worst defeat in the history of US Indian fighting.

A sobered Congress decided to seek peace with the Indians of the upper Ohio, and sent out the requisite emissaries. Among them was Red Jacket of the Iroquois. He was jeered and hooted at by the Northwestern tribes, for being a messenger boy of the Whites. So had the once mighty fallen. [The Iroquois would, however, endure better than most tribes, sustained as they later were by the vision of the Seneca Skanyadariyoh, or Handsome Lake, whose "Good Message" allowed the Iroquois to adopt aspects of White culture, like domestic animals, but retain their identity through revitalized religion.]

Another peace effort followed, in the summer of 1793, with the Americans promising to give up most of the lands north of the Ohio, save for Cincinnati and other large settlements, for which it would pay fifty thousand dollars in goods, plus an annual annuity of ten thousand dollars. The reply of the tribes was brief. All Whites north of the Ohio had to leave.

Washington had expected such a response. On standby was General "Mad Anthony" Wayne, a former tanner turned Revolutionary hero, the victor of Stoney Point. Wayne was instructed to take "vigorous offensive action" against the hostile nations of the Ohio country. Patiently Wayne drilled his men, perfected their marksmanship and then led them into battle on 20 August 1794 in the Fallen Timbers along the Maumee River.

Everything went wrong for the Indians at Fallen Timbers. Little Turtle, noting the calibre of Wayne's approaching army, had urged peace; when this was rejected by the tribes he fought at Fallen Timbers, but not as leader. Then, the Great Lakes and Ottawa Indians made a premature charge, before a mass ambush could be sprung on the "Long Knives".

Although the Americans initially panicked as the Great Lakes and Ottawa Indians fell upon them, Wayne steadied his Legion of the United States, then hurled it in a screaming bayonet charge into the thickets. Blue Jacket's allied Indian force disintegrated and fled to the safety of the British Fort Miami, only to have the gate shut in their faces. The British commander was not prepared to openly violate Britain's neutrality. The rejection broke the Indians' morale.

On 3 August 1795, the Miami, Delaware, Shawnee, Ottawa, Wyandot, Wea, Kickapoo, Potawatomi, Kaskaskia, Chippewa and Piankashaw tribes signed a peace treaty at Wayne's Greenville headquarters. Under its terms, the Indians forfeited a slice of southeastern Indiana and nearly all of Ohio. White settlers flooded. By 1803 the wilderness the Indians had warred for was a state of the Union.

The Vision of Tecumseh

"Accursed be the race that has seized on our country and made women of our warriors. Our forefathers from their tombs reproach us as slaves and cowards. I hear them now in the wailing skies. Let the white race perish. They seize your land, they corrupt your women, they trample on the ashes of your dead! Back hence they came, upon a trail of blood, they must be driven."

Tecumseh, October 1811

After the Treaty of Greenville, a great darkness descended on the Indians of the Northwest. Some, like Little Turtle, who had signed at Greenville stating, "I am the last to sign – I shall be the last to break it," accepted annuities in exchange for land and allowed Quakers to build model farms on their land. Such "accommodationism" delighted the Whites of the East, who under Washington and his secretary of war, Henry Knox, pioneered a "civilization" answer to the so-called Indian problem. A majority of the Northwest Indians, however, struggled to live in the old manner, which became ever harder to do as game was depleted, Whites overran the lands the Indians still held, and epidemics rampaged. Alcohol became a frequent refuge. Ceremonial life waned, so did dignity, as formerly proud warriors and hunters were forced to live upon the hand outs of the White man.

Of the many alcoholic Indians in the Northwest, none seemed more hopeless than the Shawnee Lalawethika, whose name meant "Noisemaker" in mark of his liquor-fuelled bragging. To feed his family, Lalawethika relied on his older brother Tecumseh ("Celestial Panther Lying in Wait"), a war chief with an honoured reputation. Tecumseh had refused to sign the Treaty of Greenville.

One spring night in 1805, Lalawethika experienced a vision in which he encountered the Creator, who revelled to him that the Whites "grew from the scum of the great water, when it was troubled by an evil spirit and the froth was driven into the woods by a strong east wind. They are numerous, but I hate them. They are unjust; they have taken away your lands, which were not made for them." According to the Creator, the Indians had transgressed by following White ways, and he had chosen to punish them by shutting the game in the ground. If the Indians rejected the Whites' influences – liquor, domestic animals, traders' goods and the like – a supernatural force would remove the Whites.

Taking the name Tenskwatawa ("Open Door") and vowing never to touch alcohol again, Lalawethika preached to the Shawnees, admonishing them for their depravity and urging them, like Handsome Lake of the Iroquois, to favour the old religion. Soon the Shawnee Prophet's message spread, to the tribes of the region, but also to the ears of William Henry Harrison, the ramrod governor of Indian Territory. "Who is this pretended prophet who dares to speak in the name of the Great Creator?" Harrison wrote to the Indians. "Demand of him some proofs at least of his being the messenger of the Deity . . . ask him to cause the sun to stand still – the moon to alter its course – or the dead to rise from their graves. If he does these things, you may then believe that he has been sent by God."

It was an epistle Harrison would rue writing. Tenskwatawa – probably through an almanac – learned when an eclipse of the sun was due, and "foretold" it. When the Prophet's miracle duly occurred, many more Indians flocked to join Tenswatawa's Nativist revival.

In 1808 Tenskwatawa and his brother Tecumseh founded the "Prophet's Town", near the junction of the Wabash and Tippecanoe Rivers in Indiana. At "Prophet's Town", where Indians from different nations lived together insulated from White influences, Tecumseh begin to spin out his brother's religious revivalism into something bigger: a Pan-Indian military and political movement. The Whites had been conspicuously able to buy off or fight off the tribes one by one, but the tribes combined would be an unbreakable fist. Moreover, Tecumseh asserted that the Indians should own their land in common, and no tribe could sell the common patrimony.

Initially, Tecumseh did not urge war on the Whites, for he hoped they would be sufficiently admiring of Indian unification – it was not unlike, after all, their own united states – to allow a permanent, all-nations Indian state behind the Ohio. It was not to be.

For a year after the founding of Prophet's Town, the charismatic Tecumseh ceaselessly journeyed America, from the northwest down to Florida, preaching his vision of Pan-Indianism. His absence was cannily exploited by Governor Harrison, who gathered a group of compliant chiefs at Fort Wayne, plied them with alcohol ("mellowed them" said Harrison) and conned them into selling three million acres of Indiana for $7,600. Some it it they did not even own.

On his return to Prophet's Town, Tecumseh was outraged by the Fort Wayne "treaty". So were hundreds of other Indians, who crowded around him, listening to his fine oratory and his proclamations of Indian unity. Warriors from many tribes joined Tecumseh and Tenskwatawa at Prophet's Town, where they practised the arts of war. The Indians would defend their lands by force of arms if necessary.

Seeking to dampen the fiery Indians of Prophet's Town, in August 1810 Harrison invited Tecumseh to parlay at Vincennes, the Indiana capital. Accompanied by one hundred painted warriors, Tecumseh sailed down the Wabash and met Harrison to protest the land sales. He refused to enter the Governor's mansion:

Houses are built for you to hold councils in; Indians hold theirs in the open air. I am a Shawnee. My forefathers were warriors. Their son is a warrior. From them I take my only existence. From my tribe I take nothing. I have made myself what I am. And I would that I could make the red people as great as the conceptions of my own mind, when I think of the Great Spirit that rules over us all . . . I would not then come to Governor Harrison to ask him to tear up the treaty. But I would say to him. "Brother, you have the liberty to return to your own country."

You wish to prevent the Indians from doing as we wish them, to unite and let them consider their lands as the common property of the whole. You take the tribes aside and advise them not to come into this measure . . . You want by your distinctions of Indian tribes, in allotting to each a particular, to make them war with each other. You never see an Indian endeavor to make the white people do this. You are continually driving the red people, when at last you will drive them onto the great lake, where they can neither stand nor work.

Since my residence at Tippecanoe, we have endeavored to level all distinctions, to destroy village chiefs, by whom all mischiefs are done. It is they who sell the land to the Americans. Brother, this land that was sold, and the goods that was given for it, was only done by a few . . . In the future we are prepared to punish those who propose to sell land to the Americans. If you continue to purchase them, it will make war among the different tribes, and, at last I do not know what will be the consequences among the white people. Brother, I wish you would take pity on the red people and do as I have requested. If you will not give up the land and do cross the boundary of our present settlement, it will be very hard, and produce great trouble between us.

The way, the only way to stop this evil is for the red men to unite in claiming a common and equal right in the land, as it was at first, and should be now – for it was never divided, but belongs to all. No tribe has the right to sell, even to each other, much less to strangers . . . *Sell a country! Why not sell the air, the great sea, as well as the earth?* Did not the Great Spirit make them all for the use of his children?

How can we have confidence in the white people?

When Jesus Christ came upon the earth you killed Him and nailed Him to the cross. You thought He was dead, and you were mistaken. You have Shakers among you and you laugh and make light of their worship.

Everything I have told you is the truth. The Great Spirit has inspired me.

Tecumseh was probably the greatest Indian orator of them all.

When Harrison replied, he sought to defend the Fort Wayne treaties. So heated did the argument then become that Harrison drew his sword, and Tecumseh's warriors their tomahawks. A fight was avoided. For a while.

A year later, Tecumseh was again invited to Vincennes, and again the meeting broke up without agreement. Afterwards, Harrison recorded his observations of Tecumseh – the "uncommon genius" – and his mission:

> The implicit obedience and respect which the followers of Tecumseh pay to him is really astonishing and more than any other circumstance bespeaks him one of those uncommon geniuses, which spring up occasionally to produce revolutions and overturn the established order of things. If it were not for the vicinity of the United States, he would perhaps be the founder of an Empire that would rival in glory that of Mexico or Peru.
>
> No difficulties deter him. His activity and industry supply the want of letters. For four years he has been in constant motion. You see him today on the Wabash and in a short time you hear of him on the shores of Lake Erie or Michigan, or on the banks of the Mississippi, and wherever he goes he makes an impression favourable to his purpose.

Shortly after this second council at Vincennes, Tecumseh set out to the South, accompanied by thirty warriors, visiting the Chickasaws, Choctaws, Creeks, Seminoles, Cherokees before going north to address the Delawares, Shawnees, Osages, Iowas, the Sauks and the Foxes. In town after town, thousands turned up to hear Tecumseh, his cheeks bright with lines of red war paint, tell them to unite and fight for their land:

Where today are the Pequot? Where are the Narragansett, the Mohican, the Pocanet, and other powerful tribes of our people? They have vanished before the avarice and oppression of the white man, as now before the summer summer sun . . . Will we let ourselves be destroyed in our turn, without making an effort worthy of our race? Shall we, without a struggle. give up our homes, our lands. bequeathed to us by the Great Spirit? The graves of our dead and everything that is dear and sacred to us? . . . I know you will say with me, Never! Never! . . .

Sleep not longer, O Choctaws and Chickasaws, in false security and delusive hopes . . . Will not the bones of our dead be plowed up, and their graves turned into plowed fields?

Tecumseh's oratory and message did not convert everyone, especially amongst the Choctaws, Cherokees and the other southern tribes who were already, by blood or by acculturation, wedded to White America.

In the early spring of 1812 Tecumseh returned home to to Prophet's Town. He found it a ruin. Harrison had once again taken advantage of Tecumseh's absence to drive through his own design, putting Prophet Town to the flame. There was worse news for Tecumseh; his brother admitted to a precipitate attack on Harrison, instead of maintaining the peace as instructed. (Harrison would later use his victory at Tippecanoe as a ticket to the Presidency.) In consequence, Tecumseh was at war before he had finished his pan-Indian confederation. Furiously, he "seized his brother by the hair and almost shook the life out of him". The rage passed, but henceforth the Prophet was cast to the dim sidelines of history, and died in obscurity in Kansas.

Patiently, Tecumseh gathered in his chiefs and sent out ernissaries, seeking to to rebuild the coalition. Time was running too fast, however. In June 1812 war broke out between Britain and America. "Here is a chance," Tecumseh told a meeting of chiefs, "such as will never occur again – for us Indians of North America to form ourselves into one great combination." Raising a war party, Tecumseh marched to Fort Maiden and joined the British. It was a large war party – with Kickapoos, Potawatomis, Shawnees, Delawares, Wynadots, Chippewas, Sioux, Winnebagos, Sauk and Fox – but it was not a "great combination" of all the tribes.

Impressed, nonetheless, the British made Tecumseh a brigadier general. Tecumseh and his warriors played important roles in the British capture of Detroit, of Fort Dearborn. All this was achieved under Tecumseh's able friend Sir Isaac Brock; when Brock was killed in battle, the incompetent Henry Proctor took over as British commander. It was Proctor who allowed the massacre of American prisoners at River Raisin on January 22 1813, and would have allowed the slaughter of American prisoners at Fort Meigs – if Tecumseh had not intervened. "You are not fit to command," Tecumseh shouted at Proctor. "Go and put on petticoats." Shortly afterwards, against Tecumseh's advice, Proctor lifted the siege of Fort Meigs.

If Tecumseh had any doubts about the ability and will of the British to fight the war they were well founded. On 10 Sepember 1813, Commodore Oliver Hazard Perry annihilated the British fleet on Lake Erie, and cut the western army from its supply line. Secretly, Proctor planned a retreat of his army back across Canada – leaving the northwest, and its Indians, to the Americans. When Tecumseh found out Proctor's hidden design, he upbraided him in public:

Father! Listen to your children: you have them now all before you. In the old war our British father gave the hatchet to his red children when our old chiefs were alive. They are now dead. In that war our British father was thrown on his back by the Americans, and he took them by the hand without our knowledge. We are afraid our father will do so again this time. In the summer before last, when I came forward with my red brethren, and was ready to take up the hatchet in favor of our British father, we were told not to be in a hurry, for he had not yet determined to fight the Americans.

Listen! – When war was declared, our father stood up and gave us the tomahawk, and told us that he was then ready to strike the Americans; that he wanted our assistance: and that he would certainly get our lands back which the Americans had taken from us.

Father, listen! – The Americans have not yet beaten us by land, nor are we sure they have done so by water. We therefore wish to stay here and fight the enemy if they come. If they beat us, we will then retreat with our father. At the battle of the Rapids [Fallen Timbers], in the last war, the Americans certainly defeated us, and when we retreated to our father's fort at that place, the gates were shut against us. We were afraid this would happen again; but, instead of this, we now see our British father preparing to march out of his garrison.

Father! – You have got the arms and ammunition which our great father sent for his red children. If you mean to go away, give them to us, and you may go and welcome. Our lives are in the hands of the Great Spirit. We are determined to defend our lands, and, if it be his will, we wish to leave our bones upon them.

Despite Tecumseh's plea to Proctor to stand and fight, the British began a retreat along the north side of the lake. With William Harrison, now elevated to General, approaching with 3,000 Americans, Tecumseh had little option but to withdraw across Ontario with the British.

At Thames River, on 5 October 1813, Tecumseh decided to halt the unseemly retreat, and compelled Proctor to do the same. "Father," Tecumseh said to Proctor, "tell your men to be firm, and all will be well."

It was good place for a fight against a superior force. The Shawnee chief positioned his men on the right in a swampy wood, the British on the left with their flank to their river. Soon the pursuant Harrison was upon them, and launched a cavalry charge against the regulars in the British line. They broke almost immediately, running terrified from the battlefield, Proctor overtaking them on his horse.

Tecumseh rallied his warriors, and they fought on in fierce and desperate fighting in the swamp. Before the battle Tecumseh had told his warriors, "I shall never come out alive." He achieved his desire to die fighting. Minutes after his death, his faithful companions, men who had been with him since the beginning, spirited away his body so it could not be defiled and paraded by his enemy.

Alongside Tecumseh in the swamp of Thames River there died a great vision, a vision of an American Indian nation.

More prosaically, at Thames River died meaningful Indian resistance to the white settlement of the Old West. Old Black Hawk (Makataimeshekiakiak) of the Sauk and Fox went on the warpath in 1832 to defend his sacred Rock River lands, but it was a gesture as futile as it was tragic. He surrendered the same year, and his people were removed to Iowa. His address to his captors at Prairie du Chien, Wisconsin, bears repeating:

You have taken me prisoner with all my warriors. I am much grieved, for I expected, if I did not defeat you, to hold out much longer, and give you more trouble before I surrendered. I tried hard to bring you into ambush, but your last general understands Indian fighting. The first one was not so wise. When I saw I could not beat you by Indian fighting, I determined to rush on you, and fight you face to face. I fought hard. But your guns were well aimed. The bullets flew like birds in the air, and whizzed by our ears like the wind through the trees in the winter. My warriors fell around me; it began to look dismal. I saw my evil day at hand. The sun rose dim on us in the morning, and at night it sunk in a dark cloud, and looked like a ball of fire. That was the last sun that shone on Black Hawk. His heart is dead, and no longer beats quick in his bosom. He is now a prisoner to the white men; they will do with him as they wish. But he can stand torture, and is not afraid of death. He is no coward. Black Hawk is an Indian.

He has done nothing for which an Indian ought to be ashamed. He has fought for his countrymen, the squaws and papooses, against white men, who came year after year, to cheat them and take away their lands. You know the cause of our making war. It is known to all white men. They ought to be ashamed of it. Indians are not deceitful. The white men speak bad of the Indian and look at him spitefully. But the Indian does not tell lies; Indians do not steal.

An Indian who is as bad as the white men could not live in our nation; he would be put to death, and eaten up by the wolves. The white men are bad schoolmasters; they carry false books, and deal in false actions; they smile in the face of the poor Indian to cheat him; they shake them by the hand to gain their confidence, to make them drunk, to deceive them, and ruin our wives. We told them to leave us alone, and keep away from us; but they followed on, and beset our paths, and they coiled themselves among us, like the snake. They poisoned us by their touch. We were not safe. We lived in danger. We were becoming like them, hypocrites and liars, adulterous lazy drones, all talkers, and no workers.

We looked up to the Great Spirit. We went to our great father. We were encouraged. His great council gave us fair words and big promises; but we got no satisfaction. Thing were growing worse. There were no deer in the forest. The opossum and beaver were fled; the springs were drying up; and our squaws and papooses were without victuals to keep them from starving. We called a great council, and built a large fire. The spirit of our fathers arose and spoke to us to avenge our wrongs or die. We all spoke before the council fire. It was warm and pleasant. We set up the war-whoop, and dug up the tomahawk; our knives were ready, and the heart of Black Hawk swelled high in the bosom, when he led his warriors to battle. He is satisfied. He will go to the world of spirits contented. He has done his duty. His father will meet him there and commend him.

Black Hawk is a true Indian, and disdains to cry like a woman. He feels for his wife, his children and friends. But he does not care for himself. He cares for his nation and the Indians. They will suffer. He laments their fate. The white men do not scalp the head; but they do worse – they poison the heart. It is not pure with them. His countrymen will not be scalped, but they will, in a few years, become like the white men, so that you can't trust them, and there must be, as in the white settlements, nearly as many officers as men to take care of them and keep them in order.

Farewell, my nation! Black Hawk tried to save you, and avenge your wrongs. He drank the blood of some of the whites. He has been taken prisoner, and his plans are stopped. He can do no more. He is near his end. His sun is setting, and he will rise no more. Farewell to Black Hawk.

And such was the farewell of the Indians to the Old Northwest.

The Fall of Leaves

"Murder is murder and somebody must answer, somebody must explain the streams of blood that flowed in the Indian country in the summer of 1838. Somebody must explain the 4,000 silent graves that mark the trail of the Cherokees to their exile. I wish I could forget it all, but the picture of the 645 wagons lumbering over the frozen ground with their cargo of suffering humanity still lingers in my memory."

John G. Burnett, United States Army interpreter

In the South, the big tribes had long seen that armed resistance to Whites was useless. Even so, there was a clamouring traditionalist faction among the Creeks, notably those impassioned by Tecumseh's vision and the Creek religious revival of the early nineteenth century. It was these dissenters who led the last great hurrah against the Whites in the South. This was the Creek War of 1812–13, as bitterly fought as it was vain in purpose.

The Creeks, also known as the Muskogees, took their name from the inland waterways amongst which they lived, and led a confederacy as powerful in the South as that of the Iroquois in the North. At its zenith before the American Revolution, the Creek confederacy – which enjoyed by dint of geographical providence, a strategic location between the imperial claims of England, France and Spain – could muster upwards of 10,000 fighting men from its hundred towns.

Although the newly minted United States of America concluded a treaty with the Creeks in 1790 which solemnly guaranteed the borders of the Creek nation (present-day Georgia, Alabama and South Carolina), Creek lands were steadily eaten at by speculators, cotton planters and hardscrabble farmers. Out of outrage at this unceremonious land-grabbing came the Creek anti-American faction, which gave a ready ear to Tecumseh's militant message. When the United States entangled itself in the War of 1812 with the British, the anti-American faction judged it prudent to strike.

On 30 August 1813 hostile Creeks from the Upper Towns fell on the American Fort Mims, near Mobile, in Alabama, where a less than prudent comander had left the gate open. The hostiles – known as "Red Sticks" after the magic clubs given them by Tecumseh's supporters – rushed in and slew 160 civilians, 107 soldiers and 100 black slaves. Retribution was quick and gigantic. Federal forces, Tennessee and Georgia militia, Choctaws and Cherokees all invaded the Upper Towns; so too did the pro-American Lower Creeks under their principal chief William MacIntosh. The unmitigated tragedy of the Creek War was that it was as much a civil war as it was one of rebellion against the whites.

After being beaten back and beaten back, Tennessee militia – led by an obscure volunteer general, Andrew Jackson – finally cornered the Red Sticks at Horseshoe Bend on the Tallapoosa River on 27 March 1814. For two hours, Jackson pounded the Red Sticks under Chief Menawa with artillery, before letting loose Cherokee and American Creek auxiliaries, who burned the Red Stick encampment but were unable to seize the hostiles' main position. This finally fell to militia mass assault, the warriors dropping "like the fall of leaves", with a scattered remnant of Red Sticks fleeing to a picket, upon which Jackson turned his cannon. The picket was fired, the handful of remaining Red Sticks shot as they ran from the flames.

Around the battlefield lay some 900 Red Stick dead; Jackson had their corpses mutilated, strips of their skin turned into bridle reins for horses. Among the few Red Stick warriors who survived was Menawa himself. He had been shot eight times, with one bullet fired into his face at near point blank range and blowing away part of his jaw. Under cover of darkness he crawled away to the river, found a canoe and floated with the current to join some some Red Stick women and children hiding out in a swamp. At length, the Red Stick survivors and their families escaped to Spanish-contolled Florida and joined the Seminoles.

If any of the Lower Creeks were expecting reward for their part in hunting down the Red Sticks they were to be sorely disappointed. In August Jackson called the Creek chiefs together and forced them to hand over two-thirds of their territory. He also obliged them to accept responsibility for the Creek War.

Jackson's days of Creeks-fighting were not over, however. In Florida, the Red Stick refugees and Seminole were embroiled in border skirmishes with illegal white occupants. To settle the matter in favour of the whites, Jackson – who considered Indians nothing but "savage dogs" – invaded Florida in 1818, torched the villages of the Red Sticks and Seminoles, and captured Pensacola from the Spaniards. At this, Spain decided to cut her losses and sold Florida to the United States in 1819. With a flood of white settlers into Florida, the Red Sticks and Seminoles were pushed into the swamps. By 1835 the Seminoles and Red Sticks were again at war with the US, in the protracted "Second Seminole War" to resist settlement west of the Mississippi. Although American forces enjoyed a notable success in their treacherous capture under a white flag of Osceola, the main Seminole war leader, the resoluteness of the Seminole and difficulty of the malaria-ridden terrain required them to quit in 1842 before the job was done; several hundred Seminole and Mikasukis held out in the Everglades, where their descendants continue to live until this day.

The Trail of Tears

While the Red Sticks and Seminoles had been engaged in
their long war with the United States the main tribes of the
South had been progressing far down the path of the white
man's ways. In this "acculturation" – or becoming "civilized"
as the Whites saw it – the Cherokees were in the van. Under
the teachings of missionaries from the Moravian Brethren
and the American Board of Commissioners, the Cherokees
were Christianized, introduced to agriculture and literacy.
Education was hastened by Sequoyah's invention in 1821 of
the Cherokee alphabet, which assigned a letter to eighty-six
Cherokee syllables; almost overnight the whole Cherokee
tribe became literate. By 1828 the Cherokee had their own
weekly newspaper, the *Cherokee Phoenix*, printed in both the
syllabary of Sequoyah (sometimes called George Guess or
Gist) and English. The selfsame year saw the Cherokee elect
delegates to a constitutional convention, modelled on the
American republic, with the eighth-white John Ross chosen
as principal chief.

Unfortunately for the Cherokee, their impressive acculturation – which received concrete, visible form in the buildings
and squares of their capital New Echota – did nothing to
lessen either the land-hunger of the Whites, nor the latter's

perception of the Cherokee as racial inferiors. By pressure and by fraud, the Cherokees, along with Creeks, Choctaws and Chickasaws (who, plus the Seminole formed the "Five Civilized Tribes") were steadily driven off their lands and to resettlement west of the Mississippi. But the pace and scale of resettlement was too slow for most whites.

Enter Andrew Jackson, elected to the presidency in 1828. Two years later Jackson signed into law the Indian Removal Act, a purposeful piece of chicanery, which in fine detail disavowed the forced removal of the eastern Indian but in spirit allowed it. Specifically, Jackson failed to protect Indians of the Five Civilized tribes from state-sponsored land-grabs and the illegal extension of white laws into the nations.

The Choctaws were the first to feel the brunt of the Indian Removal Act. In 1830, the peaceable Choctaws signed a provisional treaty of removal to Oklahoma. The first exodus of Choctaws, four thousand of them, left Mississippi in November 1831, the wailing emigrants touching their beloved trees, streams, and rocks in farewell before they tramped off westwards. It happened to be an especially harsh winter, with deep snow in the Great Arkansas swamp, through which the near-naked Choctaw had to wade. A number of Choctaws elected to remain behind, on individual "allotments", as their new treaty allowed, but swindled out of their land, which was promptly taken over by White families.

Next came the Chickasaws and the Creeks. The former left without strife, but many Creeks refused to move, at which White speculators and cotton-planters drove them from homes and slaughtered their livestock. In response, some starving Lower Creeks turned "hostile" and raided White settlements for food. Once again, the Creeks fell into internecine conflict, with the Upper Creek chief Opothle Yahola assisting the American army in putting down the "uprising". (Ironically enough, at Opothle Yahola's side was Menewa, the former Red Stick leader, now reconciled to America, and even the proud wearer of an US Army general's uniform). No sooner was the uprising vanquished than the government ordered the entire Creek nation – Opothle Yahola included – off to Arkansas. Before the journey, the Creeks' medicine men, the *hillis hayas*, put out the sacred fires in the town squares, and silently the Creeks began the forlorn march westwards. Some Creeks later wrote in complaint: "We were drove off like wolves . . . and our peoples' feet were bleeding with long marches . . . We are men . . . we have women and children, and why should we come like wild horses?" According to some historians, the tribe lost 10,000 of their 22,000 population in the removal.

Tragedy also awaited the Cherokees. Under John Ross's leadership, the Cherokees mounted a tenacious legal challenge to their removal, and in 1832 won their case in the Supreme Court when Chief Justice John Marshall ruled emphatically that Georgia had no authority to pass laws affecting the Cherokee. "The whole intercourse between the United States and this nation [the Cherokees]", Marshall wrote, "is by our constitution and laws, vested in the government of the United States."

But Jackson simply ignored the Court's ruling, and winked at Georgia to do the same. Reputedly Jackson sniped, "John Marshall has rendered his decision, now let him enforce it."

So came about the 1833 great Georgia lottery of confiscated Cherokee property, with winners of lucky tickets winning Cherokee farms, plantation houses, even the government buildings of New Echota. Some Cherokee moved west after the fraudulent New Echota Treaty, which forfeited all Cherokee lands, but the majority under John Ross stayed put. At length, the army, under General Winfield Scott was sent in; James Mooney, who interviewed Scott's soldiers, painted the scene that ensued:

Under Scott's orders the troops were disposed at various points throughout the Cherokee country, where stockade forts were erected for gathering in and holding the Indians preparatory to removal. From these, squads of troops were sent to search out with rifle and bayonet every small cabin hidden away in the coves or by the sides of mountain streams, to seize and bring in as prisoners all the occupants, however or wherever they might be found. Families at dinner were startled by the sudden gleam of bayonets in the doorway and rose up to be driven with blows and oaths along the weary miles of trail that led to the stockade. Men were seized in their fields or going along the road, women were taken from their wheels and children from their play. In many cases, on turning for one last look as they crossed the ridge, they saw their homes in flames, fired by the lawless rabble that followed on the heels of the soldiers to loot and pillage. So keen were these outlaws on the scent that in some instances they were driving off the cattle and other stock of the Indians almost before the soldiers had fairly started their owners in the other direction. Systematic hunts were made by the same men for Indian graves, to rob them of the silver pendants and other valuables deposited with the dead. A Georgia volunteer, afterward a colonel in the Confederate service, said: "I fought through the civil war and have seen men shot to pieces and slaughtered by thousands, but the Cherokee removal was the cruelest work I ever knew."

In what became known to the Cherokee as "The Trail of

Tears", the six-month walk west claimed about 30 per cent of the lives of the 18,000 Cherokee rounded up by Scott. Among those who died was Ross' wife, Quatie, who had given her blanket to a cold, sick child. One White traveller stumbling upon the Cherokee's death march noted: "We learned from the inhabitants on the road where the Indians passed, that they buried fourteen or fifteen at every stopping place, and they make a journey of ten miles per day only on average."

A few hundred Cherokee escaped to the Smoky Mountains. Scott ignored them, in return for their leader, Tsali, giving himself and his sons up to execution by firing squad. With cruel irony, Scott had the shooting done by Cherokee who supported the New Echota treaty.

In their new home, the so-called "Indian Territory" (centred on present-day Oklahoma), the southern tribes resolutely rebuilt the accultured life they had established in the east, though factionalism amongst the Cherokees saw the assassination in 1839 of prominent signatories to New Echota Treaty, such as Major John Ridge and Elias Boudinot, the former editor of the *Cherokee Phoenix*. With the commencement of the Civil War, division again came to the Civilized Tribes, some fighting for the south, others for the north; something of the fierceness of the whirlwind which caught up the tribes is captured in the fact that the Cherokee Mounted Rifles of the diminuitive, bow-legged Stand Watie (Degataga) fought more engagements than any other unit in the western theatre. Stand Watie was also the last Confederate general to surrender in the war, not laying down his arms at Doaksville, Indian Territory, until 23 June 1865.

The Civil War left the prosperity of Indian Territory in ruins. But the peace brought worse problems, because all the tide of White settlement dammed up by the war was let go; by 1879 there were no less than 12,287 Whites illegally settling on the lands of the Five Civilized Tribes. Then the railways invaded, headed by the "Katy" (the Missouri, Kansas and Texas) and the Atlantic and Pacific. More than that, the territory became a dumping ground for tribes from the north – among them the Shawnee, the Delaware, and Kickapoo – impacted by the Removal Act and the Civil War, and later for tribes from the west defeated in the Indian Wars; in all, Indian Territory became home to Indians from no less than fifty nations. All the while, government officials steadily stripped the Territory in size, and then in 1893, with the Dawes Commission, went all the way and effectively sequestered Indian Territory and opened it up to legal white settlement. In 1907 what had been given to the Indians "for ever" became the state of Oklahoma

PART III

The Losing of the West

Native America, from Creation until AD 1492

clear the way
in a sacred manner
I come
the earth
is mine

Sioux war song

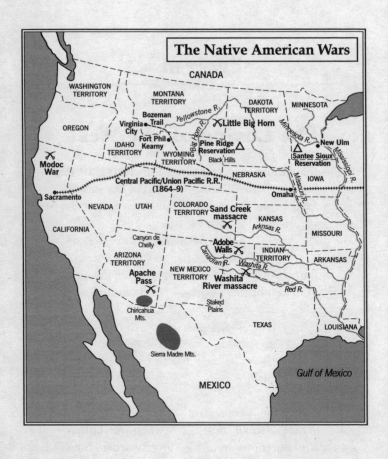

The Native American Wars

CANADA

WASHINGTON TERRITORY

MONTANA TERRITORY

DAKOTA TERRITORY

MINNESOTA

OREGON

Yellowstone R.

Bozeman Trail

Virginia City

✗ Little Big Horn

New Ulm

Fort Phil Kearny

Big Horn R.

Minnesota R.

IDAHO TERRITORY

WYOMING TERRITORY

Pine Ridge Reservation △

△ Santee Sioux Reservation

✗ Modoc War

Black Hills

Missouri R.

Mississippi R.

Central Pacific/Union Pacific R.R. (1864–9)

NEBRASKA

IOWA

Sacramento

NEVADA

UTAH

COLORADO TERRITORY

Omaha

Sand Creek massacre

KANSAS

MISSOURI

CALIFORNIA

Canyon de Chelly

Arknsas R.

Adobe Walls ✗

INDIAN TERRITORY

ARKANSAS

ARIZONA TERRITORY

NEW MEXICO TERRITORY

Canadian R.

Washita R.

✗ Apache Pass

Washita River massacre

Red R.

Chiricahua Mts.

Staked Plains

TEXAS

LOUISIANA

Sierra Madre Mts.

MEXICO

Gulf of Mexico

Prologue

. . . these tribes cannot exist surrounded by our settlements and in continual contact with our citizens. They have neither the intelligence, the industry, the moral habits, nor the desire of improvement. They must necessarily yield to the force of circumstance and, ere long, disappear.

President Andrew Jackson, 1832

Behold, my brothers, the spring has come; the earth has received the embraces of the sun and we shall soon see the results of that love!

Every seed is awakened and so has all animal life. It is through this mysterious power that we too have our being and we therefore yield to our neighbors, even our animal neighbors, the same right as ourselves, to inhabit this land.

Yet hear me, people, we have now to deal with another race – small and feeble when our fathers first met them but now great and overbearing. Strangely enough they have a mind to till the soil and the love of possession is a disease with them. These people have made many rules that the rich may break but the poor may not. They take tithes from the poor and weak to support the rich who rule. They claim this mother of ours, the earth, for their own and fence their neighbors away; they deface her with their buildings and their refuse. That nation is like a spring freshet that overruns its banks and destroys all who are in its path.

We cannot dwell side by side. Only seven years ago we made a treaty by which we were assured that the buffalo country should be left to us forever. Now they threaten to take that away from us. My brothers, shall we submit or shall we say to them; "First kill me before you take possession of my Fatherland . . ."

Sitting Bull (Talanka Yotanka), Huncpapa Sioux,
Powder River Council, 1877

By 1840, there were only 400,000 Indians left in North America. All the eastern tribes had been annihilated, subdued or forcibly removed, west of the Mississippi. This was to be a permanent Indian domain, inviolable.

No sooner had the eternal Indian frontier been declared than it began to crumble. The westward movement of White settlement had a momentum behind it that could not be stopped by paper declarations. As if in proof, in spring 1843 one thousand pioneers stepped into the wilderness from Independence, Missouri, bound for California and Oregon. It was the beginning of the end for the Indian of North America.

The pioneers made it to the Pacific, against all doubts. Soon there was an endless stream of emigrant covered wagons going across the plains, scarring a highway that reached a mile across, devastating the grasslands and scaring away the buffalo so necessary to the life of the Plains Indian.

Then, in 1848, came the discovery of California gold at Sutter's sawmill. Incredibly, the white man's traffic increased. It seemed, to the Indians of the Plains, that the entire white world was crossing before their eyes.

The "Diggers" as the whites contemptuously called the root-gathering Indians of California, were simply overrun. In the five years up to 1850, when California was admitted to the union, its non-Indian population increased by over 1,000 per cent to 92,000. Even the Indians of the backhills who had resisted the Spanish Missions were incapable of resisting the White tide.

An American holocaust visited the Indians of California. They were dispossessed and starved. They were enslaved. More than 10,000 Indians between 1850 and 1863 were sold or indentured to mines and *rancherias*. Women were taken into concubinage in miners' camps. Children did not escape, either. "Abducting children," noted one Californian newspaper in 1854, "has become quite a common practice."

It was all legal, by various devices and strategems. The duplicitous ordinance adopted by the Pueblo of Los Angeles was typical: Indian criminal prisoners (especially drunks) were sold to the highest bidder "and in that manner . . . disposed of for a sum which shall not be less than for the amount of their fine for double the time which they were to serve as hard labour."

The Indians' slavery was perpetual. As a contemporary noted: "For years past it has been the practice of (our farmers] . . . to hang around the Mayor's court on Monday morning and advance the degraded Indian a few dollars with which to pay his nominal fine . . . and on Saturday night, after deducting the sum advanced, pay him a couple of dollars, which insures him a place in the station house on the following Monday . . . and thus the process goes on." Not until 1869 was anti-Indian slavery ended in California. And this in a state where blacks were never enslaved.

The massacres committed against the Indians of California make long, bloody and unsettling reading. It was open season on the Indians. Some settlers went hunting Indians like they were game, shooting twenty or thirty a trip. "Good Haul of Diggers: Thirty-eights Bucks Killed" boasted Eureka's *Humboldt Times* after one such spree. The worst atrocities had official imprimatur.

In May 1850, an army detachment led by Captain Nathaniel Lyon, sought five Pomo men for the killing of their brutal white owners, ranchers Charles Stone and Andrew Kelsey. When Lyon failed to find the Pomo perpetrators, he ordered the slaying of some unconnected Pomos who were innocently fishing in Clear Lake. Although the Indians tried to surrender: ". . . the soldiers did not give them time. The soldiers went in the camp and shot them down as if they were dogs. Some of them escaped by going down a little creek leading to the river. And some of them hid in the brush. And those who hid in the brush most of them were killed . . . They mostly killed women and children."

More than 130 Pomos were killed at Clear Lake.

The Indians of California were not passive in the face of armed genocide. There were sustained fightbacks, especially in the north of the state on the Oregon border, notably the Rogue River War of 1853 involving the Modocs and Cayuses among others. As late as 1873 Kentipoos (known to Whites as Captain Jack) of the Modoc held out against US troops in the lava beds around Lake Tule. With Captain Jack were 250 Modocs, of whom a mere 80 were warriors. The US forces ranged against them, who were led by no less than General William Tecumseh Sherman, numbered 1,000. It took five months of siege, 100 casualties and an artillery campaign to force the Modocs into surrender. Captain Jack was hanged for murder. The survivors of his band were taken to the malarial Quapaw agency in Indian Territory.

Yet the Indians of California never stood a chance. There were too few of them. Between 1852 and 1860 alone, the indigenous population of the state free-fell, through killing and disease, from 85,000 to 35,000. By 1890 there were just 15,000 Indians left in California. Whole tribes had been erased from the face of the land.

On the Great Plains, the Indians had better odds. The whites had not yet come to stay. They were merely passing through. They were also needy and vulnerable.

Initially, Plains tribes confined themselves to besting the White man at his own pecuniary game. They charged passage and pilotage. (The Chinook, when leading horses over the Columbia River, liked to stop in mid-stream to demand more payment to finish the job.) But as the wagons rolled and rolled, things soured. The overlanders overhunted, overgrazed, exhausted the water supply, fired the grasslands, and deleted the precious tree stocks. For their part, the Whites were disgusted by the Indians' demanded tolls. It was against the racial order of things for the Red Man to have rights over the White. Violent confrontations became commonplace, with the Pawnee toll at Shell Creek a notable hot spot. Something approaching a battle took place there in May 1852. Emigrants refused the 25 cents per wagon toll, and rushed the bridge – only to find that the Pawnee had cut a hole in its centre. The lead wagon fell into the river and the shooting started. The Pawnee got the worst of it, with nine dead.

The deterioration in Indian–White relations in the West caused government agents to fear a generalized Indian uprising. "What then will be the consequences," wrote Thomas Fitzpatrick, a former trapper, to his superiors in Washington, "should twenty thousand Indians, well armed, well mounted, and the most . . . expert in war . . . turn out in hostile array against all American travellers?" To forestall this dread possibility, in September 1851 the government called a meeting of all the northern tribes at Horse Creek, 35 miles from Fort Laramie, a remote outpost on the Oregon Trail.

It was the greatest gathering of tribes in history attended by 10,000 American Indians, camped in the valley in a forest of tipis. The mighty Teton (from *Titowa*, "plains") Sioux were there, so were their time-honoured enemies, the Crow. Also in attendance were the Arikara, Shoshoni, Cheyenne, Assinboine, Arapaho, and the Gros Ventre. Colonel Thomas Fitzpatrick addressed the tribesmen telling them that the Great Father was "aware that your buffalo and game are driven off, and your grass and timber consumed by the opening of roads and the passing of emigrants through your countries. For these losses he desires to compensate you." The compensation offered the tribes by the Great Father was $50,000 a year, plus guns, if the Indians would keep away from the trail and confine themselves to designated tracts of land. (Thus began the reservation system, though no one yet called it that.)

The Indians "touched the pen", and many went away in the belief that an age of harmony between the White and Red people was about to begin. Cut Nose of the Arapaho declared: "I will go home satisfied. I will sleep sound, and not have to watch my horses in the night, or be afraid for my women and children. We have to live on these streams and in the hills, and I would be glad if the Whites would pick out a place for themselves and not come into our grounds."

Two years later a similar council was held with bands of the Comanche and Kiowa in Kansas. They agreed to refrain from molesting emigrants on the Santa Fe Trail in return for the annuity of $18,000 in goods.

The treaties were doomed to failure. Invariably, the political organization of an Indian tribe did not allow a chief to speak for all his people. And some chiefs, anyway, did not fully understand what they had been required to give up: their freedom to roam on the wind, to hunt buffalo, and to wage war with their ancient enemies. Such freedom required immense space; the Blackfoot from Montana are known to have raided as far south as the Mexican province of Durango. More serious were the White man's failures. Congress almost immediately reduced the number of years the stipend would be paid. Supplies delivered were inadequate. To avoid starvation, the Indians were forced to range far and wide in pursuit of a dwindling supply of game. Tension along the emigrant trails increased. There were frequent instances of petty thieving. To defend the emigrants, the Army sent more troops west.

Nearly 40 years of war between the United States and the Plains Indians was set off by an argument over a cow. On 18 August 1854 a young Miniconjou Sioux warrior called High Forehead butchered a lame cow that an emigrant on the Oregon Trail had either lost or abandoned. Hearing this, the owner demanded that the Sioux pay him $25 for his loss. An amiable Sioux leader, Bear

That Scatters, offered two cows as reparation. This was refused. Furthermore, the Army at nearby Fort Laramie intervened to insist on High Forehead's surrender. The next day, brash young Brevet Second Lieutenant John L. Grattan, a West Pointer who had bragged that he could handle the red hordes single-handedly, marched into the Sioux camp accompanied by 31 men. Negotiations broke down when Bear That Scatters refused to surrender High Forehead, who was a guest in his village. Suddenly, Grattan's patience snapped, and he ordered his men to fire into the Sioux village at point-blank range. Bear That Scatters fell mortally wounded. After a second or two of silence, hundreds of Lakota warriors leaped into battle and every White man in the force was killed. Grattan's face was smashed to a pulp with stones.

One year later, Brigadier-General William S. Harney was sent to punish the "hostile" Sioux and fell on a village on Blue Water Creek in Nebraska. Eighty-six Indians were killed, and the village razed to the ground. The Indians were staggered, for never before had a village been destroyed by the Whites' army. Watching the massacre from the safety of a hill was a young Sioux boy, Curly. Afterwards, he went into the Sand Hills to find a vision, and when it came it was a vision of himself as a warrior aboard a flying horse, both untouched by the bullets and arrows which thickened the air. Later the boy's father helped him understand the dream: he would be a warrior who never fell in battle, a warrior who would lead his people against the Whites. He would also be given a new name: Crazy Horse.

The peace of the plains was broken. But before the full fury of Whites could be loosed on the Indians, the United States began to rip itself apart in the debate over slavery.

In 1860 seven states (South Carolina, Mississippi, Florida, Alabama, Louisiana, Georgia, and Texas) had passed ordinances of secession and formed the Confederate States of America, later extended to include Virginia, North Carolina, Tennessee, and Arkansas. A year later, North and South were at war.

The conflict between the Union and the Confederacy was both a disaster and a respite for the Native Americans. Those closest to the Whites' turmoil, the settled tribes located in Indian Territory (Oklahoma), were those most affected by it. Under threats and entreaties, the tribes were obliged to sign to the respective causes of the north and south. Stand Watie's Cherokees signed to the south, as did the Choctaws, Osage, Senecas and Shawnees, believing that the Confederacy would offer them a better deal in the long run. (A not altogether foolish hope: delegates from the Choctaw-Chickasaw, Creek-Seminole and Cherokee nations sat in the Confederate Congress throughout the war; the US had extended the prospect of Indian seats in Congress as early as 1778 but had never delivered on it.) Several tribes had their own Grey vs Blue conflict. Along with the Whites, the Indians bled plenty too between 1861 and 1865.

Less adversely affectected by the Civil War were the Indians of the Far West. When the conflict commenced, the Army's forces in the West numbered around 10,000 men. The majority were quickly summoned to the East, which would be the main theatre of the war. Eventually, these regulars were replaced by large numbers of volunteers, highly motivated young men, keen on adventure, and keenest of all to "crack it to the Indians."

But in the meantime, some of the tribes of the West enjoyed the breathing space. And some decided to take advantage of the reduction in numbers of "blue coats" to go on the warpath.

Among them were the Apache of the endless lands of the southwest.

War Comes to the Land of Little Rain

The Apache arrived in the arid, rugged country of the Southwest in a time before memory. Nomadic Athapascan-speakers from Northern Canada and Alaska, the Apache ruthlessly drove out the tribes already living there, the Comanche and the Zuni.

In their new home, the Apache retained distinctive Athapascan habits. They practiced an intense shamanic religion, their society was matrilineal. They lived in small, autonomous bands under a dominant chief (there were no Apache *tribes*, until they politicked with the Americans). Not that the Apache were immune to their neighbours' charms. The Lipan Apache, for instance, became followers of the Plains bison like the Comanche; further west the Navajo branch of the Apache learned agriculture from the Pueblos. In between the Chiricahua, Mescalero and Jicarilla lived mainly as old-fashioned hunter-gatherers.

Wherever they settled, the Apache added to their economic base by raiding. Which is how the Apache got their nomenclature. The Apache called themselves "N'de" or "Dineh" (meaning "people"), but the newcomers were known to others by the Zuni word for enemy, *apachu*. The *apachu* were infamously hardy. A Chiricahua brave was expected to be able to run and walk seventy miles a day. Horses – which the Apache took to readily – could not keep up. Even when he was in his forties the warrior Geronimo, a member of the Bedonkohe band of the Chiricahua, still ran on raids, trotting endlessly hour after hour.

If the Apache valued brawn and the ability to endure beyond anything their enemies could conceive, they esteemed another quality more: cunning. This was the greatest virtue to the Apache. It ranked even higher than courage. Kudos for the Apache brave came not from killing, or scalping (they didn't do it) but from silent stealing.

Hostile and wily, the Apache were the despair of the black-robed Spanish Missions as they pushed northwards out of Mexico. Only the Lipan Apache were ever missionized – and then only for a brief moment in the eighteenth century – and so the Spanish opted for a *realpolitik* of arms and false treaties. Ever expedient, the Apache flirtingly allied themselves with the Spanish when it suited, such as when Spain warred against the Pawnee. Suffice it to say, by 1850 the Apache had uniquely lived for 200 years on the frontier of European civilization without being conquered.

At first, relations between the Apache and the Anglo-Americans were cordial. The bow-and-arrow wielding, wild-haired Apache (they washed their locks every day, which made for cleanliness but not for high coiffeur) hardly merited a mention in the annual reports of the War Department in Washington. For their part, the Apache were more interested in pursuing their heriditary opponents, the Comanche, the Pima and the Mexicans, than the few "White Eyes" prospecting for metals in their New Mexico–Arizona–Texas homeland. Even the ferocious Chiricahua were friendly to the

Americans, cutting wood for a stage station in the Chiricahua mountains.

Alas, cordiality broke down because the Americans picked up the Spanish-Mexican habit of enslaving Indians. By official estimate, 2,000 Indian slaves were held by the White Eyes in New Mexico and Arizona in 1866. Of particular hurt to the Apache was the forced prostitution of Apache girl captives.

Enslaving the Apache was not enough for many White Eyes on the Southwest frontier. Wrote Sylvester Mowry in 1863:

> Governor Pesquiera of Sonora has offered a bounty of $100 per scalp for Apaches, and a proportionate sum for animals retaken from them. This should be imitated by the Authorities of Arizona. The Pimos (Pimas) and Papago Indians would be most valuable auxiliaries in the pursuit of these "human wolves". They lately killed about sixty Apaches and took several prisoners in a single campaign. The children of the Apaches when taken young, make good servants and are sold by the Pimos in the Territory [Arizona] and in Sonora.
>
> There is only one way to wage war against the Apaches . . . They must be surrounded, starved into coming in, surprised or inveigled – by white flags or any other method, human or divine – and then put to death.
>
> If these ideas shock any weak-minded individual, who thinks himself a philanthropist, I can only say that I pity, without respecting, his sympathy. A man might as well have sympathy for a rattlesnake or a tiger.

The White Eyes made their crucial error when they disturbed the sleeping tigers that were the Chiricahua.

One day in the 1850s Mangas Coloradas ("Red Sleeves"), a sexagenarian chief of the Mimbreno band of the Chiricahua, made a friendly visit to miners at Pinos Altos in southwestern New Mexico. The miners tied him to a tree and lashed him unconscious with a bullwhip. To no great surprise, Mangas Coloradas went on the warpath. He also requested the help of his son-in-law, Cochise, the great Chiricahua warrior chief.

The six-foot-tall Cochise soon had his own grudge against the Americans. In early 1861, Cochise was accused of stealing a White boy named Ward from a ranch near Buchanan. The boy (who later became a government scout known as Mickey Free) had in fact been stolen by Pinal Apaches. A Second Lieutenant George Bascom of the 7th Cavalry refused to believe Cochise's protestations of innocence, and took Cochise and his family hostage. Cochise escaped by pulling his knife, slashing a gash in the tent wall and jumping through. In an effort to free his relatives, Cochise captured a stage driver and two Americans from a wagon train and offered Bascom an exchange of prisoners. Bascom refused. The affair ended with Cochise killing the Whites he had taken and Bascom hanging three Indian hostages. (Hanging was the worst form of death for an Indian, because it shut him out from the warrior's afterlife.)

And so Cochise joined Mangas Coloradas on the warpath. "I was at peace with the Whites," said Cochise, "until they tried to kill me for what other Indians did; now I live and die at war with them."

It was a good time for war. The Whites were beginning to shoot each other in their civil conflict, and New Mexico was stripped of its troops and its forts evacuated. Ranging from their mountain strongholds, the Chiricahuas brought swift-striking death to wagon trains, mines, ranches and small settlements. Estimates of White dead were as high as 150 within two months. Many were tortured, some burned alive, others having small pieces of their body cut away until they died from shock or loss of blood.

Settlers fled for their lives to safer regions – if they could find them. For the Apache were not the only people laying claim and waste to the Southwest. Confederate and Union forces began to manoeuvre and skirmish in the region. In 1862, in an effort to seize the desert country for the federal cause, the Union sent out 1,800 Californian Volunteers under General James Carleton. Their eastwards route lay through Apache Pass.

Alerted by his scouts, Cochise decided to ambush the White soldiers in the gorge. He was joined by Mangas Coloradas and 700 Apaches, the largest force the People had ever raised. Many were armed with rifles, taken from dead Whites.

On 14 July 1862, an advance party of 123 Californian Volunteers entered the pass. The ambush should have been deadly, but the Volunteers under Captain Thomas L. Roberts had two mountain howitzers in tow. Quickly Roberts trained these on the Apache positions. The Indians had never encountered shellfire before, and withdrew.

Mangas Coloradas, as he retreated, was shot in the chest. The wound was not fatal, but it caused him to tire of fighting. Less than a year after Apache Pass, he decided to take up the American offer of peace. The old chief walked trustingly and alone into Pinos Altos. Brevet General Joseph West ordered him seized, telling his guards: "I want him dead or alive tomorrow morning. Understand? I want him dead."

A miner walking about the camp related what happened next: "About 9 o'clock I noticed the soldiers were doing something to Mangas. I discovered that they were heating their bayonets in the fire and burning his feet and legs. Mangas rose upon his left elbow, angrily protesting that he was no child to be played with." Whereon the guards shot him dead. Afterwards, he was scalped and decapitated. The official euphemism for the event was "resisting arrest". Even other Army soldiers were appalled. General Nelson Miles declared Mangas Coloradas "foully murdered".

The fate of Mangas Coloradas only encouraged Cochise to stay on the warpath. Apache Pass had taught him a valuable, if harsh, lesson – never to confront well-armed troops in open combat. Henceforth, Cochise's war would be a guerrilla struggle, in which the Apache would come and go like the wind. He was joined by other Apache notables, among them the Warm Springs chiefs Victorio and Nana, and the warrior leader Geronimo. Soon the Gila River country of south Arizona was swept clean of ranchers. The exception was Pete Kitchen, who turned his hilltop adobe ranch into a fortress, and was left alone. Elsewhere Apache raids continued unabated.

In the the big year of fighting, 1864, the White-eyes and the Apache fought hundreds of recorded skirmishes. The Americans recruited miners, Pimas, Maricopas, Papagos anyone and else who would tote a gun for money in their campaign to exterminate the Apache. Despite all the effort, the official toll of Apache dead in that year was just 216.

For a long decade Cochise fought the Americans, trading atrocity for atrocity, until the war staggered to stalemate. The US Army was unable to best Cochise, but whatever the Chiricahua chief did White emigrants still came through the "land of little rain" and miners still dug for metal. "We kill ten; a hundred come in their place," Cochise lamented to his warriors.

Then something happened which brought a softening in

government attitude to the Apache. Early in the morning of 30 April 1871, a mob of Americans, Mexicans and Papago Indians massacred 128 unarmed Aravaipa Apache near Tucson in revenge for raids carried out by other Apache. Twenty-nine of the Aravaipa children were taken as slaves. First Lieutenant Royal E. Whitman, the commander of Camp Grant, described the scene of the massacre in his report:

The camp was burning and strewn with their dead and mutilated women and children. I immediately mounted a party of about twenty soldiers and citizens and sent them with the post surgeon, with a wagon to bring in any wounded, if any could be found. The party returned late in the p.m. having found no wounded and without having been able to communicate with any of the survivors. Early the next morning I took a similar party, with spades and shovels, and went out and buried all the dead in and immediately about the camp . . . While at the work many of them came to the spot and indulged in their expressions of grief, too wild and terrible to be described.

Many of the men, whose families have been killed, when I spoke to them and expressed sympathy for them, were obliged to turn away, unable to speak and too proud to show their grief. The women whose children had been killed or stolen were convulsed with grief, and looked at me appealingly, as though I was their last hope on earth. Children who two days before had been full of fun and frolic kept at a distance, expressing wondering horror . . .

Although the participants in the massacre at Camp Grant

were acquitted after less than half an hour's deliberation at Tucson, Eastern humanitarians applied pressure on the government to stop such genocidal slaughters. Congress voted $70,000 for the "collecting of the Apaches of Arizona and New Mexico upon reservations, furnishing them with subsistence and other necessary articles and to promote peace and civilization among them". In truth, the government had little option but to switch to conciliation instead of extermination. The war with the Apache had already cost 1,000 American lives and $40 million.

Entrusted with the mission of dealing fairly but firmly with the Apache was General George Crook. Crook was an Indian fighter, but no Indian hater. Astutely recruiting scouts from conciliated Apache bands, Crook began rounding up and treating with the bands which insisted on hostility. When Crook was moved north to Sioux country, he was succeeded by the one-armed General Oliver O. Howard.

For help, Howard sought out Thomas Jeffords, the superintendent of mail between Tucson and Fort Bowie. The flame-haired New Yorker was the one White man Cochise called friend, a friendship begun when Jeffords had courageously ridden alone into Cochise's camp and asked the chief not to kill his drivers. In respect to Jeffords' personal courage, he did not.

The intensely moral General Howard won Jefford's approval, and the two went to meet Cochise in the mountains. After 11 days of negotiation, a deal was struck. Cochise agreed to stop fighting and enter a reservation in the Dragoon mountain if Jeffords was appointed agent for the Chiricahua. The terms were met. Also entering into the agreement was the warrior leader Geronimo, whose small band of Bedonkohe Apache had been virtually assimilated into the Chiricahua. Geronimo served as escort to Howard as he left the mountains, riding double on the general's horse. The Apache war was visibly over.

Cochise was not privileged to enjoy his peace for long. In 1874, in his fifty-first year, he was taken mortally ill. He died with Jeffords by his side. Cochise's warriors painted him in yellow, black and vermilion, shrouded him in a red blanket, propped him on his favourite horse and took him deep into the mountains. His body was buried in a crevice whose location they never revealed.

The great chief of the Chiricahua Apache was dead, but the peace he agreed for his people endured.

For a while.

The Long Walk

In the azure-skied lands of the Southwest, one branch of the Apache found a separate destiny. Their embrace of agriculture and their resolution before the vicissitudes of history would make them the most populous tribe in North America. When the Spanish came across these Idians in 1629 they named them after the nearby Tewa pueblo of *Nabaju* ("cultivated field").

These "Navajo" were considerable farmers, like the Pueblo peoples whose ancestral lands they settled. Not just in the cultivation of corn and peaches, but in the herding of sheep and goats. (The seed stock for Navajo ovine herds were pilfered from the Spanish and the Pueblo Indians; some old Apache habits died hard). Out of the fleeces of their sheep and goats, the Navajo women wove sublime, colourful blankets that were highly sought after by Whites and Native Americans alike. Something about the Navajo's environment, the primeval mesas and the painted deserts, inspired a mystical reverence for beauty in The People.

Isolated in their canyon fastnesses, the Navajo were of little interest to the United States until she annexed the southwest after the Mexican War. Then came a wail of complaints by Anglo settlers of Navajo raids and thefts. To settle the matter, the governor of New Mexico marched his troops westward from the Rio Grande. Although nothing like an overall leader existed amongst the Navajo, a local patriarch, Narbona, came with three hundred or so followers to meet the Americans. To show good heart, Narbona turned over to the Whites 130 sheep and 5 horses. A treaty of "perpetual peace and friendship" duly followed.

It lasted for five minutes. Someone with the American party demanded an extra horse. The Navajo refused, climbed up on their horses and rode out. As they sped off, the governor ordered the soldiers to open fire. Among the six or seven Navajo dead was the eighty-year-old Narbona.

Having partaken of American diplomacy, the Navajo went back to marauding. In response, the US decided to architecturally awe the Navajo into submission, and built Fort Defiance plum in the middle of Dineh land. Alas, the existence of Fort Defiance – the name said everything – only antagonized the Navajo more, while the cattle and horses of the US Army directly competed for grazing with the Navajo's livestock. The local headman of the Navajo, Manuelito, informed the fort commander: "Your army has horse and wagons, mules and many soldiers. They are capable of hauling in feed for their own livestock. We . . . have only our feet, and must take our sheep and cattle wherever there is good grazing. The land around the fort has been ours for many years."

Major T. H. Brooks, the commandant, was moved – but to punish Manuelito for his impudence in protesting, Brooks ordered his men to shoot sixty head of Navajo livestock and drive off the rest. Fighting soon followed. In October 1858 US soldiers and Zuni mercenaries torched Manuelito's village. Six months later Manuelito took his revenge, leading 1,000 Navajo in a mass attack on Fort Defiance which was barely beaten off. Eventually, the commencement of the Civil War caused the abandonment of Fort Defiance as soldiers were withdrawn to the east. The Navajo took advantage of the soldiers' absence to commit some profitable plundering. A single raid in 1863 netted them 20,000 sheep.

The withdrawal of the White Eyes, however, was merely temporary. When Union victory at Glorieta Pass (the largest Civil War battle in the West) effectively ended the chances of Confederate control in the region, the US raised volunteer regiments from western states and territories and dispatched them to the newly built Forts Canby and Wingate. Brigadier-General James H. Carleton directed his old friend, the famous scout Colonel Kit Carson, then the commander of the New Mexico volunteers, to subdue hostile Apaches and Navajos. By the end of March 1863, Carson had rounded up more than 400 Mescalero Apaches and sent them to the new reservation at Bosque Redondo, a tract of forty square miles of semi-arid land next to the military outpost of Fort Sumner.

Next, Carson moved on the 10,000 people of the Navajo nation. His message to the Navajo was brief: "Go to Bosque Redondo, or we will pursue and destroy you. We will not make peace with you on any other terms."

Carson was as good as his word. After razing *hogans* (the Navajo's domed earth-houses), orchards and fields, and seizing Navajo livestock, the Americans invaded the Navajo strong-hold of Canyon de Chelly. The scorched-earth campaign continued: 3,000 peach trees were cut down, and fields of corn were trampled. In the spring of 1864 8,000 starving and dejected Navajo surrendered. They were marched 300 miles to Bosque Redondo ("Hweeldi" in the tongue of the Dineh), an event that became known to them as the "Long Walk". The land at Bosque Redondo was too poor to support the Indians incarcerated there. Navajo died from malnutrition, disease, and drought in their hundreds. (They also disputed fiercely with the Mescalero, traditional enemies.) Many times was heard their healing chant, the "Blessing Way", the concluding lines of which run:

> May it be beautiful before me
> May it be beautiful behind me
> May it be beautiful all around me
> In beauty may I walk
> In beauty it is finished

Such words fortified not only the patient but also the whole people. The Navajo endured.

By 1868 even Washington realized that Bosque Redondo was a disaster. A delegation led by General William Tecumseh Sherman found that the Navajo at Bosque Redondo were "sunk into a condition of absolute poverty and despair". On behalf of the Navajo Barboncito put an eloquent case as to why the Navajo should be allowed to return to their own land:

> If we are taken back to our own country, we will call you our father and mother. If you should only tie a goat there, we would all live off it, all of the same opinion. I am speaking for the whole tribe, for their animals from the horse to the dog, also the unborn . . . It appears to me that the General commands the whole thing as a god. I hope therefore he will do all he can for my people . . . and I wish you to tell me when you are going to take us to our own country.

Washington granted permission for a return to the Chuska mountains. With the Navajo went $100,000 worth of sheep and equipment. A treaty obliged them to never again possess arms and to educate their children in White schools.

To this day the Navajo have kept to the terms of the 1868 treaty. Some 200,00 strong, they are the largest Indian nation in the United States, in population and the area of their reservation lands.

The Great Sioux Uprising

When men are hungry they help themselves.

Little Crow

In the Civil War summer of 1862, the agricultural state of Minnesota looked to be one of the quieter places on the continent. The bulk of the internecine fighting was going on in the East and in the Missouri–Kansas border country, while the Indian frontiers were far away on the Great Plains and in the Southwest. The most unexpected event was a rising by the peaceful Santee Sioux who lived on a reservation along the Minnesota River.

The Santee (or eastern) Sioux had remained in Minnesota when their relatives migrated to the buffalo plains in the eighteenth century. Over time, the government had acquired all their land, save for a barren strip 150 miles long and 10 miles wide on the south side of the Minnesota River. The payment for the Santee's many land cessions, which totalled 26 million acres, was an annual government cash allotment that barely kept them alive.

In June 1862, the annuity failed to arrive. To make matters worse, cutworms had devastated the tribe's previous year's corn crop. Local merchants refused to extend credit, or to equip the Indians for their privilege of an annual summer buffalo hunt on the Dakota range. "If they are hungry," the trader Andrew Myrick said of the Santee Sioux, "let them eat grass or their own dung."

By August, the 12,000 Santee crowded on the reservation were starving. The 52-year-old leader of the Santee, Little Crow (Ta-oya-te-duta), tried to warn the Whites that trouble was coming: "We have waited a long time. We have no food, but here are stores, filled with food. We ask you: make some arrangement by which we can get food, or we will keep ourselves from starving." On 8 August, bands of Santee at the Upper Agency looted the government warehouse. But still nobody expected an uprising. It began with an incident that would have been trivial but for its bitter consequences.

On Sunday 17 August, a small group of Sioux warriors returned from an unsuccessful hunt in the "Big Woods" along the Mississippi. As they passed through the settlements, one found some eggs belonging to a farmer's hen. Another cautioned him against taking the property of a White man. The group then fell to arguing and boasting, with one warrior insisting that he would prove he was unafraid of the White inan by killing one – and dared his comrades to do the same. Arriving at a farm where some families had gathered for a Sunday visit, the Santee warriors challenged the White men gathered there to a shooting contest. When the White men had emptied their rifles, the Indians turned on the hosts and killed three men and two women. The murderers then rode to the reservation and reported their crime to Little Crow. A council was called.

The Indians debated all night. Some chiefs, among them Wabasha and Wacouta, spoke for peace. So did Little Crow.

"The White men," said Little Crow, "are like the locusts when they fly so thick that the whole sky is a snowstorm. You may kill one – two – ten; yes, as many as the leaves in the forest yonder, and their brothers will not miss them. Kill one – two – ten, and ten will come to kill you. Count your fingers all day long and White men with guns . . . will come faster than you can count . . . Yes: they fight among themselves but if you strike at them they will all turn on you and devour you and your women and little children just as the locusts in their time fall on the trees and devour all the leaves in one day."

Some argued that the time for war was never better, with so many able-bodied Whites away on battlefields fighting each other. Finally, the council declared for war. Little Crow, to retain his leadership, put himself at the head of the hostiles. "Little Crow is not a coward," he said, "he will die with you."

At dawn the next day, Monday 18 August scores of braves attacked the Lower Agency. "Kill the Whites! Kill all the Whites!" shouted Little Crow. Twenty-three White men were shot and stabbed. One of the first to die was Andrew Myrick, his body mutilated, his mouth stuffed full with prairie grass.

From the Lower Agency, bands of Santee fanned out to the Upper Agency and into the surrounding countryside. Whites were hauled from their homes and fields. Few had time to pull a gun. Men – unless judged to be friends – were summarily dispatched. Women were held captive and raped. "They came down upon us like the wind," one survivor remembered.

A few fugitives reached Fort Ridgely on the north side of the Minnesota River and raised the alarm. With more courage than judgement, the commander took out 47 of his men – more than half of his depleted force – to engage the Sioux. At the river, he ran into an ambush and his men were all but wiped out. The Santee lost one brave – their only casualty in the whole of the first day. White losses ran at 400.

By Wednesday 20 August, when Little Crow finally

mounted an attack on Fort Ridgely, the post had been reinforced. (Among the reinforcements were the guards of the coach carrying the delayed annuity.) The defenders threw back the Santee, who lost over a hundred warriors. As one of the Santee said years later: "But the defenders of the fort were very brave and kept the door shut." Frustrated at the fort, Little Crow launched an all-out attack on the town of New Ulm. Throughout 23 August, Little Crow's men besieged New Ulm, despite withering fire from the militia. The town was reduced to ashes. Thirty-six Whites died. The survivors abandoned the town and picked their way eastward to Mankato.

The settlements of Western Minnesota and Eastern Dakota were now in a state of fear. Thirty thousand settlers evacuated their homes and fled to Mankato and other White population centres. "You have no idea," wrote General John Pope to the War Department, "of the uncontrollable panic everywhere in this country. The most horrible massacres have been committed; children nailed alive to trees and houses; women violated and then disembowelled – everything that horrible ingenuity could devise."

It took two weeks for Minnesota to calm down enough to organize a militia to take the field against the Santee. This was placed under the command of Colonel Henry Sibley, a former fur trader, who advanced towards the Santee at a snail's pace. The Indians continued their raids, adding more to their toll of dead Whites. By conservative estimate, the Santee eventually killed 500 Whites.

The Indians won several skirmishes with the slowly approaching militia. Then, on 22 September, after failing to spring a planned ambush, Little Crow was beaten in battle by the 1,600-strong militia near Wood Lake. The warring Santee fled back to the reservation, packed their tipis and debated what to do with their pitiful captives. Eventually, these were left in the care of those Santee who had not embarked on hostilities. Little Crow and most of his warriors left for the Plains.

If Colonel Sibley was slow to fight, he was quick to avenge. By October 2,000 Santee had been rounded up, many of them Santees from the Upper Agency who had refused to participate in the rising. Four hundred of the gathered Santee were tried by military commission, some cases receiving as few as five minutes. The trials ended with 307 Santee sentenced to die, who were hauled to Mankato for hanging.

Most Minnesotans were eager to see the convicted Indians hang, but one kept his humanity. Episcopal Bishop Henry B. Whipple appealed to President Lincoln for mercy: "I ask," he wrote, "that the people shall lay the blame . . . where it belongs, and . . . demand the reform of an atrocious Indian system which has always garnered for us . . . anguish and blood."

Lincoln commuted the sentences of those Sioux condemned to die merely because they had partaken of battle. Still, 38 were taken out into the chilly morning of 26 December and hanged from a special scaffold, constructed so that all the traps would drop by the cutting of a single rope. Those who died, their bodies jerking grotesquely in the air, included Cut Nose, who claimed he had killed Whites "till his arm tired." Alongside him were three innocent men accidentally put to death when their names were confused with those of the condemned. While waiting to die a warrior called Little Six (Shakapee) is said to have heard the shriek of a train whistle in the distance and said: "As the White man comes in, the Indian goes out."

Thereafter there were a few desultory raids by Santee still free and hostile, but in the summer of 1863 two settlers near

Hutchinson, Minnesota, caught Little Crow picking raspberries in a field and shot him dead. They shot him not because he was Little Crow but because he was an Indian. When his body was identified, the Minnesota legislature paid $575 for Little Crow's scalp, and then put it on display in a museum. Another chief was caught and hanged at Fort Snelling.

The Santee reservation by the Minnesota River was then removed from the map, and 2,000 Santee – hostile or otherwise – were herded into a tiny reservation along the Missouri River, alongside 3,000 Winnebago Indians. During the first winter, 400 Indians died of starvation and disease.

The Great Sioux Uprising – the biggest Indian insurrection since Wampanoag King Philip had set the Massachusetts frontier aflame in 1675 – was over. But the climactic struggle between the Indians and Whites had barely passed its first rounds.

Sand Creek

I have come to kill Indians, and believe that it is right
and honourable to use any means under God's heaven
to kill Indians.

Colonel John Chivington, 3rd Colorado Volunteers

All we ask is that we may have peace with the Whites
. . . I want you to give all the chiefs of the soldiers here
to understand that we are for peace, and that we have
made peace, that we may not be mistaken by them for
enemies.

Black Kettle, Cheyenne Chief

The area around Pike's Peak in Colorado had long been
rumoured to be rich in gold, and in 1858 a small group of
prospectors hit pay dirt. The cry went up "Gold in
Colorado!" and wagon trains of frenzied prospectors rolled
west in wagons daubed with the defiant slogan "Pike's Peak
or Bust!"

To the prospectors swarming into Colorado one thing
was apparent: the region's Indians were an obstacle,
possibly a dangerous one. They would have to go.

The Southern Cheyenne and the Arapaho were themselves relatively recent arrivals to the plains, both being Algonquin-speakers from the Great Lakes area. Not until the early 1800s had the Cheyenne accumulated enough horses to become a truly equine people of the interior plains. Their nomadic scattered lifestyle meant that the Cheyenne avoided some of the worst smallpox and cholera epidemics. In the mid-nineteenth century their population stood at around 20,000. A people with a highly elaborate moral code, the Cheyenne were relatively free of crime, and any transgressors were more likely to be rehabilitated than punished. But a murderer left undiscovered, they believed, would smell bad and keep away the buffalo.

The Cheyenne and Arapaho might have been late in getting to Colorado country, but they were determined to keep it. As more and more prospectors swarmed onto tribal land – more than 50,000 of them by 1859 – the Indians became resentful and hostile. Treaty commissioners managed to persuade some Cheyenne and Arapaho to move onto a small reservation in eastern Colorado, but the younger war leaders refused.

All through the winter of 1864 wisps of rumour of an Indian war floated up and down the Denver road. These were deliberately fanned by Major-General Samuel R. Curtis, Army commander of the Kansas and Colorado department, who wanted any pretext to drive the Indians out. So did Colonel John Chivington, the fiery Methodist-preacher-turned-soldier who had led the Union to victory at Glorieta Pass. Now commander of the District of Colorado, Chivington was eager to try out his new-found appetite for war on the Cheyenne.

NOTHING LIVES LONG

The excuse to "punish" the Cheyenne and Arapaho came on 7 April 1864. Chivington reported to Curtis that the Cheyenne had raided 175 cattle from a ranch on the Smoky Hill trail. Later, a thorough investigation would find no evidence of Indian theft.

Chivington was in the field within days of reporting the "theft". In his pocket he had an order from Governor John Evans, another ruthless Indian-hater, to "burn villages and kill Cheyenne whenever and wherever found."

By early June, Chivington's brutal campaign had razed four unsuspecting Cheyenne villages. One of his junior officers had also shot Chief Lean Bear, a peaceful Cheyenne who had walked up to the White man proudly wearing a medal the Great Father in Washington had given him. Arapahoes, who had tried to intercede in a dispute between the Army and some Kiowa, were fired on. Soon half the Cheyenne and Arapaho in Colorado were on the warpath.

The first retaliatory blow was struck at a ranch outside Denver. A family named Hungate was murdered, their bodies mutilated. The corpses were taken to Denver and placed on display. The town went wild with fear and fury. Traffic on the trails was attacked, Cheyenne and Arapaho bands virtually cutting Denver off from the outside world. During three weeks in August, 50 people were killed on the Platte route alone.

With Denver near famine, the War Department authorized Governor Evans to raise a special regiment of Indian fighting volunteers who would serve for 100 days. The 3rd Colorado Regiment (the "Hundred Dazers") under the command of "the Fighting Parson" Colonel Chivington was still being mustered, however, when peace suddenly broke out.

Some of the Cheyenne chiefs had tired of war; some had never wanted it. Using the offices of George Bent, a half-White living with the Cheyenne, the chiefs sent a letter to Major Edward W. Wynkoop at Fort Lyon offering an end to hostilities:

> We held a counsel . . . and all came to the conclusion to make peace with you providing you make peace with the Kiowas, Comences, Arropohoes Apaches and Siouxs. We are going to send a message to the Kiowas . . . about our going to make [peace] with you We heard that you [have] some prisoners in Denver. We have seven prisoners of you which we are willing to give up providing you give up yours. There are three war parties out yet, and two of Arropohoes; they have been out some time and expected in soon. When we held this counsel there were few Arropohoes and Siouxs present; we want news from you in return. (That is a letter)
>
> *Signed* BLACK KETTLE and Other Chiefs

Wynkoop, a decent and able officer, saw a chance to avert bloodshed. He visited Black Kettle, persuaded him to release four prisoners, and encouraged him to go to Denver and consult with the Governor.

On 28 September, the genial and aged Black Kettle rode into Camp Weld near Denver to talk peace. After conceding his inability to control some of his younger warriors, Black Kettle agreed to settle at Fort Lyon with those Cheyenne and Arapaho who would follow him. There he would be protected by Major Wynkoop. The

Indian left the meeting believing he had made a peace deal.

Peace was the last thing the Indian-hating Colonel Chivington wanted. If he was to use his hundred-day men he had to use them soon. He complained to General Curtis about Wynkoop's conciliatory policy and got him replaced at Fort Lyon by Major Scott J. Anthony. In the presence of other officers at Fort Lyon, the newly arrived Anthony told Black Kettle that he would continue to be protected by the Army. Allegedly to enable the surrendered Cheyenne and Arapaho to do some hunting, Anthony directed them to move their village to an almost dry watercourse about 40 miles to the north-east: Sand Creek.

Anthony had moved the Indians to a place where they could be inconspicuously massacred. Chivington and his 3rd Colorado Volunteers reached Fort Lyon on 28 November. Major Anthony and 125 men of his garrison joined them. Some officers protested violently when they learned what Chivington and Anthony intended to do. Chivington cursed them as spies and traitors, no better than Indians.

At daybreak on the clear frosty morning of 29 November 1864, Colonel Chivington and 700 soldiers approached Black Kettle's camp. When a junior officer, Lieutenant Cramer, again protested that the Cheyenne were at peace, Chivington roared back: "I have come to kill Indians, and believe that it is right and honourable to use any means under God's heaven to kill Indians." His troops were ordered to "Kill and scalp all, big and little; nits make lice."

The sleeping Indians were given no warning, no chance for talk. Chivington's men simply bore down on them, firing their rifles, slashing into the sleeping tents. There was confusion and noise. Black Kettle, unable to comprehend what was

happening, ran up the Stars and Stripes outside his tent.
Then a white flag of surrender. Still the killing continued.

Some of the Indians ran into the sand hills and frantically dug pits in the banks in which to hide. The troops
pursued them, and shot into the pits. To prevent an escape,
the Americans cut off the horse herd. Nevertheless, a few
Indians ran as far as five miles to escape the slaughter –
and were still cut down. A lost child crying for its family
was used for target practice.

There was little chance for the dazed Cheyenne and
Arapaho to fight back. They had surrendered most of their
guns to Wynkoop days before. Those warriors who had arms
and could use them fought desperately. Major Anthony
himself said: "I never saw such bravery displayed by any set
of people on the face of the earth than by these Indians. They
would charge on the whole company singly, determined to
kill someone before being killed themselves." Chief White
Antelope refused to flee or fight. He stood in front of his tipi
and sang his death song, "Nothing lives long/Except the
earth and the mountains," until he was killed.

The horror of Sand Creek is only truly borne by the
words of those who were there.

Robert Bent, Chivington's guide:

After the firing the warrriors put the squaws and children
together, and surrounded them to protect them. I saw five
squaws under a bank for shelter. When the troops came up
to them they ran out and showed their persons, to let the
soldiers know they were squaws and begged for mercy, but
the soldiers shot them all . . . There were some thirty or
forty squaws collected in a hole for protection; they sent
out a little girl about six years old with a white flag on a

stick, she had not proceeded but a few steps when she was shot and killed. All the squaws in that hole were afterwards killed, and four or five bucks outside. The squaws offered no resistance. Every one I saw dead was scalped. I saw one squaw cut open with an unborn child, as I thought lying by her side. Captain Soule afterwards told me that such was the fact . . . I saw quite a number of infants in arms killed with their mothers.

First Lieutenant James D. Connor, New Mexico Volunteers:

About day break on the morning of the 29th of November we came in sight of the camp of the friendly Indians aforementioned, and were ordered by Colonel Chivington to attack the same, which was accordingly done. The command of Colonel Chivington was composed of about one thousand men; the village of the Indians consisted of from one hundred to one hundred and thirty lodges, and, as far as I am able to judge, of from five hundred to six hundred souls, the majority of which were women and children; in going over the battleground the next day I did not see a body of man, woman, or child but was scalped, and in many instances their bodies were mutilated in the most horrible manner – men, women, and children's privates cut out, etc.; I heard one man say that he had cut out a woman's private parts and had them for exhibition on a stick . . . according to the best of my knowledge and belief these atrocities that were committed were with the knowledge of J. M. Chivington, and I do not know of his taking any measures to prevent them; I heard of one instance of a child a few months old being thrown in the feed-box of a wagon, and after being carried some distance left on the ground to perish; I also heard of numerous instances in which men had cut out the private parts of females and stretched them over the saddle-boxes, and wore them over their hats while riding in the ranks . . .

Lieutenant Cramer:

We arrived at the Indian village about daylight . . . Colonel Chivington moved his regiment to the front, the Indians retreating up the creek, and hiding under the banks . . .White Antelope ran towards our columns unarmed, and with both arms raised, but was killed. Several other of the warriors were killed in like manner. The woman and children were huddled together, and most of our fire was concentrated on them . . . The Indian warriors, about 100 in number, fought desperately; there were about 500 all told. I estimated the loss of the Indians to be from 125 to 175 killed; no wounded fell into our hands and all the dead were scalped. The Indian who was pointed out as White Antelope had his fingers cut off. Our force was so large that there was no necessity of firing on the Indians. They did not return the fire until after our troops had fired several rounds . . . I told Colonel Chivington . . . that it would be murder, in every sense of the word, if he attacked those Indians. His reply was, bringing his fist down close to my face, "Damn any man who sympathizes with Indians" . . . he had come to kill Indians and believed it to be honorable to kill Indians under any and all circumstances.

Ashbury Bird, Company D, 1st Colorado Cavalry:

I went over the ground soon after the battle. I should judge there were between 400 and 500 Indians killed . . . Nearly all, men, women, and children were scalped. I saw one woman whose privates had been mutilated.

Corporal Amos C. Miksch, 1st Colorado Cavalry, Company C:

Next morning after the battle, I saw a little boy covered up among the Indians in a trench, still alive. I saw a major in the 3rd regiment take out his pistol and blow off the top of his head. I saw some men unjointing figers to get rings off, and cutting off ears to get silver ornaments. I saw a party with the same major take up bodies that had been buried in the night to scalp them and take off ornaments. I saw a squaw with her head smashed in before she was killed. Next morning, after they were dead and stiff, these men pulled out the bodies of the squaws and pulled them open in an indecent manner. I heard men say they had cut out the privates, but did not see it myself.

Sergeant Lucien Palmer, 1st Colorado Cavalry, Company C:

The bodies were horribly cut up, skulls broken in a good many; I judge they were broken in after they were killed, as they were shot besides. I do not think I saw any but what was scalped; saw fingers cut off [to get the rings off them], saw several bodies with privates cut off, women as well as men.

David Louderbeck, 1st Colorado Cavalry:

The dead bodies of women and children were afterwards mutilated in the most horrible manner. I saw
only eight. I could not stand it; they were cut up too
much . . . . they were scalped and cut up in an awful
manner . . . White Antelope's nose, ears, and privates
were cut off.

John S. Smith, interpreter:

All manner of depredations were inflicted on their
persons, they were scalped, their brains knocked out;
the men used their knives, ripped open women, clubbed
little children, knocked them in the head with their
guns, beat their brains out, mutilated their bodies in
every sense of the word . . . worse mutilated than any I
ever saw before, the women all cut to pieces . . .
[C]hildren two or three months old; all ages lying there,
from sucking infants up to warriors.

By the end of the day, 28 men and 105 women and
children lay dead at Sand Creek. Among those who
escaped was Black Kettle, his badly injured wife on his
back.

When the soldiers returned to Denver the town went into
a delirium of joy. "Colorado Soldiers", the *Rocky Mountain
News* declared, "have again covered themselves with glory
. . . the Colonel [Chivington] is a credit to Colorado and
the West." Cheyenne scalps were strung across the stage of
the Denver Opera House during intermission, to standing
applause.

On the Great Plains, the shock waves from Sand Creek

rolled westwards. Already agitated by the Minnesota Sioux uprising, the tribes fell to anger and a desperate revenge. Plains Indians rarely fought in winter, but now they made an exception. In January 1865, a combined military expedition of Cheyenne, Northern Arapaho, Oglala and Brulé Sioux – 1,600 picked warriors and one of the greatest cavalry forces the world had ever seen – whipped into Colorado. Fort Rankin suffered severe losses. The town of Julesburg was sacked twice, the outskirts of Denver threatened. Seventy-five miles of the South Platte Trail was wrecked. Ranches and stations were burnt, wagon trains captured and more people killed than Chivington had slain at Sand Creek.

The Sand Creek massacre caused outrage in the east, and bolstered the movement for Indian reform. A Military Investigation Commission condemned Chivington and his soldiers, but the colonel escaped punishment because he had left the army. (The most damaging witness, Captain Silas Soule, was murdered before the Commission finished its business, probably with Chivington's connivance.) Congress approved the report, and added more testimony to it.

In July 1865, Senator James Doolittle of Wisconsin went out to Denver to argue the case for a peaceful solution to the Indian problem. The choice, he told a capacity crowd at the Denver Opera House, was to put the Indians on adequate reservations where they might support themselves, or to exterminate them. The audience, Doolittle later wrote, gave "a shout almost loud enough to raise the roof of the Opera House – 'Exterminate them! Exterminate them! Exterminate them!'"

PUNISHMENT

Three months before Senator Doolittle had the roof of the Denver Opera House raised on him, the Civil War had come to an end. On 9 April 1865, in the front parlour of Wilmer McLean's farm at Appomattox Courthouse, Virginia, Robert E. Lee surrendered to Ulysses S. Grant. Now the North versus South conflict was over, Union officers turned their faces towards the land of the setting sun to unite the nation east and west.

Top of their agenda was "punishment" of the Sioux, Northern Cheyenne and Arapaho, whose rampage through Colorado had been followed by a mass raid on the great overland trail on the Platte and North Platte. In July 1865 3,000 Warriors had fallen on the Platte Bridge (now Casper, Wyoming), wiping out a train of dismounted cavalry.

The Army began a determined effort to defeat the Indians of the North Plains, sending General Patrick E. Connor and 3,000 troops to destroy the Indians in their Powder River camps. Connor instructed his junior officers not to "receive overtures of peace or submission" but "to kill every male Indian over 12 years of age." Connor was a seasoned Indian fighter, having defeated the trail-harassing Shoshonis at Bear River (Idaho) in 1863, but he would not have his way in the Powder River country. All summer the Indians harried his columns, took his horses and vanished into the buttes before they could be engaged. Some of his detachments got hopelessly lost, the men died of scurvy and were lamed by cactus spines. Already exhausted by the Civil War, soldiers deserted by the drove.

General Connor was deprived of his command for failing to punish the elusive Indians. But before he left the northern plains he built a fort, Fort Reno, on a road which had recently been blazed to the goldfields of Montana by John M. Bozeman. The Bozeman Trail would be the subject of the next great fight between the Whites and the Cheyenne, Arapaho and their Sioux allies A fight the Indians would win.

Red Cloud's War

They made us many promises more than I can remember, but they never kept but one. They promised to take our land, and they took it.

Red Cloud (Makhpiya-Luta), Oglala Sioux chief

With eighty men I could ride through the entire Sioux nation.

Captain William J. Fetterman

Fort Phil Kearny was established amid hostilities. No disaster other than the usual incidents to border warfare occurred, until gross disobedience of orders sacrificed nearly eighty of the choice men of my command . . . In the grave I bury disobedience.

Colonel Henry B. Carrington, US Army

The Fort Laramie council held in June 1866 was a magnificent spectacle. To either side of the fort, set between the Laramie and Platte rivers in the heart of Sioux country, tipis stretched for a mile or more, smoke wisping out of their tops into the sunshine. Hundreds of ponies were corralled, knots of Indians came and went, and from a staff at the corner of the sod parade ground the Stars and Stripes flapped languidly in the breeze. On a temporary platform sat officials of the federal government and the leading chiefs of the Cheyenne, Arapaho, and the Brulé, Miniconjou and Oglala sub-bands of the Teton Sioux. Prominent on the platform was the 44-year-old Oglala chief Red Cloud (Makhpiya-Luta), a warrior with 80 coups to his name. For three years "Bad Faces" led by Red Cloud had been attacking parties of Whites travelling the Bozeman Trail to the Montana goldfields. The Trail ran through the heart of the Powder River country, the last unviolated buffalo range of the Sioux and their allies. The Laramie council had been called to bribe Red Cloud and the other warring bands into selling the road.

The talks began promisingly. In return for the safe passage of Whites on the Bozeman Trail, the government promised the Indians $75,000 a year and an assurance that their land would never be taken by force. Then Colonel Henry Beebe Carrington rolled into the fort at the head of a long column of wagons and men. When a chief asked where he was going, Carrington explained that he was to construct two more forts on the trail, both deep into Teton Sioux country. At this news, Red Cloud exploded with anger: "The Great Father sends us presents and wants us to sell him the road, but White chief goes with soldiers to steal the road before Indians say Yes or No! I will talk with you no more! I will go now, and I will fight you! As long as I live I will fight you for the last hunting grounds of my people!"

Red Cloud stormed off the platform. Many in the Sioux nation felt the same desperate anger as Red Cloud. Over sixty years later two Lakota warriors recalled why they decided to take up arms against the US:

. . . I felt that the white men would just simply wipe us

out and there would be no Indian nation . . . We wouldn't have fought the White men if they hadn't fought us. We would have allowed them to live among us in peace.

When I was about fourteen, I remember that the White men were coming and that they were going to fight us to the finish and take away our land, and I thought it was not right. We are humans too and God created us all alike, and I was going to do the best I could to defend my nation. So I started out on the warpath when I was sixteen years old.

From what I heard from old people, I thought I would just have to do my part. We roamed the country freely, and this country belonged to us in the first place. There was plenty of game and we were never hungry. But since the white men came we were fighting all the time. The white man was just going to kill all of us. I was so scared that I rode one horse all night just guarding . . . The band I was in got together and said they were not going to let the white men run over them and down deep m my heart I was going to defend my fellow men to the last. At the age of ten or eleven I had a six-shooter and a quiver full of arrows to defend my nation.

Red Cloud had promised to fight the White men. He kept his word.

"CHARACTER OF INDIAN AFFAIRS HOSTILE"

On 22 June, Colonel Carrington and the 700-strong Eighteenth Infantry, plus assorted civilian woodchoppers and a number of wives and children, marched out of Fort

Laramie for the Powder River country. On the 28th, Carrington reached Fort Reno on the Bozeman Trail. The next afternoon Indians ran off nearly all the fort's horses and mules.

Security was tightened. The expedition went on, through a heat so profound that it caused the wheels of the wagons to shrink and fall apart. At Crazy Woman's Creek nine men deserted for the Montana goldfields. A detail sent after them was stopped on the Trail by a band of Cheyenne who refused to let them pass.

Still Carrington pressed on. At the fork to the Little Piney he pitched camp and started to build Fort Phil Kearny. The scout Jim Bridger, accompanying the expedition, argued against it: the hills on all sides shut out any view, and the nearest wood was five miles away. He was overruled by the military.

While Fort Phil Kearny was being built, Carrington dispatched two companies north to build a smaller stockade, Fort C. F. Smith, on the Bighorn. With Fort Reno, Carrington then had three forts to guard the Bozeman Trail. But his men were spread terribly thin.

Red Cloud used a familiar Indian strategy. There were no full frontal attacks. There were ambushes, lightning raids, and constant sniping. A steady attrition of White men and morale.

Some of Red Cloud's tactics, however, were dangerously novel. He even taught some of his warriors a few words of English and dressed them in captured blue uniforms, all the better to confuse the enemy when they pursued him. Most often, however, as Standing Bear remembered, the Sioux fought in bare skin:

We went into battle naked because it is more handy. You can get around quickly and are more swift in every way. With clothes on you would be much slower. We had the pony's bridle fastened to our belt to keep the pony from getting away when the rider would fall off.

The white cavalry did not know how to fight. They stuck together and thus made an easy target for us. When we started fighting, we would probably be under the horse's belly and after we were on the ground we would jump around, and it was pretty hard to hit us. We'd zigzag toward them. It was open order fighting. We fought in circles because when we go around them it would scare the soldiers and then we would charge on them . . . Some would go one way and the other would go another way, thus disorganizing the soldiers. We would hang on our ponies at times with one leg. This is a real trick to know how to do. Then we would shoot under the horse's neck while the other leg is cramped up on the side.

By August, Carrington's soldiers at Fort Phil Kearny were being scalped and wounded at the rate of one per day. When the photographer-correspondent Ridgeway Glover of Frank Leslie's *Illustrated Paper* wandered away from the post he was found naked, his back cleaved open by a tomahawk. (The naive, daydreaming Glover had survived a desperate ambush by 160 Sioux at Crazy Woman's Creek only days before and thought he was "Indianproof".) But even soldiers inside the growing fort were not safe. One was shot as he sat in the latrine. The garrisons were too besieged to protect traffic. In his first five weeks in the Powder River country, Carrington reported that 33 travellers were killed on the Bozeman road.

Carrington was reduced to ever more desperate orders to

tighten vigilance. After a sequence of attacks on his wood-cutters, hay mowers and the driving off of the fort's beef herd, Carrington issued a special order on 13 September (to the Indians, the month of the "Drying Grass Moon"):

1. Owing to recent depredation of Indians near Fort Philip Kearny, Dak., the post commander [Ten Eyck] will issue such regulation and at once provide such additional escorts for wood trains, guard for stock and hay and the steam saw-mills as the chief quartermaster [Brown] may deem essential. He will also give

2. Instructions, so that upon Indian alarm no troops leave the post without an officer or under the antecedent direction of an officer, and the garrison will be so organized that it may at all times be available and disposable for exterior duty or interior defence.

3. One relief of the guard will promptly support any picket threatened at night, and the detail on posts should be visited hourly by a non-commissioned officer of the guard between the hours of posting successive reliefs.

4. Stringent regulations are enjoined to prevent camp rumors and false reports, and any picket or soldier bringing reports of Indian sign or hostilities must be required to report to the post commander or officer of the day or to the nearest commissioned officer in cases of urgent import.

5. Owing to the non-arrival of corn for the post and the present reduced condition of the public stock, the quarter-master is authorized upon the approval of the post commander, to purchase sufficient corn for moderate issues, to last until a supply already due, shall arrive, but the issue will be governed by the condition of the stock, and will only be issued to horses unless the same in half

ration shall be necessary for such mules as are daily in use
and can not graze or be furnished with hay.

6. Reports will be made of all Indian depredations, with the
   results, in order that a proper summary may be sent to
   department headquarters.

7. Soldiers while on duty in the timber or elsewhere are
   forbidden to waste ammunition in hunting, every hour of
   their time being indispensable in preparing for their own
   comfort and the well-being of the garrison during the
   approaching winter.

More Indian attacks brought more instructions from
Carrington to tighten defensive measures. The Commander
was in a dithering panic, reduced to ever more obsessional
treatises on security. A special order of 21 September 1866
read:

The fastenings of all gates must be finished this day; the
locks for large gates will be similar, and the district
cornrnander, post commander, officer of the day, and
quartermaster will alone have keys. Keys for the wicket
gates will be with the same officers.

Upon a general alarm or appearance of Indians in
force or near the gates, the same will be closed, and no
soldier or civilian will leave the fort without orders.

No large gate will be opened, except the quartermaster gate, unless it shall be necessary for wagons.
Stock must invariably pass in and out of that gate.

The west or officers' gate will not be opened without
permission, even for wagons, unless for timber wagons
or ambulances, or mounted men.

Upon a general alarm the employees in the sutlers'
department will form at the store and wait for orders and

assignment to some part of the interior defence, but will not be expected to act without the fort unless voluntarily, and then after sanction is given, and under strict military control.

All soldiers, however detailed or attached, or in whatever capacity serving, will, upon a general alarm, take arms and be subject to immediate disposal with their companies or at the headquarters or department with which serving.

All horses of mounted men will be saddled at reveille.

It is also expressly enjoined that in no case shall there be needless running in haste upon an alarm. Shouting, tale-bearing, and gross perversion of facts by excited men does more mischief than Indians. And the duty of guards being to advise of danger, soldiers who have information must report to the proper officer, and not to comrades.

At the sounding of assembly the troops of the garrison not on daily duty will form in front of their respective quarters.

The general alarm referred to in foregoing paragraph will be indicated by the sound of the assembly, followed by three quick shots from the guard-house, which latter will be the distinction between the general alarm and the simple alarm for turning out the troops of the garrison.

This order will be placed upon a bulletin-board for early and general information.

Officers and non-commissioned officers are charged with its execution, and the soldiers of the 18th Infantry are especially called upon to vindicate and maintain, as they ever have, the record of their regiment.

This will require much hard work, much guard duty,

and much patience, but they will have an honorable field to occupy in this country, and both Indian outrages and approaching winter stimulate them to work, and work with zeal and tireless industry.

Their colonel will with his officers share all, and no idling or indifference can, under these circumstances, have any quarters in the breast of a true soldier.

In addition to his instructions on fort security, Carrington kept up a steady stream of complaining missives to his superiors. A report to General Philip St George Cooke, Commander of the Department of the Platte, informed him:

Character of Indian affairs hostile. The treaty does not yet benefit this route [Some tribes did sign the 1866 Fort Laramie agreement] . . . My ammunition has not yet arrived; neither has my Leavenworth supply train . . . My infantry make poor riders . . . I am equal to any attack they [the Indians] may make, but have to build quarters and prepare for winter, escort trains, and guaranty the whole road from the Platte to Virginia City with eight companies of infantry. I have to economize ammunition . . . I sent two officers out on recruiting service, under peremptory orders from Washington, leaving me crippled and obliged to trust too much to non-commissioned officers . . .

Carrington's pleas fell on deaf ears. Cooke fully understood the impossibility of his Colonel's position.

But if Cooke was deaf and Carrington a ditherer, the special responsibility for the disaster that was to ensue lay elsewhere.

SLAUGHTER AT LODGE TRAIL RIDGE

In November 1866 a young infantry captain named William Judd Fetterman joined Carrington's staff at Fort Phil Kearny. A dashing Civil War hero who had been breveted Lieutenant-Colonel, Fetterman had little respect for his cautious commanding officer, a former attorney who had served the conflict behind a desk as an administrator. Fetterman had even less regard for the Indians around the fort. "Give me a single company of regulars," he bragged "and I can whip a thousand Indians. With eighty men I could ride through the Sioux nation."

By December 1866, Red Cloud and the other senior chief of the Oglala Sioux, Man-Afraid-of-His-Horses (more accurately translated as "the mere sight of his horses inspires fear"), were ready to give Fetterman his opportunity to prove his boast. They were joined by Black Shield of the Miniconjou, Roman Nose and Medicine Man of the Cheyenne, and Little Chief and Sorrel Horse of the Arapaho. Around 2,000 warriors moved into the foothills around Fort Phil Kearny. For two weeks they tantalized the soldiers, riding on the skyline just out of rifle range, creeping around the fort at night howling like wolves, springing small attacks, but always keeping their main force hidden.

The soldiers' nerves were stretched to breaking point.

Then on 20 December the Sioux and their allies camped on Prairie Dog Creek and began the ceremonies which preceded battle. A hermaphrodite medicine man rode off over the hills and returned to tell of a vision in which he had caught a hundred soldiers in his hands. The warriors beat the ground with their hands in approval and selected the leaders for the next day's battle. The task of leading the all-important decoy party fell to a young warrior named Crazy Horse.

At daybreak on 21 December, the Indians moved into position. The decoy rode towards Fort Phil Kearny, while the remainder prepared an ambush on either side of Lodge Trail Ridge. The Cheyenne and Arapaho took the west side, and some Sioux hid in the grass opposite. Still more Sioux remained mounted, hidden behind rocks.

Meanwhile, at the fort, Carrington had sent out the customary train of wagons to cut wood. The morning was beautiful, with the snow around the fort sparkling in the brilliant sunshine, but as though he had some premonition of danger, Carrington attached an extra guard to the train. About eleven o'clock look-outs on top of Pilot Hill started signalling frantically that the wood train was under attack.

Carrington ordered a relief party of cavalry and infantry to assemble. As it was about to move out under the command of Captain J. W. Powell, Fetterman stepped before Carrington and demanded permission to lead the relief instead of Powell. Fetterman pointed out that because of his brevet rank of Lieutenant-Colonel he technically outranked Powell. For a second Carrington hesitated, then gave Fetterman the command.

Then matters unfolded as though in an Ancient Greek tragedy. Fetterman had seventy six men under his command. But then Captain Brown rode up and asked to join the detail. Seventy seven. So did the armourer Private Maddeon. They were joined by two civilian employees, the Civil War veterans James Wheatley and Isaac Fisher. Wheatley and Fisher were armed with new sixteen-shot Henry rifles. They were anxious to try them out.

Knowing Fetterman's rashness, Carrington warned him that the Indians were a cunning and desperate enemy. Then he gave him exact orders: "Support the wood train, relieve it and report to me. Do not engage or pursue the Indians at its expense. Under no circumstances pursue over Lodge Trail Ridge."

As the relief started to move out, Carrington sprang up onto the sentry walk by the gate and repeated his order to Fetterman: "Under no circumstances must you cross Lodge Trail Ridge." Fetterman acknowledged the order, and the relief moved quickly out of sight. Fetterman had with him 80 men – all he needed to "ride through the Sioux nation."

When Fetterman got to the wood train, the Indians had apparently disappeared. But moments later, the decoy party under Crazy Horse rushed out of the brush, yipping and waving blankets. The soldiers opened fire, but the Indians merely cantered up close, taunting the White men. At least once, Crazy Horse dismounted within rifle range and admired the view, pretending that the soldiers were not there. Then the warriors began to retreat slowly in a zig-zagging path up the slope to Lodge Trail Ridge, always tantalizingly just out of reach.

The frustrated Fetterman ordered his men to follow them.

The trap worked perfectly. A little before noon, Fetterman's command followed Crazy Horse over Lodge Trail Ridge.

The earth must have seemed alive with warriors. Two thousand Indians sprang from behind their cover, their cries of "Hoka hey, hoka hey" filling the chill air.

It was over in minutes. Wheatley and Fisher, the two Civil War veterans toting 16-shot Henrys managed, with several infantrymen, to form a defensive wall that blunted the first charge. Using downed ponies as breastworks they kept up a rattling fire. Dead Indians were ringed around them. Then they were overwhelmed.

Some of the infantry ran back up the slope to a rock formation and held off their attackers for a quarter of an hour before running out of ammunition. Fetterman and Captain Fred Brown committed suicide, shooting each other in the head with their revolvers.

Above the infantry in the rock formation, a group of dismounted cavalry tried to get over the ice which covered the ridge top and found Indians on the other side. Few Sioux or Cheyenne carried rifles but they fired up showers of arrows. As the cavalry slipped and scrabbled towards a cluster of boulders they were cut to pieces. A few knots of survivors took up position in the boulders.

Around this time, Indian Scouts reported that soldier reinforcements were riding out from the fort. Desperate for a quick victory, the warriors charged the dismounted cavalrymen. It was now so cold that blood froze as it spurted from wounds. Among the last of the soldiers to die was the bugler Adolph Metzger, who beat off attackers with his bugle until it was a shapeless mass. A dog belonging to a cavalryman came running out of the rock. Even this was killed, a Sioux arrow through its neck.

When the reinforcements from the fort under Captain Ten Eyck reached the top of the ridge at 2.45 all sounds of firing had ceased. Looking down into the Peno valley they could see literally thousands of Indians moving about, some picking up the wounded and their 60 or so dead, others salvaging any of the 40,000 arrows fired which were still usable. A few Indians rode up towards the reinforcements, slapping their buttocks, and calling obscenities.

Gradually, the Indians began to move off westwards. As they cleared the battlefield, one of the reinforcements suddenly pointed to the Bozeman Trail: "There're the men down there, all dead!"

And they were. None of Fetterman's command survived. They had been annihilated. Warily going down to retrieve the bodies, Ten Eyck's men found them mutilated beyond their belief. In Colonel Carrington's official report, suppressed for 20 years after the event, there were no details spared:

> Eyes torn out and laid on rocks; noses cut off; ears cut out; chins hewn off; teeth chopped out; joints of fingers, brains taken out and placed on rocks with other members of the body; entrails taken out and exposed; hands cut off; feet cut off; arms taken out from sockets; private parts severed and indecently placed on the person; eyes, ears, mouth and arms penetrated with spear-heads, sticks, and arrows; ribs slashed to separation with knives; skulls severed in every form, from chin to crown; muscles of calves, thighs, stomach, breast, back, arms and cheek taken out. Punctures upon every sensitive part of the body, even to the soles of the feet and palms of the hand.*

All had been scalped, save for, two, whose heads had been placed in buffalo-skin bags, a signal dishonour reserved by the Sioux for cowardly foe.

The so-called Fetterman Massacre so reduced the Fort Phil Kearny garrison that Carrington feared that his entire command might be destroyed. Despite a raging blizzard, a miner staying at the fort volunteered to ride the 235 miles to Fort Laramie to obtain reinforcements. This was John ("Portugee") Phillips. He refused pay, but took one of the colonel's horses. Before riding off, Phillips visited the pregnant

---

*Mutilation by the Plains Indian had religious basis. A dead man entered the afterworld in the form he held just after death. It followed, then that if the dead enemy was shorn of his fingers, of his feet, of his eyes, he would be unable to menace in the hereafter.

wife of Lieutenant Grummond, killed alongside Fetterman, and told her: "I will go if it costs my life. I am going for your sake."

John Phillips's ride, through snow and Indians, is an epic in the folklore of the frontier. With only hardtack to eat and temperatures reaching 20 below, he somehow made the 190 miles to Horse Shoe Station in four days, from where the news was flashed to Fort Laramie. For good measure, he rode on to Fort Laramie to report in person. He arrived on Christmas night, as the officers were holding a ball.

Less well known is that Carrington sent out another volunteer messenger from the fort, George Bailey, who also made it through the blizzards and hostile Native Americans, meeting up with Philips sometime before Horse Shoe Station. Both men arrived together at the telegraph office and later at Fort Laramie.

Within hours of their arrival, reinforcements were struggling towards Fort Phil Kearny. With them went orders relieving Carrington of his command.

These fresh troops did not intimidate the Sioux, who continued to besiege Fort Phil Kearny and virtually halt travel along the Bozeman Trail.

VICTORY OUT OF DEFEAT

In the late summer of 1867 there came another battle at Fort Phil Kearny. At dawn on 2 August Red Cloud and a thousand Sioux warriors, wearing their white and green and yellow warpaint, attacked a 36-man detail working under Captain James Powell at the pinery. Anticipating such a fight, Powell had taken the precaution of building an oval barricade of the large wooden boxes from the wagon beds. Thirty-two of the detail made it to shelter behind the wagon boxes. For four hours, to the vast surprise of the Sioux, the soldiers kept up an almost continuous fire. Braves fell in futile charge after charge.

Unknown to Red Cloud, the soldiers had the new breech-loading Springfield rifles instead of muzzle-loaders. "Instead of drawing ramrods and thus losing precious time," recalled Sergeant Samuel Gibson, "we simply threw open the breech-blocks of our new rifles to eject the empty shell and slapped in fresh ones." These Springfield rifles, along with Powell's wagon boxes, enabled the work detail to hold off the Indians until reinforcements arrived. Years afterwards Red Cloud said he lost the flower of his fighting warriors in the Wagon Box Fight.

The day preceding the Wagon Box Fight, an attack by Cheyenne at Fort C. F. Smith – the Hayfield Fight – had also been beaten off with Springfields.

For weeks, Red Cloud believed he had suffered a fatal defeat. But the government in Washington had been so shocked by the previous disasters on the Trail – especially the Fetterman Massacre – that it wanted to make peace. A commission was sent out to Wyoming to draw up a treaty. Red Cloud refused to sign. Sensing his advantage, he demanded that the blue-coat soldiers abandon their forts in Sioux country. Wearied of a war that was costly – President Grant's Secretary of the Interior, Carl Schurz, estimated it took $1 million to kill each Indian – and unpopular in the east, the government took the unprecedented step of agreeing to an Indian's terms. Forts C. F. Smith, Phil Kearny and Reno were abandoned in the summer of 1868.

As the soldiers departing Fort Phil Kearny looked back, they saw a band of Indians under Little Wolf set fire to the buildings.

When he saw that the posts had truly been evacuated, Red Cloud rode into Fort Laramie and signed the treaty. Under its terms, the government agreed to abandon the Bozeman Trail, and define the Powder River country as "unceded Indian territory" from which White persons would be excluded. Red Cloud had won his war to retain his people's traditional hunting grounds. In return, the Indians agreed to settle on a giant reservation in Dakota and cease hostilities. "From this day forward," the treaty began, "all wars between the parties to this agreement shall forever cease."

A pious hope. But peace of a sort held for eight years on the northern plains. And when it was finally broken, it was broken by the White man.

Just as he had broken the other 370 treaties made with the Indian in the 90 years since Independence.

Blood on the Grasslands

"They have run over our country; they have destroyed the growing wood and green grass; they have set fire to our lands. They have devastated the country and killed animals, the elk, the deer, the antelope, my buffalo. They do not kill them to eat them; they leave them to rot where they fall. Fathers, if I went into your country to kill your animals, what would you *say*? Would I not be wrong, and would you not make war on me?"

Bear Tooth

THE BUFFALO AND THE IRON HORSE

White emigrants had been streaming into the trans-Mississippi West since the 1840s, along roads which disfigured the landscape and scared away the buffalo. To keep them in contact with the East, stagecoach lines and telegraph poles sprang up in the wilderness, stretching to Santa Fe, Salt Lake, Denver and beyond. But not until 1862 were the forces set in motion which would transform the Wild West beyond redemption. In that year, Lincoln's Congress passed the Homestead Act, which offered parcels of 160 acres of free land to anyone willing to work it. Millions took up the offer, and began pushing out into the Great Plains. In the same year, Congress passed the Pacific Railroad Act, which made possible the first transcontinental railway.

The iron horse had already penetrated to Omaha. Now it would push westwards from Omaha into the wilderness, while a line would come eastwards from Sacramento, California to meet it. With the end of the Civil War in 1865, the pace of expansion quickened at a fantastic rate. National energies which had been directed North and South were now focused West. Emigration boomed. Demobbed soldiers and men desperate for work flooded to work on the transcontinental railroad. By the end of 1866, the Union Pacific was advancing into Nebraska at the rate of a mile a day. Another railroad, the Kansas Pacific, was started towards Denver, Colorado.

The railway was the engine of ultimate destruction for the Native American. The railway would bind East and West the plains across in bands of steel. It would make possible the settlement of the interior frontier, and it would give the Army an added mobility in the Indian Wars. And it would bring the buffalo to near extinction.

Unknown to the Plains Indians, the buffalo on which they had based their lifestyle, culture and religion was already in crisis before the railroads came, At their peak there were probably 25 million buffalo on the Great Plains (50 million less than the traditional estimate), and by the early 1800s these were suffering competition from mustang and Indian horse herds for water and grazing. The cattle brought to the Plains by Native American raiders and White migrants gave the buffalo brucellosis and tuberculosis. Emigrant trails – which cut the immense herds in two – and White settlement on the edges of the grasslands obliterated areas of range which were critical in times of drought.

The buffalo only appeared to be infinite. By the mid-nineteenth century the animal was struggling to maintain its numbers. And then came the railroads.

The iron horse scared away the herds and destroyed the range. To feed the railroad crews with meat, the companies hired hunters to slaughter the conveniently placed bison. A discovery that buffalo hides made cheap machine belts for Eastern factories increased the demand for the animal's skin – which could now be shipped back on the railroads. Buffalo hunters galloped to the end of the line, and the carnage began.

A skilled marksman, using a heavy Sharps rifle and staying downwind from the herd, could kill – with luck – around 150 of the short-sighted animals per day. A former Pony Express rider and crack-shot called William F. Cody killed 4,280 buffalo for the Kansas-Pacific in eight months in 1867–8. This feat won him the soubriquet "Buffalo Bill". Hide hunters took an estimated 4,374,000 from the southern plains alone between 1872 and 1874. The Great Plains were being turned into a wasteland and a charnel-house,

Great Plains Indians began to attack the railroad, striking at Union Pacific grading crews, even speeding locomotives. Rails were ripped up, obstacles tied to the track. Once, a group of braves tried to capture a moving locomotive by pulling a rawhide lariat taut in front of it. Several were pulled under the wheels. A more effective attack came in the late summer of 1867.

On the night of 6 August 1867, the telegraph wire at Plum Creek, Nebraska, went dead. William Thompson and a crew of five went down the Union Pacific line in the dark to investigate – and ran headfirst into a Cheyenne barricade made from a section of ripped-up track. Within moments the crew were dead, and Thompson had been knocked unconscious.

He woke to feel himself being scalped, but feigned death. Lying inert, he witnessed another attack by the Cheyenne nearby. This time a freight train came along and piled up on the barricade; the driver and fireman were killed by the Indians, but four men travelling in the caboose escaped. Still pretending death, Thompson watched the Cheyenne loot the cars. When the war party finally moved on, Thompson retrieved his bloody scalp and stumbled back to Plum Creek, from where he caught a train to Omaha. Among those who visited the scalpless repairman there was the journalist Henry Stanley: "In a pail of water by his side, was his scalp, somewhat resembling a drowned rat, as it floated, curled up, on the water. At Omaha, people flocked from all parts to view the gory baldness which had come upon him so suddenly."

CUSTER AND THE CHEYENNE

As the attacks on the railroad increased, the Army turned its attention to the central and southern plains. To protect railcrews and emigrants in Kansas and Nebraska, the irascible commander of the Military Division of the Missouri, General William Tecumseh Sherman, wanted to remove all Indians from a wide corridor between the Platte and the Arkansas. Sherman was itching for war, complaining in 1866: "God only knows when, and I do not see how, we can make a decent excuse for an Indian war." Desultory attacks on the iron horses did not quite justify wholesale war on the Indians, but Sherman got his excuse when his subordinate, Major General Winfield Scott Hancock, burned a Cheyenne village because it was a "nest of conspirators". Scott added that it was not "of much importance" whether the villagers had actually committed depredations. Thus provoked, the Cheyenne took to the warpath. Sherman got his Indian War.

To fight the war against the Cheyenne, Sherman employed the talents of Hancock and another celebrated officer, George Armstrong Custer. Although Custer had graduated 34th of a class of 34 at West Point (and collected 726 demerits), he had gone on to establish a Civil War reputation as an able cavalry leader, being breveted Major-General of Volunteers at the age of 25. Sherman held Custer in high esteem, but was not blind to his failures:

> G. A. Custer, Lieutenant Colonel, Seventh Cavalry, is young, very brave, even to rashness – a good trait for a cavalry officer. His outstanding characteristics are his youth, health, energy and extreme willingness to act and fight. But he has not too much sense.

As if to prove the truth of Sherman's latter assessment, Custer mounted one of the most capricious and ineffectual cavalry campaigns seen on the plains. Pained at being separated from his wife, Libby, Custer became moody and erratic. Men were given brutal punishments for the slightest reason. Rather than engage the enemy he went buffalo-hunting. When his men, exhausted by four months of fruitless careering about the plains, began to desert, he sent out a posse with the order to "shoot them down, and bring none in alive."

Eventually, Custer broke off the campaign completely and force-marched his men across Kansas so that he could be with Libby. Two men were killed by Indians en route but Custer refused to stop to bury them. A week after being reunited with Libby, Custer was arrested and charged with inhumane treatment of his men and abandoning his command. He was convicted on both counts, and suspended from his post for one year.

An expedition into Kansas headed by Hancock fared little better. In four months of active campaigning, Hancock's command killed four Indians, two of them friendly. The other two were Sioux, casualties in a fight that saw one of Hancock's detachments annihilated.

There were other Indian victories. On 26 June 1867, a war party of 300 Cheyenne and their Arapaho and Sioux allies descended on Fort Wallace in Western Kansas, where a company of the 7th Cavalry was stationed. "They [the Indians] came literally sailing," recalled Captain Albert Barnitz, "uttering their peculiar 'Hi! Hi! Hi!' and terminating it with the warwhoop – their ponies, gaily decked with feathers and scalplocks, tossing their heads high in the air, and looking wildly from side to side."

Seven soldiers died in the attack, including Sergeant Frederick Wyllyams, an English Eton graduate who had come West for adventure. Another Englishman, Dr William Abraham Bell, working for the Kansas Pacific Survey, came upon his countryman's body shortly afterwards and photographed it. Bell also recorded the scene in words:

> I shall minutely describe this horrid sight, characteristic of a mode of warfare soon – thank God – to be abolished. We shall have no difficulty in recognizing some meaning in the wounds. The muscles of the right arm hacked to the bone speak of the Cheyennes; the nose slit denotes the Arapahoes; and the throat cuts bear witness that the Sioux were also present. I have not discovered what tribe was indicated by the incisions down the thighs, and the laceration of the calves of the legs, in oblique parallel gashes. Warriors from several

tribes purposely left one arrow each in the dead man's body.

Bell sent copies of his photograph to Washington so that "the authorities should see how their soldiers were treated on the Plains." Few in the 7th Cavalry forgot the fate of Frederick Wyllyams.

Military policy was a self-evident failure. The Indians on the northern plains had been even more successful by this date, having wreaked havoc to the Bozeman Trail and wiped out Fetterman's command.

A peace commission was established which met first with the northern tribes at Fort Laramie, then in October 1867 with the central and southern plains tribes at Medicine Lodge Creek in Kansas.

More than 5,000 Indians were present at the council, which was conducted with much pomp and ceremony. On both sides. Soldiers drilled. Indians rode around in milling circles, their horses painted for war. The only ones who remained aloof were the Quahadi Comanche of the Staked Plains, fearsome raiders led by the half-breed Quanah. Indian chief after chief made eloquent, impassioned speeches on behalf of their cause and their desire.

The Kiowa chief Satanta (white Bear), wearing a blue officer's uniform coat given him as a present, told the commission:

I love the land and the buffalo and will not part with it . . . I want the children raised as I was. I have heard that you want to settle us on a reservation near the [Wichita] mountain. I don t want to settle. I want to roam over the prairies. There I feel free and happy but when I settle down I feel pale and die . . . These soldiers cut down my timber; they kill my buffalo; and when I see that it feels as if my heart would burst with sorrow.

As for the commission's offer to build the Indians "civilized" homes, Satanta added: "This building of homes for us is all nonsense. We don't want you to build any for us."

At the end of the council some chiefs signed, and some did not. Black Kettle of the southern Cheyenne, despite the massacre of his people at Sand Creek, still wanted friendship with the Whites, and signed. So did Kicking Bird of the Kiowa and, after protestations, Chief Ten Bears of the Comanche. Just before he left, the ageing Satank, noted chief of the Kiowa, came up to the commissioners to bid them farewell. He stood there with his pony, and made a little speech that moved even the most Indian-hating of the White men gathered.

I come to say that the Kiowas and the Comanches have made you a peace, and they intend to stick to it . . . We have warred against the White man, but never because it gave us pleasure . . . In the far distant past there was no suspicion among us. The world seemed large enough for both . . . But its broad plains seem now to contract, and the White man grows jealous of his Red brother . . . You have patiently heard our many complaints . . . For your sakes the green grass shall not be stained with the blood of Whites . . .

Little more than a year later, the ranges were running with White blood. Despite the hopes of Satank, Black Kettle, and other tribal leaders peace was impossible. The Indians had promised to stay away from the trails and the railroads, but these things were not static. They spread over the hunting grounds almost by the day. And now the farmer had arrived, eating land with his plough and his vision of a land turned to agriculture. The iron horse and the sodbuster: these were the ultimate enemies. They had to be stopped.

During the summer of 1868, bands of hostile Indians attacked settlements and trails in western Kansas and Colorado, killing 124 people. By fall, the grasslands from Kansas to Texas were criss-crossed by war parties.

Following the disastrous campaigns of the previous year, Sherman replaced Hancock with his old colleague, General Philip H. Sheridan, a black-eyed, brilliant and profane cavalry officer. Sheridan authorized Major George A. Forsyth to enlist 50 volunteer frontiersmen who would give the Indians a taste of their own free-booting warfare. The result was the famous fight at Beecher Island in the Arikaree River, Colorado.

Hot on the trail of a Cheyenne war party, Forsyth made camp beside the Arikaree on 6 September. The water was shallow and good, and there was grass aplenty for the horses. Unknown to the impetuous Forsyth – who had something of the Grattan and Fetterman about him – he was only ten or so miles from Cheyenne, who had been joined by Sioux and northern Arapahos.

Next morning, as Forsyth was blearily talking to his sentry, the Indians came screaming along the creek bed. Fortuitously for Forsyth, the flatness of the landscape meant he saw the enemy far enough away to sound the alarm and scram his men onto a low island in the centre of the creek. The Indians – as many as 600 of them – came pounding through the water.

Probably they intended to ride over the island, but the volume of bullets pumped out by Forsyth's command deterred all but a handful of warriors. Most of the Indians passed alongside the island, hanging from the offside of their horse and firing under its neck. They caused a number of early casualties – Forsyth himself took non-mortal wounds to his head, and both legs – before the white men dug pits in the soft sand for cover. Over the next nine days, Forsyth's scouts withstood repeated assaults.

It was leading one such mounted charge that the legendary Cheyenne war chief Roman Nose (Woqini) was killed. Roman Nose had a black-and-white war bonnet whose supernatural ability to protect him from harm depended on his not eating food touched by metal. But before the battle, whilst visiting a Sioux chief, an unknowing hostess had taken his food from the skillet with an iron fork. Initially, Roman Nose refrained from a part in the fight against Forsyth but an elder, White Contrary, came and shamed him: "All those people fighting out there feel that they belong to you, and they will do all that you tell them, and here you are behind this hill." Knowing he was to die, Roman Nose painted himself and put on his war bonnet. He was shot in the spine as he rode at the white men. Falling into the willow brush, he crawled to cover until some braves found him in the evening, and carried him back to the tents. Roman Nose died later the same night.

For all the bravery shown by the Plains Indians in the battle on the Arikaree, no engagement so plainly showed the limitations of their way of war. The White man in the West fought with single-minded, sometimes genocidal, purpose; the Plains Indian was in two minds. He wanted to deal death. But more than that he wanted to "count coup" – to be the first to touch one of the enemy, dead or alive. Counting coup brought special honour. Killing the enemy did not.

There was no kudos to be gained in starving Whites to

death. After a few days, the warriors at the Arikaree fight began to drift away. When Forsyth was relieved on day nine of the battle by black soldiers of the 10th US Cavalry there was not an Indian in sight. Forsyth had sustained a mere handful of casualties.

Forsyth's stand at Beecher Island (named after one of his volunteers who was killed there, authoress Harriet Beecher Stowe's nephew, Frederick) was a singular bright episode for the Army. Elsewhere the picture on the central and southern plains was bleak. Sheridan called in the one officer he believed had the motivation to crush Indian resistance: George Custer. "If there was any poetry or romance in war he could develop it," said Sheridan of his protégé. In October 1887, the flamboyant Custer rejoined the 7th Cavalry and marched them into hostile country determined to restore his glorious reputation.

On 23 November, Custer's Osage scouts picked up the trail of a war party of young men returning from a plundering raid in the Kansas settlements. The story of the ensuing "Battle of the Washita" – at least from the point of view of the 7th Cavalry – was later told by Edward S. Godfrey, one of Custer's lieutenants:

November 23rd – Reveille at 3 o'clock. Snowed all night and still snowing very heavily. The darkness and heavy snowfall made the packing of the wagons very difficult, but at dawn the wagons were assembled in the train and daylight found us on the march, the band playing, "The Girl I Left Behind me," but there was no woman there to interpret its significance. The snow was falling so heavily that vision was limited to a few rods. All landmarks were invisible and the trails were lost. "We didn't know where we were going, but we were on the way." Then General Custer, with compass in hand, took the lead and became our guide.

As the day wore on the weather became warmer and I have never seen the snowflakes as large or fall so lazily as those that fell that day. Fortunately there was no wind to drift the snow to add to our discomfort. They melted on the clothing so that every living thing was wet to the skin. The snow balled on the feet of our shod animals causing much floundering and adding to the fatigue of travel. About two o'clock we came to Wolf Creek, crossed to the right side of the valley and continued to march till we came to a clump of fallen timbers and there went into camp with our wagon train far behind. As soon as the horses were unsaddled everyone except the horse holders was gathering fuel for fires. The valley was alive with rabbits and all messes were supplied with rabbit stew. Our rawhide-covered saddles were soaked. The unequal drying warped the saddle trees which subsequently caused that bane of cavalry – many sore backs. Snow, eighteen inches "on the level"; distance marched, about fifteen miles.

The snowfall ceased during the night. The sun rose on the 24th with clear skies and with warmer weather. The snow melted rapidly. The glare of the bright sunshine caused much discomfort and a number of cases of snowblindness. Some buffalo were killed and many rabbits. Some deer were seen. We camped on Wolf Creek. Distance marched, about 18 miles.

November 25th we marched some distance up Wolf Creek and then turned in a southerly direction toward the Canadian. As we approached the summit of the divide, the peaks of the Antelope Hills loomed up and became our marker for the rest of the day. We made camp late that evening on a small stream about a mile from the Canadian. The day's march had been tedious. The melting snows balled on our shod animals during the long pull to the divide. A number of horses and mules gave out, but were brought in late that night. Wood was very scarce, but usually the quartermaster sergeants would load some wood in the cook wagon when packing and they usually were on the lookout for fuel on the march.

At daybreak, November 26th, Major Elliott, with troops G, H, and M, some white scouts and Osage trailers, started up the north side of the Canadian to scout for a possible trail of war parties. The remainder of the command and the wagon train marched to the Canadian to cross to the south side. To "California Joe" had been given the task of finding a ford. The river was high and rising, current swift and full of floating snow and slush ice. After much floundering he found a practical ford. The cavalry crossed first and assembled on the plain. Owing to the quicksand bottom each wagon was double teamed and rushed through without halting. A mounted man preceded each team and other mounted men were alongside to "whoop 'em up".

While this tedious crossing and parking was going on General Custer and a number of officers went to the tops of the hills to view the country. The highest peak was about three hundred feet above the plain. Suddenly we were enveloped in a cloud of frozen mist. Looking at the sun we were astonished to see it surrounded by three ellipses with rainbow tints, the axes marked by sundogs, except the lower part of the third or outer ellipse which seemingly was below the horizon, eleven sundogs. This phenomenon was not visible to those on the plain below.

As the last of the wagons had crossed and the rear guard was floundering in crossing, someone of our group on the hills called out, "Hello, here comes somebody." But General Custer had already seen him and had focused his field glasses on the galloping scout, but he said nothing. It was a tense moment when Jack Corbin rode up and began his report.

Major Elliott had marched up the Canadian about twelve miles when he came to the abandoned camp of a war party of about one hundred and fifty; he had crossed the river and was following the trail which was not over twenty-four hours old, and asked for instructions. Corbin was given a fresh horse to return to Major Elliott with instructions to follow the trail till dark, then halt till the command joined him.

Officers' call was sounded and when assembled we were told the news and ordered to be prepared to move as soon as possible. One wagon was assigned to each squadron (two troops), one to Troop G and the teamsters, and one to headquarters; seven in all, and one ambulance under the quartermaster, Lieutenant James M. Bell. These were to carry light supplies and extra ammunition. I cannot recall of just what the limited supplies consisted. Each trooper was ordered to carry one hundred rounds of ammunition on his person. (They were armed with the Spencer magazine carbine and Colt revolver, paper cartridges and caps.) The main train guarded by about eighty men under the command of the officer of the day was to follow as rapidly as possible. For this guard men with weak horses were selected. Captain Louis M. Hamilton, a grandson of Alexander Hamilton, was officer of the day. He was greatly distressed because this duty fell to him and begged to go along to command his squadron, but was refused unless he could get some officer to exchange with him. Lieutenant E. G. Mathey, who was snowblind, agreed to take his place.

Soon the regiment was ready to move and we struck in a direction to intercept the trail of Elliott's advance. We pushed along almost without rest till about 9 p.m. before we came to Elliott's halting place. There we had coffee made, care being taken to conceal the fires as much as possible. Horses were unsaddled and fed. At 10 p.m. we were again in the saddle with instructions to make as little noise as possible – no loud talking, no matches were to be lighted. Tobacco users were obliged to console themselves with the quid. Little Beaver, Osage Chief, with one of his warriors, had the lead dismounted as trailers; then followed the other Indian and white scouts with whom General Custer rode to be near the advance. The cavalry followed at a distance of about a half mile. The snow had melted during the day but at night the weather had turned cold and the crunching noise could be heard for a considerable distance.

After a couple of hours' march, the trailers hurried back for the command to halt. General Custer rode up to investigate when Little Beaver informed him that he "smelled smoke." Cautious investigation disclosed the embers of a fire which the guides decided from conditions had been made by the boy herders while grazing the pony herds and from this deduced that the village could not be far distant. The moon had risen and there was little difficulty in following the trail and General Custer rode behind the trailers to watch the developments. On nearing the crest of any rise, the trailer would crawl to the crest to reconnoitre, but seeing Little Beaver exercise greater caution than usual and then shading his eyes from the moon, the General felt there was something unusual. On his return the General asked, "What is it?" and Little Beaver replied, "Heap Injuns down there." Dismounting and advancing with the same caution as the guide, he made his personal investigation, but could only see what appeared to be a herd of animals. Asking why he thought there were Indians down there, Little Beaver replied. "Me heard dog bark." Listening intently they not only heard the bark of a dog, but the tinkling of a bell, indicating a pony herd, and then the cry of an infant.

Satisfied that a village had been located, the General returned to the command, assembled the officers, and, after removing sabres, took us all to the crest where the situation was explained or rather conjectured. The barking of the dogs and the occasional cry of infants located the direction of the village and the tinkling of the bells gave the direction of the herds. Returning and resuming our sabres, the General explained his plans and assigned squadron commanders their duties and places. Major Elliott, with Troops G, H, and M was to march well to our left and approach the village from the northeast or easterly direction as determined by the ground, etc. Captain Thompson, with B and F, was to march well to our right so as to approach from the southeast, connecting with Elliott. Captain Myers, with E and I, was to move by the right so as to approach from a southerly direction. The wagons under Lieutenant Bell and Captain Benteen's squadron – H and M – had been halted about two or three miles on the trail to await the outcome of the investigations.

Just after dismissing the officers and as we were separating, General Custer called my name. On reporting, he directed me to take a detail, go back on the trail to where Captain Benteen and the wagons were, give his compliments to Captain Benteen and instruct him to rejoin the command, and Lieutenant Bell to hold the wagons where they were till he heard the attack which would be about daybreak. "Tell the Adjutant the number of men you want and he will make the detail. How many do you want?" I replied, "One orderly." He then said, "Why do you say that? You can have all you want." I replied that one was all I wanted – "to take more would increase the chances of accident and delay."

I delivered my messages and returned with Captain Benteen's squadron. The camp guard remained with the wagons.

Upon the arrival of Captain Benteen's squadron. Major Elliott proceeded to take position, also Captain Thompson and later Captain Myers.

Before the first streak of dawn, General Custer's immediate command as quietly as possible moved into place facing nearly east, Lieutenant Cooke's sharp-shooters in advance of the left dismounted. General Custer and staff were followed by the band mounted. Captain West's squadron was on the right and Captain Hamilton's on the left, the standard and guard in the center. Troop K (West's) was on the right flank and I had command of the first platoon.

With the dawn we were ordered to remove overcoats and haversacks, leaving one man of each organization in charge with orders to load them in the wagons when Lieutenant Bell came up. Following the General, the command marched over the crest of the ridge and advanced some distance to another lower ridge. Waiting till sunrise we began to feel that the village had been abandoned although the dogs continued their furious barkings. Then "little by little" we advanced. Captain West came to me with orders to charge through the village but not to stop, to continue through and round up the pony herds.

With all quiet in the early dawn, Major Elliott's command had reached a concealed position close to the village, but was waiting for the signal from headquarters. The furious barking of the dogs aroused an Indian who came from his lodge, ran to the bank of the Washita, looked about and fired his rifle. I was told that a trooper had raised his head to take aim and was seen by this Indian. With the alarm thus given, the command opened fire. The trumpeters sounded the charge and the band began to play "Garry Owen," but by the time they had played one strain their instruments froze up.

My platoon advanced as rapidly as the brush and fallen timbers would permit until we reached the Washita which I found with steep, high banks. I marched the platoon by the right flank a short distance, found a "pony crossing," reformed on the right bank, galloped through the right of the village without contact with a warrior, and then proceeded to round up the pony herds.

As I passed out of the village, Captain Thompson's and Captain Myers' squadrons came over the high ridge on my right. Both had lost their bearings during their night marching and failed to make contacts for the opening attack.

At the opening of the attack, the warriors rushed to the banks of the stream. Those in front of Custer's command were soon forced to retire in among the tepees, and most of them being closely followed retreated to ravines and behind trees and logs, and in depressions where they maintained their positions till the last one was killed A few escaped down the valley. This desperate fighting was carried on mostly by sharpshooters waiting for a head to show. Seventeen Indians were killed in one depression.

Lieutenant Bell, when he heard the firing, rushed his teams to join the oommand and while loading the overcoats and haversacks was attacked by a superior force and the greater part of them had to be abandoned. His arrival with the reserve ammunition was a welcome reinforcement.

While the fighting was going on, Major Elliott, seeing a group of dismounted Indians escaping down the valley, called for volunteers to make pursuit. Nineteen men, including Regimental Sergeant Major Kennedy responded. As his detachment moved away, he turned to Lieutenant Hale waved his hand and said: "Here goes for a brevet or a coffin."

After passing through the village, I went in pursuit of pony herds and found them scattered in groups about a mile below the village. I deployed my platoon to make the roundup and took a position for observation. While the roundup was progressing, I observed a group of dismounted Indians escaping down the opposite side of the valley. Completing the roundup, and starting them toward the village, I turned the herd over to Lieutenant Law who had come with the second platoon of the troop and told him to take them to the village, saying that I would take my platoon and go in pursuit of the group I had seen escaping down the valley.

Crossing the stream and striking the trail, I followed it till it came to a wooded draw where there was a large pony herd. Here I found the group had mounted. Taking the trail which was well up on the hillside of the valley, and following it about a couple of miles, I discovered a lone tepee, and soon after two Indians circling their ponies. A high promontory and ridge projected into the valley and shut off the view of the valley below the lone tepee. I knew the circling of the warriors meant an alarm and rally, but I wanted to see what was in the valley beyond them. Just then Sergeant Conrad, who had been a captain of Ohio volunteers, and Sergeant Hughes, who had served in the 4th U.S. Cavalry in that country before the Civil War, came to me and warned me of the danger of going ahead. I ordered them to halt the platoon and wait till I could go to the ridge to see what was beyond. Arriving at and peering over the ridge, I was amazed to find that as far as I could see down the well wooded, tortuous valley there were tepees – tepees. Not only could I see tepees, but mounted warriors scurrying in our direction. I hurried back to the platoon and returned at the trot till attacked by the hostiles, when I halted, opened fire, drove the hostiles to cover, and then deployed the platoon as skirmishers.

The hillsides were cut by rather deep ravines and I planned to retreat from ridge to ridge. Under the cavalry tactics of 1841, the retreat of skirmishers was by the odd and even numbers, alternating in lines to the rear. I instructed the line in retreat to halt on the next ridge and cover the retreat of the advance line. This was successful for the first and second ridges, but at the third I found men had apparently forgotten their numbers and there was some confusion, so I divided the skirmishers into two groups, each under a sergeant, and thereafter had no trouble.

Finally the hostiles left us and we soon came to the pony herd where the group we had started to pursue had mounted. I had not had a single casualty. During this retreat we heard heavy firing on the opposite side of the valley, but being well up on the side hills we could not see through the trees what was going on. There was a short lull when the firing again became heavy and continued till long after we reached the village, in fact, nearly all day.

In rounding up the pony herd, I found Captain Barnitz' horse, *General*, saddled but no bridle. On reaching the village I turned over the pony herd and at once reported to General Custer what I had done and seen. When I mentioned the "big village," he exclaimed, "What's that?" and put me through a lot of rapid fire questions. At the conclusion I told him about finding Captain Barnitz' horse and asked what had happened. He told me that Captain Barnitz had been severely and probably mortally wounded.

Leaving the General in a "brown study" I went to see my friend and former Captain, Barnitz. I found him under a pile of blankets and buffalo robes, suffering and very quiet. I hunted up Captain Lippincott, Assistant Surgeon, and found him with his hands over his eyes suffering intense pain from snowblindness. He was very pessimistic as to Barnitz' recovery and insisted that I tell him that there was no hope unless he could be kept perfectly quiet for several days as he feared the bullet had passed through the bowels. I went back to Captain Barnitz and approached the momentous opinion of the surgeon as bravely as I could and then blurted it out, when he exclaimed, "Oh hell! they think because my extremities are cold I am going to die, but if I could get warm I'm sure I'll be all right. These blankets and robes are so heavy I can hardly breathe." I informed the first sergeant and the men were soon busy gathering fuel and building fires.

In the midst of this, the general sent for me and again questioned me about the big village. At that time many warriors were assembling on the high hills north of the valley overlooking the village and the General kept looking in that direction. At the conclusion of his inquiry, I told him that I had heard that Major Elliott had not returned and suggested that possibly the heavy firing I had heard on the opposite side of the valley might have been an attack on Elliott's party. He pondered this a bit and said slowly, "I hardly think so, as Captain Myers has been fighting down there all morning and probably would have reported it."

I left him and a while later he sent for me again, and, on reporting, told me that he had Romeo, the interpreter, make inquiries of the squaw prisoners and they confirmed my report of the lower village. He then ordered me to take Troop K and destroy all property and not allow any looting – but destroy everything.

I allowed the prisoners to get what they wanted. As I watched them, they only went to their own tepees. I began the destruction at the upper end of the village, tearing down tepees and piling several together on the tepee poles, set fire to them. (All tepees were made of tanned buffalo hides.) As the fires made headway, all articles of personal property – buffalo robes, blankets, food, rifles, pistols, bows and arrows, lead and caps, bullet molds, etc. – were thrown in the fires and destroyed. I doubt but that many small curios went into the pockets of men engaged in this work. One man brought to me that which I learned was a bridal gown, a "one piece dress," adorned all over with bead work and elks' teeth on antelope skins as soft as the finest broadcloth. I started to show it to the General and ask to keep it, but as I passed a big fire, I thought, "What's the use, 'orders is orders'," and threw it in the blaze. I have never ceased to regret that destruction. All of the powder found I spilled on the ground and "flashed".

I was present in August 1868, at Fort Larned, Kansas, when the annuities were issued, promised by the Medicine Lodge Peace Treaties of 1867, and saw the issue of rifles, pistols, powder, caps, lead and bullet molds to these same Cheyennes.

While this destruction was going on, warriors began to assemble on the hill slopes on the left side of the valley facing the village, as if to make an attack. Two squadrons formed near the left bank of the stream and started on the "Charge" when the warriors scattered and fled. Later, a few groups were seen on the hill tops but they made no hostile demonstrations.

As the last of the tepees and property was on fire, the General ordered me to kill all the ponies except those authorized to be used by the prisoners and given to scouts. We tried to rope them and cut their throats, but the ponies were frantic at the approach of a White man and fought viciously. My men were getting very tired so I called for reinforcements and details from other organizations were sent to complete the destruction of about eight hundred ponies. As the last of the ponies were being shot nearly all the hostiles left. This was probably because they could see our prisoners and realized that any shooting they did might endanger them.

Searching parties were sent to look for dead and wounded of both our own and hostiles. A scout having reported that he had seen Major Elliott and party in pursuit of some escapes down the right side of the valley, Captain Myers went down the valley about two miles but found no trace.

A while before sunset, as the command was forming to march down the valley, the General sent for me to ride with him to show him the place from which we could see the village below. There was no attempt to conceal our formation or the direction of our march. The command in column of fours, covered by skirmishers, the prisoners in the rear of the advance troops, standard and guidons "to the breeze," the chief trumpeter sounded the advance and we were "on our way," the band playing, "Ain't I Glad to Get Out of the Wilderness." The observing warriors followed our movement till twilight, but made no hostile demonstration. Then as if they had divined our purpose there was a commotion and they departed down the valley.

When we came in sight of the promontory and ridge from which I had discovered the lower villages, I pointed them out to the General. With the departure of the hostiles our march was slowed down till after dark, when the command was halted, the skirmishers were quietly withdrawn to rejoin their troops, the advance counter-marched, joined successively by the organizations in the rear, and we were on our way on our back trail. We marched briskly till long after midnight when we bivouacked till daylight with the exception of one squadron which was detached to hurry on to our supply train, the safety of which caused great anxiety. I was detailed to command the prisoners and special guard.

At daylight the next morning, we were on the march to meet our supply train and encountered it some time that forenoon. We were glad that it was safe, but disappointed that Major Elliott and party had not come in. After supper in the evening, the officers were called together and each one questioned as to the casualties of enemy warriors, locations, etc. Every effort was made to avoid duplications. The total was found to be one hundred and three.

The Washita "battle" was one of many controversies which trailed in the wake of George Armstrong Custer. The village attacked was that of the unfortunate Black Kettle, whose tipi flew a white flag. Black Kettle and his wife were shot in the back as they tried to flee across the Washita, and died face down in the water. Contrary to the claims of the 7th Cavalry, the soldiers killed not 103 warriors but eleven. The rest of the dead were women, children and old men.

The destruction of Black Kettle's village was a Western tragedy, but it was not another Sand Creek. Black Kettle was the leading peace chief of the Cheyenne, yet his camp harboured warriors. The chief had also been informed that he would be attacked unless he surrendered to Sheridan. Black Kettle's village was a mixture of Indians who wanted war and Indians who wanted peace. It was the Indian nation in miniature.

Sheridan applauded Custer for the Washita battle, which appeared to have ended Indian resistance on the central and southern plains. All winter long, straggles of Indians appeared at Fort Cobb wanting to surrender. To encourage the recalcitrant, Custer summoned Cheyenne chiefs to a peace council – then seized three of them and threatened to hang them on the spot unless the tribe carried out his demands. More Indians surrendered and moved onto reservations. When the Comanche arrived at Fort Cobb, one of their chiefs introduced himself to Sheridan. *"Tosawi*, good Indian," he said. Sheridan replied: "The only good Indians I ever saw were dead."

In March 1869 General Philip Sheridan was able to report to the War Department that the tribes assigned to the Indian Territory were living quietly on their reservations.

Custer's victory at the Washita was not, as Sheridan thought, the end of the Indian war on the central and southern plains. But it was the beginning of the end.

The Struggle for the Staked Plains

ALWAYS AGAINST US

There was something about the Comanche and the horse. They were uncannily conjoined. Writing in the 1830s the frontier artist George Catlin, who regarded the Comanche as "homely", remarked that as soon as one of the tribe "lays his hand upon his horse, his face, even, becomes handsome, and he gracefully flies away like a different being".

All who witnessed the Comanche on horseback were amazed and scared in equal measure by their skill. A favourite Comanche feat was to hang under the neck of the horse to fire arrows or throw fourteen-foot lances. Some Comanche warriors could hang under the belly of the horse to shoot. While many Plains tribes rode to war and then got off and fought on foot, the Comanche disdained any form of pedestrian hunting or warfare. Catlin, among others, considered the Comanche as "undoubtedly the most bold and efficient warriors on horseback". He also noted their love of putting on an equine show:

After a general shake of the hand with the officers, they invited us to the great Camanchee village, some three or four days' march, to which they conducted us, and showed us daily, as we passed along, their astonishing feats in slaying the buffaloes, by which they furnished the regiment with daily food; and, in the meantime, they gave also to the officers and men, what they never before had seen, an exhibition of their powers of taking and breaking the wild horse.

Arrived on the summit of a hill, overlooking an extensive and beautiful valley, they requested the regiment to halt, and pointing, showed us the great Camanchee village, at the distance of three or four miles, with eight or ten thousand horses and mules grazing on the plains around it.* They then led us into the valley, and at the distance of a mile or so from the village, requested us to halt again, for the chief and the cavalry of the tribe were coming out to meet and welcome us.

Colonel Dodge formed his regiment in three columns, himsef occupying the front, with his staff; and after resting an hour or so in that position, two or three thousand horsemen were seen, in real military order, advancing towards us. The chief was in advance, with his body-guard around him, and his colours flying on each side – the one a white flag, a flag of truce, and the other blood red showing that he was ready for either war or peace, whichever we might propose.

The white flag was seen waving in the hands of each of our ensigns, and the red flag was lost sight of. The chief now advanced, shook hands with Colonel Dodge and the rest of the officers, and then formed his army in

*Raids and the taming of mustangs made the Comanche enormously rich in horses. An ordinary warrior often owned 250 horses, a chief a thousand.

a double column of nearly a mile in length, dressed and manoeuvred with a precision equal to any cavalry manoeuvre I ever saw, himself and his staff taking their position in the centre, and facing the officers of the dragoons.

Their equine prowess aside, the Shoshoni-speaking Comanche were originally mountain dwellers from the north ("Comanche" is derived from the Ute *kohmachts*, "always against us"), who arrived on the south plains as late as 1700. Yet as nobody took to the horse like the Comanche, their ability to fight a highly mobile warfare won them a huge 240,000-square-mile empire on the high plains, from which they evacuated the eastern Apache, the Navajo and others. The five main Comanche bands also blocked the northward expansion of the Spanish, confining them in the bulk to southern Texas. At the peak of their power, in the early nineteenth century, the Comanche were 20,000 strong. Their horses were almost countless.

And then the Anglo-Americans started to appear in east Texas. The Comanche had a reputation for belligerence, but the Whites matched it. A long and venomous war between the Anglo-Americans and the Comanche began shortly after Texas won independence from Mexico in 1836. Massacres and reprisals became commonplace on both sides.

One of the first Comanche victories in 1836 was at Parker's Fort, a stockaded cluster of homesteads in east-central Texas. The Comanche raiders killed and scalped the men, and ripped their genitals out. Some of the women were raped, and five were borne off as captives, a practice the Comanche adopted to offset their low birth rate. They included the nine-year-old Cynthia Ann Parker. When she was eighteen Cynthia Ann became the wife of Chief Peta Nocona of the

Nocona band. Early in the marriage she bore him a son Quanah ("Fragrant"). Another son, Pecos, and a daughter, Topasannah ("Prairie Flower"), followed.

In December 1860, while the Nocona band were camped near the Pease River and the men were off hunting buffalo, a force of 40 Texas Rangers and 21 US. cavalry struck. Cynthia Ann was recaptured and taken, with her daughter, back to the settlements. Cynthia Ann was welcomed by her brother and her uncle. But she mourned for her sons and several times tried to ride away to join them. When her daughter died in 1864, Cynthia Ann starved herself to death.

Meanwhile, her sons, Quanah and Pecos, had suffered other tragedies. Their father had died from an infected arrow wound. Then Pecos died of disease, probably in one of the cholera epidemics that repeatedly decimated the Comanche.

With no ties to hold him Quanah joined the Quahadi, a particularly warlike and anti-White band of the Comanche. When the Civil War stripped Texan forts of US soldiers and sent 60,000 Texan men flocking to the Confederate colours, the Quahadi Comanche were in the forefront of the devastation of central Texas. Hundreds of settlers were killed, their homes burnt to the ground.

In the course of these Comanche Wars of the 1860s, Quanah rose to become a war chief of the Quanadi band, second only to Bull Bear, the main Quahadi leader. Quanah was famed for his exploits in war, and his unbending opposition to the Whites. During a debate with other Comanche chiefs he declared: "My band is not going to live on the reservation. Tell the White chiefs that the Quahadi are warriors."

Refusing to attend the Medicine Lodge peace talks of 1867, Quanah instead marauded Texas, always afterwards retiring to the Quahadi sanctuary of the Staked Plains, a hostile arid land in the Texas Panhandle in which the Whites showed little interest. There the Quahadi were joined by other holdout bands of Comanche and Kiowa who refused to take the White road offered at Medicine Lodge, such as that of Woman Heart. On the remote Staked Plains the Indians still had freedom to live in the old ways.

It was about the last place on the southern plains where they could do so.

JUMPING THE RESERVATION

Occasionally news of the Comanche and Kiowa who had signed the Medicine Lodge Treaty came to the Texas Panhandle. The news was not good.

Government rations on the barren Comanche–Kiowa reservation in Indian Territory were pitiful. The inhabitants resented the attempts to teach them to farm, and the intrusions of Whites and eastern Indians onto their lands. Most of all these free-riding hunters of the endless plains were unable to accept confinement, or forsake the calendar joys of the buffalo hunt. Before long, Kiowa and Comanche alike were jumping the reservation to hunt. Outside reservation limits they came into violent conflict with White settlers.

In spring 1871, Satanta (White Bear) led a hundred Kiowa and Comanche off the reservation. Some of their annuity goods had been diverted to Texans, and they decided to make up the loss with a raid. They also wanted to stop a railroad being built across their old and beloved hunting grounds. On the prairie they spotted a luckless mule train and swooped down on it. Seven teamsters were killed. The Indians then plundered the train and made off with forty-one mules.

When he returned to the reservation, Satanta was

summoned before General William T. Sherman, out in the West on a tour of inspection. Before Sherman, Satanta gave a defiant account of the raid.

"The White people are preparing to build a railroad through our country, which will not be permitted . . . More recently I was arrested by soldiers and kept in confinement for several days. But that is played out now. There is never to be any more Kiowas arrested. I want you to remember that. Because of this, I led [Kiowa young braves] to Texas – to teach them how to fight."

At this, Sherman gave a sharp command and soldiers, previously hidden, appeared at the windows behind him with their rifles levelled. Satanta pulled a carbine from beneath his blanket and pointed it at Sherman's heart. For a few, brief moments it looked as though Satanta and the chiefs with him woul kill Sherman in a suicidal shooting match. The General's nerve held, however and the chiefs put up their guns. Satanta, Satank and Big Tree were arrested and sent to Texas to be tried for murder.

During the journey to Texas Satank, manacled hand and foot, began singing his death song: "O sun you remain forever, but we Ko-eet-senko must die,/O earth you remain forever, but we Ko-eet-senko must die." He made a grab for a rifle, but was shot before he could fire it. Satanta and Big Tree were tried and sentenced to death by the court in Jacksboro, Texas, in July 1871 but on the advice of Indian agents and the trial judge, who feared an Indian uprising if the chiefs were hanged, the sentences were commuted to life imprisonment.

But the Kiowas wanted Satanta, their great chief, free. When their entreaties failed, they began raiding. They captured an army ordinance train, drove off 127 mules from Camp Supply, and raided the home of a Texas family. Lone Whites on trails and in settlements were murdered.

Once again, the Kiowa were at war.

INVASION OF THE STAKED PLAINS

The tribulations of the Kiowa alarmed and agitated the Quahadi Comanche. Chief Quanah resolved ever more strongly to resist the White man. He soon had the chance to show his resolution.

Desirous of halting Quahadi raiding in Texas, the Army assigned Colonel Ranald Slidell Mackenzie to conquer the band and other holdouts operating from the Staked Plains. Unapproachable and merciless, Mackenzie was considered by Ulysses S. Grant to be the most "promising young officer in the Army". Like other Civil War heroes, however, he had much to learn about Indian fighting.

In September 1871, Mackenzie assembled 600 troopers for an invasion of the Staked Plains. But Quanah and Bull Bear did not oblige Mackenzie with the frontal fight he wanted Instead, they harried his columns and made reckless lightning thrusts, before wheeling away and vanishing. Often the war parties were led by Quanah himself. He made an impressive, unforgettable sight in battle. A cavalry officer who fought Quanah wrote in his memoirs:

A large and powerfully built chief led the bunch on a coal black racing pony. His heels nervously working in the animal's side, with a six-shooter poised in the air, he seemed the incarnation of savage brutal joy. His face was smeared with black war paint, which gave his features a satanic look. A large cruel mouth added to his ferocious appearance. Bells jingled as he rode at headlong speed, followed by the leading warriors, all eager to outstrip him in the race.

Shortly after midnight on 10 October 1871 Quanah led a charge through Mackenzie's encampment, flapping buffalo skins and ringing bells to panic the cavalry's horses. The Quahadi ran off 70 mounts, including Mackenzie's own prized animal. When Mackenzie sent a detachment of troopers after the Comanche, the Indians unceremoniously beat them off.

The relentless Mackenzie kept after the Quahadi. But in mid-October blizzards caused him to end the mission. On the way home, Mackenzie chased two Comanche who were trailing the column – and got an arrow in the hip.

But the redoubtable Mackenzie was back in the field by March 1872, hunting the Comanche. He campaigned throughout the summer, and in September his scouts came across a camp of the Kotsoteka Comanche on McClellan Creek. Mackenzie and 231 troopers attacked, killing 23 warriors and taking 124 women and children captive.

Mackenzie's victory at the creek was a crippling blow to the Kotsoteka. Most of the band trickled to the reservation. Even the Quahadi lost their morale, and raiding almost ceased. A strange quiet descended on the west Texas frontier.

It held for almost two years, but in 1874 the South Plains War set the Panhandle afire.

Having stripped Kansas of buffalo, White hunters began to drift south in March 1874 and set up a base near the deserted trading post of Adobe Walls (where Kit Carson had fought the Comanche a decade before) on the South Canadian River. The presence of these buffalo hunters enraged the Indians, for it seemed the end of their world.

Their fear was well founded. The hide hunters, in destroying the buffalo herds, were eradicating the Indians' food supply. The army cheered the hunters on. General Sheridan informed a joint session of the Texas legislature: "[They, the hunters] have done . . . more to settle the vexed Indians question than the entire regular army. They are destroying the Indians' commissary . . . For the sake of a lasting peace, let them kill, skin and sell until the buffaloes are exterminated."

For the sake of the last buffalo, the White hunters at Adobe Walls needed to be fought.

Another cause of the war was the governor of Texas. In 1873 the Kiowa chiefs Satanta and Big Tree were released from prison. This was offset by the demand of the governor of Texas that five Comanche braves on the reservation be surrendered to him as punishment for a raid which had occurred on Texas.

The Comanche refused to give up five men to an unknown fate. Instead, they moved out on the plains. So did the Cheyenne, Arapaho and some of the Kiowa and Kiowa–Apache.

In the spring of 1874, Quanah called a great council of all the Indians holding out on the south plains. They met near the mouth of Elk Creek and debated, and held a medicine dance. Isa-tai (Rear End of a Wolf), a young Quahadi medicine nan, prophesied that an all-out attack would drive the White man away. "The buffalo shall come back everywhere," said Isa-tai, "so that there shall be feasting and plenty in the lodges. The Great Spirit has taught me strong medicine which will turn away the White man's bullets."

Quanah probably thought Isa-tai a fraud, but saw how desperately the others wanted to believe his predictions. He even allowed Isa-tai to organize a sun dance, not a ceremony the Comanche observed. After the celebration, the Indians agreed to launch a combined attack on the buffalo hunters at Adobe Walls. From there they would move north, raiding all the camps in Panhandle country.

Before dawn on 27 June 1874, 700 warriors moved through the darkness and took up positions in the timber at the edge of Adobe Walls Creek. Before them were the three adobe buildings of the camp, and 30 sleeping hunters.

The hunters would have been slain in their sleep but for the luck of a ridge pole which happened to snap just before daylight. The noise awoke the hunter Billy Dixon, who chanced to go outside. In the grey dawn he saw hundreds of warriors moving towards the camp and shouted the alarm.

The hunters, now alert, took up positions in the buildings, and staved off repeated assaults with their new long-range Sharps rifles, fitted with telescopic sights. A warrior was knocked off his horse by one of the hunters – who included the soon-to-be-famous lawman Bat Masterson – at a distance of nearly a mile. As Red Cloud had found in the Wagon Box Fight on the Bozeman Trail, numbers or even unlimited courage were no match for innovations in gun technology. Although Quanah led the warriors to the very doors of the stockade, so that they could beat upon them with their rifle butts, the Indians could not break in.

After three days of desultory siege, Quanah called his warriors off. He was injured in the shoulder, and many of his best braves were dead. The remainder had lost all heart.

Superstition made the Plains Indian a mercurial fighter. He lived by magic, but if the magic failed he simply gave up the fight. Isa-tai had proven to be a false prophet. When his horse, which was covered in bullet-proof paint, was shot from under him, the Comanche at Adobe Walls jeered.

The buffalo hunters had lost only three men, one of them

killed by Quanah. When the Indians withdrew, the buffalo hunters decapitated the bodies of the warriors left behind and stuck their heads on the poles of the stockade.

Quanah failed at Adobe Walls, but the Indians were still on the warpath. And more and more Indians – even some Osage – were riding off the reservations to join them. Splitting into small groups, they unleashed their frustration in raids across the southern plains from Texas to Colorado, from New Mexico to Kansas. Every time they took easy, unsuspecting pickings. About eighty Whites were killed.

The war might have fizzled out, save for the usual stupidity by some army hothead. At the Witchita agency at Anadarko, surrendering Nokoni Comanche were fired upon when their chief, Red Food, gave a whoop of greeting; it was mistaken for a war cry. In the ensuing battle, the agency school was burned down and four civilians killed. The Indians lit out for the Panhandle. A lot more people would die because of the blunder at Anadarko.

To subdue the newly enlarged host of hostiles, the army sent out columns from Fort Griffin, Fort Concho, Fort Sill, Camp Supply, and Fort Union. Three thousand troopers prosecuted a scorched-earth policy to deny the warriors essential supplies, burning their camps and killing their pony herds. Eventually the columns converged on the last holdout of the Southern Plains: the Staked Plains of the Panhandle.

The Staked Plains (named so by the Spanish, "Llano Estacado") are more than an isolated, high tableland. There are deep gashes and gorges, eroded in the rock by rivers and streams. The most stunning of these is the vast Palo Duro Canyon, gouged by the Prairie Dog Town Fork of the Red River, which runs for forty miles across the plain, eight hundred feet deep and miles wide.

The Palo Duro was almost unknown to White men when,

on September 24 1874, the 4th cavalry under Ranald Mackenzie began descending its steep sides. Below them, strung out on the canyon floor, were camps of Comanche, Kiowa and Cheyenne holdouts.

The Indians, forgetting that the White man fought even when the grass had turned dry, had posted no guard. Mackenzie's men were halfway down the canyon before the attack was discovered. Bewildered, the Indians fled in panic away down the canyon.

And so left all their possessions and supplies for Mackenzie's men to burn and break. Tipis, hides, meat, guns – anything and everything that was usable was utterly destroyed. Even kettles, which had their bottoms knocked out.

After the destruction, the regiment rounded up the horse herds. More than a thousand ponies were then duly slaughtered.

The Indians were destitute in a cold world. Within days, numbers of "hostiles" began to straggle into Fort Sill.

Meanwhile, Mackenzie kept up the pursuit. Numerous pitched battles – and a massacre of Cheyenne at Sappa River – followed, but it was the constant harrassment and deprivation that obliged the Indians to surrender. Of the surrendering Cheyenne at Darlington, their agent wrote: "A more wretched and poverty-stricken community than these people presented after they were placed in the prison camp it would be difficult to imagine. Bereft of lodges and the most ordinary cooking apparatus; with no ponies nor other means of transportation for food and water; half starved and with scarcely anything that could be called clothing, they were truly objects of pity; and for the first time the Cheyenne seemed to realize the power of government and their own inability to cope successfully therewith."

The last Indians to surrender on the Southern Plains were the wildest Comanche of all: the Quahadis. Not until April 1875 did the first Quahadi arrive at the reservation. Quanah and 400 followers continued to hold out until they received a message from Mackenzie, which informed them that if they surrendered they would be treated honourably. If they held out any longer, he would exterminate them. To the astonishment of the messenger, Quanah personally guaranteed to lead in the last of the Comanche.

On 2 June 1875 Quanah arrived at Fort Sill with his band, and over 1,500 horses in tow. The days of the free Native American on the southern plains were over for ever.

QUANAH PARKER LIVES IN PEACE

For 30 years Quanah had fought the White man. Now he took up their road. He was fortunate to escape imprisonment, which was the fate of some Comanche and Kiowa chiefs (among them Satanta, re-arrested on a fake charge; unable to endure prison, he committed suicide in 1876 by slashing his wrists and leaping from a window). After a period of model behaviour, Quanah was allowed to visit relatives of his mother, who made him welcome. He stayed with them, learned some English and studied farm tasks.

As he had once led his people in war, he began to lead them in peace. He made a big business out of the grazing rights the Comanche owned, leasing pasturage to Texas stockmen like Charles Goodnight and Burk Burnett. Burnett built Quanah Parker – as Quanah now called himself, in deference to his White blood – a large ranch house near Cache, Oklahoma, which became known as the "Comanche White House". Wearing a business suit, Quanah Parker lobbied governments, argued legal cases and invested in the railroads. He served as a judge, and in 1902 was elected deputy sheriff of Lawton, Oklahoma. Six years later, he was elected president of the local school district, which he had helped to create.

To do his duty by the Comanche, Quanah Parker was prepared to take up White ways. Yet he seldom compromised his Comanche cultural and spiritual heritage; he was a principal proponent of the ceremonial use of peyote, a spineless cactus which produces "buttons" containing a hallucinogenic drug. Over time the peyote rite became the focus for the Indian religion known as the Native American Church.

Quanah Parker died of pneumonia on 22 February 1911. In keeping with Comanche tradition, a medicine man flapped his hands over the body of Quanah like an eagle flaps its wings – and so the chief's spirit was called to the after-world.

Quanah Parker was buried next to his mother. Inside the White man's coffin, he was dressed in the full regalia of a Quahadi chief.

LITTLE BIG HORN

"We want no White men here. The Black Hills belong to me. If the Whites try to take them, I will fight."

Sitting Bull

"Come on, Lakotas! It's a good day to die."

Crazy Horse, at the battle of Little Big Horn

CLOUDS OVER THE BLACK HILLS

When the final war between the Sioux and the Whites came, it began in the Black Hills of Dakota, to the Sioux a special hallowed place. Although they had only arrived in the land themselves a century before, the Sioux had come to regard the Black Hills as the most sacred place on earth.

Under the terms of the Treaty of 1868, which the victorious Red Cloud had secured from the government, the Black Hills were promised to the Sioux for "as long as the grass shall grow." They would also hold forever the Powder River Buffalo range.

The ink of the treaty was hardly dry before small clouds of war began to hover over the Black Hills and the other lands held by the Sioux. White homesteaders were outraged that good land had been given to the Indians. Twenty Sioux chiefs, including Red Cloud, travelled east to Washington DC to put their case to President Grant.

Unlike previous Indian delegations, they refused to be diverted by sight-seeing and instead sat down for negotiation with the secretary of the interior. The secretary duly informed that they would have to locate to a new reservation in South Dakota, as agreed in the 1868 treaty. This was duly read out. So much of it was new to Red Cloud, that he erupted in anger. "I have never heard of it and do not mean to follow it. It is all lies."

Faced with Red Cloud's recalcitrance, the government dispatched him on a tourist jaunt to New York in the hope that he would be awed by the splendour of the White man's civilization. Instead Red Cloud took the opportunity to address a large audience of reformers at the Cooper Institute. He explained the reason for the current crisis:

In 1868 men came out and brought papers. We could not read them, and they did not tell us what was in them. We thought the treaty was to remove the forts, and that we should then cease from fighting . . .

When I reached Washington, the Great Father [President Grant] explained to me what the treaty was. and showed me that the interpreters had deceived me. All I want is right and just.

I wish to know why Commissioners are sent out to us who do nothing but rob us and get the riches of this world away from us.

Red Cloud's speech was a public relations triumph. A shamed government decided to compromise, and offered Red Cloud an agency thirty-two miles east of Fort Laramie.

This was as much as Red Cloud considered he could prise from the Whites. What he had seen of the white man's power in the east persuaded him that a military struggle against the US was fruitless. On his return home, Red Cloud hung up his war lance for ever. "I shall not go to war any more with the Whites," he informed the Sioux. "I shall do as my Great Father [the US president] says and make my people listen . . . I am done".

Red Cloud's decision split the Oglala Sioux. About two thirds of the Oglalas followed his path, while the rest stayed in the Powder River country and the Montana buffalo ranges, where they joined up with free bands of northern Teton Sioux. Increasingly, these holdout Sioux began to look for guidance to a Huncpapa medicine man called Sitting Bull (Tatanka Iyotake), who was as stubborn as his name suggested. In boyhood Sitting Bull had been nicknamed "Slow", for his wilful deliberation, and this aspect about him had never changed. Almost as influential as Sitting Bull was the Oglala warrior Crazy Horse. Although many found Crazy Horse strange – he believed that he lived in the world of dreams, and he always went into battle naked save for a loincloth – he was a fearless and inspired warrior. Such was his utter suspicion of and contempt for the White man that he refused to have his photograph taken by their cameras.

As each year passed, more and more little clouds of war began to accumulate over the northern plains. The slaughter of the American buffalo was continuing apace and threatening the last big herd, located in Montana–Wyoming. Settlers were edging onto Sioux lands. And then a second transcontinental railroad, the Northern Pacific began to reach out into the Far West, with surveying parties entering the Yellowstone River region – Teton Sioux land – in 1873. In the summer of that year, bands of Sioux under Crazy Horse skirmished with the cavalry assigned to protect the surveyors. The White horse soldiers were from the 7th Cavalry and were led by George Armstrong Custer. After his victory at the Washita, Custer had thrown himself into the role of frontier Indian fighter, and dressed in buckskin, complete with tassels. Custer relished fighting Indians, but was also attracted to them, to their heroic glory and their freedom. He had even taken an Indian mistress, Mo-nah-se-ta, daughter of the Cheyenne leader Little Rock.

The skirmishes in the Yellowstone were sharp probing engagements, curtain-raisers to a bigger affair. Second Lieutenant Charles Larned described one in a letter home:

At early dawn on the 10th our efforts to cross [the Tongue River] commenced, and it was not until 4 in the afternoon that they were reluctantly relinquished, after every expedient had been resorted to in vain. The current was too swift and fierce for our heavy cavalry.

We therefore went into bivouac close to the river bank to await the arrival of the main body, and slept that night as only men in such condition can sleep. We hardly anticipated the lively awakening that awaited us. Just at daylight our slumbers were broken by a sharp volley of musketry from the opposite bank, accompanied by shouts and yells that brought us all to our feet in an instant. As far up the river as we could see, clouds of dust announced the approach of our slippery foes, while the rattling volleys from the opposite woods, and the "zip," "zip" of the balls about our ears told us that there were a few evil disposed persons close by.

For half an hour, while the balls flew high, we lay still without replying, but when the occasional quiver of a wounded horse told that the range was being acquired by them, the horses and men were moved back from the river edge to the foot of the bluffs, and there drawn up in line of battle to await developments. A detachment of sharpshooters was concealed in the woods, and soon sent back a sharp reply to the thickening compliments from the other side. Our scouts and the Indians were soon exchanging chaste complimentary remarks in choice Sioux – such as: "We're coming over to give you h—;" "You'll see more Indians than you ever saw before in your life," and "Shoot, you son of a dog" from ours. Sure enough, over they came, as good as their word, above and below us, and in twenty minutes our scouts came tumbling down the bluffs head over heels, screeching: "Heap Indian come." Just at this moment General Custer rode up to the line, followed by a bright guidon, and made rapid disposition for the defence. Glad were we that the moment of action had arrived, and that we were to stand no longer quietly and grimly in line of battle to be shot at. One platoon of the first squadron on the left was moved rapidly up the bluffs, and thrown out in skirmish line on the summit, to hold the extreme left. The remainder of the squadron followed as quickly as it could be deployed, together with one troop of the Fourth Squadron.

On they came as before, 500 or 600 in number, screaming and yelling as usual, right onto the line before they saw it. At the same moment the regimental band, which had been stationed in a ravine just in rear, struck up "Garry Owen". The men set up a responsive shout, and a rattling volley swept the whole line.

The fight was short and sharp just here, the Indians rolling back after the first fire and shooting from a safer distance. In twenty minutes the squadrons were mounted and ordered to charge. Our evil-disposed friends tarried no longer, but fled incontinently before the pursuing squadrons. We chased them eight miles and over the river, only returning when the last Indian had gotten beyond our reach.

No less than a thousand warriors had surrounded us, and we could see on the opposite bluffs the scattered remnants galloping wildly to and fro. Just at the conclusion of the fight the infantry came up, and two shells from the Rodman guns completed the discomfiture of our demoralized foes. Our loss was one killed, Private Tuttle, E Troop, Seventh Cavalry, and three wounded. Among the latter, Lieutenant [Charles] Braden, Seventh Cavalry, while gallantly holding the extreme left, the hottest portion of the line, was shot through the thigh, crushing the bone badly. Four horses were killed and eight or ten wounded and deserve honorable mention, although noncombatants. Official estimates place the

Indian loss at forty killed and wounded and a large number of ponies.

To the disappointment of the 7th Cavalry they were suddenly withdrawn from the Yellowstone. So were the railwaymen. Overbuilding on the Northern Pacific had caused the bank backing the company to collapse. Within days the entire US financial system was in collapse. Within months a million Americans were out of work.

The year 1873 was destined to be a bad year for America; it also saw drought on the Great Plains, and swarms of locusts that devoured the crops, even the paint on houses.

A desperate nation began to seize on desperate solutions. There were rumours of gold in the Black Hills, the Sioux's hallowed ground, the ground given to them "forever". In July 1874, Custer, 600 soldiers and several newspapermen left Fort Abraham Lincoln near Bismarck, Dakota, on an expedition to the Black Hills. Ostensibly the purpose of the expedition was scientific and exploratory. But as everyone knew, its real mission was to determine whether there was gold in the hills; accompanying the soldiers were two prospectors.

On 27 July 1874 the prospectors found traces of gold at French Creek. By the spring of 1875 the Black Hills were alive with the sound of thousands of illegal White picks. Red Cloud and the other reservation leaders furiously demanded that the Whites should be removed, and called Custer "The Chief of all the thieves." Equally furiously, Whites demanded that the Indians be removed:

This abominable compact [the Treaty of 1868] is now pleaded as a barrier to the improvement and development of one of the richest and most fertile sections in

America. What shall be done with these Indian dogs in our manger? They will not dig gold or let others do it.

Yankton Press and Dakotian

The government tried to buy the Black Hills from the Sioux for $6 million, or lease mining rights at $400,000 a year. Red Cloud and the reservation Sioux met in council and turned the offer down.

As soon as the negotiation failed, the White invaders became totally brazen, laying out towns and organizing local governments in the Black Hills. Then they demanded troops to protect them.

Although the White settlers were acting illegally, Washington decided to remove the Indians instead. It was easier. In December, President Grant signed an executive order requiring all Indians in the "unceded land" to go voluntarily on to reservations by 31 January 1876. If they did not, they would be treated as "hostiles" and driven in. By this order, the government seized the Powder River country as well as the Black Hills.

News of the order was to be taken by messenger from the agencies to the camps of Sitting Bull, Crazy Horse, Gall, Rain-in-the-Face, Low Dog and the other Indians living up on the buffalo ranges. Blizzards and snowdrifts held up the messengers. Some camps never even received the order.

When the deadline came and the Powder River camps had not entered the reservation, the Secretary of War received a brief dispatch: "Said Indians are hereby turned over to the War Department for such action as you may deem proper."

No sooner had the snows in the northern ranges begun to thaw than General George Crook was in the field, destroying a Sioux–Cheyenne camp on the Powder River. Bad weather – including a blizzard so severe that the mercury in the expedition thermometer froze – caused Crook to return to camp unsatisfactorily early.

Meanwhile, General Phil Sheridan began to plan a three-pronged assault on the "hostiles". One column, led by Colonel John Gibbon, would drive down the Yellowstone from Fort Ellis. Crook would move up through Wyoming and strike the Indians from the south. A third column, under General Alfred Terry and Colonel Custer, would head west out of Dakota.

Throughout the spring, White soldiers gathered for the big campaign. The Army had been drastically reduced in strength since 1866, down to 27,000 men, was beset by bullying and poor pay (a mere $13 a month for privates), and weakened by alcoholism and scurvy. Disease killed more troopers than did Indians. A frequent morale-lowering lament of troopers in the 1870s was that Indians had better rifles (they seldom did). Despite all this, the 7th Cavalry, full of veterans, considered itself an elite, and was almost as good as it thought it was. On 17 May 1876, Custer – his long hair cut short for the campaign – and the 7th Cavalry marched out of Fort Lincoln towards Indian country, the regimental band striking up the familiar tones of "The Girl I Left Behind Me".

While the White soldiers had been gathering, so had the Native Americans. From all over the northern plains Indians gathered in the Powder River country. For the first time in years, more Indians left the reservation than joined it, as thousands streamed to the buffalo ranges for a joyous summer hunt. And for a war, if it was necessary.

By late May, Sitting Bull's camp had swollen to more than 7,000 people, fron the Teton Sioux (even some eastern Santee Sioux), Arapaho and other Northern tribes. Seldom before had so many Plains Indians come together.

During the second week of June, the great Indian camp moved up the Rosebud Valley to the head of Ash Creek. Here they held a Sun Dance. Among those who sought vision was Sitting Bull, whose adopted brother, Jumping Bull, cut 100 pieces of flesh from his arms with an awl and a sharp knife: then Sitting Bull danced with eyes fixed on the sun for 18 hours until he fell unconscious. At length, a great vision came: he saw many soldiers falling into the camp upside down. "These dead soldiers are the gifts of God", said Sitting Bull.

Shortly after the Sun Dance was over, Cheyenne scouts rushed into the camp to report that White soldiers headed by "Three Stars" (General Crook) were in the valley of the Rosebud. The Indians decided to intercept him.

On the morning of 17 June Crook and his 1,300 men, including Shoshoni and Crow scouts (always particularly keen to fight the Sioux), halted for coffee. Suddenly there was firing up ahead and shouts of "Sioux! Sioux!" from the scouts, and then Crazy Horse and 1,500 Sioux and Cheyenne warriors were right on top of the soldiers. All day long the battle raged over the hills, the Indians preventing Crook forming a single strong front. This was the sort of war Crazy Horse liked best, small isolated fights, a chaos in which Western military theory had no application or point. By nightfall, Crook had lost 57 men and, short of ammunition, opted to withdraw back to base camp at Goose Creek. He was immobilized for the rest of the summer.

The Indians had just beaten Crook – the Army's best Indian fighter. After a triumphal four-day scalp dance, the great Indian village moved towards the Greasy Grass River – the stream the White man called Little Big Horn.

THE BATTLE OF THE GREASY GRASS

Up on the Yellowstone the other two columns of the Army's campaign met in conference aboard the steamer *Far West*. A reconnaissance by the 7th Cavalry's Major Marcus A. Reno had located a great Indian trail leading towards Little Big Horn. General Terry, in overall command, decided to split his forces. He ordered Gibbon's infantry into the field, and sent Custer's fast-moving 7th Cavalry to pick up the Indian trail and follow it. There would be no escape for the Indians. They would be trapped between infantry and cavalry at Little Big Horn.

Custer drove his men relentlessly, a pace of 30 miles a day and more, hoping to defeat the Indians before the infantry could encounter them. On the second day out the cavalry hit the Indians' trail: it was over a mile wide. Ree and Crow scouts found scalps of Crook's soldiers which had been thrown aside. The scouts advised Custer to proceed with caution. He brushed them aside, and ordered his exhausted men to move on, towards the hills in the distance.

At dawn on 25 June, Custer's scouts climbed to the top of a mountain for a reconnaissance of the route ahead. As the light improved they could make out the Little Big Horn 15 miles away. And then they saw a pony herd which seemed to cover the distant land like a blanket. A second later they saw the hundreds upon hundreds of tipis; arranged in huge tribal circles, of the Huncpapas, the Miniconjous, the Oglalas, the San Arcs and the Cheyenne. There were nearly 7,000 Indians assembled before them, probably the greatest concentration ever of Plains Indians in one place.

Custer's scouts began singing their death songs. One told Custer that there were not enough bullets to kill all the Indians down there. Custer merely told his officers, "The largest Indian camp on the North American continent is ahead and I'm going to attack it."

A little after noon the 611 officers and men of the 7th Cavalry started down into the valley of the Little Big Horn. Not knowing the terrain or the disposition of the enemy, Custer made a fateful decision. He would reconnaissance in force – split the regiment into several components, which could be employed separately or together as circumstances dictated. It made sense but it also weakened his attacking power. Thinking the Indians might try to escape, Custer sent Captain Frederick Benteen with about 125 troopers off to scout the hills on the south. Major Marcus Reno and his battalion was ordered to cross the Little Big Horn and attack the Indian village from the South. Custer and the rest of the regiment would proceed parallel to Reno and support his action.

Fording the Little Big Horn at around 2 o'clock, Reno began advancing along the open valley bottom. Ahead, around a timbered bend in the river, was an enormous cloud of dust, thrown up by hundreds of Indian war ponies' hooves, rising up into the blazing afternoon heat. Reno signalled a charge, and his command raced forward. Occasionally he threw glances behind, looking for Custer's support, but it was nowhere to be seen. Afraid of plunging into superior Indian numbers, Reno threw up his hand to halt the galloping charge which ground to a confused halt, with Reno then ordering the men to fight on foot. They began firing ragged volleys at milling horsemen in front of them.

Without informing Reno, Custer had changed his battle plan. Instead of supporting Reno's charge, he rode north, screened by hills, and circled the Indian village so that it was between him and Reno. Presumably he intended to strike into the village through a gap in the hills, thus confronting the enemy with attacks from two directions. Indians fleeing from Reno's attack would also be cut off.

Custer and his men probably never reached the Little Big Horn River. As they descended a coulée 1,500 Huncpapa warriors led by Gall rode screaming up to meet them. Custer's men began to fall back, trying to seek higher ground. Their situation was critical, but not entirely without hope – until Crazy Horse led a thousand Oglala and Cheyenne warriors up the ridge behind them. Custer had been outflanked by Crazy Horse, who had led his warriors out of the camp in a huge swinging arc to attack the cavalry from behind. The cavalry fought desperately. They shot their horses to form breastworks, vainly trying to find shelter from the overwhelming Indians. Some troopers fought to the last. Some tried to make a break for the river. Some probably killed themselves to avoid torture. The battle took an hour, perhaps slightly less. And then all Custer's men were dead.

A eye-witness view of "Custer's Last Stand" from the Indian side was later given by Two Moon, a Cheyenne chief:

> Then the Sioux rode up the ridge on all sides, riding very fast. The Cheyenne went up the left way. Then the shooting was quick. Pop-pop-pop very fast. Some of the soldiers were down on their knees, some standing. Officers all in front. The smoke was like a great cloud, and everywhere the Sioux went the dust rose like smoke. We circled all round him – swirling like water round a stone. We shoot, we ride fast, we shoot again. Soldiers drop, and horses fall on them. Soldiers in line drop, but one man rides up and down the line – all the time shouting. He rode a sorrel horse with white face and white fore-legs. I don't know who he was. He was a brave man.

Indians keep swirling round and round, and the soldiers killed only a few. Many soldiers fell. At last all horses killed but five. Once in a while some man would break out and run towards the river, but he would fall. At last about a hundred men and five horsemen stood on the hill all bunched together. All along the bugler kept blowing his commands. He was very brave too. Then a chief was killed. I hear it was Long Hair [Custer], I don't know; and then the five horsemen and the bunch of men, may be forty, started toward the river. The man on the sorrel horse led them, shouting all the time. He wore a buckskin shirt, and had long black hair and mustache. He fought hard with a big knife. His men were all covered with white dust. I couldn't tell whether they were officers or not. One man all alone ran far down toward the river, then round up over the hill. I thought he was going to escape, but a Sioux fired and hit him in the head. He was the last man. He wore braid on his arms [sergeant].

All the soldiers were now killed, and the bodies were stripped. After that no one could tell which were officers. The bodies were left where they fell. We had no dance that night. We were sorrowful.

Next day four Sioux chiefs and two Cheyennes and I, Two Moon, went upon the battlefield to count the dead. One man carried a little bundle of sticks. When we came to dead men we took a little stick and gave it to another man, so we counted the dead. There were 388. There were thirty-nine Sioux and seven Cheyennes killed and about a hundred wounded.

Some white soldiers were cut with knives, to make sure they were dead; and the war women had mangled some. Most of them were left just where they fell. We came to the man with the big mustache; he lay down the hills towards the river. The Indians did not take his buckskin shirt. The Sioux said "That is a big chief. That is Long Hair." I don't know. I had never seen him. The man on the white-faced horse was the bravest man.

White Bull, Sitting Bull's nephew, was one of the numerous warriors who believed he had dealt Custer the mortal blow:

I charged in. A tall, well-built soldier with yellow hair and mustache saw me coming and tried to bluff me, aiming his rifle at me. But when I rushed him, he threw his rifle at me without shooting. I dodged it. We grabbed each other and wrestled there in the dust and smoke. It was like fighting in a fog. This soldier was very strong and brave. He tried to wrench my rifle from me, and nearly did it. I lashed him across the face with my quirt, striking the coup. He let go, then grabbed my gun with both hands until I struck him again.

But the tall soldier fought hard. He was desperate. He hit me with his fists on jaw and shoulders, then grabbed my long braids with both hands, pulled my face close and tried to bite my nose off. I yelled for help: "Hey, hey, come over and help me!" I thought that soldier would kill me.

Bear Lice and Crow Boy heard me call and came running. These friends tried to hit the soldier. But we were whirling around, back and forth, so that most of their blows hit me. They knocked me dizzy. I yelled as loud as I could to scare my enemy, but he would not let go. Finally I broke free.

He drew his pistol. I wrenched it out of his hand and struck him with it three or four times on the head, knocked him over, shot him in the head and fired at his heart. I took his pistol and cartridge belt. Hawk-Stays-Up struck second on his body.

Ho hechetu! That was a fight, a hard fight. But it was a glorious battle, I enjoyed it . . .

On the hill top, I met my relative, Bad Juice [Bad Soup]. He had been around Fort Abraham Lincoln and knew Long Hair by sight. When he came to the tall soldier lying on his back naked, Bad Soup pointed him out and said, "Long Hair thought he was the greatest man in the world. Now he lies there."

"Well," I said, "if that is Long Hair, I am the man who killed him."

Three miles south of Custer, Reno had been badly mauled and retreated up a hill. Benteen arrived in time to save him, and the combined companies held out for another scorching day. Reno and Benteen would have their share of blame for the debacle at Little Big Horn; Benteen, an able officer but public in his dislike of Custer, failed to respond to messages sent out by Custer to hurry to join him for the attack; Reno was indecisive, failed to keep a front at the river and failed to send Benteen, his subordinate, forward to a possible relief of Custer, whose battle he could hear.

Late in the afternoon of 26 June the exultant Indians withdrew, leaving behind their dead warriors on burial scaffolds, surrounded by a circle of dead ponies to serve the braves in the spirit land. The Battle of the Little Big Horn was over. Sitting Bull's vision had been good.

The next day Colonel Gibbon's infantry column arrived and found the ghastly piles of Custer's mutilated dead. "Long Hair" himself, had been shot twice, once through the left temple, once through the heart. According to Kate Bighead, a Cheyenne woman who was on the battlefield, his ear was punctured to enable him to hear better in the afterworld

The Sioux and Cheyenne had won an astounding victory. All five of Custer's companies, 225 men, had been killed. Reno and Benteen had lost 53 killed.

It took eight days for the news of the massacre to reach the town of Helena, Montana, and from there to be flashed by telegraph all over the world. Most Americans found out on reading their newspaper on the morning of 5 July, just a day after they had celebrated the centennial of independence.

SURRENDER

Yet, although the Indians won the battle, they lost the war. An enraged nation demanded immediate vengeance. All reservations in the northern plains were placed under military control. Congress passed a law compelling the Sioux to hand over the Black Hills, the Powder River and Big Horn mountains and to move onto reservations.

Throughout the rest of the year the free Indians of the northern plains were harassed by Crook, Mackenzie, Colonel Nelson A. Miles, and just about every seasoned Indian fighter the Army could get into the field. Throughout the winter small bands of Sioux and Cheyenne limped into the Red Cloud Agency.

On 6 May 1877 Crazy Horse led his lodges into Fort Robinson, Nebraska, and surrendered. He gave his left hand to Lieutenant W. P. Clark and said: "Friend, I shake with this hand because my heart is on this side; I want this peace to last for ever." Four months later he was dead. Peace faction Indians and the Army regarded him as too dangerous to be loose. On 6 September he was brought under guard to the army compound at Fort Robinson. Seeing that the soldiers intended to imprison him, Crazy Horse tried to escape. There was a scuffle. An officer called out, "Stab at the son of a bitch! Kill him!" A soldier named William Gentle bayoneted Crazy Horse twice.

He was taken into the adjutant's office. He refused to lie on the White man's cot, and died on the floor an hour later.

Of the mighty Sioux nation only the Huncpapa band of Sitting Bull and Chief Gall were not on the reservation. They were across the border in Canada, where they hoped to find sanctuary. Instead they found disease, diplomatic intrigues, dissension and famine. Gradually they trickled back across the border and into the reservations. In 1881 Sitting Bull himself finally gave up. At midday on 19 July, near starving and dressed in rags, Sitting Bull rode into Fort Buford in Dakota. With him were just 143 followers.

The Time of Little Wars

"I will fight no more forever."

Chief Joseph, at the surrender of the
Nez Percé after their "Long March"

"I do not wonder . . . that when these Indians see their wives and children starving, and their last supplies cut off, they go to war."

General George Crook

"The Army conquered the Sioux. You can order them around. But we Utes have never disturbed you Whites. So you must wait until we come to your ways of doing things."

Chief Ouray the Arrow

No Indians were spared in the backlash that followed Custer's Last Stand. Although the Nez Percé ("Pierced Noses") had never killed a white man, they were ordered in 1877 to leave their homeland for a new reservation in Idaho. Something of the demand was precipitated by pure anti-Indian bile; something of it was precipitated by sheer want. For over a decade the Whites in Oregon and Idaho had fraudulently laid claim to the Nez Percé's land.

At a council at Lapwai in Idaho, the local military commander Major General Oliver O. Howard, the one-armed veteran of Sherman's civil war army, delivered an "reservation or war" ultimatum to the Nez Percé bands. The elder and dreamer, Toohoolhoolzote, urged the Nez Percé to resist, at which Howard ordered him to be quiet. Toohoolhoolzote stood up in fury:

"Who are you that you ask us to talk and then tell me I shall not? . . . Are you the Creator? Did you make the World? Did you make the grass to grow? Did you make all these things that you talk to us as though we were boys?"

Howard had Toohoolhoolzote placed in the guardhouse. To avert a hopeless war, the Nez Percé did the White man's bidding. Even the the resolute Chief Joseph of the Wellamotkin band acceded. In their Wallowa Valley in northeastern Oregon the Wellamotkin wandered a million acres. Their allotment at Lapwai was 1,200 acres.

After Chief Joseph viewed the dismal Wellamotkin land at Lapwai on May 15 1877, Howard gave him one month to bring in his band and their livestock. Joseph begged for more time, pointing out that the waters of the Snake, which they needed to cross, were high with melt water and that the ponies were foaling. Howard refused even a day more.

So it was that three weeks later, Chief Joseph led his small band of 250 Wellamotkin Nez Percé out of the Wallowa country towards the Lapwai reservation, all the time harassed by Whites trying to run off the pony herds. Across the Snake River the Wellamotkin met up with other free Nez Percé bands for a last gathering in the wilderness. It was now that the trouble began. Homesick and robbed, Nez Percé temper was short and resentment tall. A young brave, Wahlitis, of the Salmon River band decided to seek revenge for the murder of his father by a White land-grabber some years before. In a night and day of mayhem Wahlitis and a group of fifteen firebrands slew nineteen White men.

Although the murderers were not of his band, Chief Joseph later elucidated the reason for their crazed actions:

> I know that my young men did a great wrong, but I ask, who was the first to blame? They had been insulted a thousand times; their fathers and brothers had been killed; their mothers and wives had been disgraced; they had been driven to madness by whisky sold to them by white men; they had been told by General Howard that all their horses and cattle . . . were to fall into the hands of White men; and, added to all this, they were homeless and desperate. I would have given my own life if I could have undone the killing of White men by my people.

Fearing reprisals, the Nez Percé encampment broke up, with many of the Indians fleeing to White Bird Canyon. It was there that Howard's troops caught up with them. Seeing the bluecoats approaching, a delegation of Nez Percé carrying a white flag advanced to negotiate. They were fired on. Although the Nez Percé numbered a bare sixty fighters, many of them aged and most of them equipped with muzzle-loaders (if that) of even greater antiquity, they proceeded in textbook military fashion to split up the attack. And then whipped each group of isolated soldiers in turn. The US 1st Cavalry took thirty-four dead. The Nez Percés suffered none.

Thus began an epic fighting retreat to rank with the Ten Thousand Greeks in Xenophon's *Anabasis*. Moving north-wards, the small band of nontreaty Nez Percé manoeuvred and outfought every US unit sent against them. All the while the fugitives picked up recruits – notably the Nez Percé chief Looking Glass, whose guiltless band had been attacked on the Lapwai reservation by revenging Whites – until they were 750 strong, counting women and children. With them went their vast herd of 3,000 horses.

Later, when the war with the Nez Percé was concluded, General Sherman wrote that it was "one of the most extraordinary Indian wars of which there is any record. The Indians throughout displayed a courage and skill that elicited universal praise. They abstained from scalping; let captive women go free; did not commit indiscriminate murder of peaceful families, which is usual, and fought with almost scientific skill, using advance and rear guards, skirmish lines, and field fortifications."

Something of the Nez Percé's martial skill and ability to endure is captured in the statistics. In the three and half months of their retreat, the Nez Percé fought 2,000 US troops and their Indian scouts and allies, in over a dozen engagements, four of them at least sizable enough to be classified as battles. They inflicted 180 fatalities, few of them "soft" targets. The Nez Percé sprang ambushes, ran guerrilla attacks, staged disappearing acts and sometimes just plain outfought the cavalry. Remembered one US officer: ". . . they [the Nez Percé horsemen] rode at full gallop along the mountainside in a steady formation by fours; formed twos, at a given signal, with perfect precision, to cross a narrow bridge; then galloped into line, reined to a sudden halt and dismounted with as much system as regulars." Also remarked on was the accuracy of Nez Percé shooting, which was unusually good for Indians.

In the popular press of the day it was Chief Joseph who was the genius "Red Napoleon" behind the Nez Percé's march through Idaho, Wyoming, the Yellowstone (already a national park; the Nez Percé on the warpath was one sight early tourists did not reckon on) and into Wyoming. But the "Red Napoleon" was a journalist's myth; in truth, the democratic Nez Percé made their strategic decisions at councils of war, where they tended to follow the advice of Chief Looking Glass until he allowed his village to suffer a surprise attack in Montana's Big Hole country. After that, the words of Lean Elk carried much weight. As civil chief Joseph participated in the councils, but in combat his duties were rearguard ones of shepherding women, children, the aged and the sick.

Sometimes Joseph fought. He did in the final battle of the Nez Percé's Long March at Eagle Creek in the Bear Paw Mountains. The Nez Percé were just thirty miles from Canada and sanctuary when they were intercepted on the last day of September, by Colonel Nelson A. Miles. Miles had been hastened ahead by the telegraph. Among the US soldiers at the denouement of the Long March was a 25-year-old West Pointer, Lieutenant Wood, who would later make a considerable reputation as a writer under the name Charles Erskine Scott Wood:

He [Chief Joseph] was stopped in his retreat by Gen. Miles, on notification sent out by Gen. Howard, but stood at bay for two days, refusing to surrender, until on the third day, Gen. Howard arrived on the scene, when, on the evening of a wintry day, the prairie powdered with snow, and a red and stormy sun almost at the horizon, Joseph surrendered, his people coming out of the burrows they had made in the hills, and where they had been living without fires, subsisting on the flesh of the dead horses . . .

In the final attack, a surprise by Gen. Miles, Joseph's

little girl, about eight or nine years old, and of whom he was very fond, fled in terror out on the prairie, and at the time of his surrender she was supposed to have perished from cold and starvation. As a matter of fact, she was afterwards found among the Sioux as a prisoner or slave, and was restored to Joseph: but with little effect, as his express condition of surrender – that he should be allowed to go back to the reservation which had been provided for him – was broken by the government, and he and his people were sent to the malarial bottoms of the Indian Territory, where all of his own children (six) and most of his band died.

At the time of the surrender, the able bodied warriors were surprisingly few, in contrast to the number of sick, aged and decrepit men and women: blind people, children, babies and wounded that poured out of their burrows in the earth as soon as it was known that they could do so with safety.

Joseph came up to the crest of the hill, upon which stood Gen. Howard. Gen. Miles, an interpreter, and myself. Joseph was the only one mounted, but five of his principal men clung about his knees and pressed close to the horse, looking at him, and talking earnestly in low tones. Joseph rode with bowed head, listening attentively, apparently, but with perfectly immobile face. As he approached the spot where we were standing, he said soemthing, and the five men who were with him halted. Joseph rode forward alone, leaped from his horse, and, leaving it standing, strode toward us. He opened the blanket which was wrapped around him, and handed his rifle to Gen. Howard, who motioned him to deliver it to Gen. Miles, which Joseph did.

Joseph then made one of the most quoted speeches in Indian literature:

Standing back, he folded his blanket again across his chest, leaving one arm free, somewhat in the manner of a Roman senator with his toga, and, half turning toward the interpreter, said:

"Tell General Howard I know his heart. What he told me before, in Idaho, I have it in my heart. I am tired of fighting . . . My people ask me for food, and I have none to give. It is cold, and we have no blankets, no wood. My people are starving to death. Where is my little daughter? I do not know. Perhaps, even now, she is freezing to death. Hear me, my chiefs. I have fought: but from where the sun now stands. Joseph will fight no more forever."

And he drew his blanket across his face, after the fashion of Indians when mourning or humiliated, and, instead of walking towards his own camp, walked directly into ours, as a prisoner.*

After long delay, and when his band was reduced to a comparatively small number of people he was [in 1885], with the remnant of his tribe allowed to come north from the Indian Territory – not to his old ground in Idaho, but to Northern Washington. No supplies were provided for them. They marched from the Indian Territory to their new home, and arrived on the edge of winter in a destitute condition, experiencing great suffering . . .

I think that, in his long career, Joseph cannot accuse

---

*About 400 Nez Percé were captured along with Chief Joseph. Two hundred died on the journey. A small number, including Chief White Bird, slipped through the army lines into Canada and exile with Chief Sitting Bull.

the Government of the United States of one single act of justice . . .

In 1904 Chief Joseph died on the alien soil of the Colville reservation in Washington Territory. Reportedly the cause was a "broken heart".

One year after the Nez Percé were "punished" by the government, it was the turn of the Bannocks of southern Idaho. The same Bannocks who had scouted for Miles against the Nez Percé. For a decade the Bannocks had subsisted on their reservation on the upper Snake River, but when Congress failed to provide their promised rations the Bannocks ordered off the settlers who had illegally occupied their camas (an edible plant of the hyacinth family) prairie and used it as pasturage for hogs and cattle. As the settlers decamped, two Bannock hot-heads shot and wounded a pair of settlers.

This was the spring of 1878. Even the army had some sympathy for the starving Bannocks. General George Crook, who knew their reservation well, wrote in the *Army and Navy Journal*:

. . . I was up there last spring, and found them in a desperate condition. I telegraphed, and the agent telegraphed for supplies, but word came that no appropriation had been made. They have never been half supplied.

The agent has sent them off for half a year to enable them to pick up something to live on, but there is nothing for them in that country. The buffalo is all gone . . . and there aren't enough jackrabbits to catch. What are they to do?

Starvation is staring them in the face, and if they wait

much longer, they will not be able to fight. They understand the situation, and fully appreciate what is before them.

The encroachments upon the Camas prairies was the cause of the trouble. These prairies are the last source of subsistence . . . I do not wonder, and you will not either that when these Indians see their wives and children starving, and their last sources of supplies cut off, they go to war. And then we are sent out to kill them. It is an outrage.

The Bannock warpath led to disaster. A peace faction anyway returned to the agency, leaving the war party to tour around the Great Basin seeking allies. Aside from a handful of Paiutes and Western Shoshoni, nobody enlisted.

Within nine months the Bannock War was over. According to the Army list, White casualties were nine soldiers and thirty-one civilians. Some eighty Bannocks were reported killed, though this was certainly an underestimation, for the Bannocks, like all Indians, tried to remove their dead from the battlefield.

THE FIGHTING CHEYENNE

Even before the last Bannock hostiles were cannoned in their lodges, there was trouble on the Great Plains. This time it was the Cheyenne whose provoked patience snapped.

At the end of the war against Sitting Bull's Sioux, the northern Cheyenne had been taken to Fort Reno in Indian Territory to live with their southern relatives. Far from being accommodating, the southern Cheyenne called the arrivals "fools". Game was scarce and malaria rife. Soon the northern

Cheyenne began to die – fifty children alone through the fall of 1877 to the fall of 1878. Mostly the Cheyenne died of longing for their homeland. Said Little Chief: "Because that is the land where I was born, the land that God gave us; and because it was better than this in every way; everything was better. I have been sick a great deal of the time since I have been down here – homesick and heartsick, and sick in every way. I have been thinking of my native country, and the good home I had up there, where I was never hungry, and when I wanted anything to eat could go out and hunt the buffalo. It does not make me feel good to hang about an agency and to have to ask a white man for something to eat when I get hungry."

Endlessly they pleaded to be allowed to go back to their tribal lands. Always their words fell on deaf government ears. So the Cheyenne decided to return anyway.

On the night of 9 September 1878 the Cheyenne took down their lodges and stole through the ring of sentries around the camp. About 350 Cheyenne broke out, a scarce 70 braves among them. Led by Dull Knife (his Sioux and White name; to the Cheyenne he was Morning Star) and Little Wolf, the Cheyenne fled northwards, over the Arkansas, over the South Platte, over the North Platte, troops attacking them from every direction. For 400 miles the Cheyenne stopped only to fight and steal cattle; there was not even time for mourning.

Above the North Platte, the fugitives felt safe in their own country, and separated. Little Wolf settled down for the winter on the Lost Chokecherry stream in Nebraska's Sand Hills. Dull Knife and 148 followers turned northwest towards Camp Robinson.

Moving through a heavy snowstorm in northwestern Nebraska on 23 October, Dull Knife's band ran by pure ill luck into two companies of the 3rd Cavalry. In the swirling snow, the troopers were as surprised as the Indians.

The surrendered Cheyenne were taken to Fort Robinson and quartered in empty barracks. They gave up their oldest guns, and secretly broke down their best and hid them under the women's clothes. "I had a carbine hanging down my back", recalled the wife of Black Bear.

Life at Fort Robinson was almost congenial for the Cheyenne. They were allowed to hunt by day, as long as they returned for roll call at night.

Meanwhile, Washington deliberated over what to do with Dull Knife's band.

On 3 January 1879, as the temperature hit many degrees below zero, Dull Knife's Cheyenne were officially informed that they must return to Indian Territory. "The whole reservation system will receive a shock which will endanger its stability" if the fugitive Cheyenne were allowed to stay in Nebraska, argued Lieutenant General Philip Sheridan.

Dull Knife refused to move. "We will not go there [Indian Territory] to live," he informed Fort Robinson's commandant. "That is not a healthy country, and if we should stay we would all die. We do not wish to go back there and will not go. You may kill me here, but you cannot make me go back."

To encourage the Cheyenne into compliance, the camp commandant ordered the Indian barracks to be surrounded, and cut off their food. When this left the Indians unbowed, he cut off their water. Inside the barracks, the Cheyenne were forced to lick frost off the windows for drink.

After nearly a week of deprivation, the Cheyenne concluded that "we will not die shut up here like dogs; we will die on the prairies; we will die fighting." Accordingly, on the afternoon of 8 January the Cheyenne painted their faces, withdrew their guns from their hiding places, and improvized weapons out of cooking knives and pieces of wood. Then they kissed each other goodbye. At ten o'clock that night, five warriors of the Dog Society leaped from the barrack windows to attack the sentries and cover the escape. They had no chance of survival; they deliberately gave up their lives.

In the bright moonlight there was much shooting. Soon bodies strewed the snow. Cheyenne bodies mostly, which were mutilated where they fell by fort civilians and traders. (The soldiers behaved better; many had been moved by the Cheyenne's plight.) At daylight wagons went out from the fort and picked up fifty Cheyenne dead and sixty-five captives, many of them seriously wounded.

One group of Cheyenne made the bluffs beyond the camp, then pushed on eighteen miles – despite their considerable weakening from hunger and thirst – to a wooded knoll. There they did the unpredictable: they ambushed the pursuing soldiers. And ate their fallen horses.

For day after day, these last Cheyenne fled. Until the end came. Near the head of War Bonnet Creek, forty-five miles west of Camp Robinson, troops surrounded the thirty-one survivors on 21 January. The Indians dug deep pits and fired at the soldiers until their ammunition ran out. Then three braves charged the soldiers with all they had left – knives and an empty pistol. Some of the Indians in the pits committed suicide. The soldiers poured volleys of fire down into the remainder.

When the soldiers dared approach the pits, only three squaws were left alive.

According to the subsequent army report, eleven soldiers were killed in Dull Knife's breakout. It went on to list the Cheyenne as suffering sixty-eight dead and seventy-eight captured. Seven were unaccounted for. "These last seven," the report noted, "are women and children, and are supposed to have died on the bluffs."

Not for the first time the army got it wrong. Among the missing were Dull Knife and some of his immediate family. After hiding in a cave, they wandered for eighteen days, eating their moccasins and any roots they could find, before reaching the Pine Ridge agency, where they were taken in by the half-breed interpreter.

Fate was kinder to Little Wolf's band. After splitting with Dull Knife's Cheyenne, they spent the winter hunkered down on the Lost Chokecherry, burning only wood that made no smoke. Antelope and deer were plentiful, however, and they did not starve. In March 1879 they resumed their journey towards the hunting grounds on the Powder River. En route they were found by Lieutenant W. P. Clark, a cavalryman they trusted. He escorted them to Fort Keogh on the Yellowstone, where General Nelson Miles enlisted them as scouts.

So touched was the public by the pluck and the plight of the "fighting Cheyenne" that a reservation was donated them on the Tongue River. Dull Knife died there in 1883, home at last.

"THE UTES MUST GO"

There was one more little war to come in the north. Its cause was dismally familiar.

Most of western Colorado was a reservation for the Utes. Their wily leader Ouray, a convert to Methodism, managed to prevent major collisions with the Whites by trading land for peace. Four million acres of it in 1873 alone.

But it was never enough. The Whites didn't want some Ute land – and the gold that they prayed was in it – they wanted all of it. The governor of Colorado was elected on a "Utes

Must Go" ticket. All the Coloradoans needed was a pretext to drive out the Indians. They got one in 1879.

Nathan C. Meeker, a humourless and elderly zealot, was the agent at White River. Meeker believed that it was his duty to elevate Utes from barbarism to the "enlightened scientific and religious stage". This was to be achieved by turning the Utes from horseback hunters into farmers. Accordingly, Meeker ploughed up their lands and built new agency buildings on their horse-racing track.

Still the Utes could not be persuaded to become sod-busters. Nothing daunted, Meeker ordered the ploughing of the grassland where the Utes pastured their ponies.

Thereafter things fell quickly apart. Ute braves drove off the ploughman by shooting over his head. Meeker was shoved by Canalla (Johnson), a Ute medicine man, in an ensuing argument. The brooding agent dispatched a telegram to the Commissioner of Indian Affairs:

> I have been assaulted by a leading chief, Johnson, forced out of my own house, and injured badly. It is now revealed that Johnson originated all the trouble . . . His son shot at the plowman, and the opposition to plowing is wide. Plowing stops; life of self, family, and employees not safe; want protection immediately; have asked Governor Pitkin to confer with General Pope.

"Protection", in the form of two hundred cavalrymen, was duly dispatched to Meeker. When the cavalry arrived at Milk River, the reservation's border, the Utes assumed war had been declared on them. Led by Nicaagat, Ute warriors besieged the column, killing eleven; at the agency Meeker and nine white workmen were slain. Meeker's wife and daughter, and another white woman, were passed around the Ute men.

For the Coloradoans, the brief "Ute War" was a conspic-uous success. Governor Frederick Pitkin, the leading "Utes Must Go" politician, issued a statement to the press:

> I think the conclusion of this affair will end the depreda-tions in Colorado. It will he impossible for the Indians and whites to live in peace hereafter. This attack had no provocation and the whites now understand that they are liable to be attacked in any part of the state where Indians happen to be in sufficient force.
>
> My idea is that, unless removed by the government, they must necessarily be exterminated. I could raise 25,000 men to protect the settlers in twenty-four hours. The state would be willing to settle the Indian trouble at its own expense. The advantages that would accrue from the throwing open of 12 million acres of land to miners and settlers would more than compensate for the expenses occurred.

Unwilling for so public a holocaust, the Federal govern-ment removed all the Utes from Colorado (save for a narrow strip in the southwest) and dumped them in a tract of Utah that Mormons considered too barren for human habitation.

The Utes had gone.

All the north and the plains of the USA were now pacified. Only in the southwest were there still Indians to be reckoned with.

Geronimo, Apache Tiger

Nobody ever captured Geronimo. I know. I was with
him. Anyway, who can capture the wind?

Daklugie, Nednhi Apache

THE INVINCIBLE LEADER

Five years had passed since the Chiricahua Apache under
Cochise had entered the reservation. And gradually, imper-
ceptibly, the peace had come undone.

When Cochise died in 1874 his son Taza became chief,
tribal leadership being hereditary amongst the Apache. But
Taza, if likeable, lacked authority, and larger numbers of
Chiricahua warriors came under the influence of Geronimo,
the warrior leader of the sub-band of Bedonkohe Apache who
had become assimilated into the Chiricahua. The son of a
Nednai chief who had renounced his chieftainship to marry
into the Bedonkohe, Geronimo had been born One Who
Yawns (Goyahkia). He had been given the name Geronimo
by the Mexicans, for he had once fought them at Arispe –
after they had murdered his family – with such terrifying
ferocity that they prayed to St Geronimo for salvation. The

name had stuck, and was used by Apache, Mexicans and White alike. Geronimo had the Power; it had visited him when he had grieved for his slain family. "No gun can ever kill you," the Power had told him. He was invincible.

Geronimo had grown tired of the monotony of reservation life, and begun to sneak off to indulge his old habit of raiding Mexico. The Mexicans complained bitterly, and in 1876 the Arizonans joined the outcry when two stagecoach attendants and a rancher were killed by drunken Apaches. (That the stagecoach attendants had gotten the Apaches drunk and tried to cheat them was conveniently ignored.) The Governor of Arizona, Anson P Safford, demanded that Washington replace Thomas Jeffords as Apache Agent, while Tucsons's *Arizona Citizen* declared: "The kind of war needed for the Chiricahua Apaches is steady, unrelenting, hopeless, and undiscriminating war, slaying men, women and children, until every valley and crest and crag and fastness shall send to high heaven the grateful incense of festering and rotting Chiricahuas."

The murder of the three White men gave Washington a pretext to close the Chiricahua reservation, something it wanted to do anyway as part of its 1875 policy of "consolidation" of the reservations. The Apaches were all to be forced onto one overcrowded reservation at San Carlos. On learning of the consolidation plan, Geronimo, now aged 46, fled across the border to Mexico.

This first stint as a holdout was inauspicious. Early in 1877 he came out of Mexico, driving a herd of stolen horses, to visit the agency at Warm Springs (Ojo Caliente). The regime at Warm Springs was lax, and the place was used frequently as a refuge by "renegades" in their cross-border raids. News of Geronimo's whereabouts reached the Commissioner of Indian Affairs, who wired John Philip Clum, the young agent of the San Carlos reservation, and ordered him to arrest Geronimo. Clum immediately set out on the 400-mile journey to Warm Springs, accompanied by about 100 of his Apache Indian police.

After reaching Warm Springs, Clum sent a message to Geronimo and other "renegade" warriors, like Chief Victorio who had jumped the reservation, that he desired to talk. Having no reason to expect confrontation, the Apache rode the three miles to the agency accompanied by their wives and children. Geronimo found Clum sitting on the porch of the adobe agency building, a dozen of his police around him. Clum opened the proceedings by accusing Geronimo of killing men and violating the agreement made between Cochise and General Howard. He told Geronimo he was taking him to San Carlos. Geronimo answered defiantly: "We are not going to San Carlos with you, and unless you are very careful, you and your Apache police will not go back to San Carlos either. Your bodies will stay here at Ojo Caliente to make food for coyotes." To emphasize the point, Geronimo hitched his rifle up in his arms.

At this moment Clum gave a prearranged signal, a touch of the brim of his hat; the doors of the commissary building burst open and 80 police charged out. Geronimo's thumb began to creep towards the hammer of his rifle, but he thought better of it and stood stock-still. Clum stepped forward to disarm the Apache. This was the only time that Geronimo was ever captured, and then it was by a trick.

Conveyed to San Carlos in shackles, Geronimo found the reservation worse than he had feared. Situated alongside the Gila River, much of it was low-lying, reaching temperatures of 110 degrees in summer. White settlers were already beginning to squat the best land. There were outbreaks of malaria and smallpox.

John Clum who, despite his deceit in the capture of Geronimo, was well-liked by many Apache, believed he could work with the People and keep them peaceful on the reservation. The Army, however, because of the concentration of Apache leaders at San Carlos, sent the cavalry to guard the reservation. John Clum was forced to disband his self-regulating Apache police. He resigned in protest, and went on to edit the Tombstone *Epitaph*.

Victorio fled San Carlos almost immediately, moving back with his people to Warm Springs. The Army harassed them, and Victorio declared he would "make war forever" against the USA. He was killed in 1880 in a fight with Mexican soldiers.

Geronimo endured the reservation for a year. He had little choice, for much of the time he was incarcerated, an experience he thought "might easily have been death to me." As soon as he was able to he escaped to Mexico with a few other Chiricahuas. He returned voluntarily in 1880 following a bitter winter of starvation in the mountains, but again he did not stay long.

"THE APACHES ARE OUT!"

During the spring of 1881, a religious movement arose among the reservation Apache which preached the end of the White man and the raising again of the old Apache order. In August, the agent sent a detachment of soldiers to arrest the spiritual leader of the movement, Noch-ay-del-klinne. His followers attacked the troops; a pitched battle ensued, with dead on both sides. Army reinforcements were rushed in, and the rumour began to circulate that the Apache leaders would be arrested. More specifically, the rumours said that Geronimo – who had been sceptical about the new religion –

was to be hanged. In September of 1881, in response to these rumours, Geronimo and the Nednai chief, Juh, along with 70 warriors, jumped the reservation and made for the Sierra Madre. Their route took them past Tombstone, where a posse including three of the Earp brothers tried to head them off, to no avail.

Six months later, in April 1882, Geronimo and his band returned to the reservation but not, this time, as captives. They rode in as self-declared liberators, and persuaded most of the remaining Chiricahuas and Warm Springs Apaches to leave with them for Mexico. Near the border, at Horse Shoe Canyon, pursuing cavalry caught up with them. The warriors fought a stiff rearguard action, allowing the main body of women and children to cross into Mexico. Then disaster struck. A Mexican infantry regiment stumbled upon the Apaches, killing most of the women and children who were riding in front.

Among the warriors and chiefs who managed to escape were Naiche (a son of Cochise), Loco, Chato, and Geronimo himself. Embittered, they joined up with old Nana, chief of the Mimbrenos after the death of Victorio, to form a united guerrilla band of 80 warriors.

Over the next two years, Geronimo and the united band raided Mexican towns and villages with near impunity. The raiding life of the band was later described by Jason Betzinez, a young Chiricahua, in his memoir *I Fought with Geronimo*:

> Preparations for the raid deep into Sonora consisted of making extra pairs of moccasins, cleaning our hair, sharpening knives, and cleaning and greasing guns. We had no tomahawks, arrows or spears. The Apaches never did have tomahawks and by 1882 arrows and spears were rarely used.

We established most of the young boys, women, and children on top of the mountain where they could keep a good lookout and take care of themselves. Mother and I went with the men at least part of the way. Our job was to bring back stolen beeves to our camp so that the women and children would have plenty to eat while the men were away.

After crossing a mountain range we bivouacked for the night. The next morning our leaders told us to travel close together because of the dense timbers, briars, and cactus. The trip was to be dangerous and difficult; it would be almost impossible to travel at night. We were nearly among the enemy now but kept on going to the vicinity of the nearest town. Then our men began scouting around for horses and mules while mother and I together with five young boys waited on a hill top where we could see the surrounding country and watch out for signs of the enemy.

After a long and anxious wait, toward evening we were relieved to see our men coming, driving some horses. It had been a risky adventure for us. Even one Mexican cowboy spotting us would have meant serious trouble, we being without weapons.

The next day the men killed several head of cattle, which we cut up and loaded on horses. Late in the afternoon mother and I, together with five boys, started back toward the rest of our band. We traveled part of the night through the thick timber. In the morning we resumed our journey, our horses heavily laden with meat, arriving late in the afternoon within sight of camp. Some of the women came out to help us carry in the beef. As we climbed up the mountainside we were very careful not to leave tracks that would show. After we got to camp and unloaded the animals some of the boys drove the horses down to the river away from camp. We now had enough dried beef to last us for at least a month.

Meantime our men went on west to where a main road passed between several towns, south towards Ures, the then capital of Sonora. Where the road ran along the river through the timber was the locality in which the Apaches were accustomed to lie in wait for travelers especially pack trains laden with drygoods.

Our men were gone about fifteen days. Meanwhile we lived very quietly at camp. One day a woman standing in front of her tepee saw a white object approaching us in the distance. The women and children immediately became very excited and fearful, thinking that the enemy were coming. Two of us boys going out to investigate found that it was our warriors coming home with great quantities of dry goods, bolts of cloth and wearing apparel. When they arrived at the foot of the mountain they called up to us whereupon all the people in camp hurried down to meet them. We surely were glad to see them and they to see us. One thing we *didn't* see was scalps. The Apaches did not practice the custom of scalping a fallen enemy. There may have been exceptions to this but they were very, very rare. Concerning Geronimo I never knew him to bring in a scalp. Much nonsense has been written about this.

After our warriors returned, we hiked farther up the Yaqui River, camped for awhile, then again moved upstream. Here we had plenty of food and nothing to worry about. Nevertheless we were very careful not to disclose our presence because we were quite near a number of Mexican towns. Every day our men stationed lookouts on the hills. Our camp at this time was at the junction of the Bavispe and Yaqui Rivers.

The leaders decided to raid toward the northwest. This time we started off on foot leaving all the animals in the valley near the Bavispe River where there was plenty of good grass. We concealed in caves our saddles and the loot which the men had brought back from the earlier raid, as well as all our camp gear which we could not carry on our backs. We took only one mule, my big mule, on which Geronimo's wife and baby rode.

Our band moved straight west toward a Mexican town. Just when it appeared that we were going right on into the village the leaders stopped a few miles to the east. The plan was to avoid stealing any horses or mules while we were sneaking around in between these towns, two of which lay to the west and one to the east of our route.

From the last campsite the band turned northwest toward the mountains. Since we were about to cross the main road we were especially careful not to be seen or leave any sign that would put the soldiers on our trail. Our men knew that each town contained a garrison of troops. So we carefully covered our tracks.

We camped at the foot of a mountain a few miles from the road running between Buenavista and Moctezuma. Early next morning Geronimo told the men that they could now go out to look for horses and mules. They should drive in all that they could find, as we needed them for the expected move north into the mountains. About noon our men drove in quite a number of animals stolen from the Mexicans. We had a great time roping them and breaking them for the women and children to ride. My cousin roped a mule but it broke away from him. I chased it out into the prairie for nearly two miles. I nearly went too far. Suddenly I saw Mexican soldiers only a short distance away.

As I galloped back to the group of Apaches I heard my cousin shouting to me to hurry up, the enemy were coming along behind me. Meanwhile the Indians were taking up a position from which to attack the soldiers. As I sped over a low ridge I heard the shooting start. The Indians charged so fast toward the enemy that they failed to notice one soldier who was hiding in the bushes. This man shot and killed the last Apache to ride by him. The warriors, hearing the shot, came dashing back just in time to shoot the Mexican.

The band felt dreadfully sad over losing a warrior. He was a Warm Springs Apache who had no near relatives in the band with us.

Late that afternoon we started off to the west then camped at the foot of the mountains for supper. While we were thus engaged, a sentinel ran in to report that the enemy were at the skirmish ground of that afternoon, not far behind us. We moved out hastily into the foothills where we remained in concealment during the night. In the morning we saw the soldiers following our tracks and approaching our hill. At once the warriors took up positions ready for a fight. But the Mexicans didn't attempt to follow our trail up the mountainside.

Finally our men got tired of waiting, so we moved on, traveling very fast right on into the night. We came to a short steep canyon where we made camp and enjoyed a good night's rest.

In the morning we set a course across the wide valley of the Bavispe. Although our horses and mules were in good shape we traveled slowly, enjoying the trip and the pleasant surroundings. That night we camped beside the Bavispe River. The chiefs told the men not to shoot any deer because the Mexicans might hear the firing.

This country looked as though it belonged to us. For some days owing to the wise leadership of Geronimo we had not been disturbed by an enemy. We crossed the river and moved through the woods discussing the fact that the country seemed to be full of deer and other game. In fact the deer just stood and watched us pass. It seemed that they had never been disturbed by anyone hunting them. A person living in this favored spot would never have to go hungry. There were plenty of wild animals and other food, easily obtainable. But at this time the men all obeyed Geronimo and didn't fire a shot. Besides, we still had plenty of dried beef.

Arriving at our next objective we again settled down for an indefinite stay. It was just like peacetime. We had plenty to eat, good clothing taken from the stolen stocks, and no enemies nearby. We were about thirty miles southeast of Fronteras.

During this period the women, assisted by some of the boys, were gathering and drying the fruit of the yucca, preparing for a winter to be spent in the Sierras. It was in the late summer or early fall of 1882.

As well as raiding into Mexico, the Geronimo band attacked American settlements and ranches.

To stop the outrages, the Army once again called on George Crook ("Grey Wolf" to the Apache). On 4 September 1882 Crook assumed command at San Carlos and, on talking to the Apaches on the reservation, found that their grievances were justified. The reservation Apaches, he concluded, "had not only the best reasons for complaining, but had displayed remarkable forbearance in remaining at peace." He began a reform of the corrupt practices of White contractors and suppliers and set about re-establishing John Clum's Apache police.

Crook also gave much thought to the band of Apaches free in Mexico. He did not want another guerrilla war with the Apaches, especially in the rugged terrain of the sierras. Crook decided that he should meet with Geronimo and the other leaders, and that the best place to do this was in Mexico. But in order to cross the border, he had to wait for the Apaches to make a raid in the US. By international agreement, he could go into Mexico only in pursuit of renegade Apaches.

His justification came on 21 March 1883, when a renegade war party raided a mining camp near Tombstone. A few days later the same raiders killed federal judge H. C. McComas and his wife, and abducted their son. Crook, together with 50 soldiers and 193 civilian Apache scouts, trailed the renegades into Mexico. After searching for several weeks, the scouts located Geronimo's camp and captured the women and children, the men being on a raiding party. The Apache had believed that they were safe inside Mexico; Crook's capture of the camp was a stunning blow. Geronimo agreed to parley, and found Crook generous. Grey Wolf even allowed the Apache leader another two months of freedom, while he rounded up the rest of the Chiricahuas.

True to his word, Geronimo crossed the border voluntarily, although he stretched the two months to eight, arriving in February 1884. Before him he drove 350 head of cattle, stolen from the Mexicans. This seemed proper to Geronimo, who felt he was only supplying his people with meat. At San Carlos, Crook took a different view and confiscated the herd, ordered it sold and returned the proceeds to the original Mexican owners.

For more than a year things were quiet on the reservation, and Crook could proudly say that "not an outrage or depredation of any kind" was committed by the Apaches. Outside San Carlos, however, the citizens of Arizona were stirring up trouble. Newspapers contained lurid, and fabricated, stories about atrocities committed by Geronimo and called upon vigilantes to hang him. There was criticism of Crook for being too easy on the Apaches; some even suggested that he had surrendered to Geronimo in Mexico, and was now providing him with an easy life in return for the keeping of his scalp.

The stories made Geronimo uneasy. He also feared trouble from the reservation authorities for breaking the rule that prohibited the drinking of tiswin (corn beer), a pleasure the Apaches found unable to resist. Expecting the worst, Geronimo, Nana and 92 women and children, eight boys and 34 men departed for Mexico on the night of 17 May 1885. Before leaving, Geronimo cut the telegraph wire.

"THE APACHES ARE OUT!" warned the Arizona newspapers two days later. Whites had little to fear, however, since Geronimo was trying to avoid any confrontation with them, and was hurrying his people towards Mexico, not even stopping to make camp until they reached the safety of the Sierra Madre.

General Crook was detailed by Washington to apprehend the fugitive Geronimo, with orders to take his unconditional surrender or kill him. To fulfil his mission, Crook was obliged to mount the heaviest campaign in the Apache wars up to that date, with more than 2,500 cavalry troopers and 200 Indian scouts. (Some of these were old Apache cohorts of Geronimo, including Chato; the Apaches, understanding the boredom of reservation life, did not usually blame people who scouted for the Whites.)

Throughout the winter of 1885–6 Crook hunted Geronimo in the Sierra Madre, but having been surprised there before the Apache leader was more cautious. In January, Crook's force managed to discover and attack one renegade camp, although their quarry got away. But in March, Geronimo decided to surrender. Units of the Mexican Army, as well as the US cavalry, were combing the Sierra Madre for him. Caught between the Mexicans who only wanted to kill him and the Americans who might accept a surrender, Geronimo chose to meet with Crook at Cañon de los Embudos (Canyon of Tricksters), a few miles below the border.

When Crook arrived at the canyon, he was surprised to find neither Geronimo nor his braves looking particularly discouraged. "Although tired of the constant hounding of the campaign," Crook later recalled, "they were in superb physical condition, armed to the teeth, fierce as so many tigers. Knowing what pitiless brutes they are themselves, they mistrust everyone else."

He and Geronimo talked for two days, and Geronimo agreed once more to live on the reservation. "Do with me what you please," he said. "Once I moved about like the wind. Now I surrender to you, and that is all."

Despite his submission to Crook, within days Geronimo went fugitive. On the dark and rainy night of 28 March, as he and his surrendered Chiricahua band neared Fort Bowie, Geronimo, his young son Chappo, Naiche and 17 other warriors, and 18 women and children, slipped away from their escort. "I feared treachery," he later said, "and decided to remain in Mexico." A trader had got the hostiles drunk and filled them full of tales about how the local people were going to make "good injun" of them. It would be Geronimo's last break-out.

As a result of Geronimo's flight, the War Department severely reprimanded Crook for laxity and his over-indulgences towards the Indians. Crook resigned immediately, and was replaced by Brigadier-General Nelson A. Miles, whose orders were to "capture or destroy" Geronimo and his band of hostiles.

Miles managed to do neither, although his work amongst the Apaches would prove destructive enough. One of his first decisions was to transfer all the Mimbrenos and Chiricahuas on the reservations – including the scouts who had helped Crook – to Florida.

For the manhunt of Geronimo, Miles put 5,000 soldiers – a quarter of the entire army – in the field, and built 30 helio-graph stations to flash messages from mountain to mountain, a system of communication well known to the Apaches, who had long before shifted from smoke signals to mirrors. Meanwhile, Geronimo raided almost at will. In April of 1886, he and his warriors crossed into Arizona and killed a rancher's wife, child and an employee. A short while later, Geronimo's war party killed two men outside Nogales, and then ambushed the cavalry sent in pursuit of them. Two troopers died. The Apaches suffered not a single loss. Geronimo would later say of this period, "We were reckless of our lives, because we felt that every man's hand was against us. If we returned to the reservation we would be put in prison and killed; if we stayed in Mexico they could continue to send soldiers to fight us; so we gave no quarter to anyone and asked no favours."

Throughout the summer of 1886 Miles pursued Geronimo and his 20 warriors, but to no avail. They seemed as elusive as ghosts. Finally, Miles decided to try another tack – he would negotiate with the enemy. His appointed emissary was Lieutenant Charles Gatewood, who had met Geronimo a number of times. Accompanying Gatewood were two scouts, Martine and Kayitah.

To make contact with the renegades, Gatewood headed across the border and wandered around, listening for word of the Apaches' whereabouts. Eventually, he discovered that Geronimo was sending women into the small town of Fronteras to procure mescal. He trailed one such woman out of Fronteras and deep into the Sierra Madre. It was the end of August 1886.

Gatewood sent Geronimo a message via his scouts, and the two met near a bend in a river. The Apache laid down his rifle and walked over to Gatewood ("Big Nose"), shook his hand and asked how he was. But when they sat down to talk and smoke cigarettes in the Apache fashion, with tobacco rolled in oak leaves, Geronimo deliberately sat close enough to Gatewood for the lieutenant to feel his revolver.

Geronimo opened the council formally by announcing that he and his warriors had come to hear General Miles's message. Gatewood gave it to them straight. "Surrender, and you will be sent to join the rest of your friends in Florida, there to await the decision of the President as to your final disposition. Accept these terms or fight it out to the bitter end." At this Geronimo bristled, "Take us to the reservation [San Carlos], or fight!"

Gatewood then had to inform Geronimo that the reservation no longer existed, and that all the Chiricahuas had been removed to Florida, including members of Geronimo's own family.

The Apache were devastated by the news. They withdrew for a private council, which in the Apache way was democratic, with everyone having a voice. Perico, Fun, Ahnandia – all of them Geronimo's cousins – indicated that they wished to surrender so that they might see their families again.

Geronimo still had a taste to fight on, but he was weakened by these defections. He stood for a few moments without speaking. At length he said, "I have been depending heavily on you three men. You have been great fighters in battle. If you are going to surrender, there is no use my going without you. I will give up with you."

Geronimo, the last of the Apache leaders, had finally surrendered.

There was a formal cessation of hostilities, signed at Skeleton Canyon. Brigadier-General Miles was in attendance, getting his first look at Geronimo: "He was one of the brightest, most resolute, determined looking men that I have ever encountered. He had the clearest, sharpest dark eye I think I have ever seen, unless it was that of General Sherman when he was at the prime of life . . . Every movement indicated power, energy and determination. In everything he did, he had a purpose."

The surrender ceremony was officially concluded on the afternoon of 4 September, and on the following day Miles flashed the news to the nation that Geronimo had finally given up arms. With a last glimpse at the Chiricahua mountains, Geronimo was taken to Fort Bowie, and from there transported, along with his hostile band, in a railway cattle car to San Antonio, Texas. From San Antonio Geronimo was shipped to Fort Pickens in Florida, a crumbling, abandoned fortification on Santa Rosa island, where he would start the first of his 23 years in captivity.

LEARNING TO BE WHITE

Probably Geronimo was not surprised after all these years of dealing with the White man, to find that he had been lied to.

He did not, as General Miles had promised him, see his family on arrival in Florida, and instead spent two years in close confinement. To the great distress of Geronimo and the other male hostiles, the women and children of their band were taken from them and sent to Fort Marion, 300 miles across the state.

The warm and humid land of Florida, so unlike the dry country of Arizona and New Mexico, was not healthy for the Apaches. Eighteen died of a disease diagnosed as consumption within only a matter of months. Their children were sent away to a school in Carlisle, Pennsylvania, where they were to be readied for integration into White man's society. Our job, said the school's founder, is to "kill the Indian and save the man."

After two years of misery in Florida, the hostile warriors were transferred to Mount Vernon Barracks in Alabama. To their great joy, there they were finally reunited with their families, with Geronimo seeing an infant daughter Lenna for the first time. To those accustomed to seeing the Apache warlord as an "inhuman monster", the care he showed for his daughter was striking. One visitor wrote: "I had luck today . . . Saw Geronimo . . . He is a terrible old villain, yet seemed quiet enough today nursing a baby." Aside from family reunions, the pleasures to be found at Mount Vernon were few. The Apaches were put to work at hard labour. Their rations were pitiful. There were several outbreaks of tuberculosis and pneumonia. Many became depressed. Nineteen of the 352 Chiricahua prisoners died within eight months.

If it had not been for the efforts of a few White friends of the Apaches such as John Clum and George Crook, many more would have died at the barracks on the Mobile River. In August 1894 the War Department was finally persuaded to move the Apaches back West, although not as far west as their original stomping grounds. They were sent to Fort Sill, in southern Oklahoma, which their old enemies, the Comanches and Cheyenne, generously offered to share with them.

Here the White men set about turning the Apache into dark-skinned White men. They were given small log houses, made to learn handiwork, made to garden, growing melons and cantaloupes on small patches of land, and made to farm. At one point, Geronimo was forced to learn how to be a cowboy. The Apaches, in fact, did well at raising cattle, but only moderately well at the other trades.

Something at which Geronimo excelled in captivity was selling himself. The Apache had always had a hard head for business and was soon making and purveying Geronimo souvenirs for the steady stream of visitors who dropped by to view him. One such visitor wrote:

> Geronimo has an eye to thrift and can drive a sharp bargain with his bows and arrows, and quivers and canes, and other work, in which he is skillful. He prides himself upon his autograph, written thus, GERONIMO, which he affixes to what he sells, usually asking an extra price for it. He had a curious headdress, which he called . . . his war bonnet . . . He seemed to value this bonnet highly, but finally in his need or greed for money, offered it for sale at $25.

In 1898, Geronimo met with General Miles at the Trans-Mississippi Exposition in Omaha, where the old warrior was the prime exhibit. He asked the former clerk to use his influence to allow him to return to Arizona.

"The acorns and piñon nuts, the quail and the wild turkey, the giant cactus and the palo verdes – they all miss me," said Geronimo.

"A very beautiful thought, Geronimo," laughed Miles. "Quite poetic. But the men and women who live in Arizona, they do not miss you. Folks in Arizona sleep now at night. They have no fear that Geronimo will come and kill them. The acorns and the piñon nuts will have to get along as best they can without you."

Later that year Miles visited Geronimo at Fort Sill. The Army man again told Geronimo that he would not be allowed home. However, he did agree to Geronimo's request that he might be excused from forced labour because of his age. He was 69 years old.

In 1905 Geronimo was taken to Washington to ride in Theodore Roosevelt's inaugural parade. People bought his autographs for 25 cents as quickly as he could write them. Geronimo stole the show. Only the president himself attracted more attention.

When the parade was over, Geronimo was able to meet with Roosevelt. He took advantage of the occasion to plead for a return to Arizona:

Great Father, other Indians have homes where they can live and be happy. I and my people have no homes. The place where we are kept is bad for us . . . We are sick there and we die. White men are in the country that was my home. I pray you to tell them to go away and let my people go there and be happy.

Great Father, my hands are tied as with a rope. My heart is no longer bad. I will tell my people to obey no chief but the Great White Chief. I pray you to cut the ropes and make me free. Let me die in my own country, an old man who has been punished enough.

Roosevelt was sympathetic, but his reply was essentially the same as Miles's. The people of Arizona would not stand for it. He told Geronimo, "I am sorry, and have no feeling against you."

In the autumn of the same year, Mr S. M. Barrett, the White Superintendent of Education in Lawton, Oklahoma, secured permission from Roosevelt to interview Geronimo about his life. Geronimo related the tale in the Apache language to Asa Dakiugie, the son of Juh, who translated it into English for Barrett to write down. More than anything in his old age Geronimo wanted to be allowed to return to the land of the Chiricahuas, and in telling his life story he politically left out most of his dealings with Americans. The book, *Geronimo's Story of His Life*, was dedicated to President Roosevelt.

By now Geronimo's years were piling up, and his rugged squat body showing signs of wear. Yet it took an accident to kill him. On a cold night in February 1909 he fell, drunk, off his horse and lay in a freezing creek all night. He developed severe pneumonia. He fought the illness for seven days, but it eventually overwhelmed him. Geronimo died at 6.15 in the morning of 17 February, and was buried the following day in Fort Sill's cemetery. He was about 80 years old, and still technically a prisoner of war.

He was never to realize his dream of returning to Arizona. But he was always proud that to finally subdue him and his band of 37 Chiricahua Apache it had taken 5,000 White soldiers

Ghost Dancers

The whole world is coming,
A nation is coming.
The Eagle has brought the message to the tribe.
Over the whole earth they are coming;
The buffalo are coming, the buffalo are coming,
The Crow has brought the message to the tribe.

Ghost Dance Song

With the final capture of Geronimo in 1886 all great chiefs were within the reservations. Some, like Quanah Parker of the Quahadi Comanche, took up White ways, trying to do their best for their people by beating the Americans at their own games, like politics, real estate deals and moneymaking. Occasionally they won. Usually they lost. Every year the reservations got smaller, as did government allotments of beef and clothing. In 1889 drought came to the West; there was starvation on the reservations, and when measles struck the children they were too weak to resist.

It was a time for hope, a time to dream. A time to remember the buffalo which used to coat the plains, the chokecherries which used to hang by the mouthwatering bunch, and the freedom to roam over the range.

There were many shaman dreamers, but the most powerful was the Paiute Wovoka. Just before dawn on New Year's Day, 1889, far out in remote Nevada, the 34-year-old Wovoka fell ill. In his delirium he dreamed he visited the Great Spirit in heaven. There, he was told that a time was coming when the buffalo would once again fill the plains and dead tribesmen would be restored to their families. If the Indians refrained from violence, and if they were virtuous and performed the proper ritual dance – the Ghost Dance – they could hasten the coming of the new world, which would cover the old, and push the White men into the sea.

Some Indians, like the Kiowa and Comanche, were sceptical. But among the former tribes of the northern plains the Ghost Dance religion took a powerful hold. It spread wildly and rapidly across the reservations, from the Arapaho, to the Cheyenne, to the Wichita. In the winter of early 1890, a holy man of the Teton Sioux, Kicking Bear, brought the new gospel to Dakota.

The Sioux began Ghost Dancing in the spring, in secret ceremonies away from White Eyes. Adapting Wovoka's original ceremony to the Sioux Sun Dance, they danced around a sacred tree. At Kicking Bear's behest, the dancers also wore "ghost shirts" painted with magical symbols to keep away White bullets.

By mid-autumn of 1890, the Sioux were in something approaching a religious frenzy. Thousands of Sioux were now participating in the Ghost Dances, shuffling around in great circles, which speeded up until the exhausted dancers reached a state of delirious ecstasy where they saw the dead "come to life". Normal life on the reservations all but stopped. Even the schools were emptied, as the Indians spent all day dancing and chanting.

In October, Kicking Bear was invited by Sitting Bull to

come to his isolated reservation at Standing Rock and teach the Huncpapa Sioux the Ghost Dance.

Sitting Bull's personal attitude to the Ghost Dance was one of disbelief. Yet, he considered that it would give succour to his people, and began to supervise personally the Huncpapa's dances.

The news that Sitting Bull, the great Sioux war leader and patriot, was Ghost Dancing caused White officials to panic. They already considered the situation out of control; with Sitting Bull involved they thought it might turn into an uprising.

On 17 November General Nelson Miles ordered troops to the Sioux reservations, including the all-Black 9th Cavalry and the late Custer's regiment, the 7th Cavalry. By December a third of the armed forces of the US was on alert. The former Indian agent Valentine McGillycuddy was dispatched by Washington to assess the gravity of the situation on the Sioux reservations. He went and saw, and counselled patience. "I should let the dance continue," he wrote to Washington. "The coming of the troops has frightened the Indians . . . If the troops remain, trouble is sure to come."

Unfortunately, the government did not listen to McGillycuddy. Instead they listened to James McLaughlin, head of the Standing Rock Agency, who urged that Sitting Bull was dangerous and should be arrested. The government acceded, and McLaughlin sent 43 Sioux policemen up to Sitting Bull's cabins on the banks of the Grand River.

Just before daybreak on the dreary morning of 15 December 1890, the Sioux police surrounded Sitting Bull's home. Some of them had ridden with him at Little Big Horn. But now the Sioux were a divided and suspicious people. The police entered Sitting Bull's cabin, and the senior policeman,

Lieutenant Henry Bull Head, found the old chief asleep on the floor. Waking him up, Bull Head brusquely informed him, "You are my prisoner. You must go to the agency."

At first, Sitting Bull agreed to go quietly. He sent one of his two wives to get his clothes, and asked one of the policemen to saddle his pony. But then the police began manhandling him and searching the house for weapons, something which upset Sitting Bull, for he then started cursing them. Meanwhile, more than 150 of Sitting Bull's most ardent followers had crowded around the police outside.

When Sitting Bull and Lieutenant Bull Head appeared outside the cabin, the situation became electric. People started shouting "You shall not take our chief! " As the 59-year-old Sitting Bull was pushed towards his pony, he suddenly declared that he was not going to Fort Yates and called upon his followers to rescue him. A brave named Catch the Bear shot Lieutenant Bull Head in the side. As he fell, he fired at Sitting Bull, hitting him in the chest. Almost in the same moment another policeman, Red Tomahawk, shot Sitting Bull through the head.

Sitting Bull was killed by his own people, as he had once been foretold by a meadowlark.

After Sitting Bull fell, a wild fight ensued in which police and Huncpapa (including women) fought and killed with guns, knives and clubs at point-blank range. The police, after suffering six dead, were only saved by the arrival of the cavalry.

Sitting Bull's body was taken away on a wagon and was buried in a pauper's grave.

WOUNDED KNEE

Following the fight at Sitting Bull's cabin, some of his Huncpapa surrendered at Fort Bennett but some, half starving and half clad, fled to other reservations. Thirty-eight joined the Miniconjou Sioux chief, Big Foot, whose village was on the forks of the Cheyenne River. The Army considered Big Foot another Ghost Dance troublemaker and he was under overt surveillance. Already disturbed by the supervision, Big Foot became deeply fearful when the Huncpapa refugees told him of Sitting Bull's death. Then troops were sighted nearby. Believing that he was going to be murdered, Big Foot led his people – 333 men, women and children – out from their camp on the night of 23 December. He headed south towards the Pine Ridge Reservation, hoping to find protection with Red Cloud.

The Army pursued the fleeing Indians, sending out three regiments, including the 7th Cavalry. As the army scoured the wintry prairie, Big Foot's band trudged south and reached the Dakota Badlands.

At two o'clock in the afternoon of 28 December, the Army caught up with Big Foot, now so ill with pneumonia that he was being carried in a wagon. He surrendered without protest, and accepted a military guard. Since the day was closing in, the Indians were directed to camp for the night at a nearby creek, Wounded Knee. The troopers took up positions in the surrounding hills to prevent any escape.

While it was still dark, Colonel George A. Forsyth (of Beecher Island fame) arrived with reinforcements from the 7th Cavalry. By the morning of the 29th there were 500 troopers ringing the Sioux.

The day dawned bright and clear. Forsyth called all the Sioux men and elder boys to stand in a semi-crcle in front of their tents. Numbering 106, they squatted on the ground, wearing their bright-coloured Ghost Dance shirts. Troopers then began searching the tents for weapons.

Women began wailing. The men sitting in the council circle immediately became alert. A shaman named Yellow Bird jumped up and told warriors: "I have made medicine of the White man's ammunition. It is good medicine, and his bullets can not harm you, as they will not go through your ghost shirts, while your bullets will kill."

Forsyth ordered the shaman to sit down. Another officer, James D. Mann, warned his men: "Be ready; there is going to be trouble."

Two soldiers began struggling with a brave named Black Coyote, who refused to hand over his rifle. Then things happened with frightening speed. The holy man Yellow Bird threw a handful of dust up into the air, which the soldiers thought was a signal for an attack on them.

Four or five Sioux warriors pulled guns out from under their blankets. An officer was shot. And then all hell broke loose. Standing only eight feet away from the braves, a line of soldiers levelled their carbines and sent a volley into their ranks. Some warriors managed to shoot back, while from a low hill four Hotchkiss guns began to spew explosive shells into the scattering Sioux at the rate of a round a second. Tents were on fire, horses screaming in pain. In a few places warriors were fighting the soldiers with whatever they had to hand, and sometimes just their hands. Sioux women and children were trying to make it to a ravine, but the shells kept bursting around them. Maddened soldiers gave chase, killing groups of Indians as they huddled in the rocks and scrub cedar – or wherever they had run to. Dead women and children would be found strung out for three miles from Wounded Knee.

Among the eye-witnesses to Wounded Knee was Black Elk, a cousin of Crazy Horse. It is worth quoting his account in full:

> In the morning I went out after my horses, and while I was out I heard shooting off toward the east, and I knew from the sound that it must be wagon guns [cannon] going off. The sounds went right through my body, and I felt that something terrible would happen.
>
> When I reached camp with the horses, a man rode up to me and said: "Hey-hey-hey! The people that are coming are fired on! I know it!"
>
> I saddled up my buckskin and put on my sacred shirt. It was one I had made to be worn by no one but myself. It had a spotted eagle outstretched on the back of it, and the daybreak star was on the left shoulder, because when facing south that shoulder is toward the east. Across the breast, from the left shoulder to the right hip, was the flaming rainbow, and there was another rainbow around the neck, like a necklace, with a star at the bottom. At each shoulder, elbow, and wrist was an eagle feather; and over the whole shirt were red streaks of lightning. You will see that this was from my great vision, and you will know how it protected me that day.
>
> I painted my face all red, and in my hair I put one eagle feather for the One Above. It did not take me long to get ready, for I could still hear the shooting over there.
>
> I started out alone on the old road that ran across the hills to Wounded Knee. I had no gun. I carried only the sacred bow of the west that I had seen in my great vision. I had gone only a little way when a band of young men came galloping after me. The first two who came up were Loves War and Iron Wasichu. I asked what they

were going to do, and they said they were just going to
see where the shooting was. Then others were coming
up, and some older men.

We rode fast, and there were about twenty of us now.
The shooting was getting louder. A horseback [scout]
from over there came galloping very fast toward us, and
he said: "Hey-hey-hey! They have murdered them!"
Then he whipped his horse and rode away faster toward
Pine Ridge.

In a little while we had come to the top of the ridge
where, looking to the east, you can see for the first time
the monument and the burying ground on the little hill
where the church is. That is where the terrible thing
started. Just south of the burying ground on the little hill
a deep dry gulch runs about east and west, very crooked,
and it rises westward to nearly the top of the ridge where
we were. It had no name, but the Wasichus [white men]
sometimes call it Battle Creek now. We stopped on the
ridge not far from the head of the dry gulch. Wagon-
guns were still going off over there on the little hill, and
they were going off again where they hit along the gulch.
There was much shooting down yonder, and there were
many cries, and we could see cavalrymen scattered over
the hills ahead of us. Cavalrymen were riding along the
gulch and shooting into it, where the women and
children were running away and trying to hide in the
gullies and the stunted pines.

A little way ahead of us, just below the head of the dry
gulch, there were some women and children who were
huddled under a clay bank, and some cavalrymen were
there pointing guns at them.

We stopped back behind the ridge, and I said to the
others: "Take courage. These are our relatives. We will

try to get them back." Then we all sang a song which went like this:

A thunder being nation I am, I have said.
A thunder being nation I am, I have said.
You shall live.You shall live.
You shall live.You shall live.

Then I rode over the ridge and the others after me, and we were crying: "Take courage! It is time to fight!" The soldiers who were guarding our relatives shot at us and then ran away fast, and some more cavalrymen on the other side of the gulch did too. We got our relatives and sent them across the ridge to the northwest where they would be safe.

I had no gun, and when we were charging, I just held the sacred bow out in front of me with my right hand. The bullets did not hit us at all.

We found a little baby lying all alone near the head of the gulch. I could not pick her up just then, but I got her later and some of my people adopted her. I just wrapped her up tighter in a shawl that was around her and left her there. It was a safe place, and I had other work to do.

The soldiers had run eastward over the hills where there were some more soldiers, and they were off their horses and lying down. I told the others to stay back, and I charged upon them holding the sacred bow out toward them with my right hand. They all shot at me, and I could hear bullets all around me, but I ran my horse right close to them, and then swung around. Some soldiers across the gulch began shooting at me too, but I got back to the others and was not hurt at all.

By now many other Lakotas, who had heard the

shooting, were coming up from Pine Ridge, and we all charged on the soldiers. They ran eastward toward where the trouble began. We followed down along the dry gulch, and what we saw was terrible. Dead and wounded women and children and little babies were scattered all along there where they had been trying to run away. The soldiers had followed along the gulch, as they ran, and murdered them in there. Sometimes they were in heaps because they had huddled together, and some were scattered all along. Sometimes bunches of them had been killed and torn to pieces where the wagon-guns hit them. I saw a little baby trying to suck its mother, but she was bloody and dead.

There were two little boys at one place in this gulch. They had guns and they had been killing soldiers all by themselves. We could see the soldiers they had killed. The boys were all alone there, and they were not hurt. These were very brave little boys.

When we drove the soldiers back, they dug themselves in, and we were not enough people to drive them out from there. In the evening they marched off up Wounded Creek, and then we saw all that they had done there.

Men and women and children were heaped and scattered all over the flat at the bottom of the little hill where the soldiers had their wagon-guns, and westward up the dry gulch all the way to the high ridge, the dead women and children and babies were scattered.

When I saw this I wished that I had died too, but I was not sorry for the women and children. It was better for them to be happy in the other world, and I wanted to be there too. But before I went there I wanted to have revenge. I thought there might be a day, and we should have revenge.

After the soldiers marched away, I heard from my friend, Dog Chief, how the trouble started, and he was right there by Yellow Bird when it happened. This is the way it was:

In the morning the soldiers began to take all the guns away from the Big Foots, who were camped in the flat below the little hill where the monument and burying ground are now. The people had stacked most of their guns, and even their knives, by the tepee where Big Foot was lying sick. Soldiers were on the little hill and all around, and there were soldiers across the dry gulch to the south and over east along Wounded Knee Creek too. The people were nearly surrounded, and the wagon-guns were pointing at them.

Some had not yet given up their guns, and so the soldiers were searching all the tepees, throwing things around and poking into everything. There was a man called Yellow Bird, and he and another man were standing in front of the tepee where Big Foot was lying sick. They had white sheets around and over them, with eyeholes to look through, and they had guns under these. An officer came to search them. He took the other man's gun, and then started to take Yellow Bird's. But Yellow Bird would not let go. He wrestled with the officer, and while they were wrestling, the gun went off and killed the officer. Wasichus and some others have said he meant to do this, but Dog Chief was standing right there, and he told me it was not so. As soon as the gun went off, Dog Chief told me, an officer shot and killed Big Foot who was lying sick inside the tepee.

Then suddenly nobody knew what was happening, except that the soldiers were all shooting and the wagon-guns began going off right in among the people.

Many were shot down right there. The women and children ran into the gulch and up west, dropping all the time, for the soldiers shot them as they ran.There were only about a hundred warriors and there were nearly five hundred soldiers. The warriors rushed to where they had piled their guns and knives. They fought soldiers with only their hands until they got their guns.

Dog Chief saw Yellow Bird run into a tepee with his gun, and from there he killed soldiers until the tepee caught fire. Then he died full of bullets.

It was a good winter day when all this happened. The sun was shining. But after the soldiers marched away from their dirty work, a heavy snow began to fall. The wind came up in the night. There was a big blizzard, and it grew very cold. The snow drifted deep in the crooked gulch, and it was one long grave of butchered women and children and babies, who had never done any harm and were only trying to run away.

It is not known how many Sioux died at Wounded Knee. The smallest estimate is 153, but it may have been as high as 300. The Army suffered twenty-five casualties, some of them killed accidentally by their own side in the frenzy of firing.

In the darkening creek of Wounded Knee, where the snow was crimson with blood, a blizzard began to threaten. So the Sioux fallen, who numbered Big Foot, were left where they lay. Not until 3 January 1891 did a burial detail go back to collect the dead. Their bodies were frozen in grotesque positions, and like this they were thrown into a common grave.

The scene was so grisly that it moved some of the civilians in the burial party to tears: "It is a thing to melt the heart of a man, if it was of stone, [wrote one] to see those little children, with their bodies shot to pieces thrown naked into the pit."

The massacre at Wounded Knee caused the Sioux at the nearby Pine Ridge Agency to run off to the Badlands, where they gathered in a huge camp of 4,000 at White Clay Creek. When the 7th Cavalry went to probe the area, they became trapped by the Sioux in a valley. They were eventually rescued by the Black buffalo soldiers of the 9th Cavalry, who made an amazing forced march of 90 miles. General Miles then surrounded the Sioux, and made overtures of peace. The Indians were hungry and outnumbered – and disillusioned over the failure of the Ghost Dance shirts, most of which had been torn off and trampled underfoot.

Gradually, Sioux were coaxed out of the Big Badlands, without any more bloodshed. On 15 January, 1891, Kicking Bear and the last of the Sioux in the Badlands laid their rifles at the feet of General Nelson Miles at Pine Ridge Agency.

The Ghost Dance was over. And so were 300 years of resistance to the White man. A few individuals, even families, would hold out into the twentieth century, but there would be no more battles, no more war against the White man.

At Wounded Knee was buried the Indian's last bid for freedom as a people.

PART IV

To Kill the Indian to Save the Man

It is probably true that the majority of our wild Indians have no inherited tendencies whatever toward morality or chastity, according to an enlightened standard. Chastity and morality among them must come from education and contact with the better element of the Whites.

Commissioner of Indian Affairs, W. A. Jones, 1903

Prologue

Hey-a-a-hey! Hey-a-a-hey! Hey-a-a-hey! Hey-a-a-hey! Grandfather, Great Spirit, once more behold me on earth and lean to hear my feeble voice. You lived first, and you are older than all need, older than all prayer. All things belong to you – the two-leggeds, the four-leggeds, the wings of the air and all green things that live. You have set the powers of the four quarters to cross each other. The good road and the road of difficulties you have made to cross; and where they cross, the place is holy. Day in and out, forever, you are the life of things.

Therefore I am sending a voice, Great Spirit, my grandfather, forgetting nothing you have made, the stars of the universe and the grasses of the earth.

You have said to me, when I was still young and could hope, that in difficulty I should send a voice four times, once for each quarter of the earth, and you would hear me.

Today I send a voice for a people in despair.

From the west, you have given me the cup of living water and the sacred bow, the power to make live and to destroy. You have given me a sacred wind and the herb from where the white giant lives – the cleansing power and the healing. The daybreak star and pipe, you have given from the east; and from the south, the nations' sacred hoop and the tree that was to bloom. To the center of the world you have taken me and showed the goodness and beauty and the strangeness of the greening earth, the only mother – and there the spirit shapes of things, as they should be, you have shown to me and I have seen. At the center of this sacred hoop you have said that I should make the tree to bloom.

With tears running, O Great Spirit, Great Spirit, my Grandfather – with running tears I must say now that the tree has never bloomed. A pitiful old man, you see me here, and I have fallen away and have done nothing. Here at the center of the world, where you took me when I was young and taught; here, old, I stand, and the tree is withered, Grandfather, my Grandfather!

Again, and maybe the last time on this earth, I recall the great vision you sent me. It may be that some little root of the sacred tree still lives. Nourish it then, that it may leaf and bloom and fill with singing birds. Hear me, not for myself, but for my people; I am old. Hear me that they may once more go back into the sacred hoop and find the good red road, the shielding tree!

In sorrow I am sending a feeble voice, O Six Powers of the World. Hear me in my sorrow, for I may never call again. O make my people live!

A Prayer of Black Elk, 1931

The Native American Movement represents the re-awakening of the Native American people and the revival of Americanist principles. It is the spiritual descendant of the earlier movements for unity organized by Tecumseh, Cuauhtemoc, Tupac Amaru, Po-pe, Cajeme, Wovoka and other great leaders.

The movement seeks to realize justice for Native Americans and all other peoples who suffer from discrimination. It does not draw any color line or exclude anyone. All persons who seek to advance the cause of true Americanism and of American unity are welcome . . . All who struggle for justice and freedom are brothers! . . . Every person in the United States and in the Americas who has a drop of Native American ancestry is a member of the Movement if he stands for freedom and justice . . .

Native American Movement pamphlet, 1963

Wounded Knee was the last military confrontation in the Indian wars. But it was not the end of the White's campaign against the Indian, which henceforth took a more invidious form.

The Native American was pacified. Now he had to be civilized.

Most Indians already had some experience of this "civilization". From 1849, the US government had been rounding up Indians and relocating them on "reservations" where they would be protected from local genocides until they were "sufficiently advanced in civilization . . . to be able to maintain themselves in close proximity with, or in the midst of, a white population."

On these reservations, everything Native had to be destroyed – even if that meant destroying the Native himself. No facet of Native American life was left untouched by the all-knowing, all-seeing Bureau of Indian Affairs. They started with the children.

With the founding of the Carlisle Indian School in 1879 by

Captain R. H. Pratt, native children were removed from their "blanket Indian" parents for Anglo-American schooling. Pratt was no blood racist; he merely considered that Indian culture was obsolete, and that the progressive future for Native Americans was to be assimilated into White society. It was, Pratt said, his intention "to kill the Indian to save the man".

At Carlisle (motto: "From Savagery to Civilization") Indian children were forcibly acculturized. Many died, and those who survived their "salvation" were scarred for perpetuity. Luther Standing Bear was one of Carlisle's first pupils:

One day [in 1879] there came to the agency a party of white people from the East. Their presence aroused considerable excitement when it became known that these people were school teachers who wanted some Indian boys and girls to take away with them . . .

I could think of no reason why white people wanted Indian boys and girls except to kill them, and not having the remotest idea of what a school was, I thought we were going East to die. But so well have courage and bravery been trained into us that it became part of our unconcious thinking and acting, and personal life was nothing when it came time to do something for the tribe . . . in giving myself up to go East I was proving to my father that he was honoured with a brave son . . .

On our way to school we saw many white people, more than we ever dreamed existed, and the manner in which they acted when they saw us quite indicated their opinion of us. It was only about three years after the Custer battle, and the general opinion was that the Plains people merely infested the earth as nuisances, and our being there simply evidenced misjudgement on the part of Wakan Tanka. Whenever our train stopped at the railway stations, it was met by great numbers of white people who came to gaze upon the little Indian "savages". The shy little ones sat quietly at the car windows looking at the people who swarmed on the platform. Some of the children wrapped themselves in their blankets, covering all but their eyes. At one place we were taken off the train and marched a distance down the street to a restaurant. We walked . . . between two rows of uniformed men whom we called soldiers, though I suppose they were policemen. This must have been done to protect us, for it was surely known that we boys and girls could do no harm . . . the white people [stood] craning their necks, talking, laughing, and making a great noise. They yelled and tried to mimic us by giving what they thought were war-whoops. We did not like this, and some of the children were naturally very much frightened . . . Back on the train the older boys sang brave songs in an effort to keep up their spirits and ours too. In my mind I often recall that scene – eighty-odd blanketed boys and girls marching down the street surrounded by a jeering, unsympathetic people whose only emotions were those of hate and fear; the conquerors looking upon the conquered. And no more understanding us than if we had suddenly been dropped from the moon.

At last at Carlisle the transforming, the "civilizing" process began. It began with clothes. Never, no matter what our philosophy or spiritual quality, could we be civilized while wearing the moccasin and blanket . . . Our accustomed dress was taken and replaced with clothing that felt cumbersome and awkward. Against trousers and handkerchiefs we had a distinct feeling – they were unsanitary and the trousers kept us from breathing well. High collars, stiff-bosomed shirts, and suspenders fully three inches in width were uncomfortable, while leather boots caused actual suffering. We longed to go barefoot, but were told that the dew on the grass would give us colds. That was a new warning for us . . . for in that time colds, catarrh, bronchitis, and *la grippe* were unknown. But we were soon to know them. Then, red flannel undergarments were given us for winter wear, and for me, at least, discomfort grew into actual torture . . . My niece once asked me what I disliked most during those first bewildering days, and I said, "red flannel" . . . I still remember those horrid, sticky garments which we had to wear next to the skin, and I still squirm and itch when I think of them. Of course, our hair was cut . . . in some mysterious way long hair stood in the path of our development. For all the grumbling among the bigger boys, we soon had our heads shaven. How strange I felt! Involuntarily, time and time again, my hands went to my head, and that night it was a long time before I went to sleep. If we did not learn much at first, it will not be wondered at, I think. Everything was queer, and it took a few months to get adjusted to the new surroundings.

Almost immediately our names were changed to those in common use in the English language. Instead of translating our names into English and calling Zinkcaziwin, Yellow Bird, and Wanbli K'leska, Spotted Eagle, which in itself would have been educational, we were just John, Henry or Maggie, as the case might be. I was told to take a pointer and select a name for myself from the list written on the blackboard. I did, and since one was just as good as another, and as I could not distinguish any difference in them, I placed the pointer on the name Luther . . .

Of all the changes we were forced to make, that of diet was doubtless the most injurious, for it was immediate and drastic. White bread we had for the first meal and thereafter, as well as coffee and sugar. Had we been allowed our own simple diet of meat, either boiled with soup or dried, and fruit, with perhaps a few vegetables, we should have thrived. But the change in clothing, housing, food, and confinement combined with lonesomeness was too much, and in three years nearly one half of the children from the Plains were dead and through with all earthly schools. In the graveyard at Carlisle most of the graves are those of little ones.

By 1900 there were 300 Indian schools. The great majority of them were boarding schools modelled on Carlisle; the remainder were reservation schools run by missionaries or government. One thing was common to them all. Native American languages were forbidden. After all, as the Commissioner of Indian Affairs noted, "teaching an Indian in his own barbarous dialect is a positive detriment to him. The impracticability, if not impossibility, of civilizing the Indians of this country in any other tongue than our own would seem obvious."

The onslaught on Native culture continued. American Indian religion was suppressed. Polygamy outlawed.* Indians were compelled even to cut their hair. Lieutenant V. E. Stottler

*Prompting a famous reply by the Comanche chief Quanah Parker: "I used to go to war in Texas and Mexico. You wanted me to stop fighting and sent messages all the time: 'You stop, Quanah. You come here. You sit down, Quanah.' You did not say anything then, "How many wives you got, Quanah?" Now I come and sit down as you want. You talk about wives; which one I throw away? . . . You little girl, you go 'way; you no papa – you pick him? You little fellow, you go 'way; you got no papa – you pick him?"

was officer in charge of barbering at the Mescalero Apache Reservation:

> As with Samson of old, the Indians' wildness lay in their long hair, which the returned educated Indians wore because, as they boasted, "It made them wild." All energies were bent to compel the adult males to cut their hair and adopt civilized attire in vain. I directed the (Indian) police to cut theirs or leave the force. They reluctantly complied, but once accomplished they were only too eager to compel the rest, and they cheerfully, under orders, arrested and brought to me every educated Indian on the [Mescalero Apache] Reservation. There were twenty of these, gorgeous in paint, feathers, long hair, breechclouts and blankets . . . The Indian Office, at my request, issued a preemptory order for all to cut their hair and adopt civilized attire; and in six weeks from the start every male Indian had been changed into the semblance of a decent man, with the warning that confinement at hard labor awaited any backsliders. [The philosophy behind this action was that] the United States has for years footed the bills that maintained them in idleness, filth, immorality, and barbarism, and where a policy for their good has been adopted, they will not be consulted.

Under such a swamping of their culture, under such pervasive institutionalization, many agency Native Americans became directionless and despairing. They suffered physically too, for they were almost always dependent on government subsistence, itself controlled by agents whose crookedness became a byword for corruption.

A small, depressing picture of reservation life comes from

the pen of an army surgeon at the Crow Creek agency in South Dakota:

> Some time about the middle of the winter a large vat was constructed of cotton-wood lumber, about six feet square and six feet deep, in connection with the steam sawmill, with a pipe leading from the boiler into the vat. Into this vat was thrown beef, beef heads, entrails of beeves, some beans, flour and pork. I think there was put into the vat two barrels of flour each time, which was not oftener than once in twenty-four hours. This mass was then cooked by the steam from the boiler passing through the vat. When that was done, all the Indians were ordered to come there with their pails and get it . . . The Santees and Winnebagos were fed from this vat; some of the Indians refused to eat it, saying they could not eat it, it made them sick . . . The Indians reported several deaths from starvation . . .

Impoverished and abject, the reservation Indian became a pitiable figure to reformist politicians in Washington. The solution was clear. He needed more civilizing. In 1888 the General Allotment Act (sometimes called the "Dawes Act", after its sponsor) was passed. A dog's dinner of avarice and do-goodery, it ushered in one of the darkest eras in American Indian history.

Allotment Act

Hailed by Theodore Roosevelt as a "mighty pulverizing engine to break up the tribal mass", the Allotment Act obliged the Indians to surrender their reservations, splinters of which were then granted to individual Indians as family-sized farms. Usually there were 160 acres apiece. Reservation acreage left over was a "surplus" to be offered to sale to Whites.

As land-grabs went, the Allotment Act was one of the great steals of history. The first allotment was the Sisseton and Wahpeton Sioux reservation in South Dakota, which yielded up a "surplus" of 660,000 acres. And so it went on, reservation by reservation. Eventually, after all the best reservation lands had been "restored to the public domain", allotment juddered to a halt. By then, of the 150 million acres owned by the Indians in 1880 – nearly all of it "guaranteed" by treaty – over 90 million acres had been plundered from them.

Many of the tribes resisted allotment, even banding together in a 22-nation council, but they were all finally cajoled, bribed and steam-rollered into doing the White man's wishes. George Bird Grinnell, a sympathetic White observer of the Indians, was a bystander to the allotment process:

The most shameful chapter of American history is that in which is recorded the account of our dealings with the Indians. The story of our government's intercourse with this race is an unbroken narrative of injustice, fraud, and robbery. Our people have disregarded honesty and truth whenever they have come in contact with the Indian, and he has had no rights because he never had the power to enforce any.

Protests against govemmental swindling of these savages have been made again and again, but such remonstrances attract no general attention. Almost everyone is ready to acknowledge that in the past the Indians have been shamefully robbed, but it appears to be believed that this no longer takes place. This is a great mistake. We treat them now much as we have always treated them. Within two years, I have been present on a reservation where government commissioners, by means of threats, by bribes given to chiefs, and by casting fraudulently the votes of absentees, succeeded after months of effort in securing votes enough to warrant them in asserting that a tribe of Indians, entirely wild and totally ignorant of farming, had consented to sell their lands, and to settle down each upon 160 acres of the most utterly arid and barren land to be found on the North American continent. The fraud perpetrated on this tribe was as gross as could be practised by one set of men upon another. In a similar way the Southern Utes were recently induced to consent to give up their reservation for another.

Americans are a conscientious people, yet they take no interest in these frauds. They have the Anglo-Saxon spirit of fair play, which sympathizes with weakness, yet no protest is made against the oppression which the Indian suffers. They are generous; a famine in Ireland, Japan or Russia arouses the sympathy and calls forth the bounty of the nation, yet they give no heed to the distress of the Indians, who are in the very midst of them. They do not realize that Indians are human beings like themselves.

Even the Five Civilized Nations – who held and governed Indian Territory under patented titles – had their lands allotted. It took an act of government to do it, the 1898 Curtis Act. But it was done.

With the breaking up of the reservations, the Indians had little sanctuary in which to maintain tribal life and tradition. Indeed, this was a prime point of allotment. Henceforth Indians were to cease to be Indians but hard-working, God-fearing Americans like all other Americans.

Since this was a self-evident good, all manner of eastern philanthropists and Western friends of the Indian, like General Crook, chorused approval of the Dawes Act.

Allotment conspicuously failed its ostensible object of "civilizing" the Indians. Allotted land was too small, too poor, and usually beguiled from the holder by White settlers. Thousands of Indians became utterly dispossessed, and crowded together in junkyard squatter camps, with the Sioux amongst the hardest hit. White reformers began to worry about the "Vanishing Indian". And they were right to worry. By 1900, the Indian population of the US was down to 237,000.

Repentance

After nearly forty years of robbery and acculturization, it occurred to Washington that allotment might not be the trick. Proof, as if proof were needed, came in the 1928 government report *The Problem of Indian Administration*: Every aspect of the Indian Service was found a failure. Nearly all Indians were living in poverty in declining lands. Education of native children was "grossly inadequate". Not one Indian Sanatorium met professional standards. Overall, Native Americans were dispossessed and discontented. As the report concluded, a deal of the blame lay with allotment itself: "It has resulted in much loss of land and an enormous increase in the details of administration without a compensating advance in the economic ability of the Indian. It almost seemed as if the government assumed that some magic in individual ownership would in itself prove an educational civilizing factor, but unfortunately this policy has for the most part operated in the opposite direction."

American Indians were dirt poor. But they had also endured as a distinct race. There was to be no more assimilation or allotment. In the aftermath of *The Problem of Indian Administration*, enlightened policies of Indian "independence" issued thick and fast from the Hoover and, especially, Franklin D. Roosevelt administrations.

One man above all others was responsible for Washington's change of heart on the "Indian Question". This was the (White) Southern idealist John Collier. Collier believed that the Indians should be preserved. More, he considered that their culture was precisely the shot-in-the-arm that materialistic Western capitalism needed. Head of the American Indian Defense Association, Collier was a consummate lobbyist for "Indian rights". It was Collier who obliged the government into compiling *The Problem of Indian Administration* report – the arrow that definitively killed assimilation and allotment. By 1932 Collier had moved from lobbyist to the man with his hands on the controls of Indian matters. Roosevelt made him Commissioner of Indian Affairs.

So influential was Collier over Native American affairs in the 20s and 30s that it is worth quoting his record of the era at length:

Moving, rapidly up the years from 1920, we witness first the defeat, in 1922–3, of the official attempt to disperse the Pueblos.* We witness the enactment of legislation to reinvest the Pueblos with land. That legislation was passed in 1924. We witness the enactment, in 1926, of legislation placing executive order reservations upon a parity with treaty reservations, thus vetoing the official plan of 1923 to transfer more than half of the then Indian estates to whites. We witness, in 1926, the invoking of the help of the United States Public Health

*Collier led Opposition to the Bursum Bill, which sought to deed 60,000 acres of Pueblo land to Hispanic and Anglo squatters. He also defeated the government's attempt at religious persecution of the pagan Taos Pueblo, termed "half animals" by the Bureau of Indian Affairs. For good measure, it called them "agents of Moscow" as well.

Service in an effort to check the rising death rates of the tribes. We see the Indians organizing the Council of All the New Mexico Pueblos, a still-continuing active organization, the first example of this Indian political renaissance. In 1924, expressly in recognition of their World War services, full citizenship was voted to all Indians by Congress. In 1927, for the first time, we see an action by the Department of the Interior to bring the light of social science to bear upon the Indian need and upon its Indian Bureau's operations. The monumental study by the Institute for Government Research, known as the Meriam Survey, resulted from the initiative of the then Secretary of the Interior. In 1928 the Senate moved into action, and the hearings and documents of the special committee upon Indian investigations of that body totaled thirty-six printed volumes by 1939.

Within the year 1929, an intellectual revolution was in full swing within the official Indian Bureau. The schooling policies of the Indian Office were fundamentally modified starting with that year. The movement was from uniformity of curriculum to diversity, and from mere classroom activity to community schools.

In 1929, the Secretary of the Interior and the Commissioner of Indian Affairs joined in memorials to Congress, asking for legislation to re-establish the local democracy of Indians, to curtail the absolutism of the government's Indian system, to apply the concept of constitutional right to Indian economic affairs, and to settle decently and promptly the host of Indian tribal claims growing out of breached treaties and compacts of the past years . . .

Public opinion could not move all at once; neither

could Indian opinion, nor administrative or congressional thinking. Active, continuous attention by the chief executive was needed; and in 1933, at last, the needed assembled data and administrative trends were made available to President Roosevelt. And in 1933, by secretarial order, the sale of Indian lands was stopped. Without public shock, the Indian cultures and religions were put in possession of the full constitutional guarantees. Without public shock, the institutionalized boarding schools for Indians were cut by one-third and the children were moved to community day schools, and thousands of children never schooled before were brought into the classroom.

Then the Indian Reorganization Act was formulated. The administrators took this proposed reform legislation to the Indians in great regional meetings, and through the Indians assembled there, back to all of the Indian communities. For the first time in history, all Indians were drawn into a discussion of universal problems of the Indians, and these universal problems focused upon the most ancient and most central Indian institution, local democracy integrated with the land.

Congress passed the Indian Reorganization Act in 1934, and it incorporated in this act a feature new in federal legislation, the referendum. The act, as passed by the Congress and signed by the President, was by its own terms merely permissive. Every Indian tribe might adopt it or reject it by majority vote by secret ballot.

The Indian Reorganization Act, under which today 74 per cent of the Indians are living and functioning, docs not contain the whole of the present Indian program. There are tribes not under the act which are realizing a creative self-determination not less than tribes that are under the act. And there are many tribes, under the act by their own choice, which have chosen to go forward with their ancient and never extinguished types of local democracy, rather than to adopt the parliamentary type of self-government.

Most tribes cooperated enthusiastically with Collier's New Deal. Indian lands, for the first time ever, were increased (by four million acres), and numerous communities utilized a revolving credit programme to purchase agricultural live and deadstock. By 1948 some 12,000 Indian families were self-supporting on their own land.

Long a devotee of Indian culture and religion, Collier also used his office to improve the spiritual lot of the Native American. The Bureau unflaggingly promoted "Indian-hood". It published books on Indian history, it marketed crafts. Against diehard clerical and Republican reaction, Collier included Indians within America's guarantee of religious freedom. Compulsory Christian services were dropped in Indian schools, while native religious ceremonies were encouraged – even the peyote cult popularized by Quanah Parker and the Native American Church.

The enlightenment came to an abrupt end in 1950. Policy towards the Indians had always been moulded by broader politics and desires. It was inevitable, then, that Indian affairs would be touched by the political reaction that took its name from Senator Joe McCarthy.

Back to the Future

If Collier had a fault, it was that he overestimated his success. When he resigned in 1945, he did so in the sure knowledge that his "New Deal" could not be undone. "Final Struggle Commences and Prevails" was the title he gave to the chapter tracing his tenure as Commissioner in his *Indians of the Americas.*

What was to last forever managed just five years more. Until, that is, President Truman installed Dillon S. Myer as Commissioner of Indian Affairs. Previously Director of the War Relocation – that is, the internment of Japanese Americans – Myer treated the Indians like they too were an enemy. A decade later a Senate Committee visiting the Klamath concluded: "The Termination of the Klamath reservation in Oregon has led to extreme social disorganization of that tribal group. Many of them can be found in state penal and mental institutions."

Any Indian made landless by termination soon found that the Bureau had an imaginative solution to their predicament. It shipped them off to urban areas, 17,500 of them, with Los Angeles, Denver and Chicago the favoured destinations. Many relocatees, wrenched from their tribe and their homes, were touched by alcoholism and depression, and in one year alone a third returned home. A number, however, made it on the White man's terms. And, to be just, many Bureau employees worked hard to place relocated Indians in employment, to find them housing. It was the coercive nature of the enterprise, the intentional separation of the Indian from his tribe and his land that was iniquitous. Land was life for the American Indian of the 1950s, as it had been for American Indians of the 1850s.

Relocation and termination were never passively accepted by the tribes. A number of them had the resources, leadership and maybe even the luck to buck the tide. They included the Northern Cheyenne who, despite bureaucratic obstacles and chicanery, manage to purchase almost the entire of their reservation in Montana after negotiating a $500,000 loan. They meant business, and paid back in full. Their plan was for "goals the Cheyenne people want to reach, and not the goals of others of good heart think we should want to reach".

This was 1960. Like other minorities in America, its Natives were beginning to organize themselves for liberation. There was change from the top, too, with the election in that year of John F. Kennedy as US president.

New Frontier

The liberal administration of JFK wasted little time in terminating termination. HCR 108 was deemed to have "died with the 83rd Congress and is of no legal effect at the present time". A "Task Force of Indian Affairs" was organized under the chairmanship of W. W. Keeler, Executive Vice President of the Phillips Petroleum Company. He was also Principal Chief of the Cherokee Nation. In July 1961 the Task Force made its report:

> The Task Force feels that recent Bureau policy has placed more emphasis on [termination] than on [development]. As a result, Indians, fearful that termination will take place before they are ready for it, have become deeply concerned. Their preoccupation was reflected in vigorous denunciation of the so-called "termination policy" during the many hearings which the Task Force conducted with Indian leaders. No other topic was accorded similar attention. It is apparent that Indian morale generally has been lowered and resistance to transition programs heightened as a result of the fear of premature Federal withdrawal. Now, many Indians see termination written into every new bill and administra-

tive decision and sometimes are reluctant to accept help which they need and want for fear that it will carry with it a termination requirement. During the Task Force hearings in Oklahoma City, Acting Commissioner Crow pointed out to those present that a few years ago it was possible for Bureau employees to sit down with Indians and talk constructively about the time when special Federal services for Indians would no longer be provided. "Now," said the Commissioner, "we have reached a point where we can't talk about it to each other; we don't want to talk about it, and if we do talk about it, we have rather harsh words on the subject."

The experience of the past few years demonstrates that placing greater emphasis on termination than on development impairs Indian morale and produces a hostile or apathetic response which greatly limits the effectiveness of the Federal Indian program. The Task Force believes it is wiser to assist the Indians to advance socially, economically and politically to the point where special services to this group of Americans are no longer justified. Then, termination can be achieved with maximum benefit for all concerned. Furthermore, if development, rather than termination, is emphasized during the transitional period, Indian cooperation – an essential ingredient of a successful program – can be expected . . .

In the opinion of the Task Force, the Bureau of Indian Affairs should seek attainment of the following related objectives:

1. Maximum Indian economic self-sufficiency.
2. Full participation of Indians in American life.
3. Equal citizenship privileges and responsibilities for Indians.

The Task Force strongly emphasizes that the aid of the tribe – or, more properly, the Indian community – is crucial to the achievement of these objectives and this support should be secured before projects are commenced. The Indians can retain their tribal identities and much of their culture while working toward a greater adjustment, and, for the further enrichment of our society, it is in our best interests to encourage them to do so.

Kennedy's "new trail" for the Indians meant more than the ending of termination and relocation. Substantial sums from government programmes – particularly the Area Development Administration – were conducted direct to the tribes themselves. For the first time in history, the Indians were regarded as being grown up enough to deal with big money. When Kennedy was assassinated, Johnson continued on the same political trail; as part of Johnson's "War on Poverty", the Office of Economic Opportunity dispatched millions of dollars to the tribes – dollars which the paternalistic BIA could not get its hands on.

Johnson was more of a "friend of the Indian" than most US presidents. He promised to put "first Americans first" in the Great Society, and to him went the record for being the first occupant of the White House to send Congress a special message on Indian matters. The influences on Johnson were several: there were his personal sympathies; there was the Kennedy legacy; and there was small but distinct political pressure put on Johnson by the Indians themselves.

This pressure had been building since 1961, when the National Congress of American Indians organized an "American Indian Conference" in Chicago. Attended by the delegates of seventy tribes, the Conference was the largest and most united gathering of Native American nations since the end of Indian Wars. A "Declaration of Indian Purpose" issued by the conference declared:

What we ask of America is not charity, not paternalism, even when benevolent. We ask only that the nature of our situation be recognized and made the basis of policy and action. In short, the Indians ask for assistance, technical and financial, for the time needed, however long that may be to regain in the America of the space age some measure of the adjustment they enjoyed as the original possessors of their native land.

The Conference was unprecedented, but it was still not radical enough for many young activists, who formed a breakaway National Indian Youth Council. Taking a leaf out of the civil rights movement handbook, the NIYC led a campaign of civil disobedience "fish-ins" to protest against curbs on the fishing rights of tribes in Washington state. Soon, militants from NIYC were leading fish-ins throughout the northwest, and although many were arrested the campaign caused the federal Department of Justice, in 1966, that it would defend Indians "who fish in accordance with . . . treaty and tribal regulations" against state interference.

In the wake of the "fish-ins" came a spate of Indian direct actions, some organized by the NIYC, some organized by local militant groups. Populating them mainly were city Indians, the children of relocatees. (There was irony in this, since relocation was designed to assimilate the Indian, not turn him or her against White society.) Such urban activists led the famous 1969 occupation of Alcatraz, when seventy-eight Native Amencans – from fifty tribes – "reclaimed" the island with the intention of building a cultural, religious and educational centre. They issued the following "Proclamation: To the Great White Father and All His People".

PROCLAMATION TO THE
GREAT WHITE FATHER AND ALL HIS PEOPLE

We, the native Americans, claim the land known as Alcatraz Island in the name of all American Indians by right of discovery.

We wish to be fair and honorable in our dealings with the Caucasian inhabitants of this land, and hereby offer the following treaty:

We will purchase said Alcatraz Island for twenty-four dollars ($24) in glass beads and red cloth, a precedent set by the white man's purchase of a similar island about 300 years ago. We know that $24 in trade goods for these 16 acres is more than was paid when Manhattan Island was sold, but we know that land values have risen over the years. Our offer of $1.24 per acre is greater than the 47¢ per acre that the White men are now paying the California Indians for their land. We will give to the inhabitants of this island a portion of that land for their own, to be held in trust by the American Indian Affairs and by the bureau of Caucasian Affairs to hold in perpetuity – for as long as the sun shall rise and the rivers go down to the sea. We will further guide the inhabitants in the proper way of living. We will offer them our religion, our education, our life-ways, in order to help them achieve our level of civilization and thus raise them and all their white brothers up from their savage and unhappy state. We offer this treaty in good faith and wish to be fair and honorable in our dealings with all white men . . .

We feel that this so-called Alcatraz Island is more

than suitable for an Indian Reservation, as determined by the white man's own standards. By this we mean that this place resembles most Indian reservations in that:

1. It is isolated from modern facilities, and without adequate means of transportation.
2. It has no fresh running water.
3. It has inadequate sanitation facilities.
4. There are no oil or mineral rights.
5. There is no industry and so unemployment is very great.
6. There are no health care facilities.
7. The soil is rocky and non-productive; and the land does not support game.
8. There are no educational facilities.
9. The population has always exceeded the land base.
10. The population has always been held as prisoners and dependent upon others.

Further, it would be fitting and symbolic that ships from all over the world, entering the Golden Gate, would first see Indian land, and thus be reminded of the true history of the great lands once ruled by free and noble Indians.

For seven months, the occupiers held out on Alcatraz, until federal marshals retook the island, gun in hand.

By the 1970s a new pressure group had emerged to arrow-head Indian protest. This was the American Indian Movement, which melded urban activism with appreciation of traditional tribal culture. AIM had spectacular early success in its occupation of the town of Gordon, Nebraska, to force the authorities to arrest the Army veteran murderers of a local Lakota, Raymond Yellow Thunder, in 1972. In that same year, AIM joined the "Trail of Broken Treaties" march on

Washington, stopping at reservations on route to spread the Red Power word. Remembered Mary Crow Dog, in her book *Lakota Woman*: "The American Indian Movement hit our reservation like a tornado, like a new wind blowing out of nowhere, a drumbeat from far off getting louder and louder. It was almost like the Ghost Dance fever that had hit the tribes in 1890, old uncle Dick Fool Bull said spreading like a prairie fire".

AIM's protests of 1972, however, were but curtain-raisers for its most spectacular demonstration: the occupation in February 1973 of Wounded Knee on the Pine Ridge (Oglala) Reservation. For 72 days AIM protestors were besieged by 300 federal forces, with considerable shooting by both sides. Two protestors died, and one US marshal was seriously injured before the AIM protestors surrendered.

As the first Wounded Knee had brought one era of American Indian history to a close, so did Wounded Knee II. It was the zenith of Red Power. AIM itself was repressed, infiltrated by the FBI, its leaders jailed, while supporters disillusioned by the failure of dissidence turned away.

The "New Indians" left little trace of their coming and their going. Or did they? Surely it was no accident that government passed in 1975 the Indian Self-Determination and Educational Assistance Act, which permitted the tribes to run their own federal programmes.

If this was not the giant leap to freedom that many militants had wanted, it was at least a small but definite step on the trail of empowerment.

INDIAN LAW

After Red Power, Indian activism underwent a change of armoury. Out went the placard, and in came the briefcase.

Led by the Native American Rights Fund (NARF), Indian attorneys fought numerous legal battles over treaty violations. Perhaps the most spectacular of the victories was that of the Passamaquoddies and Penobscots, who were able to prove ownership of most of the state of Maine. To settle the case in 1980, the federal government granted the two tribes 300,000 acres and $27.5 million.

As well as unsettled land claims, legal activism during the 1980s focused on the rights of the tribes to regulate their reservation's resources (water and game in particular), and the long-standing Indian grievance over the despoilation of native burial and sacred sites by white archaeologists and anthropologists. In a watershed moment, the Smithsonian Institution returned hundreds of artefacts to the tribes in 1989. A year later, the Native American Graves Protection and Repatriation Act gave the tribes wide powers to reclaim human remains and sacred objects from America's museums.

The white man's law was being used against himself. No longer were the Indian activists fighting the system. They were working it to their advantage.

To the present time, the most conspicuous example of Indian utilization of the American Way has been the growth of casinos on the reservations. The idea was smart: with Reaganite cuts in government funding in the 1980s, the tribes had to find a new way to gather a buck. Since Indian land was (and is) under federal jurisdiction, gaming was legal there no matter what prohibitions obtained in the adjacent state. And so, casinos and bingo halls opened up all over Indian Country. And millions of non-Indian punters rolled up to lose their money to the tribes.

They still do. The biggest casino in America is the property of the Mashantucket Pequots, who opened up their Ledyard high-stakes and bingo joint just as soon as they had sued the

US government for recognition as an Indian tribe. Indian casinos – which are exempt from taxation – have brought lucre to the tribes on undreamed of levels. Whereas, for example, the 362-member Agua Caliente tribe of Palm Springs once subsisted by hardscrabble farming and government handouts their casino (a tent initially, before taking more luxurious form) allowed them to buy a 45% share of the local bank. According to the US Census, between 1997 and 1999 the average median income of Native Americans was $30,784, making them the nation's second-wealthiest minority after Asians.

Not that gaming has been an unmitigated success. On some reservations, the casino and its attendant influx of non-Indian gamblers have nigh on obliterated their distinctive "Indianness". Traditionalists have taken umbrage, and the fall-out has not always been pretty. During the 1980s, the Mohawk reservation at Akwesne was the scene of violent confrontation – murder even – between "Traditionals" and pro-casino "Warriors".

But it is not just the casino that is threatening "Indianness" on the reservations. So is TV, with its constantly beamed images of Amero-euro culture. So is education, which is invariably conducted in a foreign tongue (English), and leaves just 23% of American Indian families speaking their native language at home. As a result, all the familiar problems of spiritual and psychological alienation – increased suicide rates, drug abuse, violence, and generational conflict – have taken hold in Indian Country.

Along with "Indianness", the "blood" Indian himself is an endangered species. More than 50% of Native Americans marry outside their race. By some estimates, only 8% of "Native Americans" in the year 2080 will be half-bloods or more.

TRICKSTER PEOPLE

Will the American Indian vanish? It is a question that has hung over Native Americans before.

Over the last five hundred years, after all, Native Americans have endured the white man's microbes, genocide, acculturation, termination, relocation, "melting pots". And the Indians are still here. They are even making a comeback. Against the contemporary permeation of English throughout Indian Country, numerous tribes have founded native language schools. Meanwhile, a reservation-based revitalization of Native American religion has, for many Indians, put religion at the centre of what it means to be an Indian. Sweat lodges, the use of sacred pipes and the purification ceremonies of the Sun Dance have become enormously popular. So popular, in fact, that hundreds of thousands of "New Age" whites, with no trace of "redman's blood" have taken them up. As the acerbic Sioux commentator Vine Deloria Jr noted in his *Red Earth, White Lies*: "When multitudes of young whites roam the West convinced they are Oglala Sioux Pipe Carriers and on a holy mission to protect 'Mother Earth', and when priests and ministers, scientists and drug companies, ecologists and environmentalists are crowding the reservations in search of new ritual, new medicines, or new ideas about the land, it would appear as if American Indians finally have made it."

Meanwhile, Native Americans who once found it embarrassing or inexpedient to admit their Indian blood, have become proud of the fact. According to the 2000 Census more than four million Americans classify themselves as Natives – many more than can be accounted for by the rising birth rate.

One of the most widespread myths of the North American

Indians concerns the cunning, shape shifting Trickster – often likened to a supernatural coyote – who reforms and rebounds no matter the challenge.

The Natives of America, it might be said, are the Trickster people.

Envoi

What the Indian Means
to America

Luther Standing Bear

Luther Standing Bear became hereditary chief of the
Oglala Sioux in 1905. The following chapter comes
from his classic *Land of the Spotted Eagle*.*

The feathered and blanketed figure of the American Indian
has come to symbolize the American continent. He is the
man who through centuries has been moulded and sculpted
by the same hand that shaped its mountains, forests, and
plains, and marked the course of its rivers.

The American Indian is of the soil, whether it be the region
of forests, plains, pueblos, or mesas. He fits into the
landscape, for the hand that fashioned the continent also
fashioned the man for his surroundings. He once grew as
naturally as the wild sunflowers; he belongs just as the buffalo
belonged.

With a physique that fitted, the man developed fitting skills
– crafts which today are called American. And the body had

Land of the Spotted Eagle, Houghton Mifflin Company, Boston, 1933.

a soul, also formed and moulded by the same master hand of harmony. Out of the Indian approach to existence there came a great freedom – an intense and absorbing love for nature, a respect for life; enriching faith in a Supreme Power. and principles of truth, honesty, generosity, equity, and brotherhood as a guide to mundane relations.

Becoming possessed of a fitting philosophy and art, it was by them that native man perpetuated his identity; stamped it into the history and soul of this country – made land and man one.

By living – struggling, losing, meditating, imbibing, aspiring, achieving – he wrote himself into inerasable evidence – an evidence that can be and often has been ignored, but never totally destroyed. Living – and all the intangible forces that constitute that phenomenon – are brought into being by Spirit, that which no man can alter. Only the hand of the Supreme Power can transform man; only Wakan Tanka can transform the Indian. But of such deep and infinite graces finite man has little comprehension. He has, therefore, no weapons with which to slay the unassailable. He can only foolishly trample.

The white man does not understand the Indian for the reason that he does not understand America. He is too far removed from its formative processes. The roots of the tree of his life have not yet grasped the rock and soil. The white man is still troubled with primitive fears; he still has in his consciousness the perils of this frontier continent, some of its fastnesses not yet having yielded to his questing footsteps and inquiring eyes. He shudders still with the memory of the loss of his forefathers upon its scorching deserts and forbidding mountain-tops. The man from Europe is still a foreigner and an alien. And he still hates the man who questioned his path across the continent.

But in the Indian the spirit of the land is still vested; it will be until other men are able to divine and meet its rhythm. Men must be born and reborn to belong. Their bodies must be formed of the dust of their forefathers' bones.

The attempted transformation of the Indian by the white man and the chaos that has resulted are but the fruits of the white man's disobedience of a fundamental and spiritual law. The pressure that has been brought to bear upon the native people, since the cessation of armed conflict, in the attempt to force conformity of custom and habit has caused a reaction more destructive than war, and the injury has not only affected the Indian, but has extended to the white population as well. Tyranny, stupidity, and lack of vision have brought about the situation now alluded to as the "Indian Problem".

There is, I insist, no Indian problem as created by the Indian himself. Every problem that exists today in regard to the native population is due to the white man's cast of mind, which is unable, at least reluctant, to seek understanding and achieve adjustment in a new and a significant environment into which it has so recently come.

The white man excused his presence here by saying that he had been guided by the will of his God; and in so saying absolved himself of all responsibility for his appearance in a land occupied by other men.

Then, too, his law was a written law; his divine decalogue reposed in a book. And what better proof that his advent into this country and his subsequent acts were the result of divine will! He brought the Word! There ensued a blind worship of written history, of books, of the written word, that has denuded the spoken word of its power and sacredness. The written word became established as a criterion of the superior man – a symbol of emotional fineness. The man who could write his name on a piece of paper, whether or not he possessed the spiritual fineness to honor those words in speech, was by some miraculous formula a more highly developed and sensitized person than the one who had never had a pen in hand, but whose spoken word was inviolable and whose sense of honor and truth was paramount. With false reasoning was the quality of human character measured by man's ability to make with an implement a mark upon paper. But granting this mode of reasoning be correct and just, then where are to be placed the thousands of illiterate whites who are unable to read and write? Are they, too, "savages"? Is not humanness a matter of heart and mind, and is it not evident in the form of relationship with men? Is not kindness more powerful than arrogance; and truth more powerful than the sword?

True, the white man brought great change. But the varied fruits of his civilization, though highly colored and inviting, are sickening and deadening. And if it be the part of civilization to maim, rob, and thwart, then what is progress?

I am going to venture that the man who sat on the ground in his tipi meditating on life and its meaning, accepting the kinship of all creatures, and acknowledging unity with the universe of things was infusing into his being the true essence of civilization. And when native man left off this form of development, his humanization was retarded in growth.

Another most powerful agent that gave native man promise of developing into a true human was the responsibility accepted by parenthood. Mating among Lakotas was motivated, of course, by the same laws of attraction that motivate all beings; however, considerable thought was given by parents of both boy and girl to the choosing of mates. And a still greater advantage accrued to the race by the law of self-mastery which the young couple voluntarily placed upon themselves as soon as they discovered they were to become parents. Immediately, and for some time after, the sole thought of the parents was in preparing the child for life. And true civilization lies in the dominance of self and not in the dominance of other men.

How far this idea would have gone in carrying my people upward and toward a better plane of existence, or how much of an influence it was in the development of their spiritual being, it is not possible to say. But it had its promises. And it cannot be gainsaid that the man who is rising to a higher estate is the man who is putting into his being the essence of humanism. It is self-effort that develops, and by this token the greatest factor today in humanizing races is the manner in which the machine is used – the product of one man's brain doing the work for another. The hand is the tool that has built man's mind; it, too, can refine it.

THE SAVAGE

After subjugation, after dispossession, there was cast the last abuse upon the people who so entirely resented their wrongs and punishments, and that was the stamping and the labeling of them as savages. To make this label stick has been the task of the white race and the greatest salve that it has been able to apply to its sore and troubled conscience now hardened through the habitual practice of injustice.

But all the years of calling the Indian a savage has never made him one; all the denial of his virtues has never taken them from him; and the very resistance he has made to save the things inalienably his has been his saving strength – that which will stand him in need when justice does make its belated appearance and he undertakes rehabilitation.

All sorts of feeble excuses are heard for the continued

subjection of the Indian. One of the most common is that he is not yet ready to accept the society of the white man – that he is not yet ready to mingle as a social entity.

This, I maintain, is beside the question. The matter is not one of making-over the external Indian into the likeness of the white race – process detrimental to both races. Who can say that the white man's way is better for the Indian? Where resides the human judgement with the competence to weigh and value Indian ideals and spiritual concepts; or substitute for them other values?

Then, has the white man's social order been so harmonious and ideal as to merit the respect of the Indian, and for that matter the thinking class of the white race? Is it wise to urge upon the Indian a foreign social form? Let none but the Indian answer!

Rather, let the white brother face about and cast his mental eye upon a new angle of vision. Let him look upon the Indian world as a human world; then let him see to it that human rights be accorded to the Indians. And this for the purpose of retaining for his own order of society a measure of humanity . . .

THE LIVING SPIRIT OF THE INDIAN – HIS ART

The spiritual health and existence of the Indian was maintained by song, magic, ritual, dance, symbolism, oratory (or council), design, handicraft, and folk-story.

Manifestly, to check or thwart this expression is to bring about spiritual decline. And it is in this condition of decline that the Indian people are today. There is but a feeble effort among the Sioux to keep alive their traditional songs and dances, while among other tribes there is but a half-hearted attempt to offset the influence of the Government school and at the same time recover from the crushing and stifling regime of the Indian Bureau.

One has but to speak of Indian verse to receive uncomprehending and unbelieving glances. Yet the Indian loved verse and into this mode of expression went his deepest feelings. Only a few ardent and advanced students seem interested; nevertheless, they have given in book form enough Indian translations to set forth the character and quality of Indian verse.

Oratory receives a little better understanding on the part of the white public, owing to the fact that oratorical compilations include those of Indian orators.

Hard as it seemingly is for the white man's ear to sense the differences, Indian songs are as varied as the many emotions which inspire them, for no two of them are alike. For instance, the Song of Victory is spirited and the notes high and remindful of an unrestrained hunter or warrior riding exultantly over the prairies. On the other hand, the song of the *Cano unye* is solemn and full of urge, for it is meant to inspire the young men to deeds of valor. Then there are the songs of death and the spiritual songs which are connected with the ceremony of initiation. These are full of the spirit of praise and worship, and so strong are some of these invocations that the very air seems as if surcharged with the presence of the Big Holy.

The Indian loved to worship. From birth to death he revered his surroundings. He considered himself born in the luxurious lap of Mother Earth and no place was to him humble. There was nothing between him and the Big Holy. The contact was immediate and personal, and the blessings of Wakan Tanka flowed over the Indian like rain showered from the sky. Wakan Tanka was not aloof, apart, and ever seeking to quell evil forces. He did not punish the animals and the birds, and likewise He did not punish man. He was not a punishing God. For there was never a question as to the supremacy of an evil power over and above the power of Good. There was but one ruling power, and that was *Good.*

Of course, none but an adoring one could dance for days with his face to the sacred sun, and that time is all but done. We cannot have back the days of the buffalo and beaver; we cannot win back our clean blood-stream aud superb health, and we can never again expect that beautiful *rapport* we once had with Nature. The springs and lakes have dried and the mountains are bare of forests. The plow has changed the face of the world. Wi-wila is dead! No more may we heal our sick and comfort our dying with a strength founded on faith, for even the animals now fear us, and fear supplants faith.

And the Indian wants to dance! It is his way of expressing devotion, of communing with unseen power, and in keeping his tribal identity. When the Lakota heart was filled with high emotion, he danced. When he felt the benediction of the warming rays of the sun, he danced. When his blood ran hot with success of the hunt or chase, he danced. When his heart was filled with pity for the orphan, the lonely father, or bereaved mother, he danced. All the joys and exaltations of life, all his gratefulness and thankfulness, all his acknowledgments of the mysterious power that guided life, and all his aspirations for a better life, culminated in one great dance – the Sun Dance.

Today we see our young people dancing together the silly jazz – dances that add nothing to the beauty and fineness of our lives and certainly nothing to our history, while the dances that record the life annals of a people die. It is the American Indian who contributes to this country its true folk-dancing, growing, as we did, out of the soil. The dance is far older than his legends, songs, or philosophy.

Did dancing mean much to the white people they would better understand ours. Yet at the same time there is no attraction that brings people from such distances as a certain tribal dance, for the reason that the white mind senses its mystery, for even the white man's inmost feelings are unconsciously stirred by the beat of the tomtom. They are heartbeats, and once all men danced to its rhythm.

When the Indian has forgotten the music of his forefathers, when the sound of the tomtom is no more, when noisy jazz has drowned the melody of the flute, he will be a dead Indian. When the memory of his heroes are no longer told in story, and he forsakes the beautiful white buckskin for factory shoddy, he will be dead. When from him has been taken all that is his, all that he has visioned in nature, all that has come to him from infinite sources, he then, truly, will be a dead Indian. His spirit will be gone, and though he walk crowded streets, he will, in truth, be – *dead!*

But all this must not perish; it must live, to the end that America shall be educated no longer to regard native production of whatever tribe – folk-story, basketry, pottery, dance, song, poetry – as curios, and native artists as curiosities. For who but the man indigenous to the soil could produce its song, story, and folk-tale; who but the man who loved the dust beneath his feet could shape it and put it into undying, ceramic form; who but he who loved the reeds that grew beside still waters, and the damp roots of shrub and tree, could save it from seasonal death, and with almost superhuman patience weave it into enduring objects of beauty – into timeless art!

Regarding the "civilization" that has been thrust upon me since the days of reservation, it has not added one whit to my sense of justice; to my reverence for the rights of life; to my love for truth, honesty, and generosity; not to my faith in Wakan Tanka – God of the Lakotas. For after all the great religions have been preached and expounded, or have been revealed by brilliant scholars, or have been embellished in fine language with finer covers, man – all man – is still confronted with the Great Mystery.

So if today I had a young mind to direct, to start on the journey of life, and I was faced with the duty of choosing between the natural way of my forefathers and that of the white man's present way of civilization, I would, for its welfare, unhesitatingly set that child's feet in the path of my forefathers. I would raise him to be an Indian!

APPENDIX I

The American Indian Nations of North America

Here are listed 300 and more tribes and sub-tribes, and their primary area of settlement. Some of the tribes are long gone, their existence only remembered in place names and consumer goods.

Abitbi (Sub-Arctic)
Abnaki (Eastern Woodlands)
Accohannock (East Coast)
Achomawi/Atsugewi (Northwest Plateau)
Alabama (Southeast)
Aleut (Alaska)
Alsea (Northwest Coast)
Apache (Southwest)
Arapaho (Great Plains)
Arikara (Great Plains)
Assiniboin (Great Plains)
Atakapa (Southeast)
Atsina (Great Plains)
Attiwandaronk (Eastern Woodlands)
Bannock (Great Basin)
Beaver (Sub-Arctic)
Bella Coola (Northwest Coast)
Biloxi (Southeast)
Blackfoot (Great Plains)

Caddo (Great Plains)

Cahuilla (California)

Calusa (Southeast)

Caribou (Sub-Arctic)

Carrier (Sub-Arctic)

Catawba (Southeast)

Cayuse (Northwest Plateau)

Chemehuevi (Great Basin)

Cherokee (Southeast)

Cheyenne (Great Plains)

Chickasaw (Southeast)

Chicora (Southeast)

Chilcotin (Northwest Plateau)

Chinook (Northwest Coast)

Chipewyan (Sub-Arctic)

Chitimacha (Southeast)

Choctaw (Southeast)

Chumash (California)

Coahuiltec (Southwest)

Cocopa (Southwest)

Coeur d'Alene (Northwest Plateau)

Coharie (Eastern Woodlands/Southeast)

Comanche (Great Plains)

Conoy (East Coast)

Coos (Northwest Coast)

Costanoa (California)

Cowlitz (Northwest Coast)

Cree (Sub-Arctic)

Creek (Southeast)

Crow (Great Plains)

Delaware (East Coast)

Dieguno (California)

Dogrib (Sub-Arctic)

Edisto (Southeast)

Erie (Eastern Woodland/Great Lakes)

Eskimo (Sub-Arctic/Arctic Circle)

Esselen (California)

Eyak (Northwest Coast)

Flathead (Northwest Plateau)

Fox (Eastern Woodlands/Great Lakes)

Gabrielino (California)

Gitskan (Northwest Coast)

Goshute (Great Basin)

Gros Ventres of the Prairie (Great Plains)

Gros Ventres of the River (Great Plains)

Haida (Northwest Coast)

Haisla (Northwest Coast)

Halchidhoma (Southwest)

Han (Sub-Arctic)

Heiltsuk (Northwest Coast)

Hohokam (Southwest)

Hopi (Southwest)

Houma (Southeast)

Hupa (California)

Huron (Eastern Woodland/Great Lakes)

Illinois (Eastern Woodlands)

Ingalik (Alaska)

Inupiaq (Alaska)

Iowa (Great Plains)

Iroquois (including
    Mohawk, Oneida,
    Onondaga, Cayuga,
    Seneca) (Eastern
    Woodlands/Great Lakes)

Jemez (Southwest)

Kalapuya (Northwest Coast)

Kalispel (Northwest Plateau)

Kansa (Great Plains)

Karankawa (Great Plains)

Karok (California)

Kaw (Great Plains)

Keres (Southwest)

Kickapoo (Eastern
    Woodlands/Great Lakes)

Kiowa (Great Plains)

Kiowa-Apache (Great
    Plains)

Klamath (Northwest
    Plateau)

Klikitat (Northwest Plateau)

Koyukon (Alaska)

Kutchin (Sub-Arctic)

Kutenai (Northwest Plateau)

Kwakiutl (Northwest Coast)

Lillooet (Northwest Plateau)

Lipan (Great Plains)

Luiseno (California)

Mahican (East Coast)

Maidu (California)

Makah (Northwest Coast)

Malisit (East Coast)

Mandan (Great Plains)

Maricopa (Southwest)

Mascouten (East Coast)

Massachuset (East Coast)

Mattabesic (East Coast)

Menomini (Eastern
    Woodlands/Great Lakes)

Metoac (East Coast)

Miami (Eastern Woodlands)

Micmac (East Coast)

Minga (Eastern Woodlands)

Missouri (Great Plains)

Miwok (California)

Modoc (Great Plains)

Mohegan (East Coast)

Mojave (Southwest)

Mono (California)

Montagnais (Sub-Arctic)

Mountain (Sub-Arctic)

Nansemond (Southeast)

Narragansett (East Coast)

Naskapi (Sub-Arctic)

Natchez (Southeast)

Navajo (Southwest)

Nespelem (Northwest
    Plateau)

Netsilik (Arctic Circle)

Nez Percé (Great Plains)

Notka (Northwest Coast)

Ojibwa (Eastern
    Woodlands/Great Lakes)

Okanagan (Northwest
  Plateau)
Omaha (Great Plains)
Osage (Great Plains)
Oto (Great Plains)
Ottawa (Eastern
  Woodlands/Great Lakes)
Paiute (Great Basin)
Palus (Northwest Plateau)
Pamlico (East Coast)
Pamunkey (Southeast)
Papago (Southwest)
Patwin (California)
Pawnee (Great Plains)
Pennacook (East Coast)
Penobscot (East Coast)
Pequot (East Coast)
Pericu (California)
Pima (Southwest/Mexico)
Plains Cree (Great Plains)
Plains Objiwa (Great Plains)
Pomo (California)
Ponca (Great Plains)
Potawatomi (Eastern
  Woodlands)
Powahatan (East Coast)
Quapaw (Southeast)
Quileute (Northwest Coast)
Quinault (Northwest Coast)
Salinan (California)
Salish (Northwest Coast)
Santee Sioux (East Coast)
  Great Plains)

Sarsi (Great Plains)
Sauk (Eastern Woodlands/
  Great Lakes)
Secotan (Eastern
  Woodlands)
Sekani (Sub-Arctic)
Seminole (Southeast)
Seri (Southwest)
Serrano (California)
Shasta (California)
Shawnee (Eastern
  Woodlands/Great
  Plains)
Shoshoni (Great Basin)
Shuswap (Northwest
  Plateau)
Skidi (Great Plains)
Slave (Sub-Arctic)
Sobaipuri (Southwest)
Spokan (Southwest)
Susquehanna (Eastern
  Woodlands)
Sutaio (Great Plains)
Taensa (Southeast)
Tagish (Sub-Arctic)
Tahltan (Sub-Arctic)
Tanaina (Alaska)
Tanoan Pueblos (Southwest)
Tekesta (Southeast)
Teton Sioux (Great Plains)
Thompson (Northwest
  Plateau)
Timucua (Southeast)

Tionontati (Eastern
  Woodlands)
Tlingit (Northwest Coast)
Tobacco (Eastern
  Woodlands/Great Lakes)
Tolowa (Northwest Coast)
Tonkawa (Great Plains)
Tsetsaut (Sub-Arctic)
Tsimshian (Northwest
  Coast)
Tubatulabal (California)
Tunica (Southeast)
Tuscarora (East Coast)
Tutchone (Sub-Arctic)
Tutelo (Eastern Woodlands)
Umatilla (Northwest
  Plateau)
Ute (Great Basin)
Walapai (Southwest)
Wampanoag (Eastern
  Woodlands)
Wappinger (Eastern
  Woodlands)
Washo (Great Basin)

Wenro (Eastern
  Woodlands/Great Lakes)
Wind River Shoshoni
  (Great Basin)
Winnebago (Eastern
  Woodlands/Great Lakes)
Wintun (California)
Wishram (Northwest
  Plateau)
Witchita (Great Plains)
Wiyot (California)
Yakima (Northwest Plateau)
Yakutat (Northwest Coast)
Yana (California)
Yankton Sioux (Eastern
  Woodlands/Great Plains)
Yaqui (Southwest/Mexico)
Yavapai (Southwest)
Yellowknife (Sub-Arctic)
Yokuts (California)
Yuchi (Southeast)
Yuma (Southwest)
Yurok (California)
Zuni (Southwest)

APPENDIX II

The Soul of the Indian*

An Interpretation by
Charles Eastman (Ohiyesa)

Dr Eastman (1858–1939) was a member of the Santee
Sioux and a graduate of the Carlisle Indian School.

CHAPTER 1 – THE GREAT MYSTERY

Solitary Worship

The original attitude of the American Indian toward the
Eternal, the "Great Mystery" that surrounds and embraces
us, was as simple as it was exalted. To him it was the supreme
conception, bringing with it the fullest measure of joy and
satisfaction possible in this life.

The worship of the "Great Mystery" was silent, solitary,
free from all self-seeking. It was silent, because all speech is of

*The Soul of the Indian, Charles Eastman, Houghton Mifflin Co., Boston, 1911 necessity feeble and imperfect; therefore the souls of my ancestors ascended to God in wordless adoration. It was solitary, because they believed that He is nearer to us in solitude, and there were no priests authorized to come between a man and his Maker. None might exhort or confess or in any way meddle with the religious experience of another. Among us all men were created sons of God and stood erect, as conscious of their divinity. Our faith might not be formulated in creeds, nor forced upon any who were unwilling to receive it; hence there was no preaching, proselytising, nor persecution, neither were there any scoffers or atheists.

There were no temples or shrines among us save those of nature. Being a natural man the Indian was intensely poetical. He would deem it sacrilege to build a house for Him who may be met face to face in the mysterious, shadowy aisles of the primeval forest, or on the sunlit bosom of virgin prairies, upon dizzy spires and pinnacles of naked rock, and yonder in the jeweled vault of the night sky! He who enrobes Himself in filmy veils of cloud, there on the rim of the visible world where our Great-Grandfather Sun kindles his evening camp-fire, He who rides upon the rigorous wind of the north, or breathes forth His spirit upon aromatic southern airs, whose war-canoe is launched upon majestic rivers and inland seas – He needs no lesser cathedral!

That solitary communion with the Unseen which was the highest expression of our religious life is partly described in the word *bambeday*, literally "mysterious feeling," which has been variously translated "fasting" and "dreaming". It may better be interpreted as "consciousness of the divine".

The Savage Philosopher

The first *bambeday*, or religious retreat, marked an epoch in the life of the youth, which may be compared to that of confirmation or conversion in Christian experience. Having first prepared himself by means of the purifying vapour-bath, and cast off as far as possible all human fleshly influences, the young man sought out the noblest height, the most commanding summit in all the surrounding region. Knowing that God sets no value upon material things, he took with him no offerings or sacrifices other than symbolic objects, such as paints and tobacco. Wishing to appear before Him in all humility, he wore no clothing save his moccasins and breech-clout. At the solemn hour of sunrise or sunset he took up his position, overlooking the glories of earth and facing the "Great Mystery", and there he remained, naked, erect, silent, and motionless, exposed to the elements and forces of His arming, for a night and a day to two days and nights, but rarely longer. Sometimes he would chant a hymn without words, or offer the ceremonial "filled pipe". In this holy trance or ecstasy the Indian mystic found his highest happiness and the motive power of his existence.

When he returned to the camp, he must remain at a distance until he had again entered the vapour-bath and prepared himself for intercourse with his fellows. Of the vision or sign vouchsafed to him he did not speak, unless it had included some commission which must be publicly fulfilled. Sometimes an old man, standing upon the brink of eternity, might reveal to a chosen few the oracle of his long-past youth.

The native American has been generally despised by his white conquerors for his poverty and simplicity. They forget, perhaps, that his religion forbade the accumulation of wealth and the enjoyment of luxury. To him, as to other single-minded men in every age and race, from Diogenes to the brothers of Saint Francis, from the Montanists to the Shakers, the love of possessions has appeared a snare, and the burdens of a complex society a source of needless peril and temptation. Furthermore, it was the rule of his life to share the fruits of his skill and success with his less fortunate brothers. Thus he kept his spirit free from the clog of pride, cupidity, or envy, and carried out, as he believed, the divine decree – a matter profoundly important to him.

It was not, then, wholly from ignorance or improvidence that he failed to establish permanent towns and to develop a material civilization. To the untutored sage, the concentration of population was the prolific mother of all evils, moral no less than physical. He argued that food is good, while surfeit kills; that love is good, but lust destroys; and not less dreaded than the pestilence following upon crowded and unsanitary dwellings was the loss of spiritual power inseparable from too close contact with one's fellow-men. All who have lived much out of doors know that there is a magnetic and nervous force that accumulates in solitude and that is quickly dissipated by life in a crowd; and even his enemies have recognized the fact that for a certain innate power and self-poise, wholly independent of circumstances, the American Indian is unsurpassed among men.

The Dual Mind

The red man divided mind into two parts – the spiritual mind and the physical mind. The first is pure spirit, concerned only with the essence of things, and it was this he sought to strengthen by spiritual prayer, during which the body is subdued by fasting and hardship. In this type of prayer there was no beseeching favor or help. All matters of personal or selfish concern, as success in hunting or warfare, relief from sickness, or the sparing of a beloved life, were definitely relegated to the plane of the lower or material mind, and all ceremonies, charms, or incantations designed to secure a benefit or to avert a danger, were recognized as emanating from the physical self.

The rites of this physical worship, again, were wholly symbolic, and the Indian no more worshipped the Sun than the Christian adores the Cross. The Sun and the Earth, by an obvious parable, holding scarcely more of poetic metaphor than of scientific truth, were in his view the parents of all organic life. From the Sun, as the universal father, proceeds the quickening principle in nature, and in the patient and fruitful womb of our mother, the Earth, are hidden embryos of plants and men. Therefore our reverence and love for them was really an imaginative extension of our love for our immediate parents, and with this sentiment of filial piety was joined a willingness to appeal to them, as to a father, for such good gifts as we may desire. This is the material or physical prayer.

The elements and majestic forces in nature, Lightning, Wind, Water, Fire, and Frost, were regarded with awe as spiritual powers, but always secondary and intermediate in character. We believed that the spirit pervades all creation and that every creature possesses a soul in some degree, though not necessarily a soul conscious of itself. The tree, the waterfall, the grizzly bear, each is an embodied Force, and as such an object of reverence.

The Indian loved to come into sympathy and spiritual communion with his brothers of the animal kingdom, whose inarticulate souls had for him something of the sinless purity that we attribute to the innocent and irresponsible child. He had faith in their instincts, as in a mysterious wisdom given from above; and while he humbly accepted the supposedly voluntary sacrifice of their bodies to preserve his own, he paid homage to their spirits in prescribed prayers and offerings.

Spiritual Gifts versus Material Progress

In every religion there is an element of the supernatural, varying with the influence of pure reason over its devotees. The Indian was a logical and clear thinker upon matters within the scope of his understanding, but he had not yet charted the vast field of nature or expressed her wonders in terms of science. With his limited knowledge of cause and effect, he saw miracles on every hand – the miracle of life in seed and egg, the miracle of death in lightning flash and in the swelling deep! Nothing of the marvellous could astonish him; as that a beast should speak, or the sun stand still. The virgin birth would appear scarcely more miraculous than is the birth of every child that comes into the world, or the miracle of the loaves and fishes excite more wonder than the harvest that springs from a single ear of corn.

Who may condemn his superstition? Surely not the devout Catholic even Protestant missionary, who teaches Bible miracles as literal fact! The logical man must either deny all miracles or none, and our American Indian myths and hero stories are perhaps, in themselves, quite as credible as those of the Hebrews of old. If we are of the modern type of mind, that sees in natural law a majesty and grandeur far more impressive than any solitary infraction of it could possibly be, let us not forget that, after all, science has not explained everything. We have still to face the ultimate miracle – the origin and principle of life! Here is the supreme mystery that is the essence of worship, without which there can be no religion, and in the presence of this mystery our attitude cannot be very unlike that of the natural philosopher, who beholds with awe the Divine in all creation.

It is simple truth that the Indian did not, so long as his native philosophy held sway over his mind, either envy or desire to imitate the splendid achievements of the white man. In his own thought he rose superior to them! He scorned them, even as a lofty spirit absorbed in its stern task rejects the soft beds, the luxurious food, the pleasure-worshiping dalliance of a rich neighbor was clear to him that virtue and happiness are independent of these things, if not incompatible with them.

The Paradox of "Christian Civilization"

There was undoubtedly much in primitive Christianity to appeal to this man, and Jesus' hard sayings to the rich and about the rich would have been entirely comprehensible to him. Yet the religion that is preached in our churches and practiced by our congregations, with its element of display and self-aggrandizement, its active proselytism, and its open contempt of all religions but its own, was for a long time extremely repellent. To his simple mind, the professionalism of the pulpit, the paid exhorter, the moneyed church, was unspiritual and unedifying, and it was not until his spirit was broken and his moral and physical constitution undermined by trade, conquest, and strong drink, that Christian missionaries obtained any real hold upon him. Strange as it may seem, it is true that the proud pagan in his secret soul despised the good men who came to convert and to enlighten him!

Nor were its publicity and its Phariseeism the only elements in the alien religion that offended the red man. To him, it appeared shocking and almost incredible that there were among this people who claimed superiority many irreligious, who did not even pretend to profess the national religion. Not only did they not profess it, but they stooped so low as to insult their God with profane and sacrilegious speech! In our own tongue His name was not spoken aloud, even with utmost reverence, much less lightly or irreverently.

More than this, even in those white men who professed religion we found much inconsistency of conduct. They spoke much of spiritual things, while seeking only the material. They bought and sold everything, labour, personal independence, the love of woman, and even the ministrations of their holy faith! The lust for money, power, and conquest so characteristic of the Anglo-Saxon race did not escape moral condemnation at the hands of his untutored judge, nor did he fail to contrast this conspicuous trait of the dominant race with the spirit of the meek and lowly Jesus.

He might in time come to recognize that the drunkards and licentious among white men, with whom he too frequently came in contact, were condemned by the white man's religion as well, and must not be held to discredit it. But it was not so easy to overlook or to excuse national bad faith. When distinguished emissaries from the Father at Washington, some of them ministers of the gospel and even bishops, came to the Indian nations, and pledged to them in solemn treaty the national honor, with prayer and mention of their God; and when such treaties, so made, were promptly and shamelessly broken, is it strange that the action should arouse not only anger, but contempt? The historians of the white race admit that the Indian was never the first to repudiate his oath.

It is my personal belief, after thirty-five years' experience of it, that there is no such thing as "Christian Civilization." I believe that Christianity and modern civilization are opposed and irreconcilable, and that the spirit of Christianity and of our ancient religion is essentially the same.

CHAPTER 2 – THE FAMILY ALTAR

Pre-Natal Influence

The American Indian was an individualist in religion as in war. He had neither a national army nor an organized church. There was no priest to assume responsibility for another's soul. That is, we believed, the supreme duty of the parent, who only was permitted to claim in some degree the priestly office and function, since it is his creative and protecting power which alone approaches the solemn function of Deity.

The Indian was a religious man from his mother's womb. From the moment of her recognition of the fact of conception to the end of the second year of life, which was the ordinary duration of lactation, it was supposed by us that the mother's spiritual influence counted for most. Her attitude and secret meditations must be such as to instill into the receptive soul of the unborn child the love of the "Great Mystery" and a sense of brotherhood with all creation. Silence and isolation are the rule for the expectant mother. She wanders prayerful in the stillness of great woods, or on the bosom of the untrodden prairie, and to her poetic mind the immanent birth of her child prefigures the advent of a master-man – a hero, or the mother of heroes – a thought conceived in the virgin breast of primeval nature, and dreamed out in a hush that is only broken by the sighing of the pine tree or the thrilling orchestra of a distant waterfall.

And when the day of days in her life dawns – the day in which there is to be a new life, the miracle of whose making has been intrusted to her, she seeks no human aid. She has been trained and prepared in body and mind for this her holiest duty, ever since she can remember. The ordeal is best met alone, where no curious or pitying eyes embarrass her; where all nature says to her spirit: *"'Tis love! 'tis love! the fulfilling of life!"* When a sacred voice comes to her out of the silence, and a pair of eyes open upon her in the wilderness, she knows with joy that she has borne well her part in the great song of creation!

Presently she returns to the camp, carrying the mysterious, the holy, the dearest bundle! She feels the endearing warmth of it and hears its soft breathing. It is still a part of herself; since both are nourished by the same mouthful, and no look of a lover could be sweeter than its deep, trusting gaze.

Early Religious Teaching

She continues her spiritual teaching, at first silently – a mere pointing of the index finger to nature; then in whispered songs, bird-like, at morning and evening. To her and to the child the birds are real people, who live very close to the "Great Mystery"; the murmuring trees breathe His presence; the falling waters chant His praise.

If the child should chance to be fretful, the mother raises her hand. *"Hush! hush!"* she cautions it tenderly, *"the spirits may be disturbed!"* She bids it be still and listen to the silver voice of the aspen, or the clashing cymbals of the birch; and at night she points to the heavenly, blazed trail, through nature's galaxy of splendour to nature's God. Silence, love, reverence, – this is the trinity of first lessons; and to these she later adds generosity, courage, and chastity.

In the old days, our mothers were single-eyed to the trust imposed upon them; and as a noted chief of our people was wont to say: *"Men may slay one another, but they can never overcome the woman, for in the quietude of her lap lies the child! You may destroy him once and again, but he issues as often from that same gentle lap – a gift of the Great Good to the race, in which man is only an accomplice!"*

This wild mother has not only the experience of her mother and grandmother, and the accepted rules of her people for a guide, but she humbly seeks to learn a lesson from ants, bees, spiders, beavers, and badgers. She studies the family life of the birds, so exquisite in its emotional intensity and its patient devotion, until she seems to feel the universal mother-heart beating in her own breast. In due time the child takes of his own accord the attitude of prayer, and speaks reverently of the Powers. He thinks that he is a blood brother to all living creatures, and the storm wind is to him a messenger of the "Great Mystery."

The Function of the Aged

At the age of about eight years, if he is a boy, she turns him over to his father for more Spartan training. If a girl, she is from this time much under the guardianship of her grandmother, who is considered the most dignified protector for the maiden. Indeed, the distinctive work of both grandparents is that of acquainting the youth with the national traditions and beliefs. It is reserved for them to repeat the time-hallowed tales with dignity and authority, so as to lead him into his inheritance in the stored-up wisdom and experience of the race. The old are dedicated to the service of the young, as their teachers and advisers, and the young in turn regard them with love and reverence.

Our old age was in some respects the happiest period of life. Advancing years brought with them much freedom, not only from the burden of laborious and dangerous tasks, but from those restrictions of custom and etiquette which were religiously observed by all others. No one who is at all acquainted with the Indian in his home can deny that we are a polite people. As a rule, the warrior who inspired the greatest terror in the hearts of his enemies was a man of the most exemplary gentleness, and almost feminine refinement, among his family and friends. A soft, low voice was considered an excellent thing in man, as well as in woman! Indeed, the enforced intimacy of tent life would soon become intolerable, were it not for these instinctive reserves and delicacies, this unfailing respect for the established place and possessions of every other member of the family circle, this habitual quiet, order, and decorum.

Our people, though capable of strong and durable feeling, were not demonstrative in their affection at any time, least of all in the presence of guests or strangers. Only to the aged, who have journeyed far, and are in a manner exempt from ordinary rules, are permitted some playful familiarities with children and grandchildren, some plain speaking, even to harshness and objurgation, from which the others must rigidly refrain. In short, the old men and women are privileged to say what they please and how they please, without contradiction, while the hardships and bodily infirmities that of necessity fall to their lot are softened so far as may be by umversal consideration and attention.

Woman, Marriage and the Family

There was no religious ceremony connected with marriage among us, while on the other hand the relation between man and woman was regarded as in itself mysterious and holy. It appears that where marriage is solemnized by the church and blessed by the priest, it may at the same time be surrounded with customs and ideas of a frivolous, superficial, and even prurient character. We believed that two who love should be united in secret, before the public acknowledgment of their union, and should taste their apotheosis with nature. The betrothal might or might not be discussed and approved by the parents, but in either case it was customary for the young pair to disappear into the wilderness, there to pass some days or weeks in perfect seclusion and dual solitude, afterward returning to the village as man and wife. An exchange of presents and entertainments between the two families usually followed, but the nuptial blessing was given by the High Priest of God, the most reverend and holy Nature.

The family was not only the social unit, but also the unit of government clan is nothing more than a larger family, with its patriarchal chief as the natural head, and the union of several clans by inter-marriage and voluntary connection constitutes the tribe. The very name of our tribe, Dakota, means Allied People. The remoter degrees of kinship were fully recognized, and that not as a matter of form only: first cousins were known as brothers and sisters; the name of "cousin" constituted binding claim, and our rigid morality forbade marriage between cousins in any known degree, or in other words within the clan.

The household proper consisted of a man with one or more wives and their children, all of whom dwelt amicably together, often under one roof, although some men of rank and position provided a separate lodge for each wife. There were, indeed, few plural marriages except among the older and leading men, and plural wives were usually, though not necessarily, sisters. A marriage might honourably be dissolved for cause, but there was very little infidelity or immorality, either open or secret.

It has been said that the position of woman is the test of civilization, and that of our women was secure. In them was vested our standard of morals and the purity of our blood. The wife did not take the name of her husband nor enter his clan, and the children belonged to the clan of the mother. All of the family property was held by her, descent was traced in the maternal line, and the honour of the house was in her hands. Modesty was her chief adornment; hence the younger women were usually silent and retiring: but a woman who had attained to ripeness of years and wisdom, or who had displayed notable courage in some emergency, was sometimes invited to a seat in the council.

Thus she ruled undisputed within her own domain, and was to us a tower of moral and spiritual strength, until the coming of the border white man, the soldier and trader, who with strong drink overthrew the honour of the man, and through his power over a worthless husband purchased the virtue of his wife or his daughter. When she fell, the whole race fell with her.

Before this calamity came upon us, you could not find anywhere a happier home than that created by the Indian woman. There was nothing of the artificial about her person, and very little disingenuousness in her character. Her early and consistent training, the definiteness of her vocation, and, above all, her profoundly religious attitude gave her a strength and poise that could not be overcome by any ordinary misfortune.

Indian names were either characteristic nicknames given in a playful spirit, deed names, birth names, or such as have a religious and symbolic meaning. It has been said that when a child is born, some accident or unusual appearance determines his name. This is sometimes the case, but is not the rule. A man of forcible character, with a fine war record, usually bears the name of the buffalo or bear, lightning or some dread natural force. Another of more peaceful nature may be called Swift Bird or Blue Sky. A woman's name usually suggested something about the home, often with the adjective "pretty" or "good", and a feminine termination. Names of any dignity or importance must be conferred by the old men, and especially so if they have any spiritual significance; as Sacred Cloud, Mysterious Night, Spirit Woman, and the like. Such a name was sometimes borne by three generations, but each individual must prove that he is worthy of it.

In the life of the Indian there was only one inevitable duty – the duty of prayer – the daily recognition of the Unseen and Eternal. His daily devotions were more necessary to him than daily food. He wakes at daybreak, puts on his moccasins and steps down to the water's edge. Here he throws handfuls of clear, cold water into his face, or plunges in bodily. After the bath, he stands erect before the advancing dawn, facing the sun as it dances upon the horizon, and offers his unspoken orison. His mate may precede or follow him in his devotions, but never accompanies him. Each soul must meet the morning sun, the new, sweet earth, and the Great Silence alone!

Whenever, in the course of the daily hunt, the red hunter comes upon a scene that is strikingly beautiful and sublime – a black thunder-cloud with the rainbow's glowing arch above the mountain; a white waterfall in the heart of a green gorge;

a vast prairie tinged with the blood-red of sunset – he pauses for an instant in the attitude of worship. He sees no need for setting apart one day in seven as a holy day, since to him all days are God's.

Every act of his life is, in a very real sense, a religious act. He recognizes the spirit in all creation, and believes that he draws from it spiritual power. His respect for the immortal part of the animal, his brother, often leads him so far as to lay out the body of his game in state and decorate the head with symbolic paint or feathers. Then he stands before it in the prayer attitude, holding up the filled pipe, in token that he has freed with honour the spirit of his brother, whose body his need compelled him to take to sustain his own life.

When food is taken, the woman murmurs a "grace" as she lowers the kettle; an act so softly and unobtrusively performed that one who does not know the custom usually fails to catch the whisper: "Spirit, partake!" As her husband receives the bowl or plate, he likewise murmurs his invocation to the spirit. When he becomes an old man, he loves to make a notable effort to prove his gratitude. He cuts off the choicest morsel of the meat and casts it into the fire – the purest and most ethereal element.

Loyalty, Hospitality, Friendship

The hospitality of the wigwam is only limited by the institution of war. Yet, if an enemy should honour us with a call, his trust will not be misplaced, and he will go away convinced that he has met with a royal host! Our honour is the guarantee for his safety, so long as he is within the camp.

Friendship is held to be the severest test of character. It is easy, we think, to be loyal to family and clan, whose blood is in our own veins. Love between man and woman is founded on the mating instinct and is not free from desire and self-seeking. But to have a friend, and to be true under any and all trials, is the mark of a man!

The highest type of friendship is the relation of "brother-friend" or "life-and-death friend". This bond is between man and man, is usually formed in early youth, and can only be broken by death. It is the essence of comradeship and fraternal love, without thought of pleasure or gain, but rather for moral support and inspiration. Each is vowed to die for the other, if need be, and nothing denied the brother-friend, but neither is anything required that is not in accord with the highest conceptions of the Indian mind.

CHAPTER 3 – CEREMONIAL AND SYMBOLIC WORSHIP

Modern Perversions of Early Religious Rites

The religious rites of the Plains Indians are few, and in large part of modern origin, belonging properly to the so-called "transition period". That period must be held to begin with the first insidious effect upon their manners and customs of contact with the dominant race, and many of the tribes were so influenced long before they ceased to lead the nomadic life.

The fur-traders, the "Black Robe" priests, the military, and finally the Protestant missionaries, were the men who began the disintegration of the Indian nations and the overthrow of their religion, seventy-five to a hundred years before they were forced to enter upon reservation life. We have no authentic study of them until well along in the transition period, when whiskey and trade had already debauched their native ideals.

During the era of reconstruction they modified their customs and beliefs continually, creating a singular admixture of Christian with pagan superstitions, and an addition to the old folk-lore of disguised Bible stories under an Indian aspect. Even their music shows the influence of the Catholic chants. Most of the material collected by modern observers is necessarily of this promiscuous character.

The Sun Dance

It is noteworthy that the first effect of contact with the whites was an increase of cruelty and barbarity, an intensifying of the dark shadows in the picture! In this manner the "Sun Dance" of the Plains Indians, the most important of their public ceremonials, was abused and perverted until it became a horrible exhibition of barbarism, and was eventually prohibited by the Government.

In the old days, when a Sioux warrior found himself in the very jaws of destruction, he might offer a prayer to his father, the Sun, to prolong his life. If rescued from imminent danger, he must acknowledge the divine favour by making a Sun Dance, according to the vow embraced in his prayer, in which he declared that he did not fear torture or death, but asked life only for the sake of those who loved him. Thus the physical ordeal was the fulfillment of a vow, and a sort of atonement for what might otherwise appear to be reprehensible weakness in the face of death. It was in the nature of confession and thank-offering to the "Great Mystery" through the physical parent, the Sun, and did not embrace a prayer for future favours.

The ceremonies usually took place from six months to a

year after the making of the vow, in order to admit of suitable preparation; always in midsummer and before a large and imposing gathering. They naturally included the making of a feast, and the giving away of much savage wealth in honour of the occasion, although these were no essential part of the religious rite.

When the day came to procure the pole, it was brought in by a party of warriors, headed by some man of distinction. The tree selected was six to eight inches in diameter at the base, and twenty to twenty-five feet high. It was chosen and felled with some solemnity, including the ceremony of the "filled pipe", and was carried in the fashion of a litter, symbolizing the body of the man who made the dance. A solitary teepee was pitched on a level spot at some distance from the village the pole raised near at hand with the same ceremony, in the centre a circular enclosure of fresh-cut.

Meanwhile, one of the most noted of our old men had carved out of rawhide, or later of wood, two figures, usually those of a man and a buffalo. Sometimes the figure of a bird, supposed to represent the Thunder, was substituted for the buffalo. It was customary to paint the man red and the animal black, and each was suspended from one end of the cross-bar which was securely tied some two feet from the top of the pole. I have never been able to determine that this cross had any significance; it was probably nothing more than a dramatic coincidence that surmounted the Sun-Dance pole with the symbol of Christianity.

The paint indicated that the man who was about to give thanks publicly had been potentially dead, but was allowed to live by the mysterious favour and interference of the Giver of Life. The buffalo hung opposite the image of his own body in death, because it was the support of his physical self, and a leading figure in legendary lore. Following the same line of thought, when he emerged from the solitary lodge of preparation, and approached the pole to dance, nude save for his breech-clout and moccasins, his hair loosened daubed with clay, he must drag after him a buffalo skull, representing the grave from which he had escaped.

The dancer was cut or scarified on the chest, sufficient to draw blood and cause pain, the natural accompaniments of his figurative death. He took his position opposite the singers, facing the pole, and dragging the skull by leather thongs which were merely fastened about his shoulders. During a later period, incisions were made in the breast or back, sometimes both, through which wooden skewers were drawn, and secured by lariats to the pole or to the skulls. Thus he danced without intermission for a day and a night, or even longer, ever gazing at the sun in the daytime, and blowing from time to time a sacred whistle made from the bone of a goose's wing.

In recent times, this rite was exaggerated and distorted into a mere ghastly display of physical strength and endurance under torture, almost on a level with the Caucasian institution of the bullfight, or the yet more modern prize-ring. Moreover, instead of an atonement or thank-offering, it became the accompaniment of a prayer for success in war, or in a raid upon the horses of the enemy. The number of dancers was increased, and they were made to hang suspended from the pole by their own flesh, which they must break loose before being released. I well remember the comments in our own home upon the passing of this simple but impressive ceremony, and its loss of all meaning and propriety under the demoralizing additions which were some of the fruits of early contact with the white man.

The Great Medicine Lodge

Perhaps the most remarkable organization ever known among American Indians, that of the "Grand Medicine Lodge," was apparently an indirect result of the labours of the early Jesuit missionaries. In it Caucasian ideas are easily recognizable, and it seems reasonable to suppose that its founders desired to establish an order that would successfully resist the encroachments of the "Black Robes". However that may be, it is an unquestionable fact that the only religious leaders of any note who have arisen among the native tribes since the advent of the white man, the "Shawnee Prophet" in 1762, and the half-breed prophet of the "Ghost Dance" in 1890, both founded their claims or prophecies upon the Gospel story. Thus in each case an Indian religious revival or craze, though more or less threatening to the invader, was of distinctively alien origin.

The Medicine Lodge originated among the Algonquin tribe, and extended gradually throughout its branches, finally affecting the Sioux of the Mississippi Valley, and forming a strong bulwark against the work of the pioneer missionaries, who secured, indeed, scarcely any converts until after the outbreak of 1862, when subjection, starvation, and imprisonment turned our brokenhearted people to accept Christianity seemed to offer them the only gleam of kindness or hope.

The order was a secret one, and in some respects not unlike the Freemasons, being a union or affiliation of a number of lodges, each with its distinctive songs and medicines. Leadership was in order of seniority in degrees, which could only be obtained by merit, and women were admitted to membership upon equal terms, with the possibility of attaining to the highest honours. No person might become a member unless his moral standing was excellent, all candidates remained on probation for one or two years, and murderers and adulterers were expelled. The commandments promulgated by this order were essentially the same as the Mosaic Ten, so that it exerted a distinct moral influence, in addition to its ostensible object, which was instruction in the secrets of legitimate medicine.

In this society the uses of all curative and herbs known to us were taught exhaustively and practiced mainly by the old, the younger members being in training to fill the places of those who passed away. My grandmother was a well-known and successful practitioner, and both my mother and father were members, but did not practise.

A medicine or "mystery feast" was not a public affair, as members only were eligible, and upon these occasions all the "medicine bags" and totems of the various lodges were displayed and their peculiar "medicine songs" were sung. The food was only partaken of by invited guests, and not by the hosts, or lodge making the feast. The "Grand Medicine Dance" was given on the occasion of initiating those candidates who had finished their probation, a sufficient number of whom were designated to take the places of those who had died since the last meeting. Invitations were sent out in the form of small bundles of tobacco. Two very large teepees were pitched facing one another, a hundred feet apart, half open, and connected by a roofless hall or colonnade of freshcut boughs. One of these lodges was for the society giving the dance and the novices, the other was occupied by the "soldiers," whose duty it was to distribute the refreshments, and to keep order among the spectators. They were selected from among the best and bravest warriors of the tribe.

The preparations being complete, and the members of each lodge garbed and painted according to their rituals, they entered the hall separately, in single file, led by their oldest man or "Great Chief". Standing before the "Soldiers' Lodge", facing the setting sun, their chief addressed the "Great Mystery" directly in a few words, after which all extending the right arm horizontally from the shoulder with open palm, sang a short invocation in unison, ending with a deep: "E-ho-ho-ho!" This performance, which was really impressive, was repeated in front of the headquarters lodge, facing the rising sun, after which each lodge took its assigned place, and the songs and dances followed in regular order.

The closing ceremony, which was intensely dramatic in its character, was the initiation of the novices, who had received their final preparation on the night before. They were now led out in front of the headquarters lodge and placed in a kneeling position upon a carpet of rich robes and furs, the men upon the right hand, stripped and painted black, with a round spot of red just over the heart, while the women, dressed in their best, were arranged upon the left. Both sexes wore the hair loose, as if in mourning or expectation of death. An equal number of grand medicine-men, each of whom was especially appointed to one of the novices, faced them at a distance of half the length of the hall, or perhaps fifty feet.

After silent prayer, each medicine-man in turn addressed himself to his charge, exhorting him to observe all the rules of the order under the eye of the Mysterious One, and instructing him in his duty toward his fellow-man and toward the Ruler of Life. All then assumed an attitude of superb power and dignity, crouching slightly as if about to spring forward in a foot-race, and grasping their medicine bags firmly in both hands. Swinging their arms forward at the same moment, they uttered their guttural "Yo-ho-ho-ho!" in perfect unison and with startling effect. In the midst of a breathless silence, they took a step forward, then another and another, ending a rod or so from the row of kneeling victims, with a mighty swing of the sacred bags that would seem to project all their mystic power into the bodies of the initiates. Instantly they all fell forward, apparently lifeless.

With this thrilling climax, the drums were vigorously pounded and the dance began again with energy. After a few turns had been taken about the prostrate bodies of the new members, covering them with fine robes and other garments which were later to be distributed as gifts, they were permitted to come to life and to join in the final dance. The whole performance was clearly symbolic of death and resurrection.

While I cannot suppose that this elaborate ritual, with its use of public and audible prayer, of public exhortation or sermon, and other Caucasian features, was practised before comparatively modern times, there is no doubt that it was conscientiously believed in by its members, and for a time regarded with reverence by the people. But at a later period it became still further demoralized and fell under suspicion of witchcraft.

Totems and Charms

There is no doubt that the Indian held medicine close to spiritual things, but in this also he has been much misunderstood; in fact everything that he held sacred is indiscriminately called "medicine", in the sense of mystery or magic. As a doctor he was originally very adroit and often successful. He employed only healing bark, roots, and leaves with whose properties he was familiar, using them in the form of a distillation or tea and always singly. The stomach or internal bath was a valuable discovery of his, and the vapour or Turkish bath was in general use. He could set a broken bone with fair success, but never practised surgery in any form. In addition to all this, the medicine-man possessed much personal magnetism and authority, and in his treatment often sought to reestablish the equilibrium of the patient through mental or spiritual influences – a sort of primitive psychotherapy.

The Sioux word for the healing art is "wah-pee-yah", which literally means readjusting or making anew. "Pay-jee-hoo-tah", literally root, means medicine, and "wakan" signifies spirit or mystery. Thus the three ideas, while sometimes associated, were carefully distinguished.

It is important to remember that in the old days the "medicine-man" received no payment for his services, which were of the nature of an honourable function or office. When the idea of payment and barter was introduced among us, and valuable presents or fees began to be demanded for treating the sick, the ensuing greed and rivalry led to many demoralizing practices, and in time to the rise of the modern "conjurer", who is generally a fraud and trickster of the grossest kind. It is fortunate that his day is practically over.

Ever seeking to establish spiritual comradeship with the animal creation, the Indian adopted this or that animal as his "totem", the emblematic device of his society, family, or clan. It is probable that the creature chosen was the traditional ancestress, as we are told that the First Man had many wives among the animal people. The sacred beast, bird, or reptile, represented by its stuffed skin, or by a rude painting, was treated with reverence and carried into battle to insure the guardianship of the spirits. The symbolic attribute of beaver, bear, or tortoise, such as wisdom, cunning, courage, and the like, was supposed to be mysteriously conferred upon the wearer of the badge. The totem or charm used in medicine was ordinarily that of the medicine lodge to which the practitioner belonged, though there were some great men who boasted a special revelation.

The Vapour-Bath and the Ceremonial of the Pipe

There are two ceremonial usages which, so far as I have been able to ascertain, were universal among American Indians, and apparently fundamental These have already been referred to as the "eneepee", or vapour-bath, and the "chan-du-hupah-za-pee", ceremonial of the pipe. In our Siouan legends and traditions these two are preeminent, as handed down from the most ancient time and persisting to the last.

In our Creation myth or story of the First Man, the vapour-bath was the magic used by The-one-who-was-First-Created, to give life to the dead bones of his younger brother, who had been slain by the monsters of the deep. Upon the shore of the Great Water he dug two round holes, over one of which he built a low enclosure of fragrant cedar boughs, and here he gathered together the bones of his brother. In the other pit he made a fire and heated four round stones, which he rolled one by one into the lodge of boughs. Having closed every aperture save one, he sang a mystic chant while he thrust in his arm and sprinkled water upon the stones with a bunch of sage. Immediately steam arose, and as the legend says, "there was an appearance of life". A second time he sprinkled water, and the dry bones rattled together. The third time he seemed to hear soft singing from within the lodge; and the fourth time a voice exclaimed: "Brother, let me out!" (It should be noted that the number four is the magic or sacred number of the Indian.)

This story gives the traditional origin of the "eneepee", which has ever since been deemed essential to the Indian's effort to purify and recreate his spirit. It is used both by the doctor and by his patient. Every man must enter the cleansing bath and take the cold plunge which follows, when preparing for any spiritual crisis, for possible death, or imminent danger.

Not only the "eneepee" itself but everything used in connection with the mysterious event, the aromatic cedar and sage, the water, and especially the water-worn boulders, are regarded as sacred, or at the least adapted to a spiritual use. For the rock we have a special reverent name – "Tunkan", a contraction of the Sioux word for Grandfather.

The natural boulder enters into many of our solemn ceremonials, such as the "Rain Dance", and the "Feast of Virgins". The lone hunter and warrior reverently holds up his filled pipe to "Tunkan", in solitary commemoration of a miracle which to him is as authentic and holy as the raising of Lazarus to the devout Christian.

There is a legend that the First Man fell sick, and was taught by his Elder Brother the ceremonial use of the pipe, in a prayer to the spirits for ease and relief. This simple ceremony is the commonest daily expression of thanks or "grace", as well as an oath of loyalty and good faith when the warrior goes forth upon some perilous enterprise, and it enters even into his "hambeday", or solitary prayer, ascending as a rising vapor or incense to the Father of Spirits.

In all the war ceremonies and in medicine a special pipe is used, but at home or on the hunt the warrior employs his own. The pulverized weed is mixed with aromatic bark of the red willow, and pressed lightly into the bowl of the long stone pipe. The worshiper lights it gravely and takes a whiff or two; then, standing erect, he holds it silently toward the Sun, our father, and toward the earth, our mother. There are modern variations, as holding the pipe to the Four Winds, the Fire, Water, Rock, and other elements or objects of reverence.

There are many religious festivals which are local and special in character, embodying a prayer for success in hunting or warfare, or for rain and bountiful harvests, but these two are the sacraments of our religion. For baptism we substitute the "eneepee", the purification by vapour, and in our holy communion we partake of the soothing incense of tobacco in the stead of bread and wine.

CHAPTER 4 – BARBARISM AND THE MORAL CODE

Silence, the Corner-Stone of Character

Long before I ever heard of Christ, or saw a white man, I had learned from an untutored woman the essence of morality. With the help of dear Nature herself, she taught me things simple but of mighty import. I knew God. I perceived what goodness is. I saw and loved what is really beautiful. Civilization has not taught me anything better!

As a child, I understood how to give; I have forgotten that grace since I became civilized. I lived the natural life, whereas I now live the artificial. Any pretty pebble was valuable to me then; every growing tree an object of reverence. Now I worship with the White man before a painted landscape whose value is estimated in dollars! Thus the Indian is reconstructed, as the natural rocks are ground to powder, and made into artificial blocks which may be built into the walls of modern society.

The first American mingled with his pride a singular humility. Spiritual arrogance was foreign to his nature and teaching. He never claimed that the power of articulate speech was proof of superiority over the dumb creation; on the other hand, it is to him a perilous gift. He believes profoundly in silence – the sign of a perfect equilibrium. Silence is the absolute poise or balance of body, mind, and spirit. The man who preserves his selfhood ever calm and unshaken by the storms of existence – not a leaf, as it were, astir on the tree; not a ripple upon the surface of shining pool – his, in the mind of the unlettered sage, is the ideal attitude and conduct of life.

If you ask him: "What is silence?" he will answer: "It is the Great Mystery!" "The holy silence is his voice!" If you ask: "What are the fruits of silence?" he will say: "They are self-control, true courage or endurance, patience, dignity, and reverence. Silence is the cornerstone of character."

"Guard your tongue in youth," said the old chief, Wabashaw, "and in age you may mature a thought that will be of service to your people!"

Basic Ideas of Morality

The moment that man conceived of a perfect body, supple, symmetrical, graceful, and enduring – in that moment he had laid the foundation of a moral life! No man can hope to maintain such a temple of the spirit beyond the period of adolescence, unless he is able to curb his indulgence in the pleasures of the senses. Upon this truth the Indian built a rigid system of physical training, a social and moral code that was the law of his life.

There was aroused in him as a child a high ideal of manly strength and beauty, the attainment of which must depend upon strict temperance in eating and in the sexual relation, together with severe and persistent exercise. He desired to be a worthy link in the generations, and that he might not destroy by his weakness that vigor and purity of blood which had been achieved at the cost of much self-denial by a long line of ancestors.

He was required to fast from time to time for short periods, and to work off his superfluous energy by means of hard running, swimming, and the vapour-bath. The bodily fatigue thus induced, especially when coupled with a reduced diet, is a reliable cure for undue sexual desires.

Personal modesty was early cultivated as a safeguard, together with a strong self-respect and pride of family and race. This was accomplished in part by keeping the child ever before the public eye, from his birth onward. His entrance into the world, especially in the case of the first-born, was often publicly announced by the herald, accompanied by a distribution of presents to the old and needy. The same thing occurred when he took his first step, when his ears were pierced, and when he shot his first game, so that his childish exploits and progress were known to the whole clan as to a larger family, and he grew into manhood with the saving sense of a reputation to sustain.

The youth was encouraged to enlist early in the public service, and to develop a wholesome ambition for the honours of a leader and feastmaker, which can never be his unless he is truthful and generous, as well as brave, and ever mindful of his personal chastity and honour. There were many ceremonial customs which had a distinct moral influence; the woman was rigidly secluded at certain periods, and the young husband was forbidden to approach his own wife when preparing for war or for any religious event. The public or tribal position of the Indian is entirely dependent his private virtue, and he is never permitted to forget that he does not live to himself alone, but to his tribe and his clan. Thus habits of perfect self-control were early established, and there were no unnatural conditions or complex temptations to beset him until he was met and overthrown by a stronger race.

To keep the young men and young women strictly to their honour, there were observed among us, within my own recollection, certain annual ceremonies of a semi-religious nature. One of the most impressive of these was the sacred "Feast of Virgins", which, when given for the first time, was equivalent to the public announcement of a young girl's arrival at a marriageable age. The herald, making the rounds of the teepee village, would publish the feast something after this fashion:

Pretty Weasel-woman, the daughter of Brave Bear, will kindle her first maidens' fire tomorrow! All ye who have never yielded to the pleading man, who have not destroyed your innocence, you alone are invited to proclaim anew before the Sun and the Earth, before your companions and in the sight of the Great Mystery, the chastity and purity of your maidenhood. Come ye, all who have not known man!

The whole village was at once aroused to the interest of the coming event, which was considered next to the Sun Dance and the Grand Medicine Dance in public importance. It always took place in midsummer, when a number of different clans were gathered together for the summer festivities, and was held in the centre of the great circular encampment.

Here two circles were described, one within the other, about a rudely heart-shaped rock which was touched with red paint, and upon either side of the rock there were thrust into the ground a knife and two arrows. The inner circle was for the maidens, and the outer one for their grandmothers or chaperones, who were supposed to have passed the climacteric. Upon the outskirts of the feast there was a great public gathering, in which order was kept by certain warriors of highest reputation. Any man among the spectators might approach and challenge any young woman whom he knew to be unworthy; if the accuser failed to prove his charge, the warriors were accustomed to punish him severely.

Each girl in turn approached the sacred rock and laid her hand upon it with all solemnity. This was her religious declaration of her virginity, her vow to remain pure until her marriage. If she should ever violate the maidens' oath, then welcome that keen knife and those sharp arrows!

Our maidens were ambitious to attend a number of these feasts before marriage, and it sometimes happened that a girl was compelled to give one, on account of gossip about her conduct. Then it was in the nature of a challenge to the scandal-mongers to prove their words! A similar feast was sometimes made by the young men, for whom the rules were even more strict, since no young man might attend this feast who had so much as spoken of love to a maiden. It was considered a high honour among us to have won some distinction in war and the chase, and above all to have been invited to a seat in the council, before one had spoken to any girl save his own sister.

"Give All or Nothing!"

It was our belief that the love of possessions is a weakness to be overcome. Its appeal is to the material part, and if allowed its way it will in time disturb the spiritual balance of the man. Therefore the child must early learn the beauty of generosity.

He is taught to give what he prizes most, and that he may taste the happiness of giving, he is made at an early age the family almoner. If a child is inclined to be grasping, or to cling to any of his little possessions, legends are related to him, telling of the contempt and disgrace falling upon the ungenerous and mean man.

Public giving is a part of every important ceremony. It properly belongs to the celebration of birth, marriage, and death, and is observed whenever it is desired to do special honour to any person or event. Upon such occasions it is common to give to the point of utter impoverishment. The Indian in his simplicity literally gives away all that he has, to relatives, to guests of another tribe or clan, but above all to the poor and the aged, from whom he can hope for no return. Finally, the gift to the "Great Mystery", the religious offering, may be of little value in itself, but to the buyer's own thought it should carry the meaning and reward of true sacrifice.

Orphans and the aged are invariably cared for, not only by their next of kin, but by the whole clan. It is the loving parent's pride to have his daughters visit the unfortunate and the helpless, carry them food, comb their hair, and mend their garments. The name "Wenonah", bestowed upon the eldest daughter, distinctly implies all this, and a girl who failed in her charitable duties was held to be unworthy of the name.

The man who is a skillful hunter, and whose wife is alive to her opportunities makes many feasts, to which he is careful to invite the older men of his clan, recognizing that they have outlived their period of greatest activity, and now love nothing so well as to eat in good company, and to live over the past. The old men, for their part, do their best to requite his liberality with a little speech, in which they are apt to relate the brave and generous deeds of their host's ancestors, finally congratulating him upon being a worthy successor of an honourable line. Thus his reputation is won as a hunter and a feast-maker, and almost as famous in his way as the great warrior is he who has a recognized name and standing as a "man of peace".

The true Indian sets no price upon either his property or his labour. His generosity is only limited by his strength and ability. He regards it as an honour to be selected for a difficult or dangerous service, and would think it shame to ask for any reward, saying rather: "Let him whom I serve express his thanks according to his own bringing up and his sense of honour!"

Nevertheless, he recognizes rights in property. To steal from one of his own tribe would be indeed disgrace if discovered, the name of "Wamanon", or Thief, is fixed upon him forever as an unalterable. The only exception to the rule is in the case of food, which is always free to the hungry if there is none by to offer it. Other protection than the moral law there could not be in an Indian community, where there were neither locks nor doors, and everything was open and easy of access to all comers.

Rules of Honourable Warfare

The property of the enemy is spoil of war, and it is always allowable to confiscate it if possible. However, in the old days there was not much plunder. Before the coming of the white man, there was in fact little temptation or opportunity to despoil the enemy; but in modern times the practice of "stealing horses" from hostile tribes has become common, and is thought far from dishonourable.

Warfare we regarded as an institution the "Great Mystery"

– an organized tournament or trial of courage and skill, with elaborate rules and "counts" for the coveted honour of the eagle feather. It was held to develop the quality of manliness and its motive was chivalric or patriotic, but never the desire for territorial aggrandizement or the overthrow of a brother nation. It was common, in early times, for a battle or skirmish to last all day, with great display of daring and horsemanship with scarcely more killed and wounded than may be carried from the field during a university game of football.

The slayer of a man in battle was expected to mourn for thirty days, blackening his face and loosening his hair according to the custom. He of course considered it no sin to take the life of an enemy, and this ceremonial mourning was a sign of reverence for the departed spirit. The killing in war of non-combatants, such as women and children, is partly explained by the fact that in savage life the woman without husband or protector is in pitiable case, and it was supposed that the spirit of the warrior would be better content if no widow and orphans were left to suffer want, as well as to weep.

A scalp might originally be taken by the leader of the war party only, and at that period no other mutilation was practised. It was a small lock not more than three inches square, which was carried only during the thirty days' celebration of a victory, and afterward given religious burial. Wanton cruelties and the more barbarous customs of war were greatly intensified with the coming of the white man, who brought with him fiery liquor and deadly weapons, aroused the Indian's worst passions, provoking in him revenge and cupidity, and even offered bounties for the scalps of innocent men, women, and children.

Murder within the tribe was a grave offence, to be atoned for as the council might decree, and it often happened that the slayer was called upon to pay the penalty with his own life. He made no attempt to escape or to evade justice. That the crime was committed in the depths of the forest or at dead of night, witnessed by no human eye, made no difference to his mind. He was thoroughly convinced that all is known to the "Great Mystery", and hence did not hesitate to give himself up, to stand his trial by the old and wise men of the victim's clan. His own family and clan might by no means attempt to excuse or to defend him, but his judges took all the known circumstances into consideration, and if it appeared that he slew in self-defence, or that the provocation was severe, he might be set free after a thirty days' period of mourning in solitude. Otherwise the murdered man's next of kin were authorized to take his life; and if they refrained from doing so, as often happened, he remained an outcast from the clan. A wilful murder was a rare occurrence before the days of whiskey and drunken rows, for we were not a violent or a quarrelsome people.

An Indian Conception of Courage

It is well remembered that Crow Dog, who killed the Sioux chief Spotted Tail, in 1881, calmly surrendered himself and was tried and convicted by the courts in South Dakota. After his conviction, he was permitted remarkable liberty in prison, such as perhaps no white man has ever enjoyed when under sentence of death.

The cause of his act was a solemn commission received from his people, nearly thirty years earlier, at the time that Spotted Tail usurped the chieftainship by the aid of the military, whom he had aided. Crow Dog was under a vow to slay the chief in case he ever betrayed or disgraced the name of the Brule Sioux. There is no doubt that he had committed crimes both public and private, having been guilty of misuse of office as well as of gross offenses against morality; therefore his death was not a matter of personal vengeance but of just retribution.

A few days before Crow Dog was to be executed, he asked permission to visit his home and say farewell to his wife and twin boys, then nine or ten years old. Strange to say, the request was granted, and the condemned man sent home under escort of the deputy sheriff, who remained at the Indian agency, merely telling his prisoner to report there on the following day. When he did not appear at the time set, the sheriff dispatched Indian police after him. They did not find him, and his wife simply said that Crow Dog had desired to ride alone to the prison, and would reach there on the day appointed. All doubt was removed next day by a telegram from Rapid City, two hundred miles distant, saying, "Crow Dog has just reported here."

The incident drew public attention to the Indian murderer, with the unexpected result that the case was reopened, and Crow Dog acquitted. He still lives, a well-preserved man of about seventy-five years, and is much respected among his own people.

It is said that, in the very early days, lying was a capital offence among us. Believing that the deliberate liar is capable of committing any crime behind the screen of cowardly untruth and double-dealing, the destroyer of mutual confidence was summarily put to death, that the evil might go no further.

Even the worst enemies of the Indian, those who accuse him of treachery, blood-thirstiness, cruelty, and lust, have not denied his courage but in their minds it is a courage that is ignorant, brutal, and fantastic. His own conception of bravery makes of it a high moral virtue, for to him it consists not so much in aggressive self-assertion as in absolute self-control. The truly brave man, we contend, yields neither to fear nor anger, desire nor agony; he is at all times master of himself; his courage rises to the heights of chivalry, patriotism, and real heroism.

"Let neither cold, hunger, nor pain, nor the fear of them, neither the bristling teeth of danger nor the very jaws of death itself, prevent you from doing a good deed," said an old chief to a scout who was about to seek the buffalo in midwinter for the relief of a starving people. This was his childlike conception of courage.

CHAPTER 5 – THE UNWRITTEN SCRIPTURES

A Living Book

A missionary once undertook to instruct a group of Indians in the truths of his holy religion. He told them of the creation of the earth in six days, and of the fall of our first parents by eating an apple.

The courteous savages listened attentively, and after thanking him, one related in his turn a very ancient tradition concerning the origin of the maize. But the missionary plainly showed his disgust and disbelief; indignantly saying: – "What I delivered to you were sacred truths, but this that you tell me is mere fable and falsehood."

"My brother," gravely replied the offended Indian, "it seems that you have not been well grounded in the rules of civility. You saw that we, who practise these rules, believed your stories; why, then, do you refuse to credit ours?"

Every religion has its Holy Book, and ours was a mingling of history, poetry, and prophecy, of precept and folk-lore, even such as the modern reader finds within the covers of his Bible. This Bible of ours was our whole literature, a living Book, sowed as precious seed by our wisest sages, and springing anew in the wondering eyes and upon the innocent lips of little children. Upon its hoary wisdom of proverb and fable, its mystic and legendary lore thus sacredly preserved and transmitted from father to son, was based in large part our customs and philosophy.

The Sioux Story of Creation

Naturally magnanimous and open-minded, the red man prefers to believe that the Spirit of God is not breathed into man alone, but that the whole created universe is a sharer in the immortal perfection of its Maker. His imaginative and poetic mind, like that of the Greek, assigns to every mountain, tree, and spring its spirit, nymph, or divinity either beneficent or mischievous. The heroes and demigods of Indian tradition reflect the characteristic trend of his thought, and his attribution of personality and will to the elements, the sun and stars, and all animate or inanimate nature.

In the Sioux story of creation, the great Mysterious One is not brought directly upon the scene or conceived in anthropomorphic fashion, but remains sublimely in the background. The Sun and the Earth, representing the male and female principles, are the main elements in his creation, the other planets being subsidiary. The enkindling warmth of the Sun entered into the bosom of our mother, the Earth, and forthwith she conceived and brought forth life, both vegetable and animal.

Finally there appeared mysteriously Ish-na-e-cha-ge, the "First-Born", a being in the likeness of man, yet more than man, who roamed solitary among the animal people and understood their ways and their language. They beheld him with wonder and awe, for they could do nothing without his knowledge. He had pitched his tent in the centre of the land, and there was no spot impossible for him to penetrate.

At last, like Adam, the "First-Born" of the Sioux became weary of living alone, and formed for himself a companion – not a mate, but a brother – not out of a rib from his side, but from a splinter which he drew from his great toe! This was the Little Boy Man, who was not created full-grown, but as an innocent child, trusting and helpless. His Elder Brother was his teacher throughout every stage of human progress from infancy to manhood, and it is to the rules which he laid down, and his counsels to the Little Boy Man, that we trace many of our most deep-rooted beliefs and most sacred customs.

Foremost among the animal people was Unk-to-mee, the Spider, the original trouble-maker, who noted keenly the growth of the boy in wit and ingenuity, and presently advised the animals to make an end of him; "for," said he, "if you do not, some day he will be the master of us all!" But they all loved the Little Boy Man because he was so friendly and so playful. Only the monsters of the deep sea listened, and presently took his life, hiding his body in the bottom of the sea. Nevertheless, by the magic power of the First-Born, the body was recovered and was given life again in the sacred vapour-bath, as described in a former chapter.

Once more our first ancestor roamed happily among the animal people, who were in those days a powerful nation. He learned their ways and their language – for they had a common tongue in those days; learned to sing like the birds, to swim like the fishes, and to climb sure-footed over rocks like the mountain sheep. Notwithstanding that he was their good comrade and did them no harm, Unk-to-mee once more sowed dissension among the animals, and messages were sent into all quarters of the earth, sea, and air, that all the tribes might unite to declare war upon the solitary man who was destined to become their master.

The First Battle

After a time the young man discovered the plot, and came home very sorrowful. He loved his animal friends, and was grieved that they should combine against him. Besides, he was naked and unarmed. But his Elder Brother armed him with a bow and flint-headed arrows, a stone warclub and a spear. He likewise tossed a pebble four times into the air, and each time it became a cliff or wall of rock about the teepee.

"Now," said he, "it is time to fight and to assert your supremacy, for it is they who have brought the trouble upon you, and not you upon them!"

Night and day the Little Boy Man remained upon the watch for his enemies from the top of the wall, and at last he beheld the prairies black with buffalo herds, and the elk gathering upon the edges of the forest. Bears and wolves were closing in from all directions, and now from the sky the Thunder gave his fearful war-whoop, answered by the wolf's long howl.

The badgers and other burrowers began at once to undermine his rocky fortress, while the climbers undertook to scale its perpendicular walls.

Then for the first time on earth the bow was strung, and hundreds of flint-headed arrows found their mark in the bodies of the animals, while each time that the Boy Man swung his stone war-club, his enemies fell in countless numbers.

Finally the insects, the little people of the air, attacked him in a body, filling his eyes and ears, and tormenting him with their poisoned spears, so that he was in despair. He called for help upon his Elder Brother, who ordered him to strike the rocks with his stone war-club. As soon as he had done so, sparks of fire flew upon the dry grass of the prairie and it burst into flame. A mighty smoke ascended, which drove away the teasing swarms of the insect people, while the flames terrified and scattered the others.

This was the first dividing of the trail between man and the animal people, and when the animals had sued for peace, the treaty provided that they must ever after furnish man with flesh for his food and skins for clothing, though not without effort and danger on his part. The little insects refused to make any concession, and have ever since been the tormentors of man; however, the birds of the air declared that they would punish them for their obstinacy, and this they continue to do unto this day.

Our people have always claimed that the stone arrows which are found so generally throughout the country are the ones that the first man used in his battle with the animals. It is not recorded in our traditions, much less is it within the memory of our old men, that we have ever made or used similar arrow-heads. Some have tried to make use of them for shooting fish under water, but with little success, and they are absolutely useless with the Indian bow which was in use when America was discovered. It is possible that they were made by some pre-historic race who used much longer and stronger bows, and who were workers in stone, which our people were not. Their stone implements were merely natural boulders or flint chips, fitted with handles of rawhide or wood, except the pipes, which were carved from a species of stone which is soft when first quarried, and therefore easily worked with the most primitive tools. Practically all the flint arrowheads that we see in museums and elsewhere were picked up or ploughed up, while some have been dishonestly sold by trafficking Indians and others, embedded in trees and bones.

We had neither devil nor hell in our religion until the white man brought them to us, yet Unk-to-mee, the Spider, was doubtless akin to that old Serpent who tempted mother Eve. He is always characterized as tricky, treacherous, and at the same time affable and charming, being not without the gifts of wit, prophecy, and eloquence. He is an adroit magician, able to assume almost any form at will, and impervious to any amount of ridicule and insult. Here we have, it appears, the elements of the story in Genesis; the primal Eden, the tempter in animal form, and the bringing of sorrow and death upon earth through the elemental sins of envy and jealousy.

The warning conveyed in the story of Unk-to-mee was ever used with success by Indian parents, and especially grandparents, in the instruction of their children. Ish-na-e-cha-ge, on the other hand, was a demigod and mysterious teacher, whose function it was to initiate the first man into his tasks and pleasures here on earth.

Another Version of the Flood

After the battle with the animals, there followed a battle with the elements, which in some measure parallels the Old Testament story of the flood. In this case, the purpose seems to have been to destroy the wicked animal people, who were too many and too strong for the lone man.

The legend tells us that when fall came, the First-Born

advised his younger brother to make for himself a warm tent of buffalo skins, and to store up much food. No sooner had he done this than it began to snow, and the snow fell steadily during many moons. The Little Boy Man made for himself snow-shoes, and was thus enabled to hunt easily, while the animals fled from him with difficulty. Finally wolves, foxes, and ravens came to his door to beg for food, and he helped them, but many of the fiercer wild animals died of cold and starvation.

One day the hungry ones appeared, the snow was higher than the tops of the teepee poles, but the Little Boy Man's fire kept a hole open and clear. Down this hole they peered, and lo! the man had rubbed ashes on his face by the advice of his Elder Brother, and they both lay silent and motionless on either side of the fire.

Then the fox barked and the raven cawed his signal to the wandering tribes, and they all rejoiced and said: "Now they are both dying or dead, and we shall have no more trouble!" But the sun appeared, and a warm wind melted the snow-banks, so that the land was full of water. The young man and his Teacher made a birch-bark canoe, which floated upon the surface of the flood, while of the animals there were saved only a few, who had found a foothold upon the highest peaks.

The youth had now passed triumphantly through the various ordeals of his manhood. One day his Elder Brother spoke to him and said: "You have now conquered the animal people, and withstood the force of the elements. You have subdued the earth to your will, and still you are alone! It is time to go forth and find a woman whom you can love, and by whose help you may reproduce your kind."

"But how am I to do this?" replied the first man, who was only an inexperienced boy. "I am here alone, as you say, and I know not where to find a woman or a mate!"

"Go forth and seek her," replied the Great Teacher; and forthwith the youth set out on his wanderings in search of a wife. He had no idea how to make love, so that the first courtship was done by the pretty and coquettish maidens of the Bird, Beaver, and Bear tribes. There are some touching and whimsical love stories which the rich imagination of the Indian has woven into this old legend.

Our Animal Ancestry

It is said, for example, that at his first camp he had built for himself a lodge of green boughs in the midst of the forest, and that there his reverie was interrupted by a voice from the wilderness – a voice that was irresistibly and profoundly sweet. In some mysterious way, the soul of the young man was touched as it had never been before, for this call of exquisite tenderness and allurement was the voice of the eternal woman!

Presently a charming little girl stood timidly at the door of his pine-bough wigwam. She was modestly dressed in grey, with a touch of jet about her pretty face, and she carried a basket of wild cherries which she shyly offered to the young man. So the rover was subdued, and love turned loose upon the world to upbuild and to destroy! When at last she left him, he peeped through the door after her, but saw only a robin, with head turned archly to one side, fluttering away among the trees.

His next camp was beside a clear, running stream, where a plump and industrious maid was busily at work chopping wood. He fell promptly in love with her also, and for some time they lived together in her cosy house by the waterside. After their boy was born, the wanderer wished very much to go back to his Elder Brother and to show him his wife and child. But the beaver-woman refused to go, so at last he went alone for a short visit. When he returned, there was only a trickle of water beside the broken dam, the beautiful home was left desolate, and wife and child were gone forever!

The deserted husband sat alone upon the bank, sleepless and faint with grief; until he was consoled by a comely young woman in glossy black, who took compassion upon his distress and soothed him with food and loving attentions. This was the bear-woman, from whom again he was afterward separated by some mishap. The story goes that he had children by each of his many wives, some of whom resembled their father, and these became the ancestors of the human race, while those who bore the characteristics of their mother returned to her clan. It is also said that such as were abnormal or monstrous in form were forbidden to reproduce their kind, and all love and mating between man and the animal creation was from that time forth strictly prohibited. There are some curious traditions of young men and maidens who transgressed this law unknowingly, being seduced and deceived by a magnificent buck deer, perhaps, or a graceful doe, and whose fall was punished with death.

The animal totems so general among the tribes were said to have descended to them from their great-grandmother's clan, and the legend was often quoted in support of our close friendship with the animal people. I have sometimes wondered why the scientific doctrine of man's descent has not in the same way apparently increased the white man's respect for these our humbler kin.

Of the many later heroes or Hiawathas who appear in this voluminous unwritten book of ours, each introduced an epoch in the long story of man and his environment. There is, for example, the Avenger of the Innocent, who sprang from a clot of blood; the ragged little boy who won fame and a wife by shooting the Red Eagle of fateful omen; and the Star Boy, who was the offspring of a mortal maiden and a Star.

It was this last who fought for man against his strongest enemies, such as Wazeeyah, the Cold or North-Wind. There was a desperate battle between these two, in which first one had the advantage and then the other, until both were exhausted and declared a truce. While he rested, Star Boy continued to fan himself with his great fan of eagle feathers, and the snow melted so fast that North-Wind was forced to arrange a treaty of peace; by which he was only to control one half the year. So it was that the orderly march of the seasons was established, and every year Star Boy with his fan of eagle feathers sets in motion the warm winds that usher in the spring.

CHAPTER 6 – ON THE BORDER-LAND OF SPIRITS

Death and Funeral Customs

The attitude of the Indian toward death, the test and background of life, is entirely consistent with his character and philosophy. Death has no terrors for him; he meets it with simplicity and perfect calm, seeking only an honorable end as his last gift to his family and descendants. Therefore, he courts death in battle; on the other hand, he would regard it as disgraceful to be killed in a private quarrel. If one be dying at home, it is customary to carry his bed out of doors as the end approaches, that his spirit may pass under the open sky.

Next to this, the matter that concerns him most is the

parting with his dear ones, especially if he have any little children who must be left behind to suffer want. His family affections are strong, and he grieves intensely for the lost, even though he has unbounded faith in a spiritual companionship.

The outward signs of mourning for the dead are far more spontaneous and convincing than is the correct and well-ordered black of civilization. Men and women among us loosen their hair and cut it according to the degree of relationship or of devotion. Consistent with the idea of sacrificing all personal beauty and adornment, they trim off likewise from the dress its fringes and ornaments, perhaps cut it short, or cut the robe or blanket in two. The men blacken their faces, and widows or bereaved parents sometimes gash their arms and legs till they are covered with blood. Giving themselves up wholly to their grief, they are no longer concerned about any earthly possession, and often give away all that they have to the first comers, even to their beds and their home. Finally, the wailing for the dead is continued night and day to the point of utter voicelessness; a musical, weird, and heart-piercing sound, which has been compared to the "keening" of the Celtic mourner.

The old-time burial of the Plains Indians was upon a scaffold of poles, or a platform among the boughs of a tree – their only means of placing the body out of reach of wild beasts, as they had no implements with which to dig a suitable grave. It was prepared by dressing in the finest clothes, together with some personal possessions and ornaments, wrapped in several robes, and finally in a secure covering of raw-hide. As a special mark of respect, the body of a young woman or a warrior was sometimes laid out in state in a new teepee, with the usual household articles and even with a dish of food left beside it, not that they supposed the spirit could use the implements or eat the food but merely as a last tribute. Then the whole people would break camp and depart to a distance, leaving the dead alone in an honourable solitude.

There was no prescribed ceremony of burial, though the body was carried out with more or less solemnity by selected young men, and sometimes noted warriors were the pall-bearers of a man of distinction. It was usual to choose a prominent position with a commanding outlook for the last resting-place of our dead. If a man were slain in battle, it was an old custom to place his body against a tree or rock in a sitting position, always facing the enemy, to indicate his undaunted defiance and bravery, even in death.

The Sacred Lock of Hair

I recall a touching custom among us, which was designed to keep the memory of the departed near and warm in the bereaved household. A lock of hair of the beloved dead was wrapped in pretty clothing, such as it was supposed that he or she would like to wear if living. This "spirit bundle", as it was called, was suspended from a tripod, and occupied a certain place in the lodge which was the place of honour. At every meal time, a dish of food was placed under it, and some person of the same sex and age as the one who was gone must afterward be invited in to partake of the food. At the end of a year from the time of death, the relatives made a public feast and gave away the clothing and other gifts, while the lock of hair was interred with appropriate ceremonies.

Reincarnation and the Converse of Spirits

Certainly the Indian never doubted the immortal nature of the spirit or soul of man, but neither did he care to speculate upon its probable state or condition in a future life. The idea of a "happy hunting-ground" is modern and probably borrowed, or invented by the white man. The primitive Indian was content to believe that the spirit which the "Great Mystery" breathed into man returns to Him who gave it, and that after it is freed from the body, it is everywhere and pervades all nature, yet often lingers near the grave or "spirit bundle" for the consolation of friends, and is able to hear prayers. So much of reverence was due the disembodied spirit, that it was not customary with us even to name the dead aloud.

Occult and Psychic Powers

It is well known that the American Indian had somehow developed occult power, and although in the latter days there have been many impostors, and, allowing for the vanity and weakness of human nature, it is fair to assume that there must have been some even in the old days, yet there are well-attested instances of remarkable prophecies and other mystic practice.

A Sioux prophet predicted the coming of the white man fully fifty years before the event, and even described accurately his garments and weapons. Before the steamboat was invented, another prophet of our race described the "Fire Boat" that would swim upon their mighty river, the Mississippi, and the date of this prophecy is attested by the term used, which is long since obsolete. No doubt, many predictions have been coloured to suit the new age, and unquestionably false prophets, fakirs, and conjurers have become the pest of the tribes during the transition period. Nevertheless, even during this period there was here and there a man of the old type who was implicitly believed in to the last.

Notable among these was Ta-chank-pee Ho-tank-a, or His War Club Speaks Loud, who foretold a year in advance the details of a great war-party against the Ojibways. There were to be seven battles, all successful except the last, in which the Sioux were to be taken at a disadvantage and suffer crushing defeat. This was carried out to the letter. Our people surprised and slew many of the Ojibways in their villages, but in turn were followed and cunningly led into an ambush whence but few came out alive. This was only one of his remarkable prophecies.

Another famous "medicine-man" was born on the Rum River about 150 years ago, and lived to be over a century old. He was born during a desperate battle with the Ojibways, at a moment when, as it seemed, the band of Sioux engaged were to be annihilated. Therefore the child's grandmother exclaimed: "Since we are all to perish, let him die a warrior's death in the field!" and she placed his cradle under fire, near the spot where his uncle and grandfathers were fighting, for he had no father. But when an old man discovered the new-born child, he commanded the women to take care of him, "for," said he, "we know not how precious the strength of even one warrior may some day become to his nation!"

This child lived to become great among us, as was intimated to the superstitious by the circumstances of his birth. At the age of about seventy-five years, he saved his band from utter destruction at the hands of their ancestral enemies, by suddenly giving warning received in a dream of the approach of a large war-party. The men immediately sent out scouts, and felled trees for a stockade, barely in time to meet and repel the predicted attack. Five years later, he repeated the service, and again saved his people from awful slaughter. There was no confusion of figures or omens, as with lesser medicine-men, but in every incident that is told of him his interpretation of the sign, whatever it was, proved singularly correct.

The father of Little Crow, the chief who led the "Minnesota massacre" of 1862, was another prophet of some note. One of his characteristic prophecies was made only a few years before he died, when he had declared that, although already an old man, he would go once more upon the war-path. At the final war-feast, he declared that three of the enemy would be slain, but he showed great distress and reluctance in foretelling that he would lose two of his own men. Three of the Ojibways were indeed slain as he had said, but in the battle the old war prophet lost both of his two sons.

The Gift of Prophecy

There are many trustworthy men, and men of Christian faith, to vouch for these and similar events occurring foretold. I cannot pretend to explain them, but I know that our people possessed remarkable powers of concentration and abstraction. I sometimes fancy that such nearness to nature as I have described keeps the spirit sensitive to impressions not commonly felt, and in touch with the unseen powers. Some of us seemed to have a peculiar intuition for the locality of a grave, which they explained by saying they had received a communication from the spirit of the departed. My own grandmother was one of these, and as far back as I can remember, when camping in a strange country, my brother and I would search for and find human bones at the spot she had indicated to us as an ancient burial-place or the spot where a lone warrior had fallen. Of course, the outward signs of burial had been long since obliterated.

The Scotch would certainly have declared that she had the "second sight," for she had other remarkable premonitions or intuitions within my own recollection. I have heard her speak of a peculiar sensation in the breast, by which, as she said, she was advised of anything of importance concerning her absent children. Other native women have claimed a similar monitor, but I never heard of one who could interpret with such accuracy. We were once camping on Lake Manitoba we received news that my uncle and his family had been murdered several weeks before, at a fort some 200 miles distant. While all our clan were wailing mourning their loss, my grandmother calmly bade them cease, saying that her son was approaching, that they would see him shortly. Although we had no other reason to doubt the ill tidings, it is a fact that my uncle came into camp two days after his reported death.

At another time, when I was fourteen years old, we had just left Fort Ellis on the Assiniboine River, and my youngest uncle had selected a fine spot for our night camp. It was already after sundown, but my grandmother became unaccountably nervous, and positively refused to pitch her tent. So we reluctantly went on down the river, and camped after dark at a secluded place. The next day we learned that a family who were following close behind had stopped at the place first selected by my uncle, but were surprised in the night by a roving war-party, and massacred to a man. This incident made a great impression upon our people.

Many of the Indians believed that one may be born more than once, and there were some who claimed to have full knowledge of a former incarnation. There were also those who held converse with a "twin spirit", who had been born into another tribe or race. There was a well-known Sioux war-prophet who lived in the middle of the last century, so that he is still remembered by the old men of his band. After he had reached middle age, he declared that he had a spirit brother among the Ojibways, the ancestral enemies of the Sioux. He even named the band to which his brother belonged, and said that he also was a war-prophet among his people.

Upon one of their hunts along the border between the two tribes, the Sioux leader one evening called his warriors together, and solemnly declared to them that they were about to meet a like band of Ojibway hunters, led by his spirit twin. Since this was to be their first meeting since they were born as strangers, he earnestly begged the young men to resist the temptation to join battle with their tribal foes.

"You will know him at once," the prophet said to them, "for he will not only look like me in face and form, but he will display the same totem, and even sing my war songs!"

They sent out scouts, who soon returned with news of the approaching party. Then the leading men started with their peace-pipe for the Ojibway camp, and when they were near at hand they fired three distinct volleys, a signal of their desire for a peaceful meeting.

The response came in like manner, and they entered the camp, with the peace-pipe in the hands of the prophet.

Lo, the stranger prophet advanced to meet them, and the people were greatly struck with the resemblance between the two men, who met and embraced one another with unusual fervour.

It was quickly agreed by both parties that they should camp together for several days, and one evening the Sioux made a "warriors' feast" to which they invited many of the Ojibways. The prophet asked his twin brother to sing one of his sacred songs, and behold! it was the very song that he himself was wont to sing. This proved to the warriors beyond doubt or cavil the claims of their seer.

Such are the beliefs in which I was reared – the secret ideals which have nourished in the American Indian a unique character among the peoples of the earth. Its simplicity, its reverence, its bravery and uprightness must be left to make their own appeal to the American of today, who is the inheritor of our homes, our names, and our traditions. Since there is nothing left us but remembrance, at least let that remembrance be just!

APPENDIX III

A Sioux Calendar of Events in the West, 1759–1925*

Ben Kindle

This is an oral calendar of the events which marked the winters of the Oglala Sioux nation, from 1759 to the year it was dictated by Ben Kindle, who was taught it by his mother, Afraid-of-Soldier.

1759 Wic'a´b.lecahą Wani^x yetu
    They are broken apart / year.
      When the tribes scattered.

1760 Hok'u´wa Wic'a´ktepi
    Fishermen / they are killed. (While engaged in fishing, they are killed.)
      Two Sioux boys went fishing in the creek and the enemy killed them.

*From Martha Warren Beckwith "Mythology of the Oglala Sioux", *Journal of American Folklore 43* (October–December 1930). Reprinted in The Portable North Ameican Indian Reader, ed. Frederick W. Turner III, The Viking Press, 1974.

1761 Wạb.li´k'uwa Wic'a´ktepi
      Eagle-trappers / they are killed.
         Two Shoshone were trapping eagles and some Sioux
         killed them.

1762 Pte A´nụwapi
      Buffalo / they swim out for them.
         Hunters chased buffaloes into the Missouri river and
         killed them there, then dragged them to land.

1763 T'uki´ mi´layapi
      Shell / they use for knives.
         The Indians had no knives, hence they brought
         shells from the Missouri and Platt rivers to use as
         knives.

1764 T'azu´skala kte´pi
      "Little ant" / they kill him.
         A Sioux called "Little Ant" was killed.

1765 Wazi´k'ute ahi´ktepi
      "He shoots at the pine" / coming they kill him.
         The Sioux Indians attack the Crow and a Sioux
         named Shooting-Pine is killed.

1766 Wale´ǧala kte´pi
      "Pouch" (made out of the rough lining of the first
      stomach) / he is killed.
         A Sioux called "Pouch" is killed.

1767 Anụk´op iya´yapi
      Both sides / in company with / they go off.
         The Crow Indians are at peace with the Sioux and

the two live together, also the Sioux are at peace with the Pawnee and they live together. When the Crow and Pawnee fight together, they find that there are Sioux on both sides and so they make peace.

1768 Iye´ska kic'i´zapi

White or clear speakers (those whose language is understandable, i.e., those in the same tribe) / they fight against each other.

The first civil war among the Sioux Indians: the Standing Rock Indians and the Cheyenne fight against the Oglala and Rosebud.

1769 Ite´hakit'ųla kte´pi

"He (little one) wears a mask" / they kill him (or, he is killed).

A Sioux named "Mask-On" is killed. The mask is made out of buckskin fastened to a willow hoop with eyes cut for a mask.

1770 Wak'ą´t'aka ihąˣb.la wįyą wąg.naśkį´yą

God / to see in vision, or dream of in sleep / woman /a / she goes crazy.

A woman has been accustomed to go to lonely places for visions and then come back and tell the people where to go for buffalo and when the enemy is coming. One morning she cannot speak, she does not know anything and soon she dies.

1771 Miwa´tani ogu´wic'ayapi

Mandans / they are burned out.

Hostile Indian dig a trench down by the creek and the Sioux are unable to drive them away. So they

build fires all about the trench and the enemy have
to escape in the night.

1772 C'ak'i´ ya´m.ni ahi´wic'aktepi
Carriers of wood on the back / three / coming to them
they kill them. (Ahi´wic'aktepi always means that an
enemy coming there from a great distance commits the
deed. It implies the killer journeying there to do it.)
The Sioux make a new camp and the Crows hide in
the timber and kill three old women sent after wood
as they are returning with the wood on their backs.

1773 Su̧´ka k'o išta´ niya̧´pi
Dogs / even / eyes / they are inflamed.
Even the dogs got snow-blindness this winter
because there was a heavy fall of snow and they had
to move camp constantly to escape attack by hostile
Indians.

1774 Heyo´k'akaǧa wa̧ kte´pi
Clown / a / he is killed.
The Sioux camp in a circle and the clowns put on
their masks, come to the circle and then go down to
the creek and back to pray for the thunder. When
they go back to the creek, hostile Indians in hiding
kill them.

1775 Paha´ta i num wic'a´ktepi
To the top of the hill / they went / two / they are
killed. (Two individuals who had gone up to the hill
were killed.)
About forty or fifty young people of the Sioux start
out on a war party. They are concealed in the heavy

timber down by the big creek. Two scouts on the hill look about and see the enemy coming down the creek, about seventy or eighty of them on foot with two Crow ahead. The Sioux mount their horses and kill the two Crow.

1776 Kig.lela hi
[This word may be K'ig.le'la – He goes back home (little one); or K'ig.le'la – He goes home carrying on his back (little one); or it may be a corruption of the white man's name] / he arrives.
 A half-breed joins the Sioux.

1777 Ho'he ahi'
Assiniboines / they arrive.
The Assiniboines make peace with the Sioux.

1778 Cana'k'sa yuha' kte'pi
"Stick broken with the foot / he carries" / he is killed.
 They were playing a game and the braves got to fightmg and this man was killed.

1779 Tuktel' wani't'i t'ai'śni awe'tupi
What place / winter camp / it is not clear / spring comes on them.
 During the winter the people generally camp by the creek with an abundance of hay and wood and move in the spring, but this year there was no feed so they had to move often throughout the winter.

1780 Slukela haka' iwo'to
(A proper name, but unidentified) / spearlike stick used in the game / he bumps into it.

Two men were playing haka'u̧'pi, or Shooting-the-Spear. They hit the umpire through the thigh with the stick so that later he died.

1781 Šųknu'ni o'ta ahi'
Stray horses / many / they come.

This year while they were in camp with their ponies in the centre of the circle, many wild horses came down from the hills and joined their ponies; so they divided up the wild horses.

1782 Nawi'c'aśli
They break out with a rash.

The first epidemic of measles.

1783 Šina'lutai wą kte'pi
Wearer of a red blanket / a / he is killed.

The man with a red blanket was killed in war.

1784 Aki'c'ita o'ta c'uwi'tat'api
Soldiers / many / they freeze to death.

White soldiers were encamped by the creek and Indians came down the creek and shot them and ran away. It was so cold that all the white men were frozen to death.

1785 Og.la'la hate' icu'pi
Og.lalas / cedar / they took.

The Sioux came west after cedar to use as medicine. "'Fraid for the Thunder" is the name of cedar smoke because if men have passed through its smoke, the lightning will not strike them in a thunderstorm They also burn cedar for the sick.

1786 P'cicu´ya zuya´ g li
   "He goes to take scalps" / on warpath / he returns
   home.

> A man vowed to go down to the Crow Indians by
> himself after a scalp. He stayed away for a week and
> then came back pretending to bring back a scalp, but
> it was only buffalo hair. He came into the tent
> carrying the scalp on a stick and singing, "I killed a
> Crow Indian." At first they believed him, but the
> brother-in-law saw the pretended scalp and recog-
> nized the fraud.

1787 O´hazi atku´kte´pi
   "Shade" / his father / they kill.

> The father of a boy named "Shade" is killed in a
> quarrel over whose arrow shot the buffalo.

1788 Heyo´k'akaǵa num wic'a´ktepi
   Clowns / two / they are killed. ("Make," in this sense.
   always means to act the part of.)

> Two clowns are killed. The Sioux have three camps
> by the river. The clowns circle the camps and when
> they come down to the last one, the Shoshone hiding
> in the timber kill the two clowns.

1789 K'aǵi´ o´ta c'uwi´tat'api
   Crows / many / they freeze to death.

> Many crows die of the cold. These are not the summer
> crows but a bigger crow that stays in the winter.

1790 Miwa´tani num c'ahc'o´ka wic'a´ktepi
   Mandans / two / out on the ice / they are killed.

> Two hostile Indians came down to the Sioux eamp

on the ice and, when the Sioux pursued, they killed them on the ice.

1791 Wo´wapi mak'o´kawih ahi´yayapi

Flag / around the earth / they carry it along.

The American flag is carried to all the Indian tribes all around the state.

1792 Wi̧´ya wa̧ ska wa̧ya´kapi

Woman / a / white / they see.

Once three Indians had gone after buffalo and were returning with the meat tied to the saddles. They looked up toward a hill just at sunset and saw a woman in white looking toward the sun. They ran back to camp and before dawn twelve young men went out to investigate and saw the woman in white at sunrise looking toward the sun. They believed this to be a spirit warning them of the approach of an enemy and they moved camp.

1793 Miwa´tani aw´c'at'ipi

Mandans / they camp close to. (They, the Sioux, camp close to the Mandans to crowd them off by making the proximity unpleasant.)

Sioux Indians camp close to hostile Indians and the two fight every day.

1794 Ite´ ci´k'a wa̧ kte´pi

Face / small / a / they kill (a small-faced enemy).

The Ponca Indians are large men with little faces, hence called "Small-Face." Three Poncas lie in hiding near the Sioux camp and try to steal horses. and the Sioux kill one "Small-Face."

1795 Pᶜehị´ haˊskaska wạ kteˊpi

Hair / long (reduplication indicates each hair is long) /
a / they kill him.

They killed a Sioux Indian with long hair.

1796 M.niˊyaye yuhaˊ wạ kteˊpi

Water container / carried / a / they killed.

A Sioux woman going after water before sunrise
with a buffalo-paunch bucket on her back is killed by
a hostile Indian in hiding near the camp.

1797 Wapᶜạˊhakitᶜụ wạ kteˊpi

Wearer of a war bonnet / a / he is killed.

A Sioux warrior kills a Blackfoot who wears a war
bonnet and thus gets possession of his war bonnet.
This event marks the introduction of the war bonnet
as well as of the buffalo horn headdress among the
Sioux.

1798 Wakᶜạtᶜạkawiyạ wạ iyeˊyapi

Great Spirit woman / a / she is found.

This year, three young men went hunting. It was in
the spring and very misty. They camped across the
creek. At midnight came a woman, but where she
entered they could not say, for the enclosure was
walled with logs like a stockade. There she stood by
the fire. She gave them three words of advice. "Grow
many and you will live" – "Pack up and run away for
two big gangs of the enemy will come after you" –
"Go in that direction and I will bring many buffalo."
Then she vanished they knew not where – up, down,
or where. The young men cried and pray'ed.

1799 Wii′g.luš′aka o′ta t′a′pi
Pregnant women / many / they die.
> Many pregnant women died.

1800 T′ac′a̧′ta Yu′tešni wae′c′ų
"Ruminant's heart / He eats not" / does a deed.
> A man named "Never-eats-buffalo-heart" made a feast for all the people. This was the first feast among the Sioux.

1801 Nawi′c′ašli
They break out with a rash.
> The second epidemic of measles.

1802 Waši′cu wą wašte′ hi
White man / a / good / he arrives.
> The first white preacher came to the Sioux.

1803 Šake′maza o′ta awi′c′ag.lipi
Horseshoes / many / they bring home. (They brought home many shoed horses.)
> The Sioux Indians were going to steal horses and for the first time saw horseshoes on them.

1804 Šukǧu′gula o′ta awi′c′ag.lipi
Horses burned all over / many / they brought home (curly-haired horses).
> The Sioux stole horses from the Blackfoot, many of them curly-haired.

1805 T′asį′ta ų aki′c′ilowąpi
Horsetail / with (as instrument) / they sang over each other. (This generally means the "Huka′" Ceremony

when the candidates are made huká by the songs sung over them by the officiating priest who at the same time waves a wand with pendant horsehair. T'a- means any ruminant; the more usual word for horsehair is šuksí'ta, but people call it t'así'ta, too.)

They first introduce the custom of adopting a member of another family by swinging the horsetail over the person thus adopted.

1806 Šag.lo´gą ahi´wic'aktepi

Eight / arriving here they kill them. (The enemy came here or near here and killed seven men.)

Nine Sioux went to war against the Crow. One of their number was posted as scout on a hill with a telescope. The Crow hid in the tent with bows drawn and when the Sioux approached they killed all but the scout, who ran two nights and a day before he reached the Sioux camp about dinnertime.

1807 Wąb.li´k'uwa eya´ wic'a´ktepi

Eagle trappers / some / they are killed (i.e. away irom home: indicates that the Sioux went off somewhere and killed some eagle trappers of another tribe).

The Sioux killed some Arapaho eagle-trappers.

1808 O´g.leluta ų wą itkop' heyo´k'a ahi´ktepi

Red Shirt / he wears / a / meeting / in an anti-natural manner / he is killed by those arriving. (A fighter who is an anti-natural, does the opposite to what the others on his side are doing, and so confuses the fighters that his own side, not realizing, of course, kill him.)

The Crow Indians are fighting the Sioux and the clown, wearing no mask but in a red shirt, runs toward the Crow and shoots at the Sioux, and the Crow kill him.)

1809 Šina´t'o atku´ku P'ala´ni ahi´ktepi
Blue-blanket / his father / Pawnee / arriving they kill.
Pawnee Indians kill Blue-Blanket's father.

1810 C'a´pa Ci´k'ala tii´le
Beaver / Little / has his house burn down. (Of itself. i.e without anyone planning it on purpose.
A white man set up a store and collected beaver-skin. The Indians called him "Little Beaver." His camp burned.

1811 Si´te wa´k'šupi o´ta awi´c'ag.lipi
Tail / decorated / many / they are brought home.
They steal horses with feathers on their tails.

1812 P'ala´ni top wic'a´ktepi
Pawnees / four / they are killed.
They kill four Pawnee.

1813 C'aku´t'a^xka atku´ku P'ala´ni kte´pi
"Road-Big" / his father / Pawnees / they kill him.
Big-Road's father is killed by Pawnees.

1814 Witapahata ų wą kahu´ḣugapi
Dweller at Island Butte / a / they break (kahu´ga means to break something with a hard shell, like an egg, a skull, a turtle's back, etc.).
A Mandan came down to the Sioux camp and talked with his hand, telling them not to kill him. A Sioux whose brother had been (killed by a Mandan) came

up to him with a concealed axe and chopped off his head.

1815 Ita´zipc‘o t‘it‘a´ka ot‘i´pi
Sans-arcs / big house / they live in.
> The No-Bow (Sans-arc) build the first log house.

1816 Nạ ak‘e´ ot’i´pi
And / again / they live in.
> The house is used for a second year.

1817 C‘ạṡe´ca ụ t‘ika´ǧapi
Dead wood / with (as material) / they build house.
> They build houses of dry wood.

1818 Nawi´c‘aṡli
They break out with rash.
> The third epidemic of measles.

1819 Sicạ´ǧu c‘ạpụ´pụ ụ t‘ica´ǧapi
Burnt-Thighs / rotten wood / with / they build house.
> Rosebud Indians build houses of rotten wood.

1820 Wạ Nụ´p.lala iwi´c‘icaṡke ki´caǧapi
Arrow / Only two" / ? // they make for him.
> Two-Arrow, who made the Crow dance as a vow for brave men, himself ran away when they went out to fight.

1821 Wic‘a´ḣpi wạ hot‘ụ´ hiya´ya
Star / a / with voice / it went by.
> A shooting star flew from east to west with a noise like thunder.

1822 Wasku´la hu s̆pa
    "He pares with a knife" (such things as pumpkin.
    potatoes, apples, wild turnips, etc.). This is a nickname,
    indicated by the la; hu, leg, / s̆pa, burn, or better, cook.
        Man with burned legs came to camp.
        He-pares-with-knife's legs got frostbitten.

1823 Wag.me´za o´ta s̆i´ce
    Corn / much / it is bad.
        Much corn spoiled. White men camped and the
        Indians took their sacks of corn to be ground and it
        got wet and moldy because they did not know how
        to keep it.

1824 Yeye´la ḣmuḣ kte´pi,
    "Unstable" / by bewitching / they kill. (Yeye´la, shaky
    and unsteady, like a table, a limb of a tree, if it is liable
    to break when climbed, etc., *ḣmuḣ*, to position by super-
    natural means.)
        "Swing-gently" was killed.

1825 M.ni wic‘a´t’e
    Water / they die. (They drown.)
        In March the people camped across the Missouri
        River. One morning before sunrise someone called
        them to wake because the water was coming. One
        heard the voice, but no one would listen. The banks
        did overflow and some of the old men and old
        women were drowned, while the able-bodied had to
        swim in the broken ice to reach high land. The
        horses were tied and could not get away, so they
        were all drowned.

1826 Ką i wą agl.it'e
Aged / he went / a / returning died.
An aged Sioux was scalped by the Crow Indians and
he returned to camp and died.

1827 P'sa ohạ'pi
Reed or rush / they wear on their feet.
The Sioux Indians first made snowshoes out of
kinnikinnick and willows.

1828 Miwa'tani o'ta wic'a'ktepi
Mandans / many / they are killed.
They kill many enemies.

1829 Ite' g.le'ga wia'k'siže
"Face / striped" / retains or keeps in his possession, a
woman.
An old man named "Spotted-face" forces a young
girl to be his wife and her father cannot get her
away.

1830 Ptesą' o'ta wic'a'opi
White buffalo / leg / it is broken. Ptesą', white buffalo.
They kill many white buffaloes.

1831 Ptesą' hu kawe'ge
White buffalo / leg / it is broken. Ptesą', white buffalo.
(Now and then, very rarely, a light-colored buffalo was
found in the herd. They were priceless because they
were rare, and some put a supernatural power to them.
Hence Ptesą' is a fine name for man or woman.)
White-Buffalo broke his leg.

1832 He Wazí´ca hu kawe´ǧe
      "Horn / only one" / it is broken.
         One-Horn broke his leg.

1833 Wic‘a´ħpi ok‘i´cam.na
      Stars / they go in all directions (crossing each other's
      path. Icam.na means "it snows." The way the stars
      seemed to fly in every way looked like snow coming down.
      Ok‘i´cam.na is used to express confusion, especially
      among a crowd, when everyone runs hither and yon).
         Stars change places. i.e., there are many shooting
         stars seen in the heavens.

1834 Śahi´yela t‘ig.le´ wa kte´pi
      Cheyenne / established in his home / a / they kill.
         A Cheyenne of good family is killed by another
         Cheyenne because he is so rich in horses.

1835 T‘at‘a´ka wa c‘e´pa o´pi
      Buffalo-bull / a / it is fat / they shoot with an arrow.
         They kill a fat buffalo bull.

1836 C‘aha´ka u aki´c‘ilowapi
      Branched stick / with / they sing over each other.
      (C‘aha´ka is a part of a bough with several branches or
      forks left on, like an elk-horn. This of course means
      such a part of the tree was used in place of the usual
      horsehair switch referred to in 1805.)
         A man about to give the sign of adoption saw some
         buffalo coming and thought they were soldiers. In
         his haste he waved a stick instead of the horsetail
         over the adopted person.

1837 Ite´hepi Sapki´ya t‘ia´paktepi

"Lower half of the face / he blackens his" / they kill him and his household right in their tepee.

Black-face, who painted half his face black from the nose down, camped away from the circle and was killed by the Crow. he and his whole family.

1838 Sųkg.na´škiyą c'ícąwą kte´pi
"Crazy Wolf" / his son / a / they kill.

Crazy-Dog's son is killed by the Crow.

1839 Wic'a´akih'ą wat'a´kpe ai´
Famine-stricken / for offensive warfare / they go.

During this year of famine they attacked a steamboat on the river, but without success.

1840 Waki´yą ci´k'ala sųka´ku num wic'a´ktepi
"Thunder / Little" / his younger brothers / two / they are killed.

Little-Thunder has two brothers who go to battle with the Crow Indians and are killed.

1841 Sųkna´kpogi o´ta t'ewi´e'ayapi
Brown-eared horses / many / they were caused to die.

Many white horses with brown ears (a colour much admired by the Sioux) are killed in quarrels over their possession.

1842 Wi´yaka Owį´ šuyu´ha na´zį wą kte
"Feather / Earring" / holding horse / he stands / a / he kills.

The Sioux called "Feather-Earrings" attacks and kills a Crow Indian who is guarding a herd, and takes the horses.

1843 Waya´ka ag.li´pi
    Captives / they bring home.
        The Sioux Indians take Crow slaves.

1844 K'agi´b.loka˟ ahi´ktepi
    "Male-crow" / coming they kill him.
        He-Crow is killed by the Crow.

1845 Nawi´c'ašli
    They break out with a rash.
        The fourth epidemic of measles.

1846 Susu´ ska wą kte´pi
    Testicles / white / a / they kill.
        White-Testicles is killed.

1847 K'agi´wab.li˟ c'ap'a´pi
    Crow-eagle / he is stabbed.
        Crow-Eagle is knifed.

1848 Wį´kte wą kte´pi
    Hermaphrodite / a / they kill.
        A hermaphrodite of the Crow dressed like a woman
        is killed.

1849 Nawi'c'at'ipa
    They cramp.
        There is an epidemic of cramp.

1850 Wic'a´hąhą
    They have sores (smallpox).
        The first smallpox epidemic.

1851 Wakpa´m.nipi t'a^xka

They pass things around / big. (Giving out of annuities on a grand scale.)

For the first time rations were distributed to the Indians.

1852 Wani´yetu waśma^x

Winter / deep snow.

A year of deep snow.

1853 Mat'o´ wą wiśą manų´hi

Bear / a / "mons veneris" / he came to steal.

A man shot a bear in his tent. He woke suddenly from sleep and looked over at the horses. They were snorting. He saw a black object right under the tent. He took his gun and said, "What you doing over here?" No answer. The bear said, "Whi-h-u-u!" It had pulled up two pickets of the tent and got inside.

1854 Mat'o´ Wayu´hi kte´pi

"Bear / he causes confusion" / they kill.

Mat'o´ Wayu´hi was killed.

1855 Wic'a´yażipa waa´k'ś'iża

"Wasp" / he refuses to have them go.

Wasp, who is a poor man, suggests after the sundance that "We have a good time here; let us stay three or four months more."

1856 K'ągi´wic'aśa ok'i´yapi

Crow Indian / they confer with.

The Sioux make peace with the Crow.

1857 K'ągi'wic'aṡa wik'ce'm.na wic'a'ktepi
  Crow Indians / ten / they are killed.
    The Sioux kill ten Crow Indians.

1858 T'aṡi'na Ġi P'sa'loka kte'pi
  "His robe / Brow" / Crows / they kill him.
    Big-Blanket is killed by Crow Indians.

1859 K'ągi'T'ącka ahi'ktepi.
  "Crow / Big" / coming they kill.
    Big-Crow is killed by the Crow.

1860 ...

1861 Hokṡic'ala hoḣpa'sotapi
  Children / by a cough they are wiped out.
    An epidemic of whooping cough among the babies
    and many died.

1862 Hokṡi'ala wą waṡpa'pi
  Boy / a / they scalp him.
    A Sioux boy crossed the creek from camp and as he
    was coming back about nine or ten o'clock some
    Shoshone Indians scalped him.

1863 Og.la'lla ṡag.lo'ġą ahi'wic'aktepi
  Oglalas / eight / coming they kill them.
    The Crow killed eight Oglala Sioux.

1864 P'sa top wic'a'ktepi
  Crow / four / they are killed.
    The Oglala killed four Crow.

1865 Šukso´tapi
Horses are wiped out, die off.
A winter of heavy snow and most of the horses died.

1866 Waši´cu opa´wiǧe wic‘a´ktepi
Whites / hundred / they are killed.
The Sioux kill a hundred whites.

1867 Šu´šula t‘ihi´ wą kte´pi
Shoshone / come right into camp / a / they kill.
A Shoshone came into the Sioux camp to steal and was killed.

1868 Waki´yą Het‘ų´ e´iḣpeyapi
"Thunder / has horns" / they take him off and leave him there.
Horned-Thunder went with a war party of Sioux to fight the Ute. His feet swelled, so they left him behind with food and wood close by the creek and went on to the war, but Horned-Thunder never came back.

1869 Winų´hcala wą c‘ąka´t‘a
Old woman / a / she is killed by a tree.
An old woman who camped under a tree was killed by the wind blowing the tree over.

1870 C‘ąku´ Waka´tuya ahi´ktepi
"Road / High" / coming they kill him.
A very brave man named "High-Road" is killed by the Crow.

1871 C‘ąha´ḣake t‘aį´šni
"Spinal column" / disappears.
Back-Bone is lost when out hunting.

1872 Nata´hlo´ka k'agi´wic'aŝa e´wic'akte
"Head with a hole in it" / Crow Indians / going he killed them.

> Hollow-Head was sleeping up on a hill with a telescope, gun, and arrows. He saw two Crow Indians and shot them both without any aid.

1873 Oma´ha num wic'a´ktepi
Omahas / two / they are killed.

> The Sioux kill two Omaha Indians.

1874 Eha´ke k'owa´kata ai´
For the last time / across the River / they went.

> The Sioux cross the Missouri for the last time.

1875 Wa´g.luhe sako´wi ahi´wic'aktepi
Camp-followers / seven / coming they kill them.

> Seven Sioux Indians from Loafer Camp go visiting to Big Horn River and are attacked by Crow Indians and killed.

1876 Mahpi´ya Lu´ta sukk'i´pi
"Cloud / Red" / they take his horses from him. (The white soldiers demanded all the horses from his tribe. This was to prevent another uprising.)

> The white soldiers take his horses from Red Cloud. the Oglala chief (Custer massacre).

1877 T'aŝu´ke Witko× kte´pi
"His horse / crazy" / they kill.

The Oglala chief Crazy Horse, who has harried the settlers in the Black Hills as they came through with oxen, is killed this year.

1878 Šahi´yela wak‘a* kte´pi

Cheyenne / Holy / they kill him. (Had it been a Cheyenne medicine man, it would have been "Sahiyela wak‘aˣ wą kte´pi.")

Cheyenne Holy Man was killed this year. He was a Sioux medicine man and at a gathering at the agency he claimed to be invulnerable. So they shot at him and killed him. (This is the year of the opening of the agency at Pine Ridge.)

1879 Sųkma´nitu G.lešká´ kte´pi

"Wolf / Spotted" / he is killed.

Spotted-Wolf is killed by a Sioux.

1880 Susu´ G.lešká´ kte´pi

"Testicles / Spotted" / they kill.

Spotted-Testicles is killed by a Sioux.

1881 Sįte´g.lešká´ kte´pi

Spotted Tail / they kill.

Spotted-Tail (chief at Rosebud) is killed.

1882 C‘ą´c‘egą k’į´la c‘įca´ wą ic’i´kte

"Drum / he carries on his back (nickname)" / his son / a / he kills himself.

Drum-on-the-back's son shoots himself.

1883 Ite´c‘aguˣgu t‘ahu´ pawe´ǵe

"Face-blackened with wood charcoal" / his neck / it is broken.

Black-paint-on-the-face broke his neck chasing the steers at the old slaughter house at Pine Ridge.

*Probably a proper name, Šahi´yela Wak‘ą´.

1884 Tʻatʻaˬˊka Ska tʻawiˊcu kikteˊ
"Buffalo-bull / White" / his wife I he kills his own.
White-Bull killed his wife.

1885 Pʻeˊtawicʻaša eˊiĥpeyapi
Fire-man (Man of fire) / they take him far and leave him.
Fire-Man went to visit the Arapaho and died there.

1886 Yuptaˊyaˬ wanuˊktepi
"Turn it over" / is accidentally killed.
Turn-them-over was killed.

1887 Wakʻaˬˊ wanuˬˊktepi
"Holy" / is accidentally killed.
Holy was killed.

1888 Woˊpʻahta yubleˊcapi
"Bundles" / they are open and exposed.
Policemen stopped the traffic in "medicine."

1889 Oˊg.le Ša tʻakʻšiˊtku waˬ icʻiˊkte
"Shirt / Red" / his younger sister / a / she hanged herself.
Red-Shirt's sister hanged herself.

1890 Si Tʻaˬˊka kteˊpi
"Big / foot" / they kill.
Chief Big-Foot came to the Ghost Dance at Oglala. The Agency stopped the dance and at Brennan the soldiers attacked them and killed the chief and many others.

1891 Maka´ ma´niakic'ita wic'a´kaġapi
Ground / walking soldiers (Infantry) / they are made.
The Indian are taken to Omaha and Fort Mink and
put into the army.

1892 C'ạ Num Yuha´ pteya´ha wic'a´kte
"Sticks / two / he has" / cattle-owners / he kills them.
Some cowboys down by White River are troubling
the cattle and Two-Sticks and his son go down and
kill the cowboys.

1893 Owa´yawat'ạka ile´ (Pine Ridge Agency)
Big school / it burns.
The first boarding school is burned at the Pine Ridge
Agency.

1894 C'ạ Num Yuha´ p'a´nak'seyapi
"Sticks / two / he has" / they behead him.
They hang Two-Sticks for killing the cowboys.

1895 Og.la´la om.ni´ciye t'ạ´ka ka´ġapi
Oglalas / gathering / great / they make.
(Om.niciye T'ạ´nka is the general term among all the
Indians for religious gatherings. It is probable this was
the first Episcopal Convocation on the Oglala
reservee.)
They call the first meeting of the big Oglala council.

1896 Zikta´la Ska Waya´su t'a
Bird / White" / judge / he dies.
White-Bird, the judge, died at the agency.

1897 T'alo´t'ipi wạ ile´yapi; Mak'a´ṡa el

Beef-house / a / they burn it; / Mak´a'ša / at.

The slaughterhouse was burned by incendiaries who did not want it there.

1898 Og.la´la t'oka´ c'ukaške ka´ǵapi

Oglalas / first time / fences / they make.

A fence is built all around the Oglala reservation.

1899 P'eta´ǵa t'a

"Live coal / he dies.

Fire (an old man who worked at the reservation) died.

1900 Wok´pam.ni nat'a´kapi

Annuities (of goods) / they lock or close or bar.

Rations are not given out.

1901 Wic'a´ḣaḣą

Smallpox.

Second smallpox epidemic.

1902 Winų´ḣcala wą t'ąi´sni

Old woman / a / she disappears.

An old man and an old woman came drunk from Chadron and the old woman disappeared.

1903 T'a´hcak'ute 'wic'a´ktepi

Antelope-hunters / they are killed.

The Sioux went down to Wyoming to hunt antelope and the policemen went after them and killed four. The Sioux killed one policeman from Newcastle.

1904 T'oka´ mak'i´yu´t'api
First time / they surveyed the land.
For the first time land was allotted in the reservation.

1905 Wap'a´ha Ho´ta c'ica´ kat'i´ye´kiya
"War-bonnet / Gray" / his son / he kills his own by shooting.
Gray-war-bonnet killed his son when he was drunk.

1906 Sa´pawic'aša owi´cayuspapi
Black-men (Utes) / they are captured.
Some Ute Indians camped within the Cheyenne River agency were transferred to the Ute reservation.

1907 Mak'i´yu´t'a wo×kazuzu icu´pi
Land survey / payment / they receive.
The first payment was made for the allotment benefit.

1908 Waši´cu T'ašu× xke t'a
"White man / His horse" / he dies.
Chief American-Horse died.

1909 Mi´wak'a Yuha´ t'a
"Sword / he has" / he dies.
Chief Sword died.

1910 Mahpi´ya Lu´ta t'a
"Cloud / Red" / he dies.
Chief Red Cloud died.

1911 Mat'o´ K'oki´p'api t'a

"Bear / they fear him" / he dies.
Afraid-of-Bear died.

1912 Wo´wapi Wąkal´ a´yapi
Flag / upward / they raise it.
Flag-raising at the agency. "The Indians and white men held the ropes. My father had one and another old Indian had another. One spoke and said, 'Always where this flag is you must fight for it; you don't want this flag down.'"

1913 Wa´ta wą m.nit'a´
Ship / a / it drowns.
The sinking of the *Titanic*.

1914 Iya´ Si´ca t'oka´ oki´c'ize
Speech / Bad* / first / there is war.
War declared with Germany.

1915 Waši´cuik'ceka oki´c'ize
Common whites (French) / there is war.
France at war with Germany.

1916 United States wa´ta nap'o´pyapi
United States / ship / they explode it.
A United States ship sunk *(the Lusitania)*.

1917 President Wilson oki´c'iżekta c'ażo´ic'iwa
President Wilson / there shall be war / he signs his name.
President Wilson wants men to enlist in the army.

---

*Because German speech was considered unintelligible.

1918 United States oki´c'ize ohi´yapi; Flu ewi´c'ac'eca
     United States / war / they win it; / Flu / they get it.
          The United States has peace from the war; flu
          epidemic.

1919 Iye´c'ika ig.lu´ha wic'a´yuṡtapi
     Of their own accord / to keep themselves / they are made.
          Some Sioux Indians become citizens.

1920 M.nita´ t'a^xka wą wak'a´heża k'o m.nit'a´pi
     Flood / great / a / children / too / they die by
     drowning.
          White Clay creek is flooded in June and horses,
          cattle and dogs are drowned. One house "drew
          away" with everything in it and two children died.

1921 July oska´te yub.le´capi
     July / celebration / they break it into parts.
          There is a fourth of July celebration at each station.

1922 Aki´c'itahokṡila ahi´
     Soldier – boys / they arrive.
          Soldiers get recruits for the army.

1923 President Wilson t'a
     President Wilson / dies.
          President Wilson died.*

1924 Ate´yapi Tidwell wic'a´k'ute
     Agent / Tidwell / he shoots at them.
          Agent Tidwell shot at Indian boys who had escaped
          from jail.

*Wilson died in 1924.

1925 Agent Jermark wo´zuok'olakic'iye ka´ga
    Agent Jermark / farming society / he makes.
    Agent Jermark makes a farming chapter.

APPENDIX IV

The Captivity of John Tanner*

Tanner's account is one of the least-known but most informative of the "captivity narratives" that were such a phenomenon in the eighteen and nineteenth centuries. Published in 1830, it was dictated by Tanner to Dr Edwin James, and recounts thirty years spent amongst the Indian tribes of the Old Northwest, principally the Ottawa and Ojibway (Chippewa). These were Alonquian-speakers who, under pressure of westwards European expansion, had pushed into the Great Lakes and Minnesota area in the 1700s and successfully contested wild rice and hunting resources with tribes of the Illinois Confederacy.

Like numerous other captives, Tanner himself was unable to readjust to "civilization" and after telling his tale disappeared back into Indian society.

The earliest event of my life, which I distinctly remember,

From *John Tanner's Narrative of His Captivity Among the Ottawa and Ojibwa Indians*, ed. James, Occasional Papers of the Sutro Branch of California State Library, Reprint Series No. 20, ed. Paul Radin, San Francisco 1940.

is the death of my mother. This happened when I was two years old, and many of the attending circumstances made so deep an impression, that they are still fresh in my memory. I cannot recollect the name of the settlement at which we lived, but I have since learned it was on the Kentucky River, at a considerable distance from the Ohio.

My father, whose name was John Tanner, was an emigrant from Virginia, and had been a clergyman. He lived long after I was taken by the Indians, having died only three months after the great earthquake, which destroyed a part of New Madrid, and was felt throughout the country on the Ohio (1811).

Soon after my mother's death, my father removed to a place called Elk Horn. At this place was a cavern – I used to visit it with my brother. We took two candles; one we lighted on entering, and went on till it was burned down; we then lighted the other, and began to return, and we would reach the mouth of the cavern before it was quite burned out.

This settlement at Elk Horn was occasionally visited by hostile parties of Shawneese Indians, who killed some white people, and sometimes killed or drove away cattle and horses. In one instance, my uncle my father's brother, went with a few men at night, and fired upon a camp of these Indians; he killed one, whose scalp he brought home; all the rest jumped into the river and escaped.

In the course of our residence at this place, an event occurred, to the influence of which I attributed many of the disasters of my subsequent life. My father, when about to start one morning to a village at some distance, gave, as it appeared, a strict charge to my sisters, Agatha and Lucy, to send me to school; but this they neglected to do until afternoon. and then, as the weather was rainy and unpleasant, I insisted on remaining at home. When my father returned at night, and found that I had been at home all day, he sent me for a parcel of small canes, and flogged me much more severely than I could suppose the offence merited. I was displeased with my sisters for attributing all the blame to me, when they had neglected even to tell me to go to school in the forenoon. From that time, my father's house was less like home to me, and I often thought and said, "I wish I could go and live among the Indians".

I cannot tell how long we remained at Elk Horn; when we moved, we traveled two days with horses and wagons, and came to the Ohio, where my father bought three flat boats; the sides of these boats had bullet holes in them, and there was blood on them, which I understood was that of people who had been killed by the Indians. In one of these boats we put the horses and cattle – in another, beds, furniture, and other property, and in the third were some Negroes. The cattle boat and the family boat were lashed together; the third, with the Negroes, followed behind. We descended the Ohio, and in two or three days came to Cincinnati; here the cattle boat sunk in the middle of the river. When my father saw it sinking, he jumped on board, and cut loose all the cattle, and they swam ashore on the Kentucky side, and were saved. The people from Cincinnati came out in boats to assist us, but father told them the cattle were all safe.

In one day we went from Cincinnati to the mouth of the Big Miami, opposite which we were to settle. Here was some cleared land, and one or two log cabins, but they had been deserted on account of the Indians. My father rebuilt the cabins, and enclosed them with a strong picket. It was early in the spring when we arrived at the mouth of the Big Miami, and we were soon engaged in preparing a field to plant corn. I think it was not more than ten days after our arrival, when my father told us in the morning, that from the actions of the horses, he perceived there were Indians lurking about in the woods, and he said to me, "John, you must not go out of the house today." After giving strict charge to my stepmother to let none of the little children go out, he went to the field with the Negroes, and my elder brother, to drop corn.

Three little children, beside myself, were left in the house with my stepmother. To prevent me from going out, my stepmother required me to take care of the little child, then not more than a few months old; but as I soon became impatient of confinement, I began to pinch my little brother, to make him cry. My mother perceiving his uneasiness, told me to take him in my arms and walk about the house; I did so, but continued to pinch him. My mother at length took him from me to give him suck. I watched my opportunity, and escaped into the yard; thence through a small door in the large gate of the wall into the open field. There was a walnut tree at some distance from the house, and near the side of the field, where I had been in the habit of finding some of the last year's nuts. To gain this tree, without being seen by my father, and those in the field, I had to use some precaution. I remember perfectly well having seen my father, as I skulked toward the tree; he stood in the middle of the field, with his gun in his hand, to watch for Indians, while the others were dropping corn. As I came near the tree, I thought to myself, "I wish I could see these Indians." I had partly filled with nuts a straw hat which I wore, when I heard a crackling noise behind me; I looked round, and saw the Indians; almost at the same instant, I was seized by both hands, and dragged off betwixt two. One of them took my straw hat, emptied the nuts on the ground, and put it on my head. The Indians who seized me were an old man and a young one; these were, as I learned subsequently, Manito-o-geezhik, and his son Kish-kau-ko. Since I returned from Red River, I have been at Detroit while Kish-kau-ko was in prison there; I have also been in Kentucky, and have learned several particulars relative to my capture, which were unknown to me at the time. It appears that the wife of Manito-o-geezhik had recently lost by death her youngest son – that she had complained to her husband, that unless he should bring back her son, she could not live. This was an intimation to bring her a captive whom she might adopt in the place of the son she had lost. Manito-o-geezhik, associating with him his son, and two other men of his band, living at Lake Huron, had proceeded eastward with this sole design. On the upper part of Lake Erie, they had been joined by three other young men, the relations of Manito-o-geezhik, and had proceeded on, now seven in number, to the settlements on the Ohio. They had arrived the night previous to my capture at the mouth of the Big Miami, had crossed the Ohio, and concealed themselves within sight of my father's house. Several times in the course of the morning, old Manito-o-geezhik had been compelled to repress the ardor of his young men, who becoming impatient at seeing no opportunity to steal a boy, were anxious to fire upon the people dropping corn in the field. It must have been about noon when they saw me coming from the house to the walnut tree, which was probably very near the place where one or more of them were concealed.

It was but a few minutes after I left the house, when my father, coming from the field, perceived my absence. My stepmother had not yet noticed that I had gone out. My elder brother ran immediately to the walnut tree, which he knew I was fond of visiting, and seeing the nuts which the Indian had emptied out of my hat, he immediately understood that I had been made captive. Search was instantly made for me, but to no purpose. My father's distress, when he found I was indeed taken away by the Indians, was, I am told, very great.

After I saw myself firmly seized by both wrists by the two Indians, I was not conscious of any thing that passed for a considerable time. I must have fainted, as I did not cry out, and I can remember nothing that happened to me, until they threw me over a large log, which must have been at a considerable distance from the house. The old man I did not now see; I was dragged along between Kish-kau-ko and a very short thick man. I had probably made some resistance, or done something to irritate this last, for he took me a little to one side, and drawing his tomahawk, motioned to me to look up. This I plainly understood, from the expression of his face, and his manner, to be a direction for me to look up for the last time, as he was about to kill me. I did as he directed, but Kish-kau-ko caught his hand as the tomahawk was descending and prevented him from burying it in my brains. Loud talking ensued between the two, Kish-kau-ko presently raised a yell; the old man and the four others answered it by a similar yell; and came running up. I have since understood that Kish-kau-ko complained to his father, that the short man had made an attempt to kill his little brother, as he called me. The old chief, after reproving him, took me by one hand, and Kish-kau-ko by the other, and dragged me betwixt them; the man who had threatened to kill me, and who was now an object of terror, being kept at some distance. I could perceive, as I retarded them somewhat in their retreat, that they were apprehensive of being overtaken; some of them were always at some distance from us.

It was about one mile from my father's house to the place where they threw me into a hickory bark canoe, which was concealed under the bushes, on the bank of the river. Into this they all seven jumped, and immediately crossed the Ohio, landing at the mouth of the Big Miami, and on the south side of that river. Here they abandoned their canoe, and stuck their paddles in the ground, so that they could be seen from the river. At a little distance in the woods, they had some blankets and provisions concealed; they offered me some dry venison and bear's grease, but I could not eat. My father's house was plainly to be seen from the place where we stood; they pointed at it, looked at me, and laughed, but I have never known what they said.

After they had eaten a little, they began to ascend the Miami, dragging me along as before. The shoes I had on when at home, they took off, as they seemed to think I could run better without them. Although I perceived I was closely watched, all hope of escape did not immediately forsake me. As they hurried me along, I endeavored, without their knowledge, to take notice of such objects as would serve as landmarks on my way back. I tried also, where I passed long grass, or soft ground, to leave my tracks. I hoped to be able to escape after they should have fallen asleep at night. When night came, they lay down, placing me between the old man and Kish-kau-ko, so close together, that the same blanket covered all three. I was so fatigued that I fell asleep immediately, and did not wake until sunrise next morning, when the Indians were up and ready to proceed on their journey. Thus we journeyed for about four days, the Indians hurrying me on, and I continuing to hope that I might escape, but still every night completely overpowered by sleep. As my feet were bare, they were often wounded, and at length much swollen. The old man perceiving my situation, examined my feet one day, and after removing a great many thorns and splinters from them, gave me a pair of moccasins, which afforded me some relief. Most commonly, I traveled between the old man and Kish-kau-ko, and they often made me run until my strength was quite exhausted. For several days I could eat little or nothing. It was, I think, four days after we left the Ohio, that we came to a considerable river, running, as I suppose, into the Miami. This river was wide, and so deep, that I could not wade across it; the old man took me on his shoulders and carried me over; the water was nearly up to his armpits. As he carried me across, I thought I should never be able to pass this river alone, and gave over all hope of immediate escape. When he put me down on the other side, I immediately ran up the bank, and a short distance into the woods, when a turkey flew up a few steps before me. The nest she had left contained a number of eggs; these I put in the bosom of my shirt, and returned towards the river. When the Indians saw me they laughed, and immediately took the eggs from me, and kindling a fire, put them in a small kettle to boil. I was then very hungry, and as I sat watching the kettle, I saw the old man come running from the direction of the ford where we had crossed; he immediately caught up the kettle, threw the eggs and the water on the fire, at the same time saying something in a hurried and low tone to the young men. I inferred we were pursued, and have since understood that such was the case; it is probable some of my friends were at that time on the opposite side of the river searching for me. The Indians hastily gathered up the eggs and dispersed themselves in the woods, two of them still urging me forward to the utmost of my strength.

It was a day or two after this that we met a party of twenty or thirty Indians, on their way toward the settlements. Old Manito-o-geezhik had much to say to them; subsequently I learned that they were a war party of Shawneese; that they received information from our party, of the whites who were in pursuit of us about the forks of the Miami; that they went in pursuit of them, and that a severe skirmish happened between them, in which numbers were killed on both sides.

Our journey through the woods was tedious and painful: it might have been ten days after we met the war party, when we arrived at the Maumee river. As soon as we came near the river, the Indians were suddenly scattered about the woods examining the trees, yelling and answering each other. They soon selected a hickory tree, which was cut down, and the bark stripped off, to make a canoe. In this canoe we all embarked, and descended till we came to a large Shawnee village, at the mouth of a river which enters the Maumee. As we were landing in this village, great numbers of the Indians came about us, and one young woman came crying directly toward me, and struck me on the head. Some of her friends had been killed by the whites. Many of these Shawneese showed a disposition to kill me, but Kish-kau-ko and the old man interposed, and prevented them. I could perceive that I was often the subject of conversation, but could not as yet understand what was said. Old Manito-o-geezhik could speak a few words of English, of which he used occasionally, to direct me to bring water, make a fire, or perform other tasks, which he now began to require of me. We remained two days at the Shawnee village, and then proceeded on our journey in the canoe. It was not very far from the village that we came to a trading house, where were three or four men who could speak English; they talked much with me, and said they wished to have purchased me from the Indians, that I might return to my friends; but as the old man would not consent to part with me, the traders told me I must be content to go with the Indians, and to become the old man's son, in place of one he had lost, promising at the same time that after ten days they would come to the village and release me. They treated me kindly while we stayed, and gave me plenty to eat, which the Indians had neglected to do. When I found I was compelled to leave this house with the Indians, I began to cry, for the first time since I had been taken. I consoled myself, however, with their promise that in ten days they would come for me. Soon after leaving this trading house, we came to the lake; we did not stop at night to encamp, but soon after dark the Indians raised a yell, which was answered from some lights on shore, and presently a canoe came off to us, in whish three of our party left us. I have little recollection of any thing that passed from this time until we arrived at Detroit. At first we paddled up in the middle of the river until we came opposite the center of the town; then we ran in near the shore, where I saw a white woman, with whom the Indians held a little conversation, but I could not understand what was said. I also saw several white men standing and walking on shore, and heard them talk, but could not understand them; it is likely they spoke French. After talking a few minutes with the woman, the Indians pushed off, and ran up a good distance above the town.

It was about the middle of the day when we landed in the woods, and drew up the canoe. They presently found a large hollow log, open at one end, into which they put their blankets, their little kettle, and some other articles; they then made me crawl into it, after which they closed up the end at which I had entered. I heard them for a few minutes on the outside, then all was still, and remained so for a long time. If I had not long since relinquished all hope of making my escape, I soon found it would be in vain for me to attempt to release myself from my confinement. After remaining many hours in this situation, I heard them removing the logs with which they had fastened me in, and on coming out, although it was very late in the night, or probably near morning, I could perceive that they had brought three horses. One of these was a large iron-gray mare, the others were two small bay horses. On one of these they placed me, on the others their baggage, and sometimes one, sometimes another of the Indians riding, we traveled rapidly, and in about three days reached Sauge-nong, the village to which old Manito-o-geezhik belonged. This village or settlement consisted of several scattered houses. Two of the Indians left us soon after we entered it; Kish-kau-ko and his father only remained, and instead of proceeding immediately home, they left their horses and borrowed a canoe, in which we at last arrived at the old man's house. This was a hut or cabin built of logs, like some of those in Kentucky. As soon as we landed, the old woman came down to us to the shore, and after Manito-o-geezhik had said a few words to her, she commenced crying, at the same time hugging and kissing me, and thus she led me to the house. Next day they took me to the place where the old woman's son had been buried. The grave was enclosed with pickets, in the manner of the Indians, and on each side of it was a smooth open place. Here they all took their seats; the family and friends of Manito-o-geezhik on the one side, and strangers on the other. The friends of the family had come provided with presents; mukkuks of sugar, sacks of corn, beads, strouding, tobacco, and the like. They had not been long assembled, when my party began to dance, dragging me with them about the grave. Their dance was lively and cheerful, after the manner of the scalp dance. From time to time as they danced, they presented me something of the articles they had brought, but as I came round in the dancing to the party on the opposite side of the grave, whatever they had given me was snatched from me: thus they continued a great part of the day, until the presents were exhausted, when they returned home.

It must have been early in the spring when we arrived at Sau-ge-nong, for I can remember that at this time the leaves were small, and the Indians were about planting their corn. They managed to make me assist at their labors, partly by signs, and partly by the few words of

English old Manito-o-geezhik could speak. After planting, they all left the village, and went out to hunt and dry meat. When they came to their hunting grounds, they chose a place where many deer resorted, and here they began to build a long screen like a fence; this they made of green boughs and small trees. When they had built a part of it, they showed me how to remove the leaves and dry brush from that side of it to which the Indians were to come to shoot the deer. In this labor I was sometimes assisted by the squaws and children, but at other times I was left alone. It now began to be warm weather, and it happened one day that having been left alone, as I was tired and thirsty, I fell asleep. I cannot tell how long I slept, but when I began to awake, I thought I heard some one crying a great way off. Then I tried to raise up my head, but could not. Being now more awake, I saw my Indian mother and sister standing by me, and perceived that my face and head were wet. The old woman and her daughter were crying bitterly, but it was some time before I perceived that my head was badly cut and bruised. It appears that after I had fallen asleep, Manito-o-geezhik, passing that way, had perceived me, had tomahawked me, and thrown me in the bushes; and that when he came to his camp he had said to his wife, "Old woman, the boy I brought you is good for nothing; I have killed him, and you will find him in such a place." The old woman and her daughter having found me, discovered still some signs of life, and had stood over me a long time, crying, and pouring cold water on my head, when I waked. In a few days I recovered in some measure from this hurt, and was again set to work at the screen, but I was more careful not to fall asleep; I endeavored to assist them at their labors, and to comply in all instances with their directions, but I was notwithstanding treated with great harshness, particularly by the old man, and his two sons She-mung and Kwo-tash-e. While we remained at the hunting camp, one of them put a bridle in my hand, and pointing in a certain direction, motioned me to go. I went accordingly, supposing he wished me to bring a horse; I went and caught the first I could find, and in this way I learned to discharge such services as they required of me.

When we returned from hunting, I carried on my back a large pack of dried meat all the way to the village; but though I was almost starved, I dared not touch a morsel of it. My Indian mother, who seemed to have some compassion for me, would sometimes steal a little food, and hide it for me until the old man was gone away, and then give it me. After we returned to the village, the young men, whenever the weather was pleasant, were engaged in spearing fish, and they used to take me to steer the canoe. As I did not know how to do this very well, they commonly turned upon me, beat me, and often knocked me down with the pole of the spear. By one or the other of them I was beaten almost every day. Other Indians, not of our family, would sometimes seem to pity me, and when they could without being observed by the old man, they would sometimes give me food, and take notice of me.

After the corn was gathered in the fall, and disposed of in the Sun-je-gwun-nun, or Ca-ches, where they hide it for the winter, they went to hunt on the Sau-ge-nong River. I was here, as I had always been, when among them, much distressed with hunger. As I was often with them in the woods, I saw them eating something, and I endeavored to discover what it was, but they carefully concealed it from me. It was some time before I accidentally found some beechnuts, and though I knew not what they were, I was tempted to taste them, and finding them very good, I showed them to the Indians, when they laughed, and let me know these were what they had all along been eating. After the snow had fallen, I was compelled to follow the hunters, and oftentimes to drag home to the lodge a whole deer, though it was with the greatest difficulty I could do so.

At night I had always to lie between the fire and the door of the lodge, and when any one passed out or came in, they commonly gave me a kick; and whenever they went to drink, they made a practice to throw some water on me. The old man constantly treated me with much cruelty, but his ill humor showed itself more on some occasions than others. One morning, he got up, put on his moccasins, and went out; but presently returning, he caught me by the hair of my head, dragged me out, rubbed my face for a long time in a mass of recent excrement, as one would do the nose of a cat, then tossed me by the hair into a snow bank. After this I was afraid to go into the lodge; but at length my mother came out and gave me some water to wash. We were now about to move our camp, and I was as usual made to carry a large pack; but as I had not been able to wash my face clean, when I came among other Indians they perceived the smell, and asked me the cause. By the aid of signs, and some few words I could now speak, I made them comprehend how I had been treated. Some of them appeared to pity me, assisted me to wash myself, and gave me something to eat.

Often when the old man would begin to beat me, my

mother, who generally treated me with kindness, would throw her arms about me, and he would beat us both together. Towards the end of winter, we moved again to the sugar grounds. At this time, Kish-kau-ko, who was a young man of about twenty years of age, joined with him four other young men, and went on a war party. The old man, also, as soon as the sugar was finished, returned to the village, collected a few men, and made his preparations to start. I had now been a year among them, and could understand a little of their language. The old man, when about to start, said to me, "Now I am going to kill your father and your brother, and all your relations." Kish-kau-ko returned first, but was badly wounded. He said he had been with his party to the Ohio River; that they had, after watching for some time, fired upon a small boat that was going down, and killed one man, the rest jumping into the water. He (Kish-kau-ko) had wounded himself in his thigh with his own spear, as he was pursuing them. They brought home the scalp of the man they had killed.

Old Manito-o-geezhik returned a few days afterward, bringing an old white hat, which I knew, from a mark in the crown, to be that of my brother. He said he had killed all my father's family, the Negroes, and the horses, and had brought me my brother's hat, that I might see he spoke the truth. I now believed that my friends had all been cut off, and was, on that account, the less anxious to return. This, it appears, had been precisely the object the old man wished to accomplish, by telling me the story, of which but a small part was true. When I came to see Kish-kau-ko, after I returned from Red River, I asked him immediately, "Is it true, that your father has killed all my relations?" He told me it was not;

that Manito-o-geezhik, the year after I was taken, at the same season of the year, returned to the same field where he had found me; that, as on the preceding year, he had watched my father and his people planting corn, from morning till noon; that then they all went into the house, except my brother, who was then nineteen years of age; he remained ploughing with a span of horses, having the lines about his neck, when the Indians rushed upon him; the horses started to run; my brother was entangled in the lines, and thrown down, when the Indians caught him. The horses they killed with their bows and arrows, and took my brother away into the woods. They crossed the Ohio before night, and had proceeded a good distance in their way up the Miami. At night they left my brother securely bound, as they thought, to a tree. His hands and arms were tied behind him, and there were cords around his breast and neck; but having bitten off some of the cords, he was able to get a penknife that was in his pocket, with which he cut himself loose, and immediately run toward the Ohio, at which he arrived, and which he crossed by swimming, and reached his father's house about sunrise in the morning. The Indians were roused by the noise he made, and pursued him into the woods; but as the night was very dark, they were not able to overtake him. His hat had been left at the camp, and this they brought, to make me believe they had killed him. Thus I remained for two years in this family, and gradually came to have less and less hope of escape, though I did not forget what the English traders on the Maumee had said, and I wished they might remember and come for me. The men were often drunk, and whenever they were so, they sought to kill me. In these cases, I learned to run and hide myself in the woods, and I dared not return before their drunken frolic was over. During the two years that I remained at Sau-ge-nong, I was constantly suffering from hunger; and though strangers, or those not belonging to the family, sometimes fed me, I had never enough to eat. The old woman they called Ne-keek-wos-ke-cheem e-kwa- "the Otter woman," the otter being her *totem* – treated me with kindness, as did her daughters, as well as Kish-kau-ko and Be-nais-sa, the bird, the youngest son, of about my own age. Kish-kau-ko and his father, and the two brothers, Kwo-ta-she and Shemung, were blood-thirsty and cruel, and those who remain of this family, continue, to this time, troublesome to the whites. Be-nais-sa, who came to see me when I was at Detroit, and who always treated me kindly, was a better man, but he is since dead. While I remained with them at Sau-ge-nong, I saw white men but once. Then a small boat passed, and the Indians took me out to it in a canoe, rightly supposing that my wretched appearance would excite the compassion of the traders, or whatever white men they were. These gave me bread, apples, and other presents, all which, except one apple, the Indians took from me. By this family I was named Shaw-shaw-wa ne-ba-se (the Falcon), which name I retained while I remained among the Indians.

I had been about two years at Sau-ge-nong, when a great council was called by the British agents at Mackinac. This council was attended by the Sioux, the Winnebagoes, the Menomonees, and many remote tribes, as well as by the Ojibboways, Ottawwaws, &c. When old Manito-o-geezhik returned from this council, I soon learned that he had met there his kinswoman, Net-no-kwa, who, notwithstanding her sex, was then regarded as principal chief of the Ottawwaws. This woman had lost her son, of about my age, by death; and having heard of me, she wished to purchase me to supply his place. My old Indian mother, the Otter woman, when she heard of this, protested vehemently against it. I heard her say, "My son has been dead once, and has been restored to me; I cannot lose him again." But these remonstrances had little influence, when Net-no-kwa arrived with considerable whisky, and other presents. She brought to the lodge first a ten-gallon keg of whisky, blankets, tobacco, and other articles of great value. She was perfectly acquainted with the dispositions of those with whom she had to negotiate. Objections were made to the exchange until the contents of the keg had circulated for some time; then an additional keg, and a few more presents, completed the bargain, and I was transferred to Net-no-kwa. This woman, who was then advanced in years, was of a more pleasing aspect than my former mother. She took me by the hand, after she had completed the negotiation with my former possessors, and led me to her own lodge, which stood near. Here I soon found I was to be treated more indulgently than I had been. She gave me plenty of food, put good clothes upon me, and told me to go and play with her own sons. We remained but a short time at Sau-ge-nong. She would not stop with me at Mackinac, which we passed in the night, but ran along to Point St. Ignace, where she hired some Indians to take care of me, while she returned to Mackinac by herself, or with one or two of her young men. After finishing her business at Mackinac, she returned, and continuing on our journey, we arrived in a few days at Shab-a-wy-wy-a-gun. The corn was ripe when we reached that place, and after stopping a little while, we went three days up the river, to the place where they intended to pass the winter. We then left our canoes, and traveling over land, camped three times before we came to the place where we set up our lodges for the winter. The husband of Net-no-kwa was an Ojibbeway of Red River, called Taw-ga-we-ninne, the hunter. He was seventeen years younger than Net-no-kwa, and had turned off a former wife on being married to her. Taw-ga-we-ninne was always indulgent and kind to me, treating me like an equal, rather than as a dependant. When speaking to me, he always called me his son. Indeed, he himself was but of secondary importance in the family, as everything belonged to Net-no-kwa, and she had the direction in all affairs of any moment. She imposed on me, for the first year, some tasks. She made me cut wood, bring home game, bring water, and perform other services not commonly required of the boys of my age; but she treated me invariably with so much kindness, that I was far more happy and content, than I had been in the family of Manito-o-geezhik. She sometimes whipped me, as she did her own children; but I was not so severely and frequently beaten as I had been before.

APPENDIX V

Myths and Tales of the Native Americans

The reader coming to Native American myth for the first time is stepping into a world wholly unlike the safe and certain belief-systems of the Western science and Judeo-Christianity. It a world which is often threatening, usually fantastic, and inhabited by strange beings epitomized by the infamous shape-shifting Trickster – and inexplicable occurrences. As is obvious upon a moment's reflection, myth was the means by which American Indians made sense of an unpredictable universe and explained the past in order to understand the present. Myths were usually sacred ancient narratives. Tales, in distinction, while commonly containing a moral kernel tended to be contemporary and of a more entertaining than religious purpose. Both Native American myths and tales were, of course, *oral* narratives; the bare words reproduced here would have, in their original telling, been complemented by the teller's gestures.

THE JICARILLA APACHE

The Jicarilla were buffalo hunters of the Southern Plains, although they intermingled with the Pueblos enough to acquire some agriculture.

Origin of the Apaches*

In the under-world, U^n-gó-ya-yên-ni, there was no sun, moon, or light of any kind, except that emanating from large eagle feathers which the people carried about with them. This method of lighting proved unsatisfactory, and the head men of the tribe gathered in council to devise some plan for lighting the world more brightly. One of the chiefs suggested that they make a sun and a moon. A great disk of yellow paint was made upon the ground, and then placed in the sky. Although this miniature creation was too small to give much light, it was allowed to make one circuit of the heavens ere it was taken down and made larger. Four times the sun set and rose, and four times it was enlarged, before it was "as large as the earth and gave plenty of light." In the under-world dwelt a wizard and a witch, who were much incensed at man's presumption and made such attempts to destroy the new luminaries that both the sun and the moon fled from the lower world, leaving it again in darkness, and made their escape to this earth, where they have never been molested, so that, until the present time, they continue to shine by night and by day. The loss of the sun and moon brought the people together, that they might take council concerning the means of restoring the lost light. Long they danced and sang, and

*From "Myths of the Jicarilla Apache", Frank Russell, *The Journal of American Folklore*, Vox XI, No XLIII, 1898.

made medicine. At length it was decided that they should go in search of the sun. The Indian medicine-men caused four mountains to spring up, which grew by night with great noise, and rested by day. The mountains increased in size until the fourth night, when they nearly reached the sky. Four boys were sent to seek the cause of the failure of the mountains to reach the opening in the sky, ha-ná-za-ä, through which the sun and moon had disappeared. The boys followed the tracks of two girls who had caused the mountains to stop growing, until they reached some burrows in the side of the mountain, where all trace of the two females disappeared. When their story was told to the people, the medicine-men said, "You who have injured us shall be transformed into rabbits, that you may be of some use to mankind; your bodies shall be eaten," and the rabbit has been used for food by the human race down to the present day.

All then journeyed to the tops of the mountains, where a ladder was built which reached the aperture in the sky or roof of the under-world. The badger was then sent out to explore the earth above; the messenger soon returned, and reported water everywhere except around the margin of the opening. The legs of the badger were covered with mud, which accounts for their dark color at the present day. Four days later, the turkey was sent to see if the waters had subsided. The turkey reported no land yet to be seen above. As the turkey came in contact with the foam of the flood surrounding the opening, his tail became wet and heavy; in shaking this he scattered filmy drops upon his wings, and that is why the feathers of the turkey to the present day present an iridescent play of colors. Then the Wind came to the anxious people and said, "If you ask me to help you, I will drive back the water for you." Thus the first prayers came to be addressed to the Wind, which yet remains a powerful deity.

When the Wind had rolled back the waters to the limits of the present ocean, the Indians began to ascend the ladder; four times the ladder broke with them, and four times it was replaced by a new one. All the people reached the new world except one old woman, too old and infirm to climb the ladder, who said to them: "I do not wish to leave the land of my youth. Go your way and leave me here; you will come back to join me when you die. You have forgotten one thing; you will soon discover what it is." For four days after their emergence no one could sleep; then the people remembered the warning of the old woman, and two boys were sent down to the under-world to learn what it was that had been forgotten. The old woman said in reply to their question, "You forgot to take lice with you; without them you cannot sleep." She took two black ones from her hair and two white ones from her body, saying, "These will be all you will need, for they will increase night and day." So it has happened that the Apaches sleep well to this day because they harbor these parasites upon their bodies.

So well had the Wind performed his task of drying up the waters, that none remained for the people to drink; but prayers addressed to that deity were answered by the appearance of the present springs and rivers. The few lakes that occur in the Apache country are remnants of the primeval ocean. All the inhabitants of the earth were then Apaches, but the Cheyennes and Utes were soon created from willows. The supreme god, Yi-ná-yês-gôn-i, directed the people westward; as they journeyed, small parties became separated, and settled by the wayside. These were given different names and languages.

Death of the Great Elk Tsas

In the early days, animals and birds of monstrous size preyed upon the people; the giant Elk, the Eagle, and others devoured men, women, and children, until the gods were petitioned for relief. A deliverer was sent to them in the person of Djo-na-a`-y`-ⁿ, the son of the old woman who lives in the West and the second wife of the Sun. She divided her time between the Sun and the Waterfall, and by the latter bore a second son, named Ko-ba-tcis´-tci-ni, who remained with his mother while his brother went forth to battle with the enemies of mankind. In four days Djo-na-a`-y`-ⁿ grew to manhood, then he asked his mother where the Elk lived. She told him that the Elk was in a great desert far to the southward. She gave him arrows with which to kill the Elk. In four steps he reached the distant desert where the Elk was lying. Djo-na-a`-y`-ⁿ cautiously observed the position of the Elk from behind a hill. The Elk was lying on an open plain, where no trees or bushes were to be found that might serve to shelter Djo-na-a`-y`-ⁿ from view while he approached. While he was looking at the Elk, with dried grass before his face, the Lizard, Mai-cu-i-ti-tce-tcê, said to him, "What are you doing, my friend? Djo-na-a`-y`-ⁿ explained his mission whereupon the Lizard suggested that he clothe himself in the garments of the Lizard, in which he could approach the Elk in safety. Djo-na-a`-y`-ⁿ tried four times before he succeeded in getting into the coat of the Lizard. Next the Gopher, Mi-i-ni-li, came to him with the question, "What are you doing here, my friend?" When Djo-na-a`-y`-ⁿ told the Gopher of his intention, the latter promised to aid him. The Gopher thought it advisable to reconnoitre by burrowing his way underground to the Elk. Djo-na-a`-y`-ⁿ watched the progress of the Gopher as that animal threw out fresh heaps of earth on his way. At length the Gopher came to the surface underneath the Elk, whose giant heart was beating like a mighty hammer. He then proceeded to gnaw the hair from about the heart of the Elk. "What are you doing?" said the Elk. "I am cutting a few hairs for my little ones, they are now lying on the bare ground," replied the Gopher, who continued until the magic coat of the Elk was all cut away from about the heart of the Elk. Then he returned to Djo-na-a`-y`-ᵉⁿ and told the latter to go through the hole which he had made and shoot the Elk. Four times the Son of the Sun tried to enter the hole before he succeeded. When he reached the Elk, he saw the great heart beating above him, and easily pierced it with his arrows; four times his bow was drawn before he turned to escape through the tunnel which the Gopher had been preparing for him. This hole extended far to the eastward, but the Elk soon discovered it, and, thrusting his antler into it, followed in pursuit. The Elk ploughed up the earth with such violence that the present mountains were formed, which extend from east to west. The black spider closed the hole with a strong web, but the Elk broke through it and ran southward, forming the mountain chains which trend north and south. In the south the Elk was checked by the web of the blue spider, in the west by that of the yellow spider, while in the north the web of the many-colored spider resisted his attacks until he fell dying from exhaustion and wounds. Djo-na-a`-y`-ᵉⁿ made a coat from the hide of the Elk, gave the front quarters to the Gopher, the hind quarters to the Lizard, and carried home the antlers. He found that the results of his adventures were not unknown to his mother, who had spent the time during his absence in singing, and watching a roll of cedar bark which sank into the earth or rose in the air as danger approached or receded from Djo-na-a`-y`-ᵉⁿ, her son.

Djo-na-a`-y`-ᵉⁿ next desired to kill the great Eagle, I-tsa.

His mother directed him to seek the Eagle in the west. In four strides he reached the home of the Eagle, an inaccessible rock, on which was the nest, containing two young eaglets. His ear told him to stand facing the east when the next morning the Eagle swooped down upon him and tried to carry him off. The talons of the Eagle failed to penetrate the hard elk-skin by which he was covered. "Turn to the south," said the ear, and again the Eagle came, and was again unsuccessful. Djo-na-a`-y`-ⁿ faced each of the four points in this manner, and again faced toward the east; whereupon the Eagle succeeded in fastening its talons in the lacing on the front of the coat of the supposed man, who was carried to the nest above and thrown down before the young eagles, with the invitation to pick his eyes out. As they were about to do this, Djo-na-a`-y`-ⁿ gave a warning hiss, at which the young ones cried, "He is living yet." "Oh, no," replied the old Eagle; "that is only the rush of air from his body through the holes made by my talons." Without stopping to verify this, the Eagle flew away. Djo-na-a`-y`-ⁿ threw some of the blood of the Elk which he had brought with him to the young ones, and asked them when their mother returned. "In the afternoon when it rains," they answered. When the mother Eagle came with the shower of rain in the afternoon, he stood in readiness with one of the Elk antlers in his hand. As the bird alighted with a man in her talons, Djo-na-a`-y`-ⁿ struck her upon the back with the antler, killing her instantly. Going back to the nest, he asked the young eagles when their father returned. "Our father comes home when the wind blows and brings rain just before sunset," they said. The male Eagle came at the appointed time, carrying a woman with a crying infant upon her back. Mother and babe were dropped from a height upon the rock and killed. With the second antler of the Elk, Djo-na-a`-y`-ⁿ avenged their death, and ended the career of the eagles by striking the Eagle upon the back and killing him. The wing of this eagle was of enormous size; the bones were as large as a man's arm; fragments of this wing are still preserved at Taos. Djo-na-a`-y`-ᵑ struck the young eagles upon the head, saying, "You shall never grow any larger." Thus deprived of their strength and power to injure mankind, the eagles relinquished their sovereignty with the parting curse of rheumatism, which they bestowed upon the human race.

Djo-na-a`-y`-ᵑ could discover no way by which he could descend from the rock, until at length he saw an old female Bat, Tca-na´-mi-ᵑ, on the plain below. At first she pretended not to hear his calls for help; then she flew up with the inquiry, "How did you get here?" Djo-na-a`-y`-ᵑ told how he had killed the eagles. "I will give you all the feathers you may desire if you will help me to escape," concluded he. The old Bat carried her basket, ilt-tsai-^-z^s, by a slender spider's thread. He was afraid to trust himself in such a small basket suspended by a thread, but she reassured him, saying: "I have packed mountain sheep in this basket, and the strap has never broken. Do not look while we are descending; keep your eyes shut as tight as you can." He began to open his eyes once during the descent, but she warned him in time to avoid mishap. They went to the foot of the rock where the old Eagles lay. Djo-na-a`-y`-ᵑ filled her basket with feathers, but told her not to go out on the plains, where there are many small birds. Forgetting this admonition, she was soon among the small birds, who robbed the old Bat of all her feathers. This accounts for the plumage of the small bird klo´-kin, which somewhat resembles the color of the tail and wing feathers of the bald eagle. The Bat returned four times for a supply of feathers, but the fifth time she asked to have her basket filled, Djo-na-a`-y`-ᵑ was vexed. "You cannot take care of your feathers, so you shall never have any. This old skin on your basket is good enough for you." "Very well," said the Bat, resignedly, "I deserve to lose them, for I never could take care of those feathers".

Taos

The "Heart of the World" is supposed to be at Taos. Somewhere in that region the earth "shakes", indicating the presence of life within.

Beneath this spot are four rooms, in which an Old Man and an Old Woman imprison people.

Origin of the Animals

When the Apaches emerged from the under-world, U^n-go'-ya-yên-ni, they travelled southward on foot for four days. They had no other food than the seeds of the two plants, k'atl'-tai-ˆ, and k'atl'-tai-ˆl-tsu-yæ, from which they made a sort of flour by grinding between stones. When they camped for the fourth time, one of the tipis, called ka-ge-gôn-has-ke-ˆn-de-yê, stood somewhat apart from the others. While the owner and his wife were absent from this lodge, a Raven brought a bow and a quiver of arrows, and hung them upon the lodge poles. The children within took down the quiver, and found some meat in it; they ate this, and at once became very fat. When the mother returned, she saw the grease on the hands and cheeks of the children, and was told how the it-tsil'-te had been obtained. The woman hastened to her husband with the tale. Marvelling at the appearance of the children, the people gathered to await the reappearance of

the Raven which subsisted upon such remarkable food.
When the Raven found the it-tsil´-te had been stolen from the
quiver, he flew away toward the eastward; his destination was
a mountain just beyond the range of vision of the Indians. A
bat, however, followed the flight of the Raven, and informed
them where the Raven had alighted. That night, a council of
the whole tribe was held, and it was decided that they should
go to the home of the Raven, and try to obtain from him the
food which had wrought such a miraculous change in those
who had partaken of it. At the end of four days they came to
a place where a large number of logs were lying in irregular
heaps. Many ravens were seen, but they avoided the Indians,
and no information could be obtained from them. At one
point they discovered a great circle of ashes where the ravens
were accustomed to cook their meals. Again a council was
held, and they talked over the problem of how to spy upon
the ravens, and learn whence they obtained the precious
animal food. That night the medicine-men transformed a boy
into a puppy, and concealed him in the bushes near the
camp. After the Indians had departed, next morning the
ravens came, as is their habit, to examine the abandoned
camp. One of the young ravens found the puppy, and was so
pleased with it that he exclaimed: "Ci-chˆn-n-ja-ta" ("This
shall be my puppy"). When he carried it home his parents
told him to throw it away. He begged permission to keep it,
but agreed to give it up if the puppy winked when a splinter
of burning wood was waved before its eyes. As the puppy
possessed much more than canine intelligence, it stared
during the test without the quiver of an eyelid. So the young
raven won consent to keep the puppy, which he placed under
his own blanket, where it remained until evening. At sunset
the puppy peeped from his cover, and saw an old raven brush
aside the ashes of the fireplace, and take up a large flat stone

which disclosed an opening beneath; through this he disappeared, but arose again with a buffalo, which was killed and eaten by the ravens.

For four days the puppy remained at the camp of the ravens, and each evening he saw a buffalo brought up from the depths and devoured. Satisfied that he had discovered the source from which the ravens derived their food, the puppy resumed the form of a boy on the morning of the fifth day, and, with a white eagle feather in one hand and a black one in the other, descended through the opening beneath the fireplace, as he had seen the ravens do. In the under-world in which he found himself he saw four buffalo. He placed the white eagle-feather in the mouth of the nearest buffalo, and commanded it to follow him, but the buffalo told him to go on the last of the four and take it. This the boy tried to do, but the fourth buffalo sent him back to the first, in whose mouth the boy again thrust the feather, declaring it to be the king of all the animals. He then returned to the world above, followed by all the animals at present upon the surface of the earth, except those specially created later, such, for example, as the horse and aquatic animals. As the large herd of animals passed through the hole, one of the ravens awoke, and hastened to clap down the stone covering the opening, but he was too late to prevent their escape. Seeing that they had passed from his control into that of man, he exclaimed, "When you kill any of these animals you must at least leave their eyes for me."

Attended by the troop of beasts of many species, the boy followed the track made by the departing Apaches. On the site of their first camp he found a firestick or poker, gos-se-na´-it-tsi, of which he inquired, "When did my people leave here?" "Three days ago" was the reply. At the next camping-place was an abandoned ladder, has´-ai-ˆ, of which he asked,

"When did my people leave here?" "Two days ago," replied the ladder. Continuing his journey the boy soon reached the third camping-place, where he questioned a second firestick, and learned that the people had been gone but one day. At the fourth camp another ladder answered his question, with the news that the Indians had left there that morning. That evening he overtook them and entered the camp, the herd of animals following him like a flock of sheep. One old woman who lived in a brush lodge became vexed at the deer which ate the covering of her rude shelter. Snatching up a stick from the fire, she struck the deer over the nose, to which the white ashes adhered, causing the white mark which we see on the nose of that animal at present time. "Hereafter you shall avoid mankind; your nose tell you when you are near them," said she. Thus terminated the brief period of harmony between man and the beast: they left the camp at once, going farther each day, until on the fourth they disappeared from sight. That night the Apaches prayed for the return of the animals, that they might use them for food, and that is why animals approach nearer the camps now at night than at any other time. They never come very close, because the old woman told them to be guided by their noses and avoid the Indians.

Origin of Fire

At that early day the trees could talk, but the people could not burn them, as they were without fire. Fire was at length obtained through the instrumentality of the Fox. One day Fox went to visit the geese, têtl, whose cry he wished to learn. They promised to teach him, but it would be necessary for him to accompany them in their flights, in order to receive instruction. They gave him wings with which to fly, but cautioned him not to open his eyes while using them. When the geese rose in flight Fox flew with them. As darkness came on, they passed over the inclosure where the fire-filies, ko-na-tcic´-æ, lived. Some gleams from their flickering fires penetrated the eyelids of Fox, causing him to open his eyes. His wings at once failed to support him, and he fell within the walls of the corral in which were pitched the tents of the fireflies. Two flies went to see the fallen Fox, who gave each a necklace of juniper berries, kotl´-te-i-tsæ, to induce them to tell him where he could pass the wall which surrounded them. The fireflies showed Fox a cedar tree which would bend down at command and assist any one to pass over the wall. In the evening Fox went to the spring where fireflies obtained water, and found colored earths suitable for paint, with which he gave himself a coat of white. Returning to camp, he told the fireflies that they ought to have a feast; they should dance and make merry, and he would give them a new musical instrument. They agreed to his proposal, and gathered wood for a great camp-fire, which they ignited by their own glow. Before the ceremonies began, Fox tied shreds of cedar bark to his tail, and then made a drum, the first ever constructed, which he beat for some time. Tired of beating the drum, he gave it to one of the fireflies and moved nearer the fire, into which he thrust his tail, in opposition to the advice of those about him, who said it would surely burn. "I am a medicine-man," said Fox, "and my tail will not burn." However, he kept a close watch upon it, and when the bark was burning well he said, "It is too warm for me here; stand aside and let me go where it is cooler." Fox ran away with tail blazing, followed by the fireflies, who cried, "Stop, you do not know the road; come back." Straight to the cedar-tree Fox ran, and called, "Bend down to me, my tree, bend down." The tree lifted him out of the inclosure, and on he ran, still pursued by the fireflies. As he passed along, the brush and wood on either side was ignited by the sparks which fell from the burning cedar, and fire was widely spread over the earth. Fox became fatigued from running, and gave the firebrand to the hawk, i-tsatl´-tsu-i, which carried it on, and finally delivered it to the brown crane, tsi-nês-tso´-i. This bird flew far southward, but not so far but that one tree was not reached, and it will not burn to this day. (No name for such a tree among the Jicarilla Apaches.) The fireflies pursued Fox to his burrow and informed him that, as punishment for having stolen fire from them and spread it abroad over the land, he should never be permitted to use it himself.

Origin and Destruction of the Bear

An Apache boy, while playing with his comrades, pretended to be a bear, and ran into a hole in the hillside. When he came out his feet and hands had been transformed into bear's paws. A second time he entered the den, and his limbs were changed to the knees and elbows. Four times he entered the den, and then came forth the voracious cac-tla-yæ that devoured his former fellow-beings. One day the bear met a fox in the mountains. "1 am looking for a man to eat," said Bear. "So am I," said Fox, "but your legs are so big and thick you cannot run very fast to catch them. You ought to allow me to trim down those posts a little, so you can run as swift as I." Bear consented to have the operation performed, and Fox not only cut the flesh from the legs of Bear, but also broke the bones with his knife, thus killing the dreaded man-eater. Taking the leg bones of Bear with him, he went to the home of the bear family, and there found two other bears. These monsters preyed upon the people, who were unable to kill them, as they left their hearts at home when off on their marauding expeditions. Fox remained in hiding until the bears went away. When they ran among the Indians, Fox responded to the cries for assistance, not by flying to attack the bears, but by hastening to cut their hearts in twain. The bears were aware that their hearts had been tampered with, and rushed with all speed to rescue them, but fell dead just before they reached Fox. Thus Fox destroyed one of the most dreaded of man's enemies of that primeval time.

Fox and Porcupine

As Fox was going along he met a Porcupine, Tso^n, which he overheard saying, "I shall search for pêc´-ti, a stone knife, with which to cut up this meat." "What are you saying?" asked Fox, springing out of the bushes. "I said that I must hunt for pêc´-ti for arrow-heads," replied Porcupine. "That is not what you said." "It was," insisted Porcupine. "Where is that meat?" asked Fox, and then Porcupine admitted that he had killed a Buffalo

Porcupine had commanded a Buffalo to carry him across a river. "Don't shake your head with me, or I shall fall," said he, as he sat between the animal's horns. The Buffalo told him that, if he was afraid there, he had better crawl into his anus. In that safe retreat Porcupine was carried across the fiver, He repaid the service by gnawing the vitals of the Buffalo until it fell dead near where the Fox had come upon him. Fox was not disposed to allow Porcupine to retain possession of the Buffalo. "Come," said he, "whoever can jump over the Buffalo can have it. You try first." Porcupine jurnped, but only landed on the top of the carcase, over which Fox, of course, leaped with ease. "Now the Buffalo is mine. You can sit over there and see me cut it up." After cutting up the meat, Fox hastened away to summon all the foxes to a feast. Porcupine carried the meat piece by piece into a treetop, so that the foxes, when they came dancing in joyful anticipation, found nothing. From a safe position in the tree Porcupine told the foxes that he would throw them down some meat if they would lie down, close their eyes, and cover themselves with their blankets. They were hungry, so they obeyed the instructions of the Porcupine, who, as soon as their eyes were closed, killed them by throwing down the sharpened ribs of the Buffalo. One little fox at the end of the line had a ragged old blanket, through which he peeped in time to see and to dodge the rib hurled at him. This fox survived the massacre, and begged Porcupine to give him some meat. The Porcupine gave him some small pieces at first, and then invited him to come up and eat his fill. The Fox accepted, and, when he could eat no more, asked where he could go to relieve himself. The Porcupine directed him to the end of a branch, whence he easily shook the Fox, which fell to the ground and was killed but sprang up alive again at the moment when the first tuft of hair was blown from the putrefying carcass by the wind.

Fox and Wildcat

As soon as his life was restored, Fox went to the Buffalo head, and cut off the long pendent hair, i-yûn-e-pi-ta-ga, beneath its under jaw. Fox took this to a prairie-dog village near at hand, and told the inhabitants that it was the hair of a man, one of that race dreaded by the prairie-dogs because of its attacks upon them, which he had killed. He easily persuaded the prairie-dogs to celebrate his victory with feasting and dancing. With a stone concealed in his hand, he killed all the prairie-dogs as they circled around in the dance. Fox then placed them in a pit, and built a huge fire over them, leaving them to roast while he slept. Nj$\hat{}^{n}$-ko-j$\hat{}^{n}$, the Wildcat, came along, and stole all the roasted prairie-dogs while Fox slept, save one at the end of the pit, leaving the tails, which were pulled off. Fox awoke after some time, and flew into a great rage when he found only the tails left; the solitary dog was thrown over his shoulder in his fit of passion. The gnawings of hunger soon induced him to search for the dog he had thrown away. In the stream close by he thought he saw the roasted body; taking off his clothes, he swam for it; but could not grasp it. Again and again he tried, and finally dove for it until he bumped his nose on the stony bottom. Tired out with his efforts, he laid down upon the bank to rest, and, as he glanced upward, saw the body of the prairie-dog lying among the branches which projected over the water. Fox recovered the coveted morsel, ate it, and set off on the trail of the Wildcat. He found Wildcat asleep under a tree, around which he set a fire. With a few quick strokes he shortened the head, body, and tail of Wildcat, and then pulled out the large intestine and roasted it. Fox then awakened Wildcat and invited him to eat his (Wildcat's) flesh, but to be careful to save a small piece, and put it back in its place, for he would need it. Fox then left him.

Wildcat followed Fox, intent upon revenge. He found Fox asleep, but instead of shortening that animal's members he lengthened them; the ears were only straightened, but the head, body, and tail were elongated as we see them at the present day. The intestine scene was repeated with the Fox as victim.

Fox and Deer

As Fox was going along he met a Deer with two spotted fawns beside her. "What have you done," said he, "to make your children spotted like that?" "I made a big-fire of cedar wood and placed them before it. The sparks thrown off burned the spots which you see," answered the Deer. Fox was pleased with the color of the fawns, so he went home and told his children to gather cedar wood for a large fire. When the fire was burning well, he put the young foxes in a row before the fire, as he supposed the Deer had done. When he found that they did not change color, he pushed them into the fire and covered them with ashes, thinking he had not applied sufficient heat at first. As the fire went out, he saw their white teeth gleaming where the skin had shrivelled away and exposed them. "Ah, you will be very pretty now," said he. Fox pulled his offspring from the ashes, expecting to find them much changed in color, and so they were – black, shrivelled, and dead. Fox next thought of revenge upon the Deer, which he found in a grove of cottonwoods. He built a fire around them, but they ran through it and escape. Fox was so disappointed that he set up a cry of woe, a means of expression which he has retained from that day to this.

Fox and Kingfisher

As Fox went on his way he met Kingfisher, Kêt-la´-i-le-ti, whom he accompanied to his home. Kingfisher said that he had no food to offer his visitor, so he would go and catch some fish for Fox. He broke through six inches of ice on the river and caught two fish, which he cooked and set before his guest. Fox was pleased with his entertainment, and invited the Kingfisher to return the call. In due time the Kingfisher came to the home of the Fox, who said, "I have no food to offer you", then he went down to the river, thinking to secure fish in the same manner as the Kingfisher had done. Fox leaped from the high bank, but instead of breaking through the ice he broke his head and killed himself. Kingfisher went to him, caught him up by the tail, and swung Fox around to the right four times, thereby restoring him to life. Kingfisher caught some fish, and they ate together. "I am a medicine-man," said Kingfisher; "that is why I can do these things. You must never try to catch fish in that way again."

After the departure of Kingfisher, Fox paid a visit to the home of Prairie-dog, where he was cordially received. Prairie-dog put four sticks, each about a foot in length, in the ashes of the camp-fire; when these were removed, they proved to be four nicely roasted prairie-dogs, which were served for Fox's dinner. Fox invited the Prairie-dog to return the visit, which in a short time the latter did. Fox placed four sticks in the fire to roast, but they were consumed by it, and instead of palat-able food to set before his guest he had nothing but ashes. Prairie-dog said to Fox, " You must not attempt to do that. I am a medicine-man; that is why I can transform the wood to flesh." Prairie-dog then prepared a meal as he done before, and they dined.

Fox went to visit Buffalo, I-gûn-da, who exclaimed, "What shall I do? I have no food to offer you." Buffalo was equal to the emergency, however; he shot an arrow upward, which struck in his own back as it returned. When he pulled this out, a kidney and the fat surrounding it came out also. This he cooked for Fox, and added a choice morsel from his own nose. As usual, Fox extended an invitation to his host to return the visit. When Buffalo came to call upon Fox, the latter covered his head with weeds in imitation of the head of the Buffalo. Fox thought he could provide food for their dinner as the Buffalo had done, so fired an arrow into the air; but when it came close to him on its return flight, he became frightened and ran away. Buffalo then furnished meat for their meal as on the previous occasion. "You must not try this," said he; "I am a medicine-man; that is why I have the power."

Some time afterward, as Fox was journeying along, he met an Elk, Tsês, lying beside the trail. He was frightened when he saw the antlers of the Elk moving, and jumped to avoid what seemed to be a falling tree. "Sit down beside me," said the Elk. "Don't be afraid." "The tree will fall on us," replied Fox. "Oh, sit down; it won't fall. I have no food to offer you, but I will provide some." The Elk cut steaks from his own quarter, which the Fox ate, and before leaving Fox invited the Elk to return the visit. When Elk came to see Fox, the latter tried unsuccessfully to cut flesh from his own meagre flanks; then he drove sharpened sticks into his nose, and allowed the blood to run out upon the grass. This he tried in vain to transform into meat, and again he was indebted to his guest for a meal. "I am a medicine- man ; that is why I can do this," said Elk.

Fox and Mountain Lion

Fox could find nothing to eat for a long lime, so that he grew weak and thin. While on a journey in search of food he met the Mountain Lion, who, taking pity upon his unhappy condition, said, "I will hunt for you, and you shall grow fat again." The Fox agreed to this, and they went on together to a much frequented spring. Mountain Lion told Fox to keep watch while he slept; if a cloud of dust was to be seen arising from the approach of animals Fox was to waken him. Fox presently beheld the dust caused by the approach of a drove of horses.

Fox wakened Mountain Lion, who said, "just observe how I catch horses." As one of the animals went down to the spring to drink, he sprang upon it, and fastened his fangs in its throat, clawing its legs and shoulders until it fell dying at the water's edge. Mountain Lion brought the horse up to the rock, and laid it before the Fox. "Stay here, eat, drink, and grow fat," said he.

Fox thought he had learned how to kill horses, so when the Coyote came along he volunteered to secure one for him. Fox jumped upon the neck of the horse, as Mountain Lion had done, but became entangled in its mane and was killed.

Fox and Rabbit

Fox one day met a Rabbit who was sewing a sack. "What do you intend to do with that sack?" asked he. "I am making this coat to protect myself from being killed by the hard hail which we are going to have today," replied Rabbit. "My friend, you know how to make them; give me this coat and make another for yourself." Rabbit agreed to this, and Fox put on the sack over his head. Rabbit then hung him on a limb and pelted him with stones, while Fox, thinking it was hail striking him, endured the punishment as long as he could, but finally fell nearly dead from the tree, and looked out, to see no signs of hail, but discovered the Rabbit running away. Fox wished to avenge himself by killing Rabbit, and set off in pursuit of him. When overtaken Rabbit was chewing soft gum with which to make spectacles. Fox's curiosity was sronger than his passion for revenge. "What are you making those for?" said he. "It is going to be very hot, and I am making them to protect my eyes," answered Rabbit "Let me have this pair; you know how to make them and can make yourself another pair." "Very well," said Rabbit, and he put the eye-shields on Fox, who could then see nothing, as the gum was soft and filled his eyes. Rabbit set fire to the brush all around Fox, who was badly singed in running through it. The gum melted in the fire, and yet remains as the dark rings around his eyes. Fox again started on the trail of Rabbit, with the determination of eating him as soon as he saw him. He found Rabbit sitting beside the opening of a beehive. "I am going to eat you," said Fox; "you have tried to kill me." "You must not kill me," replied Rabbit. "I am teaching these children," and he closed the opening of the hive, so that Fox ould not see what was inside. Fox desired very much to see what was in the hive making such a noise." If you wish to see, stay here and teach them while I rest. When it is dinner time, strike them with a club, said Rabbit, who then ran away. Fox patiently awaited the dinner hour, and then struck the hive with such force that he broke into it. The bees poured out and stung him until he rolled in agony. "When I see you again, I will kill you before you can say a word!" declared he, as he started after Rabbit again. Fox tracked the Rabbit to a small hole in the fence around a field of watermelons belonging to a Mexican. The Rabbit had entered to steal, and was angered at sight of the gum figure of a man which the owner of the field had placed beside the path. "What do you desire from me?" he cried, as he struck at the figure with his forefoot, which stuck fast in the soft gum. He struck at the gum with every foot, and even his head was soon stuck in the gum. Thus Fox found him. "What are you doing here?" he asked. "They put me in here because I would not eat chicken for them," said Rabbit. "I will take your place," said Fox; "I know how to eat chicken." The Mexican found him in the morning and skinned him, and then let him go – still on the trail of the Rabbit who had so frequently outwitted him.

Origin of Corn

An Apache who was an inveterate gambler had a small tame turkey, which followed its master about everywhere One day the turkey told him that the people were tired of supporting him, as he gambled until he lost everything that they in charity gave him. They had decided to give him one more stock of supplies, and if he made away with that he should be killed. Knowing that he could not resist the temptation to gamble if he had any property in his possession, he decided to leave the tribe before their wrath should overtake him. The next day he began to chop down a tree from which to build a boat. The Woodpecker, Tsitl-ka-ta, commanded him not to cut the tree; the woodpeckers must do that for him. They also cut out the inside of the trunk, so that he could get into the cylinder, after which the spider sealed him in by making a web over each end. The woodpeckers carried the log, thus prepared, to the Rio Grande River, and threw it in. The faithful Turkey followed along the shore. In the whirlpool above San Juan the log left the main current, and spun round and round until the Turkey pushed it on into the channel again. Farther down the river the log caught in the rocks in an upright position above a fall, but the Turkey again started it on its journey. At the pueblo of Isleta, the boys hauled out the log with others for fuel. The Turkey rescued the log and placed it in the water, and again, at another pueblo far down the river, the log was returned to the stream.

Far to the southward the log drifted out of the channel into a grove of cottonwoods. The man came out of the log and found a large quantity quantity of duck feathers lying about. That night he had no blanket in which to sleep, so he covered himself with duck feathers. He killed a duck, and with the sinews of its legs made a bowstring. After he landed, the Turkey soon overtook him, and they remained there for four days. During this time the man cleared a small space and levelled it. "Why do you clear this place?" said the Turkey. "If you wish to plant something you must make a larger field." Then the Turkey ran toward the east, and the field was extended in that direction: toward the south, the west, and the north he ran, until the field was large enough. Then he ran into the field from the east side, and the black corn lay behind him; from the south side, and the blue corn appeared; from the west, and the yellow corn was made; from the north, and the seeds of every kind of cereal and vegetable lay upon the ground. The Turkey told the man to plant all these seeds in rows. In four days the growing plants appeared. The Turkey helped his master tend the crops, and in four more days everything was ripe. Then the man took an ear of corn and roasted it, and found it good.

Two Blind Old Women: Their Story

Two old women were once cooking a pot of mush which two mischievous boys were trying to steal. Both were blind, so one sat on each side of the fire, and they kept their sticks waving back and forth above the pot, to prevent any one from taking advantage of their blindness and removing the vessel or its contents. The boys found an empty pot, which they substituted for the one on the fire. Finding that the pot now had an empty ring when struck by their sticks, the old women concluded that the water had boiled away, and the mush must be sufficiently cooked. "Let us smoke while it cools," said one. "Very well," said the other, and they began to smoke alternately the single pipe in their possession: as they smoked they kept the sticks waving to and fro above the empty vessel. The boys took the pipe from the hand of one old woman as she was passing it to the other. "You are smoking all the time," said the second woman. "I gave you the pipe long ago," said the first. "You did not," said the second. Just then the boys struck the first woman in the mouth, and she, thinking it was the other woman, struck her companion, who, of course, retaliated, and they proceeded to belabor one another with their staves. When they were tired of fighting they went to eat their mush; each thought the other had eaten it, which set them to fighting again.

The Beaver and the Old Man

There was once an old man who was very fond of beaver meat. He hunted and killed beaver so frequently that his son remonstrated with him, telling him that some misfortune would surely overtake him as a punishment for his persecution of the sagacious animals, which were then endowed with the magic pewers of the medicine-men. The old man did not heed the warning, but continued to kill beaver nearly every day. Again the son said," If you kill them, they will soon catch and kill you." Not long afterward the old man saw a beaver enter a hole in the bank; disregarding his son's advice, he plunged head foremost into the burrow to catch the animal. The son saw him enter the hole, and went in after him. Catching the old man by the heels, he pushed him farther in.

Thinking another beaver had attacked him, the old man was at first too frightened to move, then he cried for mercy. "Let me go, Beaver, and I will give you my knife." He threw his knife back toward the entrance, but received no reply to his entreaty. "Let me go, Beaver, and I will give you my awl." Again no answer. "Let me go, and I will give you my arrows." The young man took the articles as they were handed to him, and hastened away without making himself known.

When the old man returned to the tipi, he said nothing of his adventures, and his son asked no questions. As soon as the old man left the tipi, the son replaced the knife and other articles in his father's fire-bag. "Where is your knife?" said the son when the old man returned. "I gave it to the beaver to induce them to let me escape with my life." "I told you they would catch you," said the son.

The old man never hunted beaver again.

The Old Beggar

There was once an old Apache who went begging from camp to camp every evening. His wife tried to reform the old beggar by playing a trick upon him. One night during his absence she fetched a bleached horse's pelvis into the tipi, and painted it so that it somewhat resembled a face. The old man came home about midnight, and beheld, as he thought, the head of a monster glaring at him in the bright moonlight from the door of the lodge. Twice the woman held up the pelvis, when he turned in terror-stricken flight, calling, "Help, help! Something has killed my woman. Bring spears, bring arrows!" With a spear he cautiously lifted the side of the tipi, but his wife threw out the bone at the back, and he could not discover the cause of the apparition.

The next night he went out to beg again. He found plenty of buffalo meat at one of the lodges, some of which was given him to carry home. There were several horses lying outside the lodge, and the old man mistook one of them for a log, and jumped upon its back. The frightened horse rose under him, and soon succeeded in bucking him off. As the Indians came out of the tipi to investigate the cause of the stampede of the ponies, the old man said, "I told you long ago to break this horse, and now I must do it myself!" Thus avoiding, in some measure, their ridicule, he groped about until he found his meat again, and then hastened home.

The next morning he decided to move his camp. His family formed a large party, and he wished to precede them on the march. His sons were alarmed, and told him that the Cheyennes would kill and scalp him. "Oh, no," said he, "nobody will attack a warrior like me," and he walked on ahead of the others. His three sons painted their faces black and white, so that they were no longer recognizable, and then ran around in front of their father. As they ran toward him he shot all his arrows, but was too frightened to shoot straight. The young men caught him; one ran his fingernail around his scalp, while another placed a fresh buffalo's heart on the old man's head. The blood from the heart ran down his face, and he thought he was scalped. His sons allowed him to go back toward the party; on the way he came to a river, where he stooped to drink, and saw the reflected image of the raw flesh upon his head. He was then sure that he had been scalped, and sat down to die. His sons made signs to him to cross the river and go back. Again frightened by their gestures, he ran until he reached the women, who all laughed at his story of being scalped by the Cheyennes. The sons had explained the joke to their mother, and when the old man appealed to his wife for sympathy she only laughed at him, as he sat and shook with fear before her. At last they pulled off the strange headcovering, and a fresh burst of ridicule of the "brave warrior" followed.

TLINGIT

The Tlingit* are a people of southern Alaska and western British Columbia, who are organized into Eagle and Raven moieties (half divisions). Linguistically they belong to the Greater Athapaskan (Na-dene) stock.

The Wolf-Chief's Son

Famine visited a certain town, and many people died of starvation. There was a young boy there who always went around with bow and arrows. One day, as he was hunting about, he came across a little animal that looked like a dog and put it under his blanket. He brought it to his mother, and his mother washed it for him. Then he took the red paint left by his dead uncles, spit upon the dog and threw paint on so that it would stick to its hair and face. When he took the dog into the woods, it would bring him all kinds of birds, such as grouse, which he carried home to his family. They cooked these in a basket pot. Afterward he brought the animal down. washed it, and put more paint upon its legs and head. This enabled him to trace it when he was out hunting.

One day after he had traced it for some distance, he found it had killed a small mountain sheep, and, when he came down, he gave it the fat part. With the meat so obtained he

*From "Tlingit Myths and Texts", J. R. Swanton, *Bureau of American Ethnology*, Bulletin 39, Washington 1909.

began to take good care of his mother and his friends. He had not yet found out whether the animal was really a dog.

The next time they went hunting they came across a large flock of sheep, and he sent the dog right up to them. It killed all of them, and he cut the best one open for it. Then he took down the rest of the sheep and dressed them. What the animal was killing was keeping some of his friends alive.

One time the husband of a sister came to him and said, "I wish to borrow your animal. It is doing great things in this place." So he brought the little dog from the house he had made for it, painted its face and feet, and said to his brother-in-law, "When you kill the first one cut it open quickly and let him have it. That is the way I always do." Then this brother-in-law took up the little dog, and, when they came to a flock of sheep, it went straight among them, killing them and throwing them down one after another. But, after he had cut one open, he took out the entrails, threw them into the dog's face, and said, "Dogs always eat the insides of animals, not the good part." The dog, however, instead of eating it, ran straight up between the mountains, yelping.

Now when his brother-in-law brought the sheep down, the man asked him, "Where is the little dog?" And he said, "It ran away from me." That was the report he brought down. Then the owner of the dog called his sister to him and said, "Tell me truly what he did with the little dog. I did not want to let it go at first because I knew people would do that thing to it." His sister said, "He threw the entrails to it to eat. That is why it ran off."

Then the youth felt very sad on account of his little animal and prepared to follow it. His brother-in-law showed him the place between the mountains where the dog had gone up, and he went up in that direction until he came to its footprints and saw the red paint he had put upon it. This animal was really the wolf-chief's son who had been sent to help him, and, because the man put red upon its head and feet, a wolf can now be told by the red on its feet and around its mouth.

After he had followed the trail for a long distance he came to a lake with a long town on the opposite side. There he heard a great noise made by people playing. It was a very large lake, so he thought, "I wonder how I can get over there." Just then he saw smoke coming out from under his feet. Then a door swung open, and he was told to enter. An old woman lived there called Woman-always-wondering (Lū wat-uwadjīgˆcānAk!ᵘ), who said to him, "Grandchild, why are you here?" He answered, "I came across a young dog which helped me, but it is lost, and I come to find where it went." Then the woman answered, "Its people live right across there. It is a wolf-chief's son. That is its father's town over there where they are making a noise." So the old woman instructed him.

Then he wondered and said to himself, "How can I get across?" But the old woman spoke out, saying. "My little canoe is just below here." He said to himself, "It might turn over with me." Then the old woman answered. "Take it down. Before you get in shake it and it will become large." Then she continued: "Get inside of the boat and stretch yourself on the bottom, but do not paddle it. Instead wish continually to come in front of that place."

He did as she directed and landed upon the other side. Then he got out, made the canoe small and put it into his pocket, after which he went up among the boys who were playing about, and watched them. They were playing with a round, twisted thing called gˆtcxAnagāʹt (rainbow). Then some one directed him to the wolf-chief's house at the farther end of the village. An evening fire, such as people used to make in olden times, was burning there, and, creeping in behind the other people, the man saw his little wolf playing about near it in front of his father.

Then the wolf-chief said, "There is some human being looking in here. Clear away from before his face." Upon this the little wolf ran right up to him, smelled him, and knew him at once. The wolf-chief said, "I feel well disposed toward you. I let my son live among you because your uncles and friends were starving, and now I am very much pleased that you have come here after him." By and by he said, "I think I will not let him go back with you, but I will do something else to help you." He was happy at the way the man had painted up his son. Now he did not appear like a wolf but like a human being. The chief said, "Take out the fish-hawk's quill that is hanging on the wall and give it to him in place of my son." Then he was instructed how to use it. "Whenever a bear meets you," he said, "hold the quill straight toward it and it will fly out of your hand." He also took out a thing that was tied up like a blanket and gave it to him, at the same time giving him instructions. "One side," he said, "is for sickness. If you put this on a sick person it will make him well. If anyone hates you, put the other side on him and it will kill him. After they have agreed to pay you for treating him put the other side on to cure him."

Then the chief said, "You see that thing that the boys are playing with? That belongs to me. Whenever one sees it in the evening it means bad weather; whenever one sees it in the morning it means good weather." So he spoke to him.

Then they put something else into his mouth and said to him, "Take this, for you have a long journey to make." He was gone up there probably two years, but he thought it was only two nights.

At the time when he came within sight of his town he met

a bear. He held the quill out toward it as he had been instructed and suddenly let it go. It hit the bear in the heart. Still closer to his town he came upon a flock of sheep on the mountain, and sent his quill at them. When he reached them, he found all dead, and, after he had cut them all open, he found the quill stuck into the heart of the last. He took a little meat for his own use and covered up the rest.

Coming to the town, he found no one in it. All had been destroyed. Then he felt very sad, and, taking his blanket out, laid the side of it that would save people upon their bodies, and they all came to life. After that he asked all of them to go hunting with him, but he kept the quill hidden away so that they would not bother him as they had before. When they came to a big flock of mountain sheep, he let his quill go at them so quickly that they could not see it. Then he went up, looked the dead sheep over, and immediately cut out the quill. All his friends were surprised at what had happened. After they had gotten down, those who were not his close friends came to him and gave payment for the meat.

The people he restored to life after they had been dead for very many years had very deep set eyes and did not get well at once.

After that he went to a town where the people were all well and killed some of them with his blanket. Then he went to the other people in that place and said. "How are your friends? Are they dead?" "Yes." "Well, I know a way of making them well." He went up to them again with his blanket and brought them back to life. They were perfectly well.

This man went around everywhere doing the same thing and became very famous. Whenever one was sick in any place they came after him and offered him a certain amount for his services, so that he became the richest man of his time.

The Woman Taken Away by the Frog People

There was a large town in the Yakutat country not very far back of which lay a big lake very full of frogs. In the middle of the lake was a swampy patch on which many frogs used to sit.

One day the town-chief's daughter talked badly to the frogs. She took one up and made fun of it, saying, "There are so many of these creatures, I wonder if they do things like human beings. I wonder if men and women cohabit among them."

When she went out of doors that night, a young man came to her and said, "May I marry you?" She had rejected very many men, but she wanted to marry this one right away. Pointing toward the lake he said, "My father's house is right up here," and the girl replied, "How fine it looks!" When they went up to it, it seemed as though a door was opened for them, but in reality the edge of the lake had been raised. They walked under. So many young people were there that she did not think of home again.

Meanwhile her friends missed her and hunted for her everywhere. Finally they gave her up, and her father had the drums beaten for a death feast. They cut their hair and blackened their faces.

Next spring a man who was about to go bunting came to the lake to bathe himself with urine. When he was done, he threw the urine among a number of frogs sitting there and they jumped into the water. When he was bathing next day he saw all the frogs sitting together in the middle of the lake with the missing woman among them. He dressed as quickly as possible, ran home to the girl's father and said,"I saw your daughter sitting in the middle of the pond in company with a lot of frogs." So her father and mother went up that evening with a number of other people, saw, and recognized her.

After that they took all kinds of things to make the frog tribe feel good so that they would let the woman return to her parents, but in vain. By and by her father determined upon a plan and called all of his friends together. Then he told them to dig trenches out from the lake in order to drain it. From the lake the frog chief could see how the people had determined, and he told his tribe all about it. The frog people call the mud around a lake their laid-up food.

After the people had worked away for some time, the trench was completed and the lake began draining away fast. The frogs asked the woman to tell her people to have pity on them and not destroy all, but the people killed none because they wanted only the girl. Then the water flowed out, carrying numbers of frogs which scattered in every direction. All the frog tribe then talked poorly about themselves, and the frog chief, who had talked of letting her go before, now had her dressed up and their own odor, which they called "sweet perfumery," was put upon her. After a while she came down the trench half out of water with her frog husband beside her. They pulled her out and let the frog go.

When anyone spoke to this woman, she made a popping noise "Hu," such as a frog makes, but after some time she came to her senses. She explained, "It was the Kˆkca´ (i.e.; KˆksA´dˆ women) that floated down with me," meaning that all the frog women and men had drifted away. The woman could not eat at all, though they tried everything. After a while they hung her over a pole, and the black mud she had eaten when she was among the frogs came out of her, but, as soon as it was all out, she died. Because this woman was taken away by the frog tribe at that place. the frogs there can understand human beings very well when they talk to them. It was a KᐟksA´dˆ woman who was taken off by the frogs, and so those people can almost understand them. They also have songs from the frogs, frog personal names, and the frog emblem. All the people know about them.

Little Felon

A certain man had a felon *(kwêq)* on his finger and suffered terribly, so that he could get no sleep. He did not know what to do for it. One day somebody said to him, "Hold it under the smoke hole of the house and get some one to poke it with something very sharp through the smoke hole. You will find that it will get well." He did so, and the two eyes of the felon came right out. Then he wrapped them up and put them away. Late in the evening he looked at it and saw a little man there about an inch long. It was the disease from his finger. He took very good care of this little man and he grew rapidly, soon becoming large enough to run about. He called the little man Little Felon (Kwêqk!ᵘ).

Little Felon was a very industrious little fellow, always at work, and he knew how to carve, make canoes, paint, and do other similar things. When he was working his master could not keep from working himself. He simply had to work. They thought it was because he had come from the hand. Little Felon was also a good shot with bow and arrows, and he was a very fast runner, running races with all the different animals. Finally he started to run a race with the heron, and everybody said the heron would prove too much for him. They raced all the way round Prince of Wales island, and, when they were through, Little Felon said to the heron, "I have been way back among the mountains of this island, and there are thirty-three lakes." The heron answered, "I have been all along the creeks, and there are fifty creeks."

By and by a youth said to Little Felon, "There is a girl living with a certain old woman. She is a very pretty girl and wants to marry, but she hasn't seen anybody she likes. Her grandmother has the dried skin of an animal and she has been making all the young fellows guess the name of it. Those that guess wrong are put to death. You ought to try for her." But Little Felon said to the boy, "I don't care to marry, and I don't want to guess, because I know. You tell her that it is the skin of a louse. It was crawling upon the woman, and she put it into a box and fed it until it grew large. Then she killed and skinned it. You will get her if you tell her. But be careful. That old woman knows a lot about medicines. When you are going toward her, go with the wind. Don't let the wind come from her. Don't go toward her when the south wind is blowing. Go toward her when the north wind is blowing. Nobody goes directly to her. People talk to her from quite a distance. A person goes to her house only to be put to death. Those persons who guess stand a great way off to do it. When they don't guess right they go to that house and are put to death. She has a large square dish in which she cooks their bodies."

After that the boy went toward the old woman's camp and remained at some distance from her for a very long time, for the south wind was blowing continually. She seemed to know that he was there, and said to her granddaughter, "There is a fellow coming who has been around here for a very long time. He is the one who is going to marry you." The little man had said to the youth he was helping, "Don't tell about me. That old woman has all kinds of dangerous things with which to kill people."

As soon as the north wind began to blow, Little Felon told him to go on, so he approached the old woman unnoticed and stood looking at her for a long time. Finally she looked up, saw him, and said, "Oh! my grandson, from how far away have you come?" He told her, and she invited him in to have something to eat. She gave him all kinds of food. Then, when they were through, she showed him the skin and said, "What kind of skin is this?" He answered, "That is a louse skin, grandma." She looked at him then for some time without speaking. Finally she said, "Where are you wise from, from your father?" "Oh!" he said, "from all around." Then she said "All right, you can marry my granddaughter. But do you see that place over there? A very large devilfish lives there. I want you to kill it."

The youth went back to Little Felon and told him what she had said. "Oh!" he answered, "there is a monster there. That is the way she gets rid of boys, is it?" So Little Felon made a hook, went to the place where the devilfish lived, made it small, and pulled it right out. He put the stick over his companion's shoulder and said to him, "Carry it this way." The youth did so and, coming to the old woman's house, he said, "Is this the devilfish you were talking about?" He threw it down, and it grew until it became a monster again that filled the entire house. The old woman felt very badly, and said, "Take it out of this house and lay it down outside." He did so, and the moment he picked it up it grew small again.

Then the old woman said, "Do you see that cliff that goes right down into the water? A monster rat lives there. If you kill it, you shall have my granddaughter." The youth went away again and told Little Felon about it, who said, "I told you so. I knew that she would give you a lot of things to do." So they got their bows and arrows ready, went to the hole of the monster, and looked in. It was asleep. They began shooting it. They blinded it first by shooting into its eyes and then they shot it through the heart. They ran in to it to school, but, as soon as they had wounded it fatally, they rushed out again, and it followed them. It ran right into the ocean, and they could hear it splashing the water about it with its tail. It sounded like thunder. Finally the rat died and drifted ashore.

Then Little Felon told the young man to take it up and carry it to the old woman, and, as soon as he had grasped it, it was very small and light. He carried it in to her and said, "Is this the rat you were talking about?" Then he threw it down, and it filled the house. So she said, "Take it up and put it outside."

Now the old woman spoke again. "Way out there in the middle of the ocean is a sculpin. Go out and fish for it, and you shall get my granddaughter." So he and Little Felon went out there and caught the sculpin, which Little Felon made very small. He threw it into the bottom of the canoe and left it there. When they reached land the youth took it up to the old woman and threw it down inside. Lo! it was an awful monster with great spines.

Now the old woman did not know what to do. She thought, "What kind of boy is this?" Then she said, "Do you see that point? A very large crab lives out there. Go and kill it." When they got out there they saw the crab floating about on its back. It looked very dangerous. Little Felon, however, told the crab to get small, and it did so. He killed it, put it into the canoe, and carried it to the old woman, who exclaimed, "Oh! he has killed everything that belongs to me."

Then the old woman. said, "Go far out to sea beyond the place where you got that sculpin. I dropped my bracelet overboard there. Go and get it." So he and Little Felon set out. But first they dug a quantity of clams and removed the shells. They took these out to that place and threw them around in the water, when all kinds of fish began to come up. Then Little Felon saw a dogfish coming up and said to it, "A bracelet was lost over there. Go and get it for me." He did so, and the youth took it to the old woman.

Then the old woman was very much surprised and said, "Well! that is the last." So she said to her granddaughter, "Come out. Here is your husband. You must have respect for him always." So he married her. After that he went over to Little Felon and asked how much he owed him. "You don't owe me anything" said Little Felon. "You remember that at the time I was sufering so badly you pricked me through the smoke hole." And the youth answered, "Oh! yes, this is the fellow." Little Felon (Kwêqk!ᵘ) is a slender fish that swims close to the beach.

After that the young man and his wife always traveled about together, for he thought a great deal of her. By and by, however, they had a quarrel and he was cruel to her. So she went away and sat down on a point, after which she disappeared and he did not know what had happened to her. He went out on the point and hunted everywhere. He is a lonely beach snipe, called ayAhᵢyiya´, which is often seen hunting about on the points today, and when they see him the Tlngit say, "There he is looking for his wife."

The Image That Came to Life

A young chief on the Queen Charlotte Islands married, and soon afterward his wife fell ill. Then he sent around everywhere for the very best shamans. If there were a very fine shaman at a certain village he would send a canoe there to bring him. None of them could help her, however, and after she had been sick for a very long time she died.

Now the young chief felt very badly over the loss of his wife. He went from place to place after the best carvers in order to have them carve an image of his wife, but no one could make anything to look like her. All this time there was a carver in his own village who could carve much better than all the others. This man met him one day and said, "You are going from village to village to have wood carved like your wife's face, and you can not find anyone to do it, can you? I have seen your wife a great deal walking along with you. I have never studied her face with the idea that you might want someone to carve it, but I am going to try if you will allow me."

Then the carver went after a piece of red cedar and began working upon it. When he was through, he went to the young chief and said, "Now you can come along and look at it." He had dressed it just as he used to see the young woman dressed. So the chief went with him, and, when he got inside, he saw his dead wife sitting there just as she used to look. This made him very happy, and he took it home. Then he asked the carver, "What do I owe you for making this?" and he replied, "Do as you please about it." The carver had felt sorry to see how this chief was mourning for his wife, so he said, "It is because I felt badly for you that I made that. So don't pay me too much for it." He paid the carver very well, however, both in slaves and in goods.

Now the chief dressed this image in his wife's clothes and her marten-skin robe. He felt that his wife had come back to him and treated the image just like her. One day, while he sat mourning very close to the image, he felt it move. His wife had also been very fond of him. At first he thought that the movement was only his imagination, yet he examined it every day, for he thought that at some time it would come to life. When he ate he always had the image close to him.

After a while the whole village learned that he had this image and all came in to see it. Many could not believe that it was not the woman herself until they had examined it closely.

One day, after the chief had had it for a long, long time, he examined the body and found it just like that of a human being. Still, although it was alive, it could not move or speak. Some time later, however, the image gave forth a sound from its chest like that of crackling wood, and the man knew that it was ill.

When he had someone move it away from the place where it had been sitting they found a small red-cedar tree growing there on top of the flooring. They left it until it grew to be very large, and it is because of this that cedars on the Queen Charlotte Islands are so good. When people up this way look for red cedars and find a good one they say, "This looks like the baby of the chief's wife."

Every day the image of the young woman grew more like a human being, and, when they heard the story, people from villages far and near came in to look at it and at the young cedar tree growing there, at which they were very much astonished. The woman moved around very little and never got to talk, but her husband dreamed what she wanted to tell him. It was through his dreams that he knew she was talking to him.

CHEROKEE

In the 17th century 30,000 Cherokee (the "real people") lived in over sixty settlements in the Allegeny region. After the Revolution, the Cherokee were on the frontline of westwards white expansionism; within decades, disease and warfare had reduced their numbers to 7,500. Despite their then accomodation to, and imitation of, white society, they were nonetheless removed to Indian Territory (Oklahoma) in the

1830s. The myths and tales below, however, are from pre-removal times.

Today, the Cherokee are again a populous nation; there are 175,000 Western Cherokee and 9,500 Eastern Cherokee.

How the World Was Made*

The earth is a great island floating in a sea of water, and suspended at each of the four cardinal points by a cord hanging down from the sky vault, which is of solid rock. When the world grows old and worn out, the people will die and the cords will break and let the earth sink down into the ocean, and all will be water again. The Indians are afraid of this.

When all was water, the animals were above in Gălûñ´lătī, beyond the arch; but it was very much crowded, and they were wanting more room. They wondered what was below the water, and at last Dâyuni´sĭ, "Beaver's Grandchild," the little Water- beetle, offered to go and see if it could learn. It darted in every direction over the surface of the water, but could find no firm place to rest. Then it dived to the bottom and came up with some soft mud, which began to grow and spread on every side until it became the island which we call the earth. It was afterward fastened to the sky with four cords, but no one remembers who did this.

At first the earth was flat and very soft and wet. The animals were anxious to get down, and sent out different birds to see if it was yet dry, but they found no place to alight and came back again to Gălûñ´lătī. At last it seemed to be time, and they sent out the Buzzard and told him to go and

*From "Myths of the Cherokee", James Mooney, *19th Animal Report of the Bureau of American Ethnology, 1897–8*, Part I, Washington, 1900.

make ready for them. This was the Great Buzzard, the father of all the buzzards we see now. He flew all over the earth, low down near the ground, and it was still soft. When he reached the Cherokee country, he was very tired, and his wings began to flap and strike the ground, and wherever they struck the earth there was a valley, and where they turned up again there was a mountain. When the animals above saw this, they were afraid that the whole world would be mountains, so they called him back, but the Cherokee country remains full of mountains to this day.

When the earth was dry and the animals came down, it was still dark, so they got the sun and set it in a track to go every day across the island from east to west, just overhead. It was too hot this way, and Tsiska´gĭlĭ, the Red Crawfish, had his shell scorched a bright red, so that his meat was spoiled; and the Cherokee do not eat it. The conjurers put the sun another handbreadth higher in the air, but it was still too hot. They raised it another time, and another, until it was seven handbreadths high and just under the sky arch. Then it was right, and they left it so. This is why the conjurers call the highest place Gûlkwâ´gine Di´gălûñ´lātiyûñ´, "the seventh height," because it is seven handbreadths above the earth. Every day the sun goes along under this arch, and returns at night on the upper side to the starting place.

There is another world under this, and it is like ours in everything – animals, plants, and people – save that the seasons are different. The streams that come down from the mountains are the trails by which we reach this underworld, and the springs at their heads are the doorways by which we enter it, but to do this one must fast and go to water and have one of the underground people for a guide. We know that the seasons in the underworld are different from ours, because the water in the springs is always warmer in winter and cooler in summer than the outer air.

When the animals and plants were first made – we do not know by whom – they were told to watch and keep awake for seven nights, just as young men now fast and keep awake when they pray to their medicine. They tried to do this, and nearly all were awake through the first night, but the next night several dropped off to sleep, and the third night others were asleep, and then others, until, on the seventh night, of all the animals only the owl, the panther, and one or two more were still awake. To these were given the power to see and to go about in the dark, and to make prey of the birds and animals which must sleep at night. Of the trees only the cedar, the pine, the spruce, the holly, and the laurel were awake to the end, and to them it was given to be always green and to be greatest for medicine, but to the others it was said: "Because you have not endured to the end you shall lose your hair every winter."

Men came after the animals and plants. At first there were only a brother and sister until he struck her with a fish and told her to multiply, and so it was. In seven days a child was born to her, and thereafter every seven days another, and they increased very fast until there was danger that the world could not keep them. Then it was made that a woman should have only one child in a year, and it has been so ever since.

The First Fire

In the beginning there was no fire, and the world was cold, until the Thunders (Ani´-Hyûñtĭkwālâs´kĭ), who lived up in Gălûñ´lătĭ, sent their lightning and put fire into the bottom of a hollow sycamore tree which grew on an island. The animals knew it was there, because they could see the smoke coming out at the top, but they could not get to it on account of the water, so they held a council to decide what to do. This was a long time ago.

Every animal that could fly or swim was anxious to go after the fire. The Raven offered, and because he was so large and strong they thought he could surely do the work, so he was sent first. He flew high and far across the water and alighted on the sycamore tree, but while he was wondering what to do next, the heat had scorched all his feathers black, and he was frightened and came back without the fire. The little Screech-owl (Wa´huhu´) volunteered to go, and reached the place safely, but while he was looking down into the hollow tree a blast of hot air came up and nearly burned out his eyes. He managed to fly home as best he could, but it was a long time before he could see well, and his eyes are red to this day. Then the Hooting Owl (U´guku´) and the Horned Owl (Tskĭlĭ´) went, but by the time they got to the hollow tree the fire was burning so fiercely that the smoke nearly blinded them, and the ashes carried up by the wind made white rings about their eyes. They had to come home again without the fire, but with all their rubbing they were never able to get rid of the white rings.

Now no more of the birds would venture, and so the little Uksu´hĭ snake, the black racer, said he would go through the water and bring back some fire. He swam across to the island and crawled through the grass to the tree, and went in by a small hole at the bottom. The heat and smoke were too much for him, too, and after dodging about blindly over the hot ashes until he was almost on fire himself he managed by good luck to get out again at the same hole, but his body had been scorched black, and he has ever since had the habit of darting and doubling on his track as if trying to escape from close quarters. He came back, and the great blacksnake, Gûle´gĭ, "The Climber," offered to go for fire. He swam over to the island and climbed up the tree on the outside, as the blacksnake always does, but when he put his head down into the hole the smoke choked him so that he fell into the burning stump, and before he could climb out again he was as black as the Uksu´hĭ.

Now they held another council, for still there was no fire, and the world was cold, but birds, snakes, and four-footed animals all had some excuse for not going, because they were all afraid to venture near the burning sycamore, until at last Kănane´skĭ Amai´yĕhi (the Water Spider) said she would go. This is not the water spider that looks like a mosquito, but the other one, with black downy hair and red stripes on her body. She can run on top of the water or dive to the bottom, so there would be no trouble to get over to the island, but the question was, How could she bring back the fire? "I'll manage that" said the Water Spider; so she spun a thread from her body and wove it into a *tusti* bowl, which she fastened on her back. Then she crossed over to the island and through the grass to where the fire was still burning. She put one little coal of fire into her bowl, and came back with it, and ever since we have had fire, and the Water Spider still keeps her *tusti* bowl.

Origin of Disease and Medicine

In the old days the beasts, birds, fishes, insects, and plants could all talk, and they and the people lived together in peace and friendship. But as time went on the people increased so rapidly that their settlements spread over the whole earth. and the poor animals found themselves beginning to be cramped for room. This was bad enough, but to make it worse Man invented bows, knives, blowguns, spears, and hooks, and began to slaughter the larger animals, birds, and fishes for their flesh or their skins, while the smaller creatures, such as the frogs and worms, were crushed and trodden upon without thought, out of pure carelessness or contempt. So the animals resolved to consult upon measures for their common safety.

The Bears were the first to meet in council in their townhouse under Kuwâ´hĭ mountain, the "Mulberry Place," and the old White Bear chief presided. After each in turn had complained of the way in which Man killed their friends, ate their flesh, and used their skins for his own purposes, it was decided to begin war at once against him. Someone asked what weapons Man used to destroy them. "Bows and arrows, of course," cried all the Bears in chorus. "And what are they made of?" was the next question. "The bow of wood, and the string of our entrails," replied one of the Bears. It was then proposed that they make a bow and some arrows and see if they could not use the same weapons against Man himself. So one Bear got a nice piece of locust wood and another sacrificed himself for the good of the rest in order to furnish a piece of his entrails for the string. But when everything was ready and the first Bear stepped up to make the trial, it was found that in letting the arrow fly after drawing back the bow, his long claws caught the string and spoiled the shot. This was annoying, but someone suggested that they might trim his claws, which was accordingly done, and on a second trial it was found that the arrow went straight to the mark. But here the chief, the old White Bear, objected, saying it was necessary that they should have long claws in order to be able to climb trees. "One of us has already died to furnish the bowstring, and if we now cut off our claws we must all starve together. It is better to trust to the teeth and claws that nature gave us, for it is plain that Man's weapons were not intended for us."

No one could think of any better plan, so the old chief dismissed the council and the Bears dispersed to the woods and thickets without having concerted any way to prevent the increase of the human race. Had the result of the council been otherwise, we should now be at war with the Bears, but as it is, the hunter does not even ask the Bear's pardon when he kills one.

The Deer next held a council under their chief, the Little Deer, and after some talk decided to send rheumatism to every hunter who should kill one of them unless he took care to ask their pardon for the offense. They sent notice of their decision to the nearest settlement of Indians and told them at the same time what to do when necessity forced them to kill one of the Deer tribe. Now, whenever the hunter shoots a Deer, the Little Deer, who is swift as the wind and cannot be wounded, runs quickly up to the spot and, bending over the bloodstains, asks the spirit of the Deer if it has heard the prayer of the hunter for pardon. If the reply be "Yes," all is well, and the Little Deer goes on his way; But if the reply he "No," he follows on the trail of the hunter, guided by the drops of blood on the ground. until he arrives at his cabin in the settlement, when the Little Deer enters invisibly and strikes the hunter with rheumatism, so that he becomes at once a helpless cripple. No hunter who has regard for his health ever fails to ask pardon of the Deer for killing it, although some hunters who have not learned the prayer may try to turn aside the Little Deer from his pursuit by building a fire behind them in the trail.

Next came the Fishes and Reptiles, who had their own com plaints against Man. They held their council together and determined to make their victims dream of snakes twining about them in slimy folds and blowing foul breath in their faces, or to make them dream of eating raw or decaying fish, so that they would lose appetite, sicken, and die. This is why people dream about snakes and fish.

Finally the Birds, Insects, and smaller animals came together for the same purpose, and the Grubworm was chief of the council. It was decided that each in turn should give an opinion, and then they would vote on the question as to whether or not Man was guilty. Seven votes should be enough to condemn him. One after another denounced Man's cruelty and injustice toward the other animals and voted in favor of his death. The Frog spoke first, saying: "We must do something to check the increase of the race, or people will become so numerous that we shall be crowded from off the earth. See how they have kicked me about because I'm ugly, as they say, until my back is covered with sores"; and here he showed the spots on his skin. Next came the Bird – no one remembers now which one it was – who condemned Man "because he burns my feet off," meaning the way in which the hunter barbecues birds by impaling them on a stick set over the fire, so that their feathers and tender feet are singed off. Others followed in the same strain. The Ground-squirrel alone ventured to say a good word for Man, who seldom hurt him because he was so small, but this made the others so angry that they fell upon the Ground-squirrel and tore him with their claws, and the stripes are on his back to this day.

They began then to devise and name so many new diseases, one after another, that had not their invention at last failed them, no one of the human race would have been able to survive. The Grubworm grew constantly more pleased as the name of each disease was called off, until at last they reached the end of the list, when someone proposed to make menstruation sometimes fatal to women. On this he rose up in his place and cried: "Wadâñ´! [Thanks!] I'm glad some more of them will die, for they are getting so thick that they tread on me." The thought fairly made him shake with joy, so that he fell over backward and could not get on his feet again, but had to wriggle off on his back, as the Grubworm has done ever since.

When the Plants, who were friendly to Man, heard what had been done by the animals, they determined to defeat the latter's evil designs. Each Tree, Shrub, and Herb, down even to the Grasses and Mosses, agreed to furnish a cure for some one of the diseases named, and each said: "I shall appear to help Man when he calls upon me in his need." Thus came medicine; and the plants, every one of which has its use if we only knew it, furnish the remedy to counteract the evil wrought by the revengeful animals. Even weeds were made for some good purpose, which we must find out for ourselves. When the doctor does not know what medicine to use for a sick man the spirit of the plant tells him.

How the Rabbit Stole the Otter's Coat

The animals were of different sizes and wore coats of various colors and pattern. Some wore long fur and others wore short. Some had rings on their tails, and some had no tails at all. Some had coats of brown, others of black or yellow. They were always disputing about their good looks, so at last they agreed to hold a council to decide who had the finest coat.

They had heard a great deal about the Otter, who lived so far up the creek that he seldom came down to visit the other animals. It was said that he had the finest coat of all, but no one knew just what it was like, because it was a long time since anyone had seen him. They did not even know exactly where he lived – only the general direction; but they knew he would come to the council when the word got out.

Now the Rabbit wanted the verdict for himself, so when it began to look as if it might go to the Otter he studied up a plan to cheat him out of it. He asked a few sly questions until he learned what trail the Otter would take to get to the council place. Then, without saying anything, he went on ahead and after four days' travel he met the Otter and knew him at once by his beautiful coat of soft dark-brown fur. The Otter was glad to see him and asked him where he was going. "Oh," said the Rabbit, "the animals sent me to bring you to the council; because you live so far away they were afraid you mightn't know the road." The Otter thanked him, and they went on together.

They traveled all day toward the council ground, and at night the Rabbit selected the camping place, because the Otter was a stranger in that part of the country, and cut down bushes for beds and fixed everything in good shape. The next morning they started on again. In the afternoon the Rabbit began to pick up wood and bark as they went along and to load it on his back. When the Otter asked what this was for the Rabbit said it was that they might be warm and comfortable at night. After a while, when it was near sunset, they stopped and made their camp.

When supper was over the Rabbit got a stick and shaved it down to a paddle. The Otter wondered and asked again what that was for.

"I have good dreams when I sleep with a paddle under my head," said the Rabbit.

When the paddle was finished the Rabbit began to cut away the bushes so as to make a clean trail down to the river.

The Otter wondered more and more and wanted to know what this meant.

Said the Rabbit, "This place is called Di´tatlâski´yĭ (The Place Where It Rains Fire). Sometimes it rains fire here, and the sky looks a little that way tonight. You go to sleep and I'll sit up and watch, and if the fire does come, as soon as you hear me shout, you run and jump into the river. Better hang your coat on a limb over there, so it won't get burned."

The Otter did as he was told, and they both doubled up to go to sleep, but the Rabbit kept awake. After a while the fire burned down to red coals. The Rabbit called, but the Otter was fast asleep and made no answer. In a little while he called again, but the Otter never stirred. Then the Rabbit filled the paddle with hot coals and threw them up into the air and shouted, 'It's raining fire! It's raining fire!'

The hot coals fell all around the Otter and he jumped up. "To the water!" cried the Rabbit, and the Otter ran and jumped into the river, and he has lived in the water ever since.

The Rabbit took the Otter's coat and put it on, leaving his own instead, and went on to the council. All the animals were there, every one looking out for the Otter. At last they saw him in the distance, and they said one to the other, "The Otter is coming!" and sent one of the small animals to show him the best seat. They were all glad to see him and went up in turn to welcome him, but the Otter kept his head down, with one paw over his face. They wondered that he was so bashful, until the Bear came up and pulled the paw away. and there was the Rabbit with his split nose. He sprang up and started to run, when the Bear struck at him and pulled his tail off, but the Rabbit was too quick for them and got away.

How the Deer Got His Horns

In the beginning the Deer had no horns, but his head was smooth just like a doe's. He was a great runner and the Rabbit was a great jumper, and the animals were all curious to know which could go farther in the same time. They talked about it a good deal, and at last arranged a match between the two, and made a nice large pair of antlers for a prize to the winner. They were to start together from one side of a thicket and go through it, then turn and come back, and the one who came out first was to get the horns.

On the day fixed all the animals were there, with the antlers put down on the ground at the edge of the thicket to mark the starting point. While everybody was admiring the horns the Rabbit said: "I don't know this part of the country; I want to take a look through the bushes where I am to run." They thought that all right, so the Rabbit went into the thicket, but he was gone so long that at last the animals suspected he must be up to one of his tricks. They sent a messenger to look for him, and away in the middle of the thicket he found the Rabbit gnawing down the bushes and pulling them away until he had a road cleared nearly to the other side.

The messenger turned around quietly and came back and told the other animals. When the Rabbit came out at last they accused him of cheating, but he denied it until they went into the thicket and found the cleared road. They agreed that such a trickster had no right to enter the race at all, so they gave the horns to the Deer, who was admitted to be the best runner, and he has worn them ever since. They told the Rabbit that as he was so fond of cutting down bushes he might do that for a living hereafter, and so he does to this day.

Ûñtsaiyĭ´, the Gambler

Thunder lives in the west, or a little to the south of west, near the place where the sun goes down behind the water. In the old times he sometimes made a journey to the east, and once after he had come back from one of these journeys a child was born in the east who, the people said, was his son. As the boy grew up it was found that he had scrofula sores all over his body, so one day his mother said to him, "Your father, Thunder, is a great doctor. He lives far in the west, but if you can find him he can cure you."

So the boy set out to find his father and be cured. He traveled long toward the west, asking of everyone he met where Thunder lived, until at last they began to tell him that it was only a little way ahead. He went on and came to Ûñtiguhĭ´, or Tennessee, where lived Ûñtsaiyĭ´, "Brass." Now Ûñtsaiyĭ´ was a great gambler, and made his living that way. It was he who invented the gatayûstĭ game that we play with a stone wheel and a stick. He lived on the south side of the river, and everybody who came that way he challenged to play against him. The large flat rock, with the lines and grooves where they used to roll the wheel, is still there, with the wheels themselves and the stick turned to stone. He won almost every time, because he was so tricky, so that he had his house filled with all kinds of fine things. Sometimes he would lose, and then he would bet all that he had, even to his own life, but the winner got nothing for his trouble, for Ûñtsaiyĭ´ knew how to take on different shapes, so that he always got away.

As soon as Ûñtsaiyĭ´ saw him he asked him to stop and play a while, but the boy said he was looking for his father, Thunder, and had no time to wait. "Well," said Ûñtsaiyĭ´, "he lives in the next house; you can hear him grumbling over there all the time" – he meant the Thunder – "so we may as well have a game or two before you go on." The boy said he had nothing to bet. "That's all right," said the gambler, "we'll play for your pretty spots." He said this to make the boy angry so that he would play, but still the boy said he must go first and find his father, and would come back afterward.

He went on, and soon the news came to Thunder that a boy was looking for him who claimed to be his son. Said Thunder, "I have traveled in many lands and have many children. Bring him here and we shall soon know." So they brought in the boy, and Thunder showed him a seat and told him to sit down. Under the blanket on the seat were long, sharp thorns of the honey locust, with the points all sticking up, but when the boy sat down they did not hurt him, and then Thunder knew that it was his son. He asked the boy why he had come. "I have sores all over my body, and my mother told me you were my father and a great doctor, and if I came here you would cure me." "Yes," said his father, "I am a great doctor, and I'll soon fix you."

There was a large pot in the corner and he told his wife to fill it with water and put it over the fire. When it was boiling, he put in some roots, then took the boy and put him in with them. He let it boil a long time until one would have thought that the flesh was boiled from the poor boy's bones, and then told his wife to take the pot and throw it into the river, boy and all. She did as she was told, and threw it into the water, and ever since there is an eddy there that we call Ûñ´tiguhĭ´, "Pot- in-the-water." A service tree and a calico bush grew on the bank above. A great cloud of steam came up and made streaks and blotches on their bark, and it has been so to this day. When the steam cleared away she looked over and saw the boy clinging to the roots of the service tree where they hung down into the water, but now his skin was all clean. She helped him up the bank, and they went back to the house. On the way she told him, "When we go in, your father will put a new dress on you, but when he opens his box and tells you to pick out your ornaments be sure to take them from the bottom. Then he will send for his other sons to play ball against you. There is a honey locust tree in front of the house. and as soon as you begin to get tired strike at that and your father will stop the play, because he does not want to lose the tree."

When they went into the house, the old man was pleased to see the boy looking so clean, and said," I knew I could soon cure those spots. Now we must dress you." He brought out a fine suit of buckskin, with belt and headdress, and had the boy put them on. Then he opened a box and said, "Now pick out your necklace and bracelets." The boy looked, and the box was full of all kinds of snakes gliding over each other with their heads up. He was not afraid, but remembered what the woman had told him, and plunged his hand to the bottom and drew out a great rattlesnake and put it around his neck for a necklace. He put down his hand again four times and drew up four copperheads and twisted them around his wrists and ankles. Then his father gave him a war club and said, "Now you must play a ball game with your two elder brothers. They live beyond here in the Darkening Land, and I have sent for them." He said a ball game, but he meant that the boy must fight for his life. The young men came, and they were both older and stronger than the boy, but he was not afraid and fought against them. The thunder rolled and the lightning flashed at every stroke, for they were the young Thunders, and the boy himself was Lightning. At last he was tired from defending himself alone against two, and pretended to aim a blow at the honey locust tree. Then his father stopped the fight, because he was afraid the lightning would split the tree, and he saw that the boy was brave and strong.

The boy told his father how Ûñtsaiyĭ´ had dared him to play, and had even offered to play for the spots on his skin. "Yes," said Thunder, "he is a great gambler and makes his living that way, but I will see that you win." He brought a small cymling gourd with a hole bored through the neck, and tied it on the boy's wrist. Inside the gourd there was a string of beads, and one end hung out from a hole in the top, but there was no end to the string inside. "Now," said his father, "go back the way you came, and as soon as he sees you he will want to play for the beads. He is very hard to beat, but this time he will lose every game. When he cries out for a drink, you will know he is getting discouraged, and then strike the rock with your war club and water will come, so that you can play on without stopping. At last he will bet his life, and lose. Then send at once for your brothers to kill him, or he will get away, he is so tricky."

The boy took the gourd and his war club and started east along the road by which he had come. As soon as Ûñtsaiyĭ´ saw him he called to him, and when he saw the gourd with the bead string hanging out he wanted to play for it. The boy drew out the string, but there seemed to be no end to it, and he kept on pulling until enough had come out to make a circle all around the playground. "I will play one game for this much against your stake," said the boy, "and when that is over we can have another game."

They began the game with the wheel and stick and the boy won. Ûñtsaiyĭ´ did not know what to think of it, but he put up another stake and called for a second game. The boy won again, and so they played on until noon, when Ûñtsaiyĭ´ had lost nearly everything he had and was about discouraged. It was very hot, and he said, "I am thirsty," and wanted to stop long enough to get a drink. "No," said the boy, and struck the rock with his club so that water came out, and they had a drink. They played on until Ûñtsaiyĭ´ had lost all his buckskins and beaded work, his eagle feathers and ornaments, and at last offered to bet his wife. They played and the boy won her. Then Ûñtsaiyĭ´ was desperate and offered to stake his life. "If I win I kill you, but if you win you may kill me." They played and the boy won.

"Let me go and tell my wife," said Ûñtsaiyĭ´, "so that she will receive her new husband, and then you may kill me." He went into the house, but it had two doors, and although the boy waited long Ûñtsaiyĭ´ did not come back. When at last he went to look for him he found that the gambler had gone out the back way and was nearly out of sight going east.

The boy ran to his father's house and got his brothers to help him. They brought their dog – the Horned Green Beetle – and hurried after the gambler. He ran fast and was soon out of sight, and they followed as fast as they could. After a while they met an old woman making pottery and asked her if she had seen Ûñtsaiyĭ´ and she said she had not. "He came this way," said the brothers. "Then he must have passed in the night," said the old woman, "for I have been here all day." They were about to take another road when the Beetle, which had been circling about in the air above the old woman, made a dart at her and struck her on the forehead, and it rang like brass – *ûñtsaiyĭ!* Then they knew it was Brass and sprang at him, but he jumped up in his right shape and was off, running so fast that he was soon out of sight again. The Beetle had struck so hard that some of the brass rubbed off, and we can see it on the beetle's forehead yet.

They followed and came to an old man sitting by the trail, carving a stone pipe. They asked him if he had seen Brass pass that way and he said no, but again the Beetle – which could know Brass under any shape – struck him on the forehead so that it rang like metal, and the gambler jumped up in his right form and was off again before they could hold him. He ran east until he came to the great water; then he ran north until he came to the edge of the world, and had to turn again to the west. He took every shape to throw them off the track, but the Green Beetle always knew him, and the brothers pressed him so hard that at last he could go no more and they caught him just as he reached the edge of the great water where the sun goes down.

They tied his hands and feet with a grapevine and drove a long stake through his breast, and planted it far out in the deep water. They set two crows on the end of the pole to guard it and called the place Kâgûñ''yĭ, "Crow Place." But Brass never died, and cannot die until the end of the world, but lies there always with his face up. Sometimes he struggles under the water to get free, and sometimes the beavers, who are his friends, come and gnaw at the grapevine to release him. Then the pole shakes and the crows at the top cry *Ka! Ka! Ka!* and scare the beavers away.

Nûñ´yunúwĭ the Stone Man

This is what the old men told me when I was a boy.

Once when all the people of the settlement were out in the mountains on a great hunt one man who had gone on ahead climbed to the top of a high ridge and found a large river on the other side. While he was looking across he saw an old man walking about on the opposite ridge, with a cane that seemed to be made of some bright, shining rock. The hunter watched and saw that every little while the old man would point his cane in a certain direction, then draw it back and smell the end of it. At last he pointed it in the direction of the hunting camp on the other side of the mountain, and this time when he drew back the staff he sniffed it several times as if it smelled very good, and then started along the ridge straight for the camp. He moved very slowly, with the help of the cane, until he reached the end of the ridge, when he threw the cane out into the air and it because a bridge of shining rock stretching across the river. After he had crossed over upon the bridge it became a cane again, and the old man picked it up and started over the mountain toward the camp.

The hunter was frightened, and felt sure that it meant mischief, so he hurried on down the mountain and took the shortest trail back to the camp to get there before the old man. When he got there and told his story the medicine man said the old man was a wicked cannibal monster called Nûñ´yunúwĭ, "Dressed in Stone," who lived in that part of the country, and was always going about the mountains looking for some hunter to kill and eat. It was very hard to escape from him, because his stick guided him like a dog, and it was nearly as hard to kill him, because his whole body was covered with a skin of solid rock. If he came he would kill and eat them all, and there was only one way to save themselves. He could not bear to look upon a menstrual woman, and if they could find seven menstrual women to stand in the path as he came along the sight would kill him.

So they asked among all the women, and found seven who were sick in that way, and with one of them it had just begun. By the order of the medicine man they stripped themselves and stood along the path where the old man would come. Soon they heard Nûñ´yunúwĭ coming through the woods, feeling his way with his stone cane. He came along the trail to where the first woman was standing, and as soon as he saw her he started and cried out: "Yu! my grandchild; you are in a very bad state!" He hurried past her, but in a moment he met the next woman, and cried out again: "Yu! my child; you are in a terrible way," and hurried past her, but now he was vomiting blood. He hurried on and met the third and the fourth and the fifth woman, but with each one that he saw his step grew weaker until when he came to the last one, with whom the sickness had just begun, the blood poured from his mouth and he fell down on the trail.

Then the medicine man drove seven sourwood stakes through his body and pinned him to the ground, and when night came they piled great logs over him and set fire to them, and all the people gathered around to see. Nûñ′yunúwĭ was a great ada′wehĭ and knew many secrets, and now as the fire came close to him he began to talk, and told them the medicine for all kinds of sickness. At midnight he began to sing, and sang the hunting songs for calling up the bear and the deer and all the animals of the woods and mountains. As the blaze grew hotter his voice sank low and lower, until at last when daylight came, the logs were a heap of white ashes and the voice was still.

Then the medicine man told them to rake off the ashes, and where the body had lain they found only a large lump of red wâ′dĭ paint and a magic u′lûñsû′ti stone. He kept the stone for himself, and calling the people around him he painted them, on face and breast, with the red wâ′dĭ, and whatever each person prayed for while the painting was being done – whether for hunting success, for working skill, or for a long life – that gift was his.

IROQUOIS

A confederation of five (later six) nations, the Iroquois were indisputably the most powerful Indian group of the Northeast, controlling a territory which stretched from Niagara Falls to Albany, New York, from New England to Ohio. Their legendary prowess as warriors has tended to overshadow their novel political organization, which was democratic and discernibly influenced the writers of the US constitution.

The Creation*

The Council Tree

In the faraway days of this floating island there grew one stately tree that branched beyond the range of vision. Perpetually laden with fruit and blossoms, the air was fragrant with its perfume, and the people gathered to its shade where councils were held.

One day the Great Ruler said to his people: "We will make a new place where another people may grow. Under our council tree is a great cloud sea which calls for our help. It is lonesome. It knows no rest and calls for light. We will talk to it. The roots of our council tree point to it and will show the way."

Having commanded that the tree be uprooted, the Great Ruler peered into the depths where the roots had guided, and surmoning Ata-en-sic, who was with child, bade her look down. Ata-en-sic saw nothing, but the Great Ruler knew that the sea voice was calling, and bidding her carry its life, wrapped around her a great ray of light and sent her down to the cloud sea.

*From "Myths and Legends of the New York State Iroquois", Harriet Maxwell Converse, *New York State Museum Bulletin 124*, ed. Arthur C. Parker, Albany, 1908.

Hah-nu-nah, the Turtle

Dazzled by the descending light enveloping Ata-en-sic, there was great consternation among the animals and birds inhabiting the cloud sea, and they counseled in alarm.

"If it falls it may destroy us," they cried.

"Where can it rest?" asked the Duck.

"Only the oeh-da (earth) can hold it," said the Beaver, "the oeh-da which lies at the bottom of our waters, and I will bring it." The Beaver went down but never returned. Then the Duck ventured, but soon its dead body floated to the surface.

Many of the divers had tried and failed when the Muskrat, knowing the way, volunteered to obtain it and soon returned bearing a small portion in his paw. "But it is heavy," said he, "and will grow fast. Who will bear it?"

The Turtle was willing, and the oeh-da was placed on his hard shell.

Having received a resting place for the light, the water birds, guided by its glow, flew upward, and receiving the woman on their widespread wings, bore her down to the Turtle's back.

And Hah-nu-nah, the Turtle, became the Earth Bearer. When he stirs, the seas rise in great waves, and when restless and violent, earthquakes yawn and devour.

Ata-en-sic, the Sky Woman

The *oeh-da* grew rapidly and had become an island when Ata-en-sic, hearing voices under her heart, one soft and soothing, the other loud and contentious, knew that her mission to people the island was nearing.

To her solitude two lives were coming, one peaceful and

patient, the other restless and vicious. The latter, discovering
light under his mother's arm, thrust himself through, to
contentions and strife, the right born entered life for freedom
and peace.

These were the Do-ya-da-no, the twin brothers, Spirits of
Good and Evil. Foreknowing their powers, each claimed
dominion, and a struggle between them began, Hah-gweh-di-
yu claiming the right to beautify the island, while Hah-gweh-
da-ĕt-găh determined to destroy. Each went his way, and
where peace had reigned discord and strife prevailed.

The Sun, Moon, and Stars

At the birth of Hah-gweh-di-yu his Sky Mother, Ata-en-sic,
had died, and the island was still dim in the dawn of its
new life when, grieving at his mother's death, he shaped
the sky with the palm of his hand, and creating the Sun
from her face, lifted it there, saying, "You shall rule here
where your face will shine forever." But Hah-gweh-da-ĕt-
găh set Darkness in the west sky, to drive the Sun down
behind it.

Hah-gweh-di-yu then drew forth from the breast of his
Mother, the Moon and the Stars, and led them to the Sun as
his sisters who would guard his night sky. He gave to the
Earth her body, its Great Mother, from whom was to spring
all life.

All over the land Hah-gweh-di-yu planted towering
mountains, and in the valleys set high bills to protect the
straight rivers as they ran to the sea. But Hah-gweh-da-ĕt-găh
wrathfully sundered the mountains, hurling them far apart,
and drove the high hills into the wavering valleys, bending the
rivers as he hunted them down.

Hah-gweh-di-yu set forests on the high hills, and on the low plains fruit-bearing trees and vines to wing their seeds to the scattering winds. But Hah-gweh-da-ĕt-găh gnarled the forests besetting the earth, and led monsters to dwell in the sea, and herded hurricanes in the sky which frowned with mad tempests that chased the Sun and the Stars.

The Animals and Birds

Hah-gweh-di-yu went across a great sea where he met a Being who told him he was his father. Said the Being, "How high can you reach?" Hah-gweh-di-yu touched the sky. Again he asked, "How much can you lift?" and Hah-gweh-di-yu grasped a stone mountain and tossed it far into space. Then said the Being, "You are worthy to be my son"; and lashing upon his back two burdens, bade him return to the earth,

Hah-gweh-di-yu swam for many days, and the Sun did not leave the sky until he had neared the earth. The burdens had grown heavy but Hah-gweh-di-yu was strong, and when he reached the shore they fell apart and opened.

From one of the burdens flew an eagle guiding the birds which followed, filling the skies with their song to the Sun as they winged to the forest. From the other there came animals led by the deer, and they sped quickly to the mountains. But Hah-gweh-da-ĕt-găh followed with wild beasts that devour, and grim flying creatures that steal life without sign, and creeping reptiles to poison the way.

Duel of Hah-gweh-di-yu and Hah-gweh-da-ĕt-găh

When the earth was completed and Hah-gweh-di-yu had bestowed a protecting Spirit upon each of his creation, he besought Hah-gweh-da-ĕt-găh to reconcile his vicious existence to the peacefulness of his own, but Hah-gweh-da-ĕt-găh refused, and challenged Hah-gweh-di-yu to combat, the victor to become the ruler of the earth.

Hah-gweh-da-ĕt-găh proposed weapons which he could control, poisonous roots strong as flint, monsters' teeth, and fangs of serpents. But these Hah-gweh-di-yu refused, selecting the thorns of the giant crab-apple tree, which were arrow pointed and strong.

With the thorns they fought. The battle continued many days, ending in the overthrow of Hah-gweh-da-ĕt-găh.

Hah-gweh-di-yu, having now become the ruler, banished his brother to a pit under the earth, whence he cannot return. But he still retains Servers, half human and half beasts, whom he sends to continue his destructive work. These Servers can assume any form Hah-gweh-da-ĕt-găh may command, and they wander all over the earth.

Hah-gweh-di-yu, faithful to the prophecy of the Great Ruler of the floating island, that the earth should be peopled, is continually creating and protecting.

Ga-oh, Spirit of the Winds

Though of giant proportions, Ga-oh, who governs the winds, is confined in the broad north sky. Were Ga-oh free, he would tear the heavens into fragments.

In the ages of his solitary confinement, he does not forget

his strength, and punishes the winds to subjection when they suddenly rear for flight.

At the entrance of his abode and reined to his hands are four watchers: the Bear (north wind), Panther (west wind), Moose (east wind), and Fawn (south wind).

When Ga-oh unbinds Bear, it leads its hurricane winter winds to Earth; when he loosens Panther, its stealthy west winds creep down and follow Earth with their snarling blasts; when Moose is released, its east wind meets the Sun and its misty breath floats over the Sun's path blinding it with rains; and when Ga-oh unlocks his reins from Fawn, its soothing south winds whisper to Earth and she summons her Spring, who comes planting the seeds for the summer sunglow.

Though in his subjugation of the winds it is Ga-oh's duty to pacify them, frequently they are influenced by his varying moods. When Ga-oh is contented and happy, gentle and invigorating breezes fan Earth; when he is irritated by his confinement and restless, strong winds agitate the waters and bend the forest trees; and when, frenzied to mighty throes, Ga-oh becomes vehement, ugly blasts go forth, uprooting trees, dashing the streams into leaping furies, lifting the sea waters to mountainous waves, and devastating the earth.

Notwithstanding these outbursts, Ga-oh is faithful in disciplining the winds to their proper seasons, and guarding Earth from the rage of the elements.

When the north wind blows strong, the Iroquois say, "The Bear is prowling in the sky"; if the west wind is violent, "The Panther is whining." When the east wind chills with its rain, "The Moose is spreading his breath"; and when the south wind wafts soft breezes, "The Fawn is returning to its Doe."

Naming the Winds

When, in the creation of the earth, Hah-gweh-di-yu limited the duties of the powerful Ga-oh to the sky, assigning to him the governing of the tempests, he blew a strong blast that shook the whole earth to trembling. and summoned his assistants to a council.

Ga-oh chose his aides from the terrestrial because of their knowledge of the earth; and when his reverberating call had ceased its thunderous echoes, he opened his north gate wide across the sky and called Ya-o-gah, the Bear.

Lumbering over the mountains as he pushed them from his path, Ya-o-gah, the bulky bear, who had battled the boisterous winds as he came, took his place at Ga-oh's gate and waited the mission of his call. Said Ga-oh, "Ya-o-gah, you are strong, you can freeze the waters with your cold breath; in your broad arms you can carry the wild tempest, and clasp the whole earth when I bid you destroy. I will place you in my far north, there to watch the herd of my winter winds when I loose them in the sky. You shall be North Wind. Enter your home." And the bear lowered his head for the leash with which Ga-oh bound him, and submissively took his place in the north sky.

In a gentler voice Ga-oh called Ne-o-ga, the Fawn, and a soft breeze as of the summer crept over the sky; the air grew fragrant with the odor of flowers, and there were voices as of babbling brooks telling the secrets of the summer to the tune of birds, as Ne-o-ga came proudly lifting her head.

Said Ga-oh, "You walk with the summer sun, and know all its paths; you are gentle, and kind as the sunbeam, and will rule my flock of the summer winds in peace. You shall be the South Wind. Bend your head while I leash you to the sky, for you are swift, and might return from me to the earth." And the gentle fawn followed Ga-oh to his great gate which opens the south sky.

Again Ga-oh trumpeted a shrill blast, and all the sky seemed threatening; an ugly darkness crept into the clouds that sent them whirling in circles of confusion; a quarrelsome, shrieking voice snarled through the air, and with a sound as of great claws tearing the heavens into rifts, Da-jo-ji, the Panther, sprang to the gate.

Said Ga-oh, "You are ugly, and fierce, and can fight the strong storms; you can climb the high mountains, and tear down the forests; you can carry the whirlwind on your strong back, and toss the great sea waves high in the air, and snarl at the tempests if they stray from my gate. You shall be the West Wind. Go to the west sky, where even the Sun will hurry to hide when you howl your warning to the night." And Da-jo-ji, dragging his leash as he stealthily crept along, followed Ga-oh to the farthermost west sky.

Yet Ga-oh rested not. The earth was flat, and in each of its four corners he must have an assistant. One corner yet remained, and again Ga-oh's strong blast shook the earth. And there arose a moan like the calling of a lost mate, the sky shivered in a cold rain, the whole earth clouded in mist, a crackling sound as of great horns crashing through the forest trees dinned the air, and O-yan-do-ne, the Moose, stood stamping his hoofs at the gate.

Said Ga-oh, as he strung a strong leash around his neck. "Your breath blows the mist, and can lead the cold rains; your horns spread wide, and can push back the forests to widen the path for my storms as with your swift hoofs you race with my winds. You shall be the East Wind, and blow your breath to chill the young clouds as they float through the sky." And, said Ga-oh, as he led him to the east sky, "Here you shall dwell forevermore."

Thus, with his assistants, does Ga-oh control his storms. And although he must ever remain in his sky lodge, his will is supreme, and his faithful assistants will obey!

Ga-Nus-Quah and Go-Gon-Sa, the Stone Giants and False Faces

Tall, fierce and hostile, they were a powerful tribe, the Stone Giants!

They invaded the country of the Iroquois during the early days of the Confederation of the Five Nations, the Mohawks, Onondagas, Oneidas, Cayugas, and Senecas, who had sent their warriors against them only to be defeated, and they threatened the annihilation of the Confederacy.

They were feared, not because of their prodigious size, but because they were cannibals as well, and would devour men, women, and children.

The Shawnees have a legend of these Giants which describes them as at one time living in a peaceful state, and although powerful, gentle and hospitable in their intercourse with the neighboring tribes; but from some disturbing cause they became restless, abandoned their home, and migrated to the far northwest snow fields, where the extreme cold of the winters "froze away their humanity," and they became "men of icy hearts."

Unable to withstand the severity of the climate, or provide themselves with sufficient food, they were again controlled by the spirit of restlessness and they became wanderers, enduring all the discomforts and hardships of a nomadic life; and subsisting on raw meat and fish, they finally drifted into cannibalism, reveling in human flesh.

In the summer they would roll in the sand to harden their

flesh, and their bodies became covered with scales which resisted the arrows of an enemy. For generations they had devastated nations before they swept down upon the Iroquois. There they found caves wherein they concealed themselves, and would sally forth, destroying some village and feasting on the people.

The Iroquois were being rapidly depleted in their numbers, when Ta-ha-hia-wa-gon, Upholder of the Heavens, who had bestowed upon them their hunting grounds and fisheries, beholding their distress, determined to relieve them of the merciless invaders, and transforming himself to a stone giant, came down to the earth and united with their tribe.

Wonderstruck at his marvelous display of power, they made him their chief; and he brandished his club high in the air, saying, "Now we will destroy the Iroquois, make a great feast of them, and invite all the Stone Giants of the sky." In pretense of this intention, the Sky Holder led them to a strong fort of the Onondagas where he bade them hide in a deep hollow in the valley and await the sunrise, when they would attack and destroy the unsuspecting people. But before day, he scaled a high place above them and overwhelmed them with a great mass of rocks. Only one escaped, who fled to the Allegheny mountains. There he secreted himself in a cave, where he remained and grew in huge strength, when he was transformed to the myth Giant, Ga-nus-quah.

Ga-nus-quah, the Depredator

He was vulnerable only on the bottom of his foot. No one could hope to destroy him without wounding the spot on his foot, and this was not in the power of a mortal to do; and thus secure, the whole earth was his path.

No human being had ever seen him. To look upon his face would be instant death. His trail could be traced in the forests by the fallen trees he had uprooted when they obstructed his way. His footprints were seen impressed on the rocks where in his travels he had leaped. If a river opposed his going, he would swoop it up with his huge hands and turn it from its course, and so cross on the dry land. Should a mountain impede his way, with his strong fists he would push a gorge through it, the more quickly to reach the other side. In the tumult of storms, his voice could be heard warning the Thunderers away from his cave, this Ga-nus-quah, the last of the Stone Giants!

It was once the fate of a young hunter to meet this fear-inspiring creature. During a terrific storm, the young hunter, a chief, blinded and bruised by the hail which fell like sharp flints, and having lost the trail, sought shelter within the hollow of a great rock.

Night with its darkness deepened the shadows, and the young hunter prepared for night's sleep, when suddenly the rock began to move, and from a far recess a strange sound approached him. At one moment, the tone was brisk as the gurgling stream, at the next, gentle as the lullaby of a singing brook, again to burst forth like the moan of a tumbling cataract or the wail of a mad torrent, then dying away as tenderly as the soft summer breeze.

During a pause in the weird harmony, the marveling young hunter heard a voice addressing him in a stentorian strain, saying: "Young warrior, beware! You are in the cave of the Stone Giant, Ga-nus-quah! Close your eyes. No human being has ever looked upon me. I kill with one glance. Many have wandered into this cave; no one lives to leave it. You did not come to hunt me; you came here for shelter; I will not turn you away. I will spare your life, which now is mine, but henceforth you must obey my commands. I will be unseen, but you will hear my voice. I will be unknown, yet will I aid you. From here you will go forth, free to live with the animals, the birds, and the fish. All these were your ancestors before you were human, and hereafter it will be your task to dedicate your life to their honoring!

"Whichever of these you meet on your way, do not pass until you have felled a strong tree and carved its image in the wood grain. When you first strike the tree, if it speaks, it will be my voice urging you and you must go on with your task. When the trees were first set in their earth mold, each was given a voice. These voices you must learn, and the language of the entire forest. Now, go on your way; I am watching and guiding you. Go, now, and teach the mankind people kindness, the brother goodness of all dumb thing, and so win your way to live forever!"

When the young hunter opened his eyes, he was standing beside a basswood tree which gradually transformed to a great mask; and related to him its power.

The Go-gon-sa (Mask)

It could see behind the stars. It could create storms, and summon the sunshine. It empowered battles or weakened the forces at will. It knew the remedy for each disease, and could overpower Death. It knew all the poison roots and could repel their strong evils. Its power was life, its peace the *o-yank-wah*, the tobacco which drowsed to rest. The venomous reptiles knew its threat and crept from its path. It would lead the young hunter back to his people when the Stone Giant directed. It said: "My tree, the basswood, is soft, and will transform for the molder. My tree wood is porous, and the sunlight can enter its darkness. The wind voice can whisper to its silence and it will hear. My tree wood is the life of the Go-gon-sa. Of all in the forest there is none other."

With this knowledge, the young hunter started on his way carving go-gon-sa-so-oh (false faces). From the basswood he hewed them. By the voice of the Stone Giant he was guided to choose; and well he learned the voices of all the forest trees before he completed his task.

In his travels he met many strange animals and birds, which he detained until he had carved them in the basswood; and inviting them to tarry, learned their language and habits; and though fearing the Giant's reproval, for he constantly heard his voice encouraging or blaming, he learned to love these descendants of his ancestors, and was loath to leave them when compelled to return to his home.

Many years had passed in the laborious task, and he who entered the cave a youth had become a bent old man when, burdened with the go-gon-sas he had carved, he set out on his return to his people. Year after year his burden had grown heavier, but his back broadened in strength, and he had become a giant in stature when he reached his home and related his story.

THE SIOUX

Originally pedestrian agriculturalists in Minnesota, the Sioux were pushed onto the Plains in the latter half of the 18th century where they adopted the horse and buffalo-hunting. The Lakota (or Dakota, the name the Sioux give themselves) are composed principally of the Teton, Brule and Oglala divisions, along with the Santee Sioux who remained in Minnesota.

The Legend of Standing Rock*

Dakota had married an Arikara Woman, and by her had one child. By and by he took another wife. The first wife was jealous and pouted. When time came for the village to break camp she refused to move from her place on the tent floor. The tent was taken down but she sat on the ground with her babe on her back. The rest of the camp with her husband went on.

At noon her husband halted the line. "Go back to your sister-in-law," he said to his two brothers. "Tell her to come on and we will await you here. But hasten, for I fear she may grow desperate and kill herself."

The two rode off and arrived at their former camping place in the evening. The woman still sat on the ground. The elder spoke:

"Sister-in-law, get up. We have come for you. The camp awaits you."

She did not answer, and he put out his hand and touched her head. She had turned to stone!

The two brothers lashed their ponies and came back to camp. They told their story, but were not believed. "The woman has killed herself and my brothers will not tell me," said the husband. However, the whole village broke camp and came back to the place where they had left the woman. Sure enough, she sat there still, a block of stone.

The Indians were greatly excited. They chose a handsome pony, made a new travois and placed the stone in the carrying net. Pony and travois were both beautifully painted and decorated with streamers and colours. The stone was thought "*wakan*" (holy), and was given a place of honor in the center of the camp. Whenever the camp moved the stone and travois were taken along. Thus the stone woman was carried

*From *Myths and Legends of the Sioux*, Marie McLaughlin, Bismarck Tribune Co., 1916.

for years, and finally brought to Standing Rock Agency, and now rests upon a brick pedestal in front of the Agency office. From this stone Standing Rock Agency derives its name.

Story of the Peace Pipe

Two young men were out strolling one night talking of love affairs. They passed around a hill and came to a little ravine or coulee. Suddenly they saw coming up from the ravine a beautiful woman. She was painted and her dress was of the very fine material.

"What a beautiful girl!" said one of the young men. "Already I love her. I will steal her and make her my wife."

"No," said the other. "Don't harm her. She may be holy."

The young woman approached and held out a pipe which she first offered to the sky, then to the earth and then advanced, holding it out in her extended hands.

"I know what you young men have been saying; one of you is good; the other is wicked," she said.

She laid down the the pipe on the ground and at once became a buffalo cow. The cow pawed the ground, stuck her tail straight out behind her and then lifted the pipe from the ground again in her hoofs; immediately she became a young woman again.

"I am come to give you this gift," she said. "It is the peace pipe. Hereafter all treaties and ceremonies shall be performrned after smoking it. It shall bring peaceful thoughts into your minds. You shall offer it to the Great Mystery and to mother earth."

The two young men ran to the village and told what they had seen and heard. All the village came out where the young woman was.

She repeated to them what she had already told the young men and added:

"When you set free the ghost (the spirit of deceased persons) you must have a white buffalo cow skin."

She gave the pipe to the medicine men of the village, turned again to a buffalo cow and fled away to the land of buffaloes.

The girl looked down; so did the youth. At last he said softly:

"Well, which is it? Shall I take up your bucket, or will you go with me?"

And she answered, still more softly: "I guess I'll go with you!"

The girl's aunt came down to the river, wondering what kept her niece so long. In the mud she found two pairs of moccasin tracks close together; at the edge of the water stood an empty keg.

The Simpleton's Wisdom

There was a man and his wife who had one daughter. Mother and daughter were deeply attached to one another, and when the latter died the mother was disconsolate. She cut off her hair, cut gashes in her cheeks and sat before the corpse with her robe drawn over her head, mourning for her dead. Nor would she let them touch the body to take it to a burying scaffold. She had a knife in her hand, and if anyone offered to come near the body the mother would wail:

"I am weary of life. I do not care to live. I will stab myself with this knife and join my daughter in the land of spirits."

Her husband and relatives tried to get the knife from her, but could not. They feared to use force lest she kill herself

They came together to see what they could do.

"We must get the knife away from her," they said.

At last they called a boy, a kind of simpleton, yet with a good deal of natural shrewdness. He was an orphan and very poor. His moccasins were out at the sole and he was dressed in wei-zi (coarse buffalo skin, smoked).

"Go to the tepee of the mourning mother," they told the simpleton, "and in some way contrive to make her laugh and forget her grief. Then try to get the knife away from her."

The boy went to the tent and sat down at the door as if waiting to be given something. The corpse lay in the place of honor where the dead girl had slept in life. The body was wrapped in a rich robe and wrapped about with ropes. Friends had covered it with rich offerings out of respect to the dead.

As the mother sat on the ground with her head covered she did not at first see the boy, who sat silent. But when his reserve had worn away a little he began at first lightly, then more heavily, to drum on the floor with his hands. After a while he began to sing a comic song. Louder and louder he sang until carried away with his own singing he sprang up and began to dance, at the same time gesturing and making all manner of contortions with his body, still singing the comic song. As he approached the corpse he waved his hands over it in blessing. The mother put her head out of the blanket and when she saw the poor simpleton with his strange grimaces trying to do honor to the corpse by his solemn waving, and at the same time keeping up his comic song, she burst out laughing. Then she reached over and handed her knife to the simpleton.

"Take this knife," she said. "You have taught me to forget my grief. If while I mourn for the dead I can still be mirthful, there is no reason for me to despair. I no longer care to die. I will live for my husband."

The simpleton left the tepee and brought the knife to the astonished husband and relatives.

"How did you get it? Did you force it away from her, or did you steal it?" they said.

"She gave it to me. How could I force it from her or steal it when she held it in her hand, blade uppermost. I sang and danced for her and she burst out laughing. Then she gave it to me," he answered.

When the old men of the village heard the orphan's story they were very silent. It was a strange thing for a lad to dance in a tepee where there was mourning. It was stranger that a mother should laugh in a tepee before the corpse of her dead daughter. The old men gathered at last in a council. They sat a long time without saying anything, for they did not want to decide hastily. The pipe was filled and passed many times. At last an old man spoke.

"We have a hard question. A mother has laughed before the corpse of her daughter, and many think she has done foolishly, but I think the woman did wisely. The lad was simple and of no training, and we cannot expect him to know how to do as well as one with good home and parents to teach him. Besides, he did the best that he knew. He danced to make the mother forget her grief, and he tried to honor the corpse by waving over it his hands.

"The mother did right to laugh, for when one does try to do us good, even if what he does causes us discomfort, we should always remember rather the motive than the deed. And besides, the simpleton's dancing saved the woman's life, for she gave up her knife. In this, too, she did well, for it is always better to live for the living than to die for the dead."

A Little Brave and the Medicine Woman

A village of Indians moved out of winter camp and pitched their tents in a circle on high land overlooking a lake. A little way down the declivity was a grave. Choke cherries had grown up, hiding the grave from view. But as the ground had sunk somewhat, the grave was marked by a slight hollow.

One of the villagers going out to hunt took a short cut through the choke cherry bushes. As he pushed them aside he saw the hollow grave, but thought it was a washout made by the rains. But as he essayed to step over it, to his great surprise he stumbled and fell. Made curious by his mishap, he drew back and tried again; but again he fell. When he came back to the village he told the old men what had happened to him. They remembered then that a long time before there had been buried there a medicine woman or conjurer. Doubtless it was her medicine that made him stumble.

The story of the villager's adventure spread through the camp and made many curious to see the grave. Among others were six little boys who were, however, rather timid, for they were in great awe of the medicine woman. But they had a little playmate named Brave, a mischievous little rogue, whose hair was always unkempt and tossed about and who was never quiet for a moment.

"Let us ask Brave to go with us," they said; and they went in a body to see him.

"All right," said Brave; "I will go with you. But I have something to do first. You go on around the hill *that* way, and I will hasten around *this* way, and meet you a little later near the grave."

So the six little boys went on as bidden until they came to a place near the grave. There they halted.

"Where is Brave?" they asked.

Now Brave, full of mischief, had thought to play a jest on his little friends. As soon as they were well out of sight he had sped around the hill to the shore of the lake and sticking his hands in the mud had rubbed it over his face, plastered it in his hair, and soiled his hands until he looked like a new risen corpse with the flesh rotting from his bones. He then went and lay down in the grave and awaited the boys.

When the six little boys came they were more timid than ever when they did not find Brave; but they feared to go back to the village without seeing the grave, for fear the old men would call them cowards.

So they slowly approached the grave and one of them timidly called out:

"Please, grandmother, we won't disturb your grave. We only want to see where you lie. Don't be angry."

At once a thin quavering voice, like an old woman's, called out: "Han, han, takoja, hechetuya, hechetuya! Yes, yes, that's right, that's right."

The boys were frightened out of their senses, believing the old woman had come to life.

"Oh, grandmother," they gasped, "don't hurt us; please don't, we'll go."

Just then Brave raised his muddy face and hands up through the choke cherry bushes. With the oozy mud dripping from his features he looked like some very witch just raised from the grave. The boys screamed outright. One fainted. The rest ran yelling up the hill to the village, where each broke at once for his mother's tepee.

As all the tents in a Dakota camping circle face the center, the boys as they came tearing into camp were in plain view from the tepees. Hearing the screaming, every woman in camp ran to her tepee door to see what had happened. Just then little Brave, as badly scared as the rest, came rushing in after them, his hair on end and covered with mud and crying out, all forgetful of his appearance:

"It's me, it's me!"

The women yelped and bolted in terror from the village. Brave dashed into his mother's tepee, scaring her out of her wits. Dropping pots and kettles, she tumbled out of the tent to run screaming with the rest. Nor would a single villager come near poor little Brave until he had gone down to the lake and washed himself.

The Bound Children

There once lived a widow with two children – the elder a daughter and the younger a son. The widow went in mourning for her husband a long time. She cut off her hair, let her dress lie untidy on her body and kept her face unpainted and unwashed.

There lived in the same village a great chief. He had one son just come old enough to marry. The chief had it known that he wished his son to take a wife, and all of the young women in the village were eager to marry the young man. However, he was pleased with none of them.

Now the widow thought, "I am tired of mourning for my husband and caring for my children. Perhaps if I lay aside my mourning and paint myself red, the chief's son may marry me."

So she slipped away from her two children, stole down to the river and made a bathing place through the ice. When she had washed away all signs of mourning she painted and decked herself and went to the chief's tepee. When his son saw her, he loved her, and a feast was made in honor of her wedding.

When the widow's daughter found herself forsaken, she wept bitterly. After a day or two she took her little brother in her arms and went to the tepee of an old woman who lived at one end of the village. The old woman's tumble down tepee was of bark and her dress and clothing was of old smoke-dried tent cover. But she was kind to the two waifs and took them in willingly.

The little girl was eager to find her mother. The old woman said to her: "I suspect your mother has painted her face red. Do not try to find her. If the chief's son marries her she will not want to be burdened with you."

The old woman was right. The girl went down to the river, and sure enough found a hole cut in the ice and about it lay the filth that the mother had washed from her body. The girl gathered up the filth and went on. By and by she came to a second hole in the ice. Here too was filth, but not so much as at the previous place. At the third hole the ice was clean.

The girl knew now that her mother had painted her face red. She went at once to the chief's tepee, raised the door flap and went in. There sat her mother with the chief's son at their wedding feast.

The girl walked up to her mother and hurled the filth in her mother's face.

"There," she cried, "you who forsake your helpless children and forget your husband, take that!"

And at once her mother became a hideous old woman.

The girl then went back to the lodge of the old woman, leaving the camp in an uproar. The chief soon sent some young warriors to seize the girl and her brother, and they were brought to his tent. He was furious with anger.

"Let the children be bound with lariats wrapped about their bodies and let them be left to starve. Our camp will move on," he said. The chief's son did not put away his wife, hoping she might be cured in some way and grow young again.

Everybody in camp now got ready to move; but the old woman came close to the girl and said:

"In my old tepee I have dug a hole and buried a pot with punk and steel and flint and packs of dried meat. They will tie you up like a corpse. But before we go I will come with a knife and pretend to stab you, but I will really cut the rope that binds you so that you can unwind it from your body as soon as the camp is out of sight and hearing."

And so, before the camp started, the old woman came to the place where the two children were bound. She had in her hand a knife bound to the end of a stick which she used as a lance. She stood over the children and cried aloud:

"You wicked girl, who have shamed your own mother, you deserve all the punishment that is given you. But after all I do not want to let you lie and starve. Far better kill you at once and have done with it!" and with her stick she stabbed many times, as if to kill, but she was really cutting the rope.

The camp moved on; but the children lay on the ground until noon the next day. Then they began to squirm about. Soon the girl was free, and she then set loose her little brother. They went at once to the old woman's hut where they found the flint and steel and the packs of dried meat.

The girl made her brother a bow and arrows and with these he killed birds and other small game.

The boy grew up a great hunter. They became rich. They built three great tepees, in one of which were stored rows upon rows of parfleche bags of dried meat.

One day as the brother went out to hunt, he met a handsome young stranger who greeted him and said to him:

"I know you are a good hunter, for I have been watching you; your sister, too, is industrious. Let me have her for a wife.

Then you and I will be brothers and hunt together."

The girl's brother went home and told her what the young stranger had said.

"Brother, I do not care to marry," she answered. "I am now happy with you."

"But you will be yet happier married," he answered, "and the young stranger is of no mean family, as one can see by his dress and manners."

"Very well, I will do as you wish," she said. So the stranger came into the tepee and was the girl's husband.

One day as they were in their tent, a crow flew overhead, calling out loudly,

"Kaw, Kaw,

They who forsook the children have no meat."

The girl and her husband and brother looked up at one another.

"What can it mean?" they asked. "Let us send for Unktomi (the spider). He is a good judge and he will know."

"And I will get ready a good dinner for him, for Unktomi is always hungry," added the young wife.

When Unktomi came, his yellow mouth opened with delight at the fine feast spread for him. After he had eaten he was told what the crow had said.

"The crow means," said Unktomi, "that the villagers and chief who bound and deserted you are in sad plight. They have hardly anything to eat and are starving."

When the girl heard this she made a bundle of choicest meat and called the crow.

"Take this to the starving villagers," she bade him.

He took the bundle in his beak, flew away to the starving village and dropped the bundle before the chief's tepee. The chief came out and the crow called loudly:

"Kaw, Kaw!

"The children who were forsaken have much meat; those who forsook them have none."

"What can he mean," cried the astonished villagers.

"Let us send for Unktomi," said one, "he is a great judge; he will tell us."

They divided the bundle of meat among the starving people, saving the biggest piece for Unktomi.

When Unktomi had come and eaten, the villagers told him of the crow and asked what the bird's words meant.

"He means," said Unktomi, "that the two children whom you forsook have tepees full of dried meat enough for all the village."

The villagers were filled with astonishment at this news. To find whether or not it was true, the chief called seven young men and sent them out to see. They came to the three tepees and there met the girl's brother and husband just going out to hunt (which they did now only for sport).

The girl's brother invited the seven young men into the third or sacred lodge, and after they had smoked a pipe and knocked out the ashes on a buffalo bone the brother gave them meat to eat, which the seven devoured greedily. The next day he loaded all seven with packs of meat, saying:

"Take this meat to the villagers and lead them hither."

While they awaited the return of the young men with the villagers, the girl made two bundles of meat, one of the best and choicest pieces, and the other of liver, very dry and hard to eat. After a few days the camp arrived. The young woman's mother opened the door and ran in crying: "Oh, my dear daughter, how glad I am to see you." But the daughter received her coldly and gave her the bundle of dried liver to eat. But when the old woman who had saved the children's lives came in, the young girl received her gladly, called her grandmother, and gave her the package of choice meat with marrow.

Then the whole village camped and ate of the stores of meat all the winter until spring came; and withal they were so many, there was such abundance of stores that there was still much left.

The Signs of Corn

When corn is to be planted by the Indians, it is the work of the women folk to see to the sorting and gleaming of the best seed. It is also the women's work to see to the planting. (This was in olden times.)

After the best seed has been selected, the planter measures the corn, lays down a layer of hay, then a layer of corn. Over this corn they sprinkle warm water and cover it with another layer of hay, then bind hay about the bundle and hang it up in a spot where the warm rays of the sun can strike it.

While the corn is hanging in the sun, the ground is being prepared to receive it. Having finished the task of preparing the ground, the woman takes down her seed corn which has by this time sprouted. Then she proceeds to plant the corn.

Before she plants the first hill, she extends her hoe heavenwards and asks the Great Spirit to bless her work, that she may have a good yield. After her prayer she takes four kernels and plants one at the north, one the south, one at the east and one at the west sides of the first hill. This is asking the Great spirit to give summer rain and sunshine to bring forth a good crop.

For different growths of the corn, the women have an interpretation as to the character of the one who planted it.

1. Where the corn grows in straight rows and the cob is full of kernels to the end, this signifies that the planter of this corn is of an exemplary character, and is very truthful and thoughtful.

2. If the rows on the ears of corn are irregular and broken, the planter is considered careless and unthoughtful. Also disorderly and slovenly about her house and person.

3. When an ear of corn bears a few scattering kernels with spaces producing no corn, it is said that is a good sign that the planter will live to a ripe old age. So old will they be that like the corn, their teeth will be few and far between.

4. When a stalk bears a great many nubbins, or small ears growing around the large one, it is a sign that the planter is from a large and respectable family.

5. After the corn is gathered, it is boiled into sweet corn and made into hominy; parched and mixed with buffalo tallow and rolled into round balls, and used at feasts, or carried by the warriors on the warpath as food.

6. When there has been a good crop of corn, an ear is always tied at the top of the medicine pole, of the sun dance, in thanks to the Great Spirit for his goodness to them in sending a bountiful crop.

Story of the Rabbits

The Rabbit nation were very much depressed in spirits on account of being run over by all other nations. They, being very obedient to their chief, obeyed all his orders to the letter. One of his orders was, that upon the approach of any other nation that they should follow the example of their chief and run up among the rocks and down into their burrows, and not show themselves until the strangers had passed.

This they always did. Even the chirp of a little cricket would send them all scampering to their dens.

One day they held a great council, and after talking over

everything for some time, finally left it to their medicine man to decide. The medicine man arose and said:

"My friends, we are of no use on this earth. There isn't a nation on earth that fears us, and we are so timid that we cannot defend ourselves, so the best thing for us to do is to rid the earth of our nation, by all going over to the big lake and drowning ourselves."

This they decided to do; so going to the lake they were about to jump in, when they heard a splashing in the water. Looking, they saw a lot of frogs jumping into the lake.

"We will not drown ourselves," said the medicine man, "we have found a nation who are afraid of us. It is the frog nation." Had it not been for the frogs we would have had no rabbits, as the whole nation would have drowned themselves and the rabbit race would have been extinct.

Bibliography

The literature on North American Indians is vast. Below is a selection of the works which have influenced the preceding pages.

Ambrose, Stephen E., *Crazy Horse and Custer: The Parallel Lives of Two American Warriors*, New York, 1975

Andrist, Ralph K., *The Long Death: The Last Days of the Plains Indians*, New York, 1964

Armstrong, Virginia I. (ed), *I have Spoken: American History through the Voices of the Indians*, Chicago, 1971

Berger, Thomas, *Little Big Man*, New York, 1964

Bergon, Frank (ed), *The Journals of Lewis & Clark*, New York, 1989

Betzinez, Jason (with W.S. Nye), *I Fought With Geronimo*, New York, 1959

Bourke, John G., *An Apache Campaign in the Sierra Madre*, New York, 1886

Brown, Dee, *The Fetterman Massacre*, London, 1972

—— *Bury My Heart at Wounded Knee: An Indian History of the American West*, New York, 1970

Capps, Benjamin, *The Great Chiefs*, Alexandria, VA., 1975

Catlin, George, *Life Among the Indians*, London, 1875

—— *Letters and Notes on the Manners, Customs, and Conditions of the North American Indians*, New York, 1973 (reprint)

Cruse, Thomas, *Apache Days and After*, Caldwell, ID., 1941

Curtis, Natalie, *The Indians Book*, New York, 1907

Custer, George A., *Wild Life on the Plains and the Horrors of Indian Warfare*, St. Louis, 1891

Davis, Britton, *The Truth About Geronimo*, New Haven, 1929

Debo, Angie, *A History of the Indians of the United States*, Norman, Oklahoma, 1971

—— *Geronimo*, London, 1993 (reprint)

—— *And Still the Waters Run: the Betrayal of the Five Civilized Tribes*, Princetown, New Jersey, 1991

Deloria, Vine, Jr., *Custer Died for Your Sins: An Indian Manifesto*, New York, 1969

—— *We Talk, You Listen*, New York, 1970

—— *Red Earth, White Lies: Native Americans and the Myth of Scientific Fact*, New York, 1988

Diaz, Bernal, *The Discovery and Conquest of New Spain* (trans A.P. Maudsley), London, 1928

Dippie, Brian W., *The Vanishing American: White Attitudes and US. Indian Policy*, Kansas, 1982

Erdoes, Richard and Alfonzo Ortiz, *American Indian Myths and Legends*, New York, 1984

Farb, Peter, *Man's Rise to Civilization as Shown by the Indian of North America from Primeval Times to the Coming of the Industrial State*, New York, 1968

Fee, Chester A., *Chief Joseph, the Biography of a Great Indian*, New York, 1936

Forbes, Jack D. (ed), *The Indian in America's Past*, Englewood Cliffs, New Jersey, 1964

Graham, William A., *The Story of the Litlle Big Horn*, Harrisburg, PA, 1941

Grinell, George B., *The Fighting Cheyennes*, New York, 1915

—— *Blackfoot Lodge Tails*, Lincoln, Nebraska, 1962

Hagan, William T., *American Indians*, Chicago, 1961

Hiesinger, Ulrich W., *Indian Lives: A Photographic Record from the Civil War to Wounded Knee*, Munich/New York, 1994

Hirschfelder, Arlene and Martha Kreipe de Montano, *The Native American Almanac: A Portrait of Native America Today*, New York, 1993

Hodge, Frederick W. (ed), *Handbook of American Indians of North of Mexico*, 2 vols, Washington, 1907, 1910

Howard, Helen A., *A Saga of Chief Joseph*, Caldwell, ID., 1965

Hoxie, Frederick, *A Final Promise: The Campaign to Assimilate the Indians, 1880–1920*, Lincoln, Nebraska, 1984

Hultkranz, Ake, *The Religions of the American Indians*, Berkeley, 1979

Hutton, Paul Andrew (ed), *The Custer Reader*, Lincoln, Nebraska, 1992

Jennings, Francis, *The Invasion of America: Indians, Colonialism and the Cant of Conquest*, New York, 1976

Jensen, Richard E., R. Eli Paul and John E. Carter, *Eyewitness at Wounded Knee*, London, 1991

John Stands in Timber and Margot Liberty, *Cheyenne Memories*, Lincoln, Nebraska, 1972

Josephy, Alvin M., *Indian Heritage of America*, London, 1971

—— *Red Power: The American Indians' Fight for Freedom*, New York, 1971

—— *The Nez Percé Indians and the Opening of the Northwest*, London, 1980

Luther Standing Bear, *Land of the Spotted Eagle*, Boston, New York, 1933

McClaughlin, James, *My Friend The Indian*, Lincoln, Nebraska, 1989 (reprint)

McCluhan, T.C., *Touch the Earth*, New York, 1971

McNickle, D'Arcy, *Native American Tribalism: Indian Survivals and Renewals*, New York, 1973

Mails, Thomas E., *Mystic Warriors of the Plains*, New York, 1972

Matthiessen, Peter, *In the Spirit of Crazy Horse*, New York, 1984
—— *Indian Country*, London, 1986

Mead, Margaret, *The Changing Culture of an Indian Tribe*, New York, 1932

Mooney, James, *The Ghost Dance Religion and the Sioux Outbreak of 1890*, Chicago, 1965

Murray, Keith A., *The Modocs and Their War*, Norman, Oklahoma, 1959

Nabokov, Peter (ed), *Native American Testimony. An Anthology of Indian and White Relations: First Encounter to Dispossesion*, New York, 1991

Niehardt, John G., *Black Elk Speaks*, Lincoln, Nebraska, 1979 (reprint)

Olson, James C., *Red Cloud and the Sioux Problem*, Lincoln, Nebraska, 1975

Payne, Doris Palmer, *Captain Jack: Modoc Renegade*, Portland, OR, 1938

Parkman, Francis, *The Conspiracy of Pontiac*, 2 vols, Boston, 1851

Radin, Paul, *The Autobiography of a Winnebago Indian*, New York, 1920
—— *The Trickster: A Study in American Indian Mythology*, New York, 1956

Sando, Joe, *Pueblo Nations: Eight Centuries of Pueblo History*, Santa Fe, 1992

Sandoz, Mari, *Crazy Horse*, New York, 1942

Snow, Dean R., *The Iroquois*, Cambridge, Mass., 1994

Spence, Lewis, *The Illustrated Guide to North American Mythology*, London, 1993 (reprint)

Spicer, Edward H., *A Short History of the Indians of the United States*, New York, 1969

Stannard, David E., *American Holocaust: The Conquest of the New World*, New York, 1992

Steiner, Stan, *The New Indian*, New York, 1968

Sturtevant, William C. (ed), *Handbook of North American Indians*, Washington, D.C., 20 volumes, various dates

Thornton, Russell, *American Indian Holocaust and Survival: A Population History Since 1492*, Norman, Oklahoma, 1987

Turner, Geoffrey, *Indians of North America*, New York, 1992

Turner, Frederick Jackson, *The Frontier in American History*, New York, 1920

Turner, Frederick W. III, *The Portable North American Indian Reader*, New York, 1974

Underhill, Ruth, *Red Men's Religion: Belief and Practices of the Indians North of Mexico*, Chicago, 1965

Utley, Robert M., *The Last Days of the Sioux Nation*, New Haven, Connecticut, 1963

—— *The Indian Frontier of the American West, 1846–1890*, Albuquerque, New Mexico, 1983

Vestal, Stanley, *Sitting Bull*, Norman, Oklahoma, 1957

Washburn, Wilcomb (ed), *The Indian and the White Man*, New York, 1964

Waters, Frank, *The Book of the Hopi*, New York, 1963

Wellman, Paul, *Indian Wars and Warriors*, 2 volumes, Boston, Mass., 1959

Wilkins, Thurman, *Cherokee Tragedy*, New York, 1970

Wilson, James, *The Earth Shall Weep*, London, 1998

Acknowledgments & Sources

A particular thanks goes to the following at Constable & Robinson Ltd for their help on this book and many others: Nick Robinson, Pete Duncan, Claire Muzzelle, Adrian Andrews, Sarah Smith and Josephine McGurk.

The editor has made every effort to locate all persons having rights in the selections which appear in this anthology, and to secure permision from the holders of such rights to reprint material. The editor apologizes in advance for any errors or omissions inadvertently made. Queries regarding the use of material should be addressed to the editor c/o the publisher.

Part I: A World Made of Dawn

"Winnebago song": John Bierhorst, *In the Trail of the Wind*, Farrar, Straus & Giroux, Inc, 1971. Copyright © 1971 John Bierhorst

"Hopi ceremony": quoted David Hurst Thomas et al, *The Native Americans: An Illustrated History*, Virgin, 1994. Copyright © 1993 Turner Publishing, Inc.

"Dekanawideh [Deganawida]" quoted David Hurst Thomas

et al, *The Native Americans: An Illustrated History*, Virgin 1994. Copyright © 1993 Turner Publishing, Inc.

"I am Dekanawidah": *The Iroquois Constitution*, The University of Oklahoma Law Center online, http://www.law.ou.edu

"All the business": *The Iroquois Constitution*, ibid.

"This string of wampum": *Iroquois Constitution*, ibid.

"Whenever a specially important matter": *Iroquois Constitution*, ibid.

"Inside of these tents": George Catlin, *Life Among the Indians*, Gall & Inglis, 1875

"An inch or more": George Catlin, *Illustrations of the Manners, Customs and Condition of the North American Indians*, Henry G. Bohn, 1848

Part II: Encounter

"But if you do not submit": quoted Jack D. Forbes (ed), *The Indian in America's Past*, Prentice-Hall, 1964

"Where today are the Pequot": quoted Frederick W. Turner III (ed), *The Portable North American Indian Reader*, The Viking Press, 1974. Copyright © The Viking Press 1973, 1974

"The Indians came presently down the river": A Gentleman of Elvas (trans. Richard Hakluyt), *The Discovery and Conquest of Terra Florida by Don Ferdinando de So*, Hakluyt Society, 1851

"[Cardenas] ordered two hundred stakes": (trans. G.P. Winship) *Narrative of Pedro de Castaneda, Fourteenth Annual report of the Bureau of American Ethnology*, US Government Printing Office, 1896

"Inasmuch as we have declared war": quoted Jack D. Forbes (ed), *The Indian in America's Past*, Prentice-Hall, 1964

"The village was very strong": *Coronado Expedition: Fourteenth Annual report of the Smithsonian Institution, 1892–3*, Part I, Bureau of Ethnology, 1896

"In the attack of the preceding Thursday": (trans. G.P. Winship) *Narrative of Pedro de Castaneda, Fourteenth Annual report of the Bureau of American Ethnology*, US Government printing Office, 1896

"Will you take by force what you may obtain by love?": Helen Hunt Jackson, *A Century of Dishonor*, 1881

"Several days before this bloodthirsty people": Anthony Chester, *Voyage of Anthony Chester to Virginia*, Peter van De Aa, 1707

"Being thus arrived at Cap-Cod":William Bradford, *History of Plymouth Plantation*, 1898

"We then marching on in a silent manner": Major John Mason, *A Brief History of the Pequot War*, S. Keeland & T. Green, 1736

"Of their Houses and Habitations": quoted Oliver J. Thatcher (ed), *The Library of Original Sources*, 1907

"On the 10th of February": quoted Katharine M. Rogers (ed), *The Meridian Anthology of Early American Women Writers*, Penguin, 1991

"These Indians by their situation": quoted James Wilson, *The Earth Shall Weep*, Picador, 1998

"The French being settled in Villages": Thomas Forsythe, "The French, British and Spanish Methods of Treating Indians &c.," *Ethnohistory*, Vol IV, Spring 1957, Wisconsin State Historical Society

"When it was evening": W.L. Grant (ed) *Voyages of Samuel de Champlain*, 1907

"The land on which you are": quoted James Wilson, *The Earth Shall Weep*, Picador, 1998

"Mr Tracy had not gone more than twenty paces":

Alexander Henry, *Travels and Adventures in Canada and the Indian Territories between the years 1760 and 1776*, I. Riley, 1809

"Those cruel men": Leonard Labaree (ed), *The Papers of Benjamin Franklin*, Yale University Press, 1967

"I appeal to any white man": quoted Jack D. Forbes (ed), *The Indian in America's Past*, Prentice-Hall, 1964

"War is war": quoted Alvin M. Josephy Jr, *500 Nations*, Hutchinson/Pimlico, 1995. Copyright © 1995 Pathways Productions, Inc.

"Houses are built for you to hold councils in": quoted Frederick W. Turner III (ed), *The Portable North American Indian Reader*, The Viking Press, 1974. Copyright © The Viking Press 1973, 1974

"The implicit obedience and respect": quoted Alvin M. Josephy Jr, *500 Nations*, Hutchinson/Pimlico, 1995. Copyright © 1995 Pathways Productions, Inc.

"Father! – Listen to your children": quoted Jack D. Forbes (ed), *The Indian in America's Past*, Prentice-Hall, 1964

"You have taken me prisoner with all my warriors": quoted T. McLuhan, *Touch the Earth*, 1971

Part III: The Losing of the West

"Clear the way": quoted Frederick W. Turner III (ed), *The Portable North American Indian Reader*, The Viking Press, 1974. Copyright © The Viking Press 1973, 1974

"Behold my brothers": ibid

"Governor Pesquira": quoted "Side Lights on Fifty years of Apache Warfare, 1836–1886", *Arizonia*, Voll II, No. 3, Fall 1961

"If we are taken back": Virginia Hoffman, *Navajo Biographies*,

Vol. I, , Navajo Curriculum Center, 1974

"After the firing": *US Senate, Reports of Committees, 39th Congress, 2nd Session*, Serial 1279, Document No. 156

"About day break": ibid

"We arrived at the Indian village": ibid

"I went over the ground soon after the battle": ibid

"Next morning after the battle": ibid

"The bodies were horribly cut up": ibid

"The dead bodies of women and children": ibid

"All manner of depredations": ibid

"I felt that the white men": quoted James Wilson, *The Earth Shall Weep*, Picador, 1998

"We went into battle naked": ibid

"Owing to recent depredations": quoted Dee Brown, *The Fetterman Massacre*, Dee Brown, Barrie & Jenkins, 1972

"Character of Indian affairs hostile": ibid

"Eyes torn out": ibid

"I love the land": quoted T. McLuhan, *Touch the Earth*, 1971

"November 23rd": quoted Paul Andrew Hutton (ed), *The Custer Reader*, University of Nebraska Press, 1997

"After a general shake of the hand": George Catlin, *Life Among the Indians*, George Catlin, Gall & Inglis, 1875

"In 1868 men came out": quoted Alvin M. Josephy Jr, *500 Nations*, Hutchinson/Pimlico, 1995. Copyright © 1995 Pathways Productions, Inc.

"At early dawn on the 10th": "Expedition to the Yellowstone River in 1873: Letters of a Young Cavalry Officer", ed George Frederick Howe, *Mississippi Valley Historical Review 39*, December 1952

"Then the Sioux rode up the ridges on all sides": Christopher Silver, *The Penguin Book of Interviews*, Penguin, 1993

"I charged in": Virginia I. Armstrong (ed), *I Have Spoken*, Swallow Press, 1971

"I know that my young men did a great wrong": quoted Alvin M Josephy, *The Nez Percé Indians and the Opening of the Northwest*, Yale Univerity Press, 1965

"He was stopped in his retreat by Gen. Miles": quoted William Brandon et al, *The American Heritage Book of Indians*, American Heritage Publishing Co., Inc., 1961

"Standing back, he folded his blanket": ibid

"Preparations for the raid": Jason Betzinez (with W.S. Nye), *I Fought with Geronimo*, The Stackpole Company, 1959

"In the morning": John G. Neihardt, *Black Elk Speaks*, University of Nebraska Press 1972. Copyright © 1961 the John G. Neihardt Trust

Part IV: To Kill the Indian to Save the Man

"It is probably true that the majority of our wild Indians": *Annual Report of the Commissioner of Indian Affairs for 1903*, US Government Printing Office, 1904

"Hey-a-a-hey! Hey-a-a-hey!": John G. Neihardt, *Black Elk Speaks*, University of Nebraska Press 1972. Copyright © 1961 the John G. Neihardt Trust

"The Native American Movement represents": quoted Jack D. Forbes (ed), *The Indian in America's Past*, Prentice-Hall, 1964

"One day [in 1879]": Luther Standing Bear, Land of the Spotted Eagle, Houghton Mifflin, 1933

"As with Samson of old": quoted C.L. Sonnrichsen, *The Mescalero Apaches*, University of Oklahoma Press, 1958

"The most shameful chapter of American history": George Bird Grinnell, *Blackfoot Lodge Tales*, University of Nebraska Press, 1962

"Moving rapidly up the years": John Collier "Introduction"

in Oliver La Farge (ed), *The Changing Indian*, ed University of Oklahoma Press, 1942.

"The Task Force feels": *Report of the Secretary of the Interior by the Task Force on Indian Affairs,* July 10, 1961

"Proclamation: To the Great White Father": quoted David Hurst Thomas et al, *The Native Americans: An Illustrated History*, Virgin 1994. Copyright © 1993 Turner Publishing, Inc.